To Karen

Contents

Acknowledgements

Bruce Springsteen, of course, was raised in Jersey – as, oddly enough, was I (the other one). Aside from twenty-five years' love of his music, that nominal fluke is the sole link I can claim to my subject. I'd like to duly thank both Springsteen and his management for their co-operation in the research and writing of *Point Blank*. Unhappily, I can't do so. Neither camp responded to my requests for a formal interview, a passion for anonymity that seems to have taken root after Dave Marsh's fine biographies. That said, every other primary source, as well as the written record and Springsteen's own archive, was tapped and/or trawled over two years. Much of the story appears here for the first time. Anyone wanting to know how a life in full can be shot from around corners should, please, read on.

Of those who did make time or comment free, I should thank, institutionally: *Asbury Park Press*, ASCAP, *Backstreets*, Badlands, BMI, Bookcase, the British Library, British Newspaper Library, Café Eckstein, Companies House, County of Los Angeles, Focus Fine Arts, Freehold High School, Gethsemane Lutheran, Helter Skelter, HMV, J. Golding Group, Lazerquick, Los Angeles County Assessor, Lucky Town, McCarthy's Geographics, *Melody Maker*,

New Jersey Department of Health, *New York Times*, Northwest Harvest, Ocean County College, Omnibus, Oregon Vital Records, Our Lady of the Lake Parish, Performing Rights Society, *Q*, St Rose of Lima Church, Seattle CC, *Seattle Post-Intelligencer*, Seattle Public Library, *Seattle Times*, *Seattle Weekly*, Shop Rite, *The Ties That Bind*, Ti-fa, Tower 801, Tower Records, Von's, Washington Mutual.

Professionally: Jean Allenbach, Mark Arax, Joan Armatrading, Stuart Belsham, Joel Bernstein, Allan Border, Bill Bradley, Randy Brecker, the late William Burroughs, Noel Chelberg, Allan Clarke, Julia Collins, Brenda Cooper, Elvis Costello, Patrick Deuchar, 'Doc', Jim Eddy, Chris Edwards, Liz Else, John Entwistle, Leah Entwistle, Chris Farlowe, Pat Fosh, Amy Frechett, Swati Gamble, Charlie Gillett, Luis Gleick, Lynn Goldsmith, Kathy Goodman, Andrew Gordon, Todd Grice, Jeff Griffin, Bob Harris, Toni Hentz, David Hepworth, Paul Jones, Lenny Kaye, Judy Kern, Robert Lamm, Barbara Levy, Woody Lock, Vince Lorimer, Nick Lowe, John Lyttle, George McDonald, Rose Macnab, Jim Mahlmann, Norman Mailer, Joey Mazo, Piers Merchant, Tom Modi, Bess Montgomery, Dave Motz, Nick from New Jersey, Graham Parker, Andy Peebles, Peter Perchard, Brian Pringle, Tim Rice, Keith Richards, Arthur Rosato, Kate Rous, Mitch Ryder, Celia Ryle, Alan Samson, Pete Seeger, Paul Sexton, Ed Shakespeare, Nancy Sinatra, David Sinclair, Andrew Smith, Kathleen Stanley, Gill Taylor, Saul Todd, Carey Trevisan, Jacob van de Rhoer, Lisbeth Vogl, George Will, Richard Williams, Phil Woodruff, Vasily Yatskin, Tony Yeo.

And socially: Arvid Anderson, the Anonymous Caller, Pete Barnes, Terry Bland, Chao Praya, Albert Clinton, the Cohns, Andrew Craig, 'Spanner' Cranfield, Celia Culpan, Bob Daugherty, Monty Dennison, John & Marie Dowdall, John Engstrom, the Gay Hussar, Mary Evans, Malcolm Galfe, Marlys Higgins, Amy Hostetter, Mick Jagger, Alan Kennington, the late Betty Knecht, the late Carl Knecht, Joan Lambert, Terry Lambert, Belinda Lawson, the late Borghild Lee, Richard Lloyd-Roberts, Lee Mattson, Al Meyersahm, Jim Meyersahm, Sheila Mohn, Bela Molnar, the late Jim Morganroth, Liz Morganroth, Chuck

Ogmund, Hugh O'Neill, Robin Parish, Chris Pickrell, the late John Riley, Amanda Ripley, April Roseman, Delia Sandford, Karen Sandford, Sefton Sandford, Peter Scaramanga, Sue Sims-Hilditch, Fred & Cindy Smith, Katie Spalding, Carrie Stacy, Debbie Standish, Ben & Mary Tyvand, Ross Viner and Victoria Willis Fleming. I owe a special debt to a great sportsman and friend, the late Godfrey Evans. DCLU, *Rent* and US Bank were no help at all.

Point Blank is the sixth and, for now, last of my rock music sagas. Buyers of this particular kind of yarn are due a well-earned break. I hope, though, the reader who can now take them in any order won't find that the last flags too badly from the modest pace of the first. Quite personally, I've enjoyed them.

C.S.
1999

List of Illustrations

Born in the USA.

After Doug Springsteen deep-sixed his plan to hitch-hike to the Monterey pop festival, Bruce donned a mortar-board and gown to graduate on 19 June 1967.

The 'New Jersey wailer' solo and flanked by Clarence Clemons and Steve Van Zandt. From a shaky start, Springsteen glossed his set into a well-rehearsed, blocked routine that was as much Broadway as boardwalk. (Both: Richie Aaron/Redferns)

The Harvard Square Theatre, where on 9 May 1974 Jon Landau saw 'rock and roll future'. (Karen Dowdall)

Those titanic early shows soon became lore. Springsteen's albums may have been on the short side, but at three hours, the gigs never were: epic rave-ups that flouted the laws of nature long before chaos theory had a name. (Richie Aaron/Redferns)

The Hammersmith Odeon, November 1975. As a slogan, it was five and a half years early.

To some, it was like looking through the pinhole of a scenic souvenir charm and seeing a whole pink-suited Apollo revue – except this was England, and the star was wearing Levi's. And that hat. (Andrew Putler/Redferns)

With 1978's *Darkness on the Edge of Town* and 118-date tour, a second-wave cult finally turned Springsteen from a novelty into a star. (Lynn Goldsmith/Corbis)

As Lynn Goldsmith, who took this shot, could bear out, the next two years were often grim, and the street was rarely easy. (Lynn Goldsmith/Corbis)

Although Springsteen alone had 'the shine', it wasn't as if his career was an effortless feat of unsculpted, free-form self-expression. Among those who helped down the way:

    The E Street Band (Van Zandt, Weinberg, Federici, BS, Clemons, Bittan, Tallent). (Lynn Goldsmith/Corbis)

    Adele Springsteen. (Sam Emerson/Sipa-Press)

    Jon Landau. (Lynn Goldsmith/Corbis)

    The Big Man. (Richie Aaron/Redferns)

By the time of 1980's *The River* – still the best, one-stop slab of what made Springsteen great – he was both a radio star and a pin-up. (Lynn Goldsmith/Corbis)

As 1984 came round, fans weren't watching him so much as adoring a god play-acting himself against a vast diorama. (Corbis/Bettmann)

Bossmania. (Rex Features)

That same year, Springsteen's 'red-headed woman' joined his boys-only band – one of the steps on their downfall, and his own saving. (Ebet Roberts/Redferns)

Meanwhile, he married the model-actress Julianne Phillips. (Alpha)

Duets – Springsteen with:

Patti Scialfa. (Rex Features)

Sting. (Mark Allan/Alpha)

Mick Jagger. (Duncan Raban/Alpha)

Springsteen's second wedding, in 1991, was a lesser world event than his first. There was no publicity strip-tease or press helicopters buzzing the reception. It did, however, set up a successful and lasting marriage. (Richard Corkery/Corbis)

Most of Springsteen's comeback gigs in 1992–93 were solid, if uninspired. On good nights, at least, he redeemed what the new band couldn't cut. Now in his forties, he still had the moves. (Both: Alpha)

Legend. (Mark Allan/Alpha)

The 'sawdust Steinbeck' who toured the world, doing some of his best and most human work, from 1995–97. (Mick Hutson/Redferns)

1998's Amnesty International reunion: Tracy Chapman, BS, Peter Gabriel, Youssou N'Dour. (Mark Allan/Alpha)

Springsteen, looking like one of his own lawyers, leaves the High

Court in London. 'I came to defend my right to my music,' he said. 'It's a big part of what you are . . . what you come up with when you're sitting alone with your guitar late at night is one of the most personal things in your life.' (Alpha)

'. . . point blank, livin' one false move just one false move away'

BRUCE SPRINGSTEEN

'For a good poet's made, as well as born'

BEN JONSON

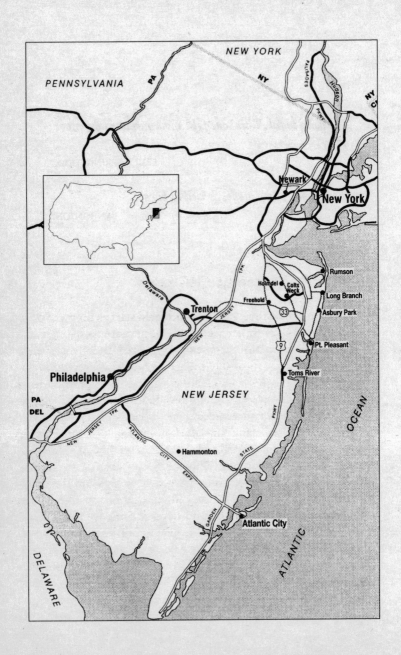

1

Across The Border

New York, September 1979

The last word on Bruce Springsteen should start as follows. Most critics, whether yea or nay, devote as much space to the myth as they do to the man. Not that the man's ignored. In 1978 *Darkness on the Edge of Town* (probably the most *craved* LP ever) brought Springsteen to the peak of his fame as a blue-collar star who wrote joyous yet grown-up songs full of 'real dudes you run into' – or at least down the Jersey turnpike and the badlands. And if they were edgy flops, so were many Americans in the late 1970s; the ones, anyway, who felt embittered and shut out in the face of a slumped economy and frayed society. This was Springsteen's power base. Add the regular-guy roots, rock-till-you-drop gigs and the fuzzy but right-on politics, and it's easy to see why he was one of the most sainted icons of pop's first thirty years. Springsteen's albums gave a glimpse of life and morality among hordes of 'real dudes' and showed the potential of an *artiste engagé*. He could turn a lyric with the best of them, weaving and spinning yarns over a booming backbeat; a hybrid god who sounded like Elvis casually colluding with Dylan in an echo-chamber. Millions responded to his farrago. They were his constituency; that, his legend.

Mythology, as usual, exalts reality. But in the man, too, there was a rare breadth. The real Springsteen was at heart a total conformist. His war with his father represents his sole tack from a course of teenage submission to petty, small-town convention. From youth through *Born to Run*-era breakthrough, his act was more prosaic than avant-garde, a notebook and thesaurus his constant companions, the guitar his most loyal friend. He neither smoked nor doped. News of Springsteen's post-Pill, pre-Aids social life – whether goosing both sexes or jittering in the klieg lights – would be tales of incongruity. In a world of foot-wide lapels and spandex, he clung to the work-shirt and Levi's. Amidst disco's and punk's dire season, he covered Mitch Ryder and Little Richard hits. His manner was to watch change and wonder why, ever worried at chaos. He was a champion brooder: cars, jobs, original sin, all were equal when it came to *Darkness*'s themes. More pertinently, in May 1979 Springsteen fretted over the near-cataclysm at the Three Mile Island reactor. Within months, he'd put down a rare political marker. That autumn, he headlined at two of the five galas, hosted by Jackson Browne and his avocado mafia, hyped as 'America's star-spangled series of gigs for a responsible future', and more popularly touted as No Nukes.

Springsteen coasted through the first night. The lights flared, the band ran on, bowing in turn, the draw with his wrangler's boots and jeans, tall, wan and bow-legged like John Wayne. When he spoke he panted as though in a state of dramatic crisis. The eighty-minute set didn't give him time to dig into subtext; the appeal had to be instant, and was. 'The response he got . . . was the most frenzied I've ever heard,' wrote the Boston stringer; 'the crowd was a Springsteen one', the New Yorker. After generous slabs of *Born* and *Darkness*, and a duet with Browne, the gig ended in a Gary Bonds knees-up as a chant, compounded of 20,000 voices, rang from the rafters. It was the urgent, force-fed lowing of an abattoir. 'Br-ooose,' it went. Then they put some lung into it. 'Br-*ooooose*.' Springsteen himself turned to the band, all of them doing their own horselaugh. 'Man,' he said, 'makes you feel like a million, don't it?' He used the word 'million' the way some people pronounce 'chump change'. Then he was off. There'd been no layers to peel back, no hint of artistic renewal or rebirth. It was classic, grainy rock, and Springsteen wiped the floor with it.

All the good vibes were reversed in the Saturday show. Both the Boss and band were uptight, as evidenced by their eyes-to-the-deck performance style. The singing was short of breath, and a screech of feedback reinforced the ugly mood. In short, things were tense. Springsteen, still in his composite cowboy-biker's garb, brought down the house with 'Thunder Road', ground through 'The Promised Land', then uttered the (normally) dread intro, 'Here's one off the new album.' As 'The River' expired in a crash of breakneck harp and mangled hi-hats – Springsteen's drummer was on probation at the time – a woman in the crowd handed up a box. Via the organ and sax, her love-gift duly hit centre stage. It was a cake. 'Well. *Fuck*,' said Springsteen. With a cartoon pitcher's wind-up, he zeroed back in on the stalls. Springsteen's aim was true. In one creamy swoop he wiped out the woman's hair and cheeks, the icing hanging there like fluffy earmuffs. The sobbing fan later called herself 'the most dumbstruck person in New York'. If so, Springsteen, who'd sounded winded all night, could have made a bid for runner-up. 'Send. Me. The. Bill,' he rasped, scowling, then cued in the riff of 'Rosalita'.

Things went downhill from there. As wailing guitar parts faded in honks of thunderous sax, and a harp also sailed into the crowd, Springsteen began jabbing wildly at the tenth row. Next, turning, he signalled to the back-line roadies. This went on over a long, clattering drum roll. The whole saga became a protracted hassle for the band, vamping away as their boss wove to and fro. Eventually Springsteen was so worked up that he slung down his Fender, cut the juice, and jumped into the pit. As he waded through the aisle he was clapped by most – save two, who never acknowledged him, leaving Springsteen still waving and yelling, 'Hey. You!' The smeared, crying fan he ignored. The other one he grabbed.

She was his ex-flame, the photographer Lynn Goldsmith. Various rationalizations for Springsteen's fit were later put forward. For one, Goldsmith (who was actually co-ordinating shots of the event) was there in apparent breach of a verbal deal. If so, that would have tapped into a moral keynote of Springsteen's life and art: the sanctity of trust and dread of deceit – a core theme for one who'd held ideals in such awe. There was the professional angle. As a friend says, 'He's superfocused on those front rows, and she was distracting him incredibly.' His own take on the scene, played out to raving, big-fun crowds, took a disarming, hurt line. 'It was just between her and me, boyfriend and girlfriend,' he said. 'She was doin' something she said she wouldn't do. I tried to handle it in other ways, but she avoided them. So I had to do it myself.'

Whatever the cause, the effect was that Springsteen (after hissing 'You had to dick me' in her ear) hauled Goldsmith back on stage. He twisted her arm so hard, she says, she thought it would break. They stood there on the lip, he hugging the mike, she blinking in the spot. There were, undeniably, a lot of cameras round her neck: a Canon; a Nikon; a lens; and a brown shoulder-bag of the kind where film's kept, stuck with a badge: 'Access All Areas. MSG. 9/23/79.' Behind this edifice of gear, Goldsmith looked strikingly glum. 'This,' Springsteen snarled, 'Is. My. Ex.' At that he whirled her into the wings. 'We're *done*,' he said. Goldsmith left open the odds that they'd meet in court. Roadies then hustled her to the exit. In *Rolling Stone*'s words, 'After the show, a clutch of them could be heard shouting "macho Boss!" Several women standing backstage were shocked. Goldsmith was intensely humiliated by the experience . . . for Bruce, though, it was just one of those things.'

That day, Springsteen hit thirty.

Seattle, October 1996

Of course, rock stars aren't ever normal. Someone with antisocial personality disorder, as we know it, shows a cool ability to split word and deed, fluid sexual *mores*, an always or usually charming front, all fuelled by a manic drive. In Springsteen's case, a strict diagnosis doesn't hold, but gives a clue to other major trends of his life: his loneliness, distrustfulness and fear of the jilt, his idealistic civics and narcissism. But along with the darker sides there was also the evolution of a soul millions loved: the arch punk, the bard, the Byronesque goods. The husbandry of this image was the nub of his fame. So, too, was the very real sweat that he brought to his work. And overriding all others was the theme of honesty, the focal point of his life. He was the sunny face of the American psyche.

For any analysis of Springsteen's CV, his thirties were the crux. He began them in a public row with one of his long list of exes; by forty he was divorced, a semi-recluse, mellow, well-read, filled with erudite goods off the national stockpile. Culturally, from 1979 to 1989 Springsteen was in chrysalis. They were busy years.

Springsteen's relations with women became 'almost normal' during the decade, and his second marriage (and fatherhood) was a hit. Musically, too, he grew without swelling. Springsteen came to a new, 'gaunt' sound, which he fought at first, then realized was him, trying to ram through. He did some of his best work. And he delved in local and state politics, donating funds, speaking out, and losing his native coyness from the days of No Nukes (when his was the sole name not to flog the shows' manifesto). Springsteen's liberal bias contained more the gist of populism than of the pristine ideological left. His goal was less one of national causes than of rooting out cases of wrong. In the face of welfare cuts, for instance, Springsteen quietly and generously gave cash to community food banks. Along with his practical activism went a matching personal growth. No longer would the Boss be the hard-eyed *capo* who flouted his moll. Springsteen's pay-back for the 'crapola road' shifted from vengeance to a pity for those he saw as fellow-travellers. 'I'll never put someone in the position of being humiliated,' he said. 'It happened to me for too long.'

Just as 1955 belonged to Elvis, 1965 to Dylan, so 1975 was Springsteen's year. Cynics would say this progression stood as a powerful rebuttal of Darwin's theory. But by the mid-1980s such sneers were either too obscurely positioned or came too late to halt the celestial trajectory of *Born in the USA*. The hype mill, in the peculiarly American sense of it, fired up. Rash claims were made on Springsteen's behalf. His cover of the hoary Motown hit

'War' was 'the one song that [can] make every implication of US policy explicit', wrote Dave Marsh. According to Father Andrew Greeley, '*Tunnel of Love* may be a more important Catholic event [in America] than the visit of the Pope.' Springsteen's deft but trite 'If I Should Fall Behind' was compared to Rousseau (Marsh again). This was surreal. However much he'd learned on the way up, on the streets of Jersey – no mean Ph.D. itself – Springsteen was poorly tutored, a pedestrian, essentially shy type for whose every entrance fans waited and on whose every word they devotedly hung. Pundits loved him. 'Real dudes', too. His lyrics were pondered in the *New York Times*, and his postman had a nervous rupture from having to haul so many bags of mail to Springsteen's door.

All this fed a critical orgasm that Springsteen, to his credit, largely ignored. He dared buck a formula. Thus the '70s street-poet became the '80s vexed soul and the '90s new man. Male bonding was junked for the less vagarious world of hearth and home. (Aptly, it was the same woman who joined Springsteen's boys-only band and then married him.) Macho posturing gave way to ruminations on wives and kids. In 1993 Springsteen's notion of brotherhood yielded the wry, haunting 'Streets Of Philadelphia', a marked artistic leap from 'Rosalita' into something more dextrous. Meanwhile, an Oedipal rage at his father blew out; anti-clericalism veered into a secularized view of redemption; even Springsteen's TV fixation was set on its ear in '57 Channels (And Nothin' On)'. Through it all, he moved one dollar's width to the left with every dollar earned. A rich and fulfilled man, he constantly probed the failed and fed-up, writing with a compassion that seemed real, witty, radiant, humane, on a par with Guthrie and Rodgers, if not Gandhi and Rousseau.

This is the Springsteen who arrives at the Paramount Theatre, Seattle, in a bus.

He looks completely changed. Springsteen semi-lopes through the black side door, a chunky, rolling-legged man with chunky, turquoise gypsy beads, the kind often linked with New Agers. His hair is swept back. He wears a full moustache and a half-beard, restored after his clean-shaven interlude, flecked with grey. Above the jeans is a lumberjack's shirt; to find such dire togs must have taken work. With his bristly-cut sideburns and slit mouth, Springsteen looks like someone on parole. He has convict's eyes. Instead of the stealth wisecrack, his only aside is a muffled grunt to the fans. When they speak, it's a throwback.

'Br-ooose.'

'You the man!'

'Bitchin'!'

'Yeah – awesome!'

Springsteen shrugs. Then he bobs in, and up comes his head, up comes a smile. *Now* he's the boss. As usual, he changes – if that word conveys reincarnation – once he lays hands on a guitar. Onstage, he's by turns ornery, fey and warm when the lyrics warrant it. He has the habit of getting in part for his songs. 'Don't clap,' he snaps at one point (earning it the tag 'Bruce's shut-the-fuck-up tour'). The intros to 'Pilgrim' and 'Red Headed Woman', by contrast, are downright bawdy. A few of the latter are allowed up to lean on the stage, still clutching their handbags. 'Sometimes you find what makes you feel alive is killin' you,' he tells them, before 'Straight Time'. 'Sometimes the old answers run out and you have to find out how to be new.'

It's the kind of unforced yet moving set that gets folk-rock a good name. In the 1940s, Hank Williams sang with just such a pity for the beaten and broke, though in a band. Springsteen works solo. He wraps his rough, full-bodied rasp around sagas full of share-croppers, Okies, doomed refugees and vets. The new wrinkle is the stark, guitar-and-harp arrangements and the neatly judged tales about migrants, notably Chicanos flooding over the California border. Springsteen brings a homespun sense and bitter wit to tunes like 'Sinaloa Cowboys' and 'The Line'. This isn't the stuff of most rich and stellar pop idols. Fellow-feeling, of course, has been in Springsteen's line-up from the off. By 1979, he'd worked it into an art form: most of *Darkness* and the new cuts from *The River* loomed as gripes on the American Dream gone awry. In those days, though, Springsteen used to be a cross, somewhere in the chasm between Pete Seeger and Mick Jagger's manic derangement. Tonight, there's John Steinbeck with a guitar. If he's the quintessential self-made man, the real 'boss' is revealed as a hyper-sensitive, easily moved soul who's hid himself behind a mask – as he did in all those soc-hop raves about cars – and learned some mint-new things in his forties, with the gratifying self-insight: 'Right now, I don't need records that are number one . . . I need to do [what's] central, vital, that sets me in the present, where I don't have to come out and count on my history or a hit I wrote twenty years ago.'

After a six-song encore, including a wiggily-done 'Blinded By The Light' (1972), Springsteen is off. He doesn't, however, leave the building. In a kind of vaulted alcove, a grey, ugly den the tone of wet cement, he signs books and albums. On one he scrawls, 'We're getting there – thanx.' He poses for amateur snaps. To a gofer he gives orders on meeting those who'd plugged the show one way or another, from wizened hacks to various DJs and movers in local clubs. One of the last calls Springsteen the 'most down to earth guy ever'. Short of having the words 'Real Dude' tattooed across his forehead, it's hard to see how much more clearly he could prove it.

First in to his dressing-room are the party from Northwest Harvest, a Seattle food-bank. They spend half an hour there, during which Springsteen soars high above the seigneurial rites of charity. He thanks *them*. One of the group, Jean Allenbach, remembers him as 'just supremely nice . . . talk[ing] about how he tried to boost causes wherever he went, instead of just writing a cheque. He wanted others to sign up in the days and weeks ahead. *They'd* make a difference.'

Behind this hope lies Springsteen's yen to move on, happier in a sea of anonymous faces than one-on-one. It also speaks to his genuine concern and acquired charm, even as his aide waves in his next date. Springsteen poses for more shots and signs posters for Allenbach to raffle. He donates the total proceeds from his T-shirt sales. When all the figures are added up, Northwest Harvest reaps $7,000.

Next in are four fans from another group, Dalmatian Dreams. One of them, a young man named Jamie, is battling cancer. A second source there calls Springsteen 'riveting'. He moves them deeply, less for the contents of his speech (mainly the commonplace of gawky clichés) than his gift to forge belief, not so much in theories, a programme or plan, as in themselves. His social analysis has a rough pragmatic note of reality. They, too, attest to Springsteen's raw humanity.

The vehicle of this power, and of his motivational nous, is his true decency, different in kind from mere do-goodery. In fact, judged by lofty political standards, Springsteen has obvious flaws as a radical. His key aesthetic is a maudlin hunger for pre-*Grapes of Wrath* America. It's nostalgia that stirs his dust-bowl reveries on *The Ghost of Tom Joad*. But that pales beside the fire and immediacy of his passions, his charisma and a style, sometimes taken for reticence, actually concealing will, a quiet nerve, guts and grit that constantly wrong-foot others: '"can-do" as well as candour', wags a friend. It's hard to read Springsteen's three decades' fame as the track record of a wimp. When a final backstage caller cites a licensing hassle going back twelve years, touching on *Born in the USA*, he 'prints' the man with a startling, cold glare. 'I'll fix it,' he says. He does.

Springsteen ducks outside to Ninth Avenue, works the line, mute again, his fleshy underlip with the hint of a curl, waves and takes off. His shoulders seem broader than ever, his dark head partly sunk between them. He wears shades against the Northwest sky. The night quickly becomes wrapped in anecdotal fable. To the loyal ones he's still the hero; to others, the latest in a firmament of rock gods to preach down. Anomalies are made to surface between the old Springsteen and the new. Quirks are seen, oddities aired. And that's the final irony of all, since neither myth nor legend can ever match the truth of the caged, wild life.

2
'You're Born, And They Bury You'

In 1949 New Jersey was in its 160th year and still struggling for a role. After the labour boom of a civil and two world wars – local factories blasted out guns, bullets, uniforms, planes and ships – industry slumped to a few chemical and drug plants. The steady exodus from town to country, euphemized as 'white flight', rent the state and ushered in banana-republic levels of disease, illiteracy and unemployment in the ghettoes, later to erupt in race riots. The migrants still came, constantly swelling suburbia. There, ironically, the American dream was self-fulfilling, made real by the willingness of each group to take its turn at the bottom for an investment cashed in by their children. If there was a melting-pot, it was toward the culture of pluralism. Rural Jersey was a stew of Lenape Indian tribes, English and German colonists, Swedes, Finns, Danes, Arabs and Czechs. Everyone was a settler.

It's rare in the careers of most Irish–Dutch to meet a Neapolitan, let alone marry her. Only slightly less rare would be to own a two-family home with a tree and a yard. In the Garden State, there were whole neighbourhoods of such mergers. One post-war union settled down in Freehold, midway between Trenton and the Atlantic shore. The groom, Doug Springsteen, was a third-generation Jerseyan; his wife, Adele Zerilli, a hard-working small-town secretary. They were there, in part, to look after his elderly parents. In time Adele, a strict Catholic, gave her husband religion and three children.

Freehold was just such a drab dormitory town as grew up near any big city between the wars, though it dated as far back as the American Revolution. In 1778, George Washington fought the British to a draw there. The name stemmed from its landowning, federalist founding fathers – freeholders. After Molly Pitcher carried jugs of water to thirsty soldiers in the Battle of Monmouth, another local word passed into lore. Later, the immigrants came with the building of the turnpikes and railroads. Appalachians jostled up against Poles and Slavs. An enormous alchemy was in the making. Freehold became a microcosm of what America was to the world.

By the time Doug and Adele Springsteen settled there the town was fully industrial. The 25,000 locals were mainly poor whites who worked in the Nestlé plant or the rug mill. Routine was all. Not since the days of the War of Independence had the words 'old' and 'fashioned' been in such close proximity. Culturally, politically, morally, it was a place of sober values. Few Freeholders veered beyond the narrow confines of Route 33. Trains hauled freight and animals west, but rarely people. Some did claim they liked to travel, but they meant to Newark, perhaps, forty miles north, or that they once visited Manhattan. It wasn't as if Freehold were some forlorn, hick town without amenities. There was harness racing, an aquarium and a museum with ceramics and tiles. Every July, the fireworks went up over Cemetery Hill. It was clean and well lit. The only pollution was the stench of the coffee factory on a wet day. In short, it was the kind of place that teaches a boy to be practical while it forces him to dream of other, headier realities.

The Springsteens' first child was born here at 10.50 p.m. on 23 September 1949; the first day of autumn. He was delivered at Monmouth Memorial hospital, down Main Street and across a cemetery from home. They named him, for two ancestors, Bruce Frederick.

That Friday's news was, in every sense of the satirical word, explosive. The very evening the boy was born, President Truman announced that a 'detonation' had occurred in the USSR. Two days later, Tass confirmed from Moscow that the Russians had a 'hot weapon'. The US monopoly ended; the arms race began. In the UN, the Soviets were flayed for 'systematic espionage' on western defence bases. In a separate row, the Chinese stigmatized the Kremlin as a 'dire threat to world peace and security'. The combined shock of bombs, spies and frustrations abroad helped to mobilize an anti-communist backlash. Union organizers became equivalent in many minds to the kind of 'reds' hounded by the Un-American Activities Committee. That same month, the New York trial wound up of eleven labour leaders accused of plotting to destabilize the US government.

Britain, meanwhile, was suffering its own perennial trauma. On 18 September the pound was devalued by 30 per cent. As a complete policy U-turn by Attlee's Cabinet, the public, still agonizing from the war, viewed the crisis as 'diabolical' (the *Evening Chronicle*): the evil spawn of some satanic pact between Westminster and Washington. Equally dazed were the world markets. In the next week, no fewer than twenty-four other states cut their currencies. The Stock Exchange shut down for a day. Traders held a frenzied impromptu session in the middle of Throgmorton Street, buying and selling gold, metal and oil shares. Even as the apparatus of the welfare state – with a new National Assistance Board paying benefits – geared up, the UK national debt was revealed as £25,620,762,600. This, too, got a Cold War spin when Russian press and radio sneered at Britain as no more than an 'IOU in Truman's pocket'.

The boy shared a birthday with Emperor Augustus, and, closer to home, the singers Ray Charles and Julio Iglesias. In Summit, a town thirty miles from Freehold, a baby called Mary Louise Streep turned three months old; she later spliced her first names into Meryl. Down the coast in Spring Lake, Jack Nicholson started high school. He'd later speak of fame being 'in the stars'. By a few hours, Springsteen himself was a Libran. According to a chart done by his grandmother, he was born, if not to run, 'to do rather than think, though [he'd] spend a long time before making a move' (a wry prediction, as it turned out, of his life in the studio). Astrologically, he was reckoned to be deep, artistic, moody, shy yet balanced. His surname (literally, the stone in a well) carried the pleasing echo of something fully alive and agile. The Dutch *springlevend* means dynamic.

The son of an angry, tart man and a kindly mother, it was Springsteen's lot to be torn evenly down the line between Doug and Adele, to behave as the one while idolizing the other. From the male side, he got his intensity, drama and fire. From the Zerillis, he learned the courtesy and wit that often stunned those who knew him as Doug's son. Schizophrenia was both the throughline and keynote. Inside, the house at 87 Randolph Street was divided, the man, in Bruce's words 'a clenched fist' while the woman, saintly in just about every account, 'did everything, everywhere, all the time'. Outside, too, Freehold was segregated, black and white symbolically split by the railroad – somewhere, downtown, men wore Irontex suits and drove boatlike Futuramics past signs reading EATS, or for the seventy-seventh straight week, *Top o' the Morning*. It was home sweet home. That's what people used to say, and for years Springsteen wondered how they could mean it.

Throughout his life, he'd be in deep conflict over his roots. Mostly, he tried to be as unlike Doug as possible. On the other hand, it was precisely his father's rusty, blue-collar norms he later adapted to the stage. He enthusiastically wore the values of conservative, '50s Freehold: cynical; unintellectual and wary of eggheads; respectful of business and determinedly patriotic. He remained, through his career, a homeboy from Jersey. Father, in turn, was untroubled by any ambiguities of the son's work. When Bruce Springsteen wrapped his 1984 album in the effigy of the Stars and Stripes, Doug told friends with obvious glee, 'The kid loves his flag.'

His early days were stark, though not the unrelieved hell some said. The eldest child and only boy, Bruce was spoilt within the limits of the family budget. His mother adored him. The 'shotgun house' on Randolph, though unlovely, was just such a home as bred millions of small tycoons, GIs and bureaucrats, and even the odd banker or lawyer. A neighbour named Judy Kern remembers him 'more often laughing than not, whirling down the street with a stick to "get doz guys". He had a wild streak.'

Springsteen, with his bandy legs and shock of dark hair, was often up and running. Another friend recalls his five-year-old boast that he could beat 'Pa' in a race – and Doug ruthlessly trouncing him, to gales of mirth from the spectators' stoop. It was another small humiliation. Bruce took solace in his mother, his sister Ginny and sundry neighbourhood girls. It was their model – soft, warm and uncritically loyal – that he came to love in his women. Meanwhile, from the displaced Alabaman next door, he got an early taste of gospel and folk hymns, along with a poker-hollow drawl and a hillbilly slang. To this day, Springsteen speaks with a twang.

His turf, for six years, was shrunk to a triangle: his duplex – a 'dumpy, two-storey house next to a gas station' – the stores down Main, and St Rose of Lima church on McLean. The Springsteens never missed Sunday mass. Variations on this regime would include an hour at the races, a park or the Howell Antique Flea Market. In summer, Doug mightn't rule out a day on the coast. Due east on 33 lay Asbury Park. When Springsteen was a boy, the resort still boasted three theatres, dozens of hotels and, of course, the board-walk – a mile-long arcade of carousel rides and neon, with its end-of-the-pier bars and the crisp tang of fatty foods. Sprayed on the rusty door of a beach café was the word JUNGLELAND. Springsteen must have seen this graffiti a hundred times. Back on the highway, daubed on an inaccessible girder over the road, a steeplejack had painted the name ROSIE. This love-tattoo loomed down on to Park Avenue as it crossed the tracks into Freehold. Despite back-seat grouses, Doug always wanted to get home early of an evening. He fell in front of the TV while Adele put her hair up in curlers. Before long, she'd be singing erratically rich notes and deep snores whose resonance Bruce would feel 'entering [his] very blood'. Her husband ignored her.

Such, in the 1950s, was Springsteen's lot. 'I lived half of my first thirteen years in a trance,' as he says. 'I was thinking of things, but I was always on the outside looking in.' This same sense of exclusion ran as a theme for forty years. At the heart of his later career wasn't a revolt but an identity crisis. 'The loner thing started early,' he adds. 'My father's entire family were outsiders.' Adele, by contrast, could say 'God bless you' in five languages. Friends recall him as both a rich child and a poor one, brought up by parents who slaved for him – 'feeding his body but starving his soul', as Kern puts it. Randolph Street was the prism through which Springsteen saw adult life. As well as the family hothouse, he was shaped by simple moral and down-home ideals, giving him a consolatory zeal for 'truth' he belted on song after song. 'People deserve it, they deserve honesty . . . and the best music is there to provide something to face the world with.'

The idea of Springsteen as parochial, beached in a time and place he used as a metaphor, became standard logic during his glory days. And it was true. His roots coloured every fibre of his being, every act, every thought. There was a strong sense of provincialism made universal. Springsteen's world was Jersey, somewhere Edison and Einstein had worked but now, post-war, sadly lapsed and satirized as the 'armpit of America'. The northern towns were all sulphurous glare and gas. In summer there was the reek of the drug labs. From Jersey City ('embroidery capital of the world'), Irish and Italian immigrants gazed over the Hudson at the rear-end of the Statue of Liberty. Frank Sinatra, who grew up there, used to call it a 'sewer'. In the south there were swamps, with miles of fetid rivers and stubbly trees. On winter nights the sea froze solid and the cold seemed to have the pygmy's power of shrinking skin. Springsteen both romanticized and hated the state, channelling it into his best work, culling a palpable chunk of Jersey and making it play in Paris or Rome: a rare gift – burrowing down the middle of the popular fancy – and sure sign of a star.

His timescape was the '50s. The boxy Nashs and Chevys, the burr-cuts and Stetsons, the oil and gas scents ground deep into the worsted suits, the red-eyed girls in overalls with scarves over their curlers trudging to the coffee mill – those were the Proustian madeleines of Springsteen's youth. Especially the cars. Doug himself, his son says, 'was a driver . . . He got everybody else, too, and made us drive. He made us all drive.' This early taste of mobility was, typically, met with a matching snag. The Springsteens' Buick wouldn't reverse. Most mornings, mother and two children pushed it backward while Doug sat grim-faced at the wheel. It was no accident that Springsteen returned to this saga time and again. He told one friend of cold, wet days 'trundling Pa round and round', like Juggernaut. In 1982, he worked it obliquely into a full song on 'Used Cars'. The son's pique was open; his father's was hidden. But both men shared a love of the road and a lust for the bolt. As a rock star, Springsteen would cruise alone for hours, ploughing the Jersey turnpike, trawling the state in the Fords that became love-objects for him; it's not exaggerating to say that he related to them as near-human, the presence of a third party like a messy *ménage à trois*. (When a roadie idly ground the gears of one model, Springsteen yelled 'as if he'd been cut'.) As a boy, the Airflytes and Dodges revving up Highway 79 and Ducky Slattery's Station on South Street were the sights and sounds he fled but never left. The Springsteens 'loved wheels'.

They weren't a close family. The father shook his religious wife by periodic drinking binges. Money, too, played a part. Doug took and lost an impressive raft of jobs, from the rug mill to a cab firm and the county jail. (Not surprisingly, the dignity, or indignity, of work became another motif of the son's songs. By 1978, the concept of 'alienated labour' ran cars a close second.) From onstage in 1985, Springsteen would talk about his mother's trips to the loan company, 'to borrow money for Christmas presents that she'd pay back in time to borrow money for school clothes . . . And [Doug] would get angry about it. He'd get angry at *us*.' On Fridays, Bruce was sent to Main Street with a quarter for fish-heads. He'd also beg some bones for a nonexistent dog – then bring them home for the main course for Saturday supper. It wasn't unknown for him to haunt the dustbins at the Borough Hall soup kitchen. The Springsteens weren't ever in danger of starving. Adele's job as a secretary usually put food on the table. But there were few extras. They never ate out. No one bothered with new clothes. During bouts of real crisis, they might lodge for a few weeks with Adele's parents. Mr Zerilli, with a long, bony face enlarged by baldness, also used to mutter about being 'stony'. One deprivation was peculiarly symbolic. 'I wasn't brought up in a house where there was a lot of reading . . . I didn't hang around with no crowd that was talking about William Burroughs.' There was enough money for TV, but not for books. Friends rarely or never called. In short, life on Randolph Street was hard. Whether husband and wife fought isn't as clear as that Springsteen felt so. 'I think when you're a kid, one of the scariest things is hearing grown-ups argue.'

Wearing the bib overalls of the era, five- and six-year-old Bruce would dog his mother downtown, or sit for hours in his room – 'a kid,' he says, 'who didn't have anything to hold on to, or any connections . . . I was just reeling through space and bouncing off walls.' By the mid-1950s, his laugh had become a nervous, party-girl's wheeze. His black flat-top tapered off into effete blond bangs. Undersized and squint-eyed, Bruce was introduced to softball in Englishtown Park, hard by the jail. He was a dab hand at pitching and hitting, though that was his one and only sporting bent. In summer, father and son would sometimes dabble in a ten-minute game of catch. Then Doug would get back to his six-pack and Camels. Later still, he'd stump up to his son's room, then lean over and beerily shake the boy's hand. Beads of moisture dripped from the tarnish and heat of the ceiling, like the sweat on Doug's lips; even at bedtime, he rarely spoke. For Bruce, already a loner, containment became a way of life. He distinguished, however, between mere seclusion and self-fulfilment. Early on, he found his niche.

The Zerillis loved music. Bruce's maternal grandmother sang 'Pony Boy' to him in the crib. Aged three, he was listening to the newly coined 'C & W' hits (the hybrid was born, like him, in 1949) from Nashville. Gene Autry, Roy Rogers and, his favourite of favourites, Hank Williams were about him as he grew up (a circle Springsteen closed on the countrified *Nebraska* and *Tom Joad*). At weekends Adele would take him down Smithburg to Appel Farm, where cowboys played 'event' songs and barn dances, all fiddles and yodelled vocals, as Bruce clapped along. Folk's streak of populism also caught his ear. He later said he 'went nuts' for Woody Guthrie. Into the mix, meanwhile, went hymns and Appalachian ballads droned from a thousand porches – every one-room shack had a radio. He could already sing along to 'Sh-Boom'. Now a new role model was filling out his education as fast as he could get it. Elvis Presley's first single hit the *Billboard* regional chart the month Springsteen turned five. 'That's All Right' may have flopped in Jersey, but it rang bells on Randolph Street. Thirty years later, Springsteen staggered a friend by his total recall of early rock lyrics. Whole aeons of his schooldays were, he said, 'hazed'. But he could quote all night – and often did – from 'Maybellene' or 'Monkey Business'. He wasn't so much entranced as infected. Pop gave him the licence to be dirty, sweaty and loud, the licence to get even, to make the real world vanish – and, ultimately, to blow town. Once Springsteen started aping the twelve-bar hits from Memphis and Detroit, it was only a matter of time for him and Freehold.

This Pauline conversion was surely a fantasy. He spent the next several years telling anyone who listened he was called 'Fats' or 'Buddy'. Springsteen lip-synched in front of a mirror. He practised pouts. What was most important, rock radiated the fragrance of the city. Even as a boy, he found Freehold 'a classic tip . . . Kids were looked on as a nuisance and a threat . . . The place choked you.' Over ten years, Springsteen's day-dreams would grow, while the small-town reality squeezed tighter. It was an interesting decade.

Springsteen's first clash with formal education came as a mutual shock. It was the start of what he still calls the 'big hate'. Overnight, the strong-but-shy six-year-old was catapulted into leering mutiny. Each weekday morning, Adele walked him around the corner to St Rose of Lima school on Lincoln.* (The ritual made it easy for him to gauge his height, since he could just reach far enough to take her

---

*Significantly, perhaps, St Rose herself had been a beautiful young nun who rubbed her face with pepper and scoured her skin with lime to disfigure herself and thus 'know the Lord'.

hand.) The place was staffed by the Sisters of St Francis of Philadelphia and a lay faculty of Catholics. It boasted a mission said by the pastor to be the 'intellectual, spiritual, emotional and physical growth of every child', by Adele 'devotion to God', and, in Springsteen's view, 'utter crap'. First thing inside, he took the oath of allegiance. The classes that followed were in religion, reading, math, English, penmanship and gym. Notably lacking was any hint of music. Bruce quickly learned what it was like to be backward, and baited, by the other kids – especially the girls. 'We ragged him,' says a St Rose graduate, Toni Hentz. 'Bruce was very sort of dorky in those days. He was dirt-poor, wore britches and liked what we still called "nigger" music. You can imagine how it set him apart.'

So, suddenly, life became bewildering, and by the time he learned to read and write he was a Valium case. Springsteen's fate to be always the outsider was blazed early on. He was slow in class, which made him a quarry for the cane-cracking nuns. One reason for this sloth was his home life. By his seventh birthday, he was squarely in the 'problem child' tradition. It became a vicious circle, the Sisters seeing only the image they foisted on him, which he in turn beamed back to them. As he moved up the school, rock and roll would become a war between him and the adult world. Even his mother thought him 'nutso' about Elvis and nagged him about it. Bruce, on the defensive, finally agreed 'Hound Dog' was silly, but later decided maybe it wasn't. Of all the singles he heard growing up, these first battle-hymns were the ones that lived.

'I remember when I was a kid. The first thing I remember is the living room of my grandparents' house . . . My grandfather had this big stuffed chair next to a kerosene stove. And I'd come running home from school and sit [there] and I remember how safe I felt.' In later years, Springsteen was skilled at softening hard memories with happy stories. His nostalgia for the lost world of 1956 hid a grim truth: the family were living with Adele's parents because Doug was broke. Despite a promising start, he'd failed to make a career in the Karagheushian rug mill. Later, he lost part of his hearing, and his job, in a plastics factory. The loan company in turn, forced an undignified exit from Randolph Street. For all his mutual love of the Zerillis, Bruce now bore the stigma – says a classmate – of 'white trash'. Another friend remembers him as 'a very weird kid'. And so it went. A Freeholder named Todd Grice says he grew up 'kind of aloof and geeky. He always carried such a weight.'

The Springsteens eventually moved a half-mile east, where they shared a two-family home on Institute Street. Doug took work at the county lock-up. Neither address could have been much worse. The duplex was in a rundown ghetto known as 'Texas', where immigrant navvies lived four to a room and dug ditches twelve hours a day, often in snow and sub-zero weather: the Nestlé packing-line, by comparison, was near-imperial status. All around were jerry-built shacks, slums whose yards gave only beer cans or the odd junked appliance as proof of life. Fifty feet from Institute Street, the freight trains made a thought-pulverizing thunder. Tracks ran like spurs in the distance, skirting the naval weapons base and Cranberry bog, ferrying chemicals and waste to the Gulf of Mexico. Those fifty feet were worlds exquisitely split. Bruce would never ride even the coal-cart south. But the railroad did, nonetheless, run the road a close second in the boy's imagination. For years, he'd lie awake at night listening to the box-cars: another aesthetic link to Steinbeck's touch of constant mobility; another connection to Joad's America. Mentally, he'd already fallen in with that part of humanity he saw all around, the part he most related to – the lost, the broke, the outcast, the ruined.

The Springsteens' home was a modest frame box in dun grey Bruce later called a 'log cabin'. It was indeed made of logs, solid balsa. Up the stoop and through the screen door were a dim-lit parlour and a kitchenette. A coal stove there gave as much heat as a sixty-watt bulb. Upstairs was the luxury of two beds. 'We had a bathroom with a big gaping hole in it,' Bruce said. 'I used to tell the other kids that during the war a plane crashed into it – to save face, y'know?' Across the scrub lay a tomato patch. At eight, his idea of fun was to lob the fruit at strangers, once splattering Grice until, he says, 'I looked like something out of *The Texas Chainsaw Massacre*'.

Another passer-by, caught in the salvo, beefed to Doug, who flogged Bruce and sent him to bed without supper. Adele collapsed in tears.

It was a bad day, the mother crying while the son smarted in an unheated bedroom. Institute Street was like that. Aside from a growing tension with Doug, there was the sheer claustrophobia. When Bruce's paternal grandparents stayed (which they did, for weeks), six would share a semi-detached made for two. Most nights, too, the Springsteens would be at the mercy of their neighbours, whose rows blared through the homes' common wall. A longing for privacy, rooted in the early years, became one of the major conflicts of Bruce's adolescence, and lasted his whole life.

In 1958 his feeling for music warped into frenzy. As he put it twenty years later, 'I remember when I was nine and I was sittin' in front of the TV and my mother had Ed Sullivan on and on came Elvis. I remember right from that time, I looked at her and I said, I wanna be just . . . like . . . that.' Adele met his fixation with a fetish. She bought him a guitar. His hands were too small for it, and the few lessons he took were 'like a coma'; but he had the tool of his trade. Bruce's precocious practising and obvious ear for melody marked him as a 'billy', local slang for the Appalachians who rocked to and fro on porches scrubbing at banjos. A cousin speaks of Springsteen's new 'jock itch' for his hero. It was more than that. It was already an identification. 'When I was nine,' he says, 'I couldn't imagine anyone *not* wanting to be Elvis.'

From then on, Bruce was busy as a pop-based pluralist or a small-town misfit. This was his life in the early 1960s: withdrawn, tense – a 'pale, sulky kid', Grice calls him – who came alive in front of WINS or *American Bandstand*. He was, by even abject local levels, undereducated. On his own admission, he read only three books in twenty years. But Springsteen would eventually drop out of community college without regret. He believed as a twelve-year-old – as he did later – that he'd chosen a course in the 'university of life', whose means and end were self-redemption. He came to this conclusion in an epiphany. 'Until I realized that rock was my connection, I felt like I was dying . . . and I didn't really know why.'

Music was the 'big, gigantic motivator', a daily surrogate for the kudos others won in shop or class. Or church. Bruce had a semi-pious way of speaking of his conversion. 'It's like [Elvis] came along and whispered a dream, and then we all dreamed it somehow.' This sense of rock-as-religion would buoy him for years, stunning Adele and bringing him untold woe at St Rose. Springsteen once handled a form project to draw Christ by showing Him crucified on a Gibson. The nuns, he said, 'went mental'.

He still used the guitar as a prop, not a springboard. Traumatized by his lessons and unable to form chords, Bruce gave up on it for four years. He studied rock like a curator. From radio and TV he learned to think in terms of musical patterns; in other words, the big picture. At thirteen he knew more about Eddie Cochran than he did of his own family. Bruce's home Ph.D. in low art was, he says, a 'whole Grand Canyon' between him and the 'straights' – especially dour, tone-deaf Doug, mired as he was in his own soul's death throe. By 1962–63, the simmering row between father and son would boil to a crisis. Meanwhile, the child's guitar went back into storage.

His feud with the Sisters of St Francis didn't, however, stay in the closet. The school's 1962 prospectus speaks of a 'warm and lovely' place for the children – 'bull' to Springsteen, whose early teens were decidedly on the ugly side. First, 'a nun stuffed me in a garbage can under her desk because, she said, that's where I belonged'. Next he had the distinction of being physically punished by a priest during mass. He was then exiled to the first-grade class and hit by a six-year-old. Finally, Bruce got in a fight with two football players, who knocked out his front tooth and demanded sex. Then things took a turn for the worse.

Seminal stuff like that can make a thirteen-year-old go either way. In the event, Springsteen grew up coiled rather than dramatically 'bad', taut, uptight, surly and pathologically anti-religion. Adele had wanted him to be an altar boy. His response to this was theatrical: he threw up. Along with his pattern of morbid seclusion with the TV or radio, there was an accompanying blast of atheism. Something in his rage at St Rose would carry over into his early songs. Springsteen was, he says, on a 'bible-burning trip'. It was doubtless this crusade that led John Hammond* to ask him, 'Bruce, were you brought up by nuns?' Parting rants about 'unholy blood' and pregnancies in the Vatican were a direct upshot of the long years, it seemed to him, of ritual abuse.

At fourteen, Springsteen moved from parochial school to Freehold Regional High. It, too, was a flop. Like many shy boys, he relied on memorizing in order to shine. A classmate recalls Bruce's 'dull, semi-dead mode' and glazed eyes as he quoted yards of Shakespeare. Rote learning, for his peers, was enlivened by the 'deez, demz and doz' tones in which he mauled the text. The muffled sniggers were yet another small snub. Mostly, though, Springsteen sleep-walked his way to graduation. His introversion brought him the fear and hatred of the staff, without ever giving him the status of 'class clown'. The gloomy, ivy-clad school never took much shine to Bruce, and he cordially returned the contempt. Other alumni would wait in vain, each summer reunion, for their most celebrated old boy to show up. For three decades, he never did. It was years before he even drove by – this time as the conquering hero, Freehold's sole export. By then whole books had been written on the 'aloof and geeky' loner who said of himself, 'I didn't have friends . . . I was quiet and shy and liked to putter with cars.'

Speaking from the far side of fame in 1998, Springsteen would introduce a reading by Paul Dunbar with the words, 'This is a poem about not feeling free to be yourself. It's about the pain of not being accepted. When I was young, I felt like I needed a mask to be accepted . . . I was a zero.' He ran into practical prejudice against his eyes-down, mumbled affect when, at Ocean College, fellow students alleged he was 'sicko'. That did for his formal education. 'I was a zero' may be more than Springsteen meant, but there's no denying he trod on the precipice of 'be[ing] a jerk. It was like I didn't exist . . . I was working on the inside all the time. A lot of rock people go through that experience.'

---

*The famed producer and A&R man at CBS, discoverer of Pete Seeger, Aretha Franklin, Bob Dylan – and, not least, Springsteen.

As well as the twin totems of cars and music, Springsteen had a hawk eye for girls. 'Pussy, always pussy,' says Grice. He may have passed on drugs, but he was dead set on sex and rock and roll. Toni Hentz adds that at school Bruce 'was almost aggressive about letting you know he was "doing it"'. Many of these early flings read like first drafts of his own songs. There were walks in the park to the west, or trips to Lake Topanemus, ringed by fields that were a dim green in the wet and a burnt gold in the summer. Springsteen liked to play baseball there. His one other known hobby was the movies. Fifty cents bought him a pass to the Roxy or Battleground Arts, where he stretched a boyish love of Roy Rogers into an adult awe of John Ford and Sergio Leone. That Springsteen related to films is obvious from the number of titles or themes he took from the screen: 'Thunder Road', 'Badlands', the 'flesh and fantasy' of 'Jungleland', 'Adam Raised A Cain', 'Point Blank', 'Nebraska', 'Atlantic City', 'Highway Patrolman' (itself making a feature), 'Used Cars', 'Murder Inc.', 'My Father's House', 'Born In The USA', 'Cautious Man', 'All That Heaven Will Allow', 'Tunnel Of Love', 'Local Hero', 'The Big Muddy', 'The Long Goodbye' and most of *Tom Joad*.

Music, meanwhile, wasn't a hobby. It was what he did. Bruce's idols came to him daily, under the covers, in recess, or loping up Main Street with his Motorola. The AM stations out of Manhattan and Trenton were the medium. Elvis and Fabian, wall-of-sound merchants like the Ronettes and Crystals and finally the British Invasion of 1963–64 were the backdrop to his second-wave research. On his fourteenth birthday, Adele duly bought him another guitar. The sunburst Kent in turn gave way to a chrome yellow Fender from a pawnshop. As well as this $60 investment, Bruce talked her into a co-venture on an RCA stereo. Between the hi-fi, the radio and TV, Springsteen now had a parallel world, where nuns and parents gave way to the likes of Dylan, the Beatles and Phil Spector's girl groups. A maternal cousin taught him the basics of twelve-bar songwriting. From sheet music and records he developed his own voice and gilded a few rough grooves into tunes. It was another Damascene moment down the road to Bruce's salvation. '[The Fender] was one of the most beautiful sights I'd ever seen . . . A magic scene . . . There it is: The Guitar. It was real and it stood for something . . . I'd found a way to do everything I wanted.'

Bruce's hands-on apprenticeship only widened the 'whole Grand Canyon' between adults and him. In particular, most of his adolescence was boxed in by two hard-liners. Doug and Freehold High made for a tight frame. When the younger Springsteen wasn't playing the Fender or rolling dice by the bike sheds, he found time to 'severely fuck up' his teachers. He hated school. One colleague recalls him 'sloughing off Broadway through the gate, with that hooded don't-dick-with-me face of his, real dark'. Trying a new look, Bruce grew his hair frizzily past his collar. Acne loomed. His voice was a drone or the loud honk of a toy accidentally trod on. By 1965, he went AWOL for days on end. The Springsteens were called constantly by the Port Authority police in New York. 'I did a lot of running away,' he says. 'And a lot of being brought back. It was terrible.' Sport held marginally more clout with him than scholastics. Bruce enjoyed softball and was something of a gym-rat. But he was never, says the same friend, 'a jock . . . I mean, Bruce didn't give a shit about teams or organization.' He could hold his own in a fight, and enjoyed the prestige of the form 'nut'. It was no place for a shy, emotionally stunted boy who wanted to ape Elvis.

Home now was 68 South Street, another squat box warmed by a weak stove and a few dim bulbs which Doug shut off each night. He banned any light or heat after ten, even when, in his own words, it was 'cold as Medusa's tit'. 'I still remember him catching Bruce with a torch,' says his cousin, and 'blasting so hard his hollering could be heard up and down the street'. Somehow, that was of a piece with the whole house. Aside from a tiny, tinny Raytheon TV, the gothic parlour was set off by a gloomy photo of Doug's dead sister. The stucco walls were almost black from smoke. It was unbearably close. Most nights, for years, there was a sullen thudding row between father and son. In one spat, Doug threw a full beer can past Bruce's head. A neighbour, fearing he was braining the boy, began yelling, 'You'll kill him, bud! You'll kill him!' The police came.

The Dickensian fog lifted just once. A dozen years after her daughter's birth, Adele got pregnant again. It was a rare thaw in the icy aura of South Street. '[Adele] took me through the whole thing,' says Springsteen. 'We used to sit on the couch and watch TV, and she'd say, "Feel this", and I'd put my hand on her stomach . . . [It was] one of the best times I can ever remember, because it changed the atmosphere of the whole house.' Doug, moody, fissile and explosive for years, became less surly and uptight around the baby. 'A ceasefire broke out when Pam was born,' says their cousin. But this seems to have been a truce, not a peace. By the mid-1960s the father's two passions, for sitting home and brooding, were met by the son's for escape and loud rock. A clash was all but ordained, and duly came. Bruce spent ten years paying Doug back, if not openly then burning down inside. Predictably, vengeance was the first source of his music, which flowed on the near-patricide of his lyrics.

The Beatles and the Stones – even Herman's Hermits and the rest – were, therefore, more than mere pin-ups. They were already a blueprint. At its core was a love of 'real' life, not the Freehold High kind ('We learned more from a three-minute record/than we ever learned in school,' sang Springsteen in 1984); and retaliation. The latter came early in Bruce's work, and resurfaced constantly. 'I pushed B-52 and bombed 'em with the blues' was just the glib end of a theme hammered home in 'Adam Raised A Cain'. The idea of his 'getting even' was neither surprising nor illogical to Bruce's friends. After first hearing *Darkness on the Edge of Town*, Grice noted, 'it sounds just like him'.

Other than school and home, Springsteen's other long-term war was with God. Most Catholic artists have dabbled in what Sting calls the 'blood and guts' imagery of their faith. Names as far-flung as Billie Holiday and Madonna have wrapped their lyrics in the iconography of the Virgin Mary, Christ and the cross. Most have tested, if not junked, the guardrails defining the limits of 'normal' ethics. So, in time, did Springsteen. He never suffered the moral trauma at the core of, for one, Holiday's life. But his rejection ran deep. 'I was raised Catholic,' he said. 'Everybody who's raised Catholic hates religion. They hate it, they can't stand it.'*

In fact, the teenager's devotion, along with his character and moods, seems to have been split down parental lines. Doug had balked when marrying Adele; and while he joined the family semi-regularly at St Rose, he was no bible-basher. As a boy, it seemed to Grice, Bruce, too, 'approved of God in principle, and in practice not at all'. The Sisters of St Francis duly turned this ambivalence into atheism. A full volte-face followed. In his twenties, Springsteen began to strafe the nuns in earnest. He'd 'soon realized the people teaching [divinity] relied on fear', he said. 'I quit that stuff when I was in eighth grade,' he told another paper. 'By the time you're older than thirteen it's too ludicrous to go along with any more . . . I just lost it all.' From semi-fame in 1975, he was blunter: 'I don't go to church. I ain't been in eight years. I don't believe in that crap.'

In short, Springsteen's assault on Freehold would be as much a blitz on mass religion as on Ma and Pa. He'd long promised himself that, when the time came, he'd settle his score with St Rose. Anti-clericalism was a strong if subtle force on half of his early songs. Only when Springsteen began to hone a stage act did he switch tack; by the early 1980s, most of the yarns were leavened with a vein of wit. Increasingly, his raps became a kind of key for 'getting' a lyric. By and large, these were dour for the 'message' songs and surrealistic when parody called. Thus the long intro to 'Pink Cadillac': 'Now *here's* one about the conflict between worldly things and spiritual health. Where did this conflict begin? Well, the Garden of Eden was originally meant to have been in Mesopotamia . . . But the latest theological studies have found out it was located off the Jersey turnpike. That's why they call it the Garden State.' Hence, his gag about the burning bush. Or the one that went, 'God said to me . . . "Moses was so scared, he went back down the mountain. What you guys don't understand is that there was supposed to be an Eleventh Commandment. And what it said

---

*'Poor boy,' Andy Warhol once told me. 'I love church myself. It's so pretty.'

was . . . Let It Rock!".' Jangled together, it was all midway from some deep Joycean stream-of-consciousness and Monty Python. The reality is that Springsteen saw he could just as easily blast the religious as blast religion. The actual targets of the skits focused more on zealotry than raw faith. As the eighties went by, he even began to take a secularized, guiltless view of redemption – indeed, to some, *was* the redeemer. It became his peculiar faculty, that of a sharp but highly abstract and isolated mind, to see things that other men didn't and to miss what was under his nose; to gloss over the present yet dwell on several major trends of the dim past. He never totally disowned Rome.

The appeal to core American ideals would play a major part in rallying fans to the cult flying under the banner and flag of Bossmania. Springsteen may have skipped '*Feinschmecker*' Catholicism – the sort catering to gourmets of religious ritual. But he was no nihilist. Many of his later songs flaunted a set of quixotic, vox pop values and greeting-card pleas for 'faith'. At bottom, these were risibly inept. On peak form, the lyrics were warm, wry and life-affirming. Springsteen was at once compassionate and convincing in his portrayal of the key imperative, of grace under pressure. The means of this credo lay in individual dignity, not in dogma. *Nebraska*'s 'Reason To Believe' was an early hint of his lay ideology. Springsteen echoed the same point a decade later, when he sang on 'Human Touch': 'Ain't no mercy on the streets of this town/Ain't no bread from heavenly skies/Ain't nobody drawin' wine from this blood/It's just you and me tonight.'

Finally, inevitably, he took on a kind of priestly role himself. The four-hour shows, full of smoke, noise and Shinto-like awe, became a *de facto* rite. Fans went to worship. Agnosticism, to them, was a mortal sin. The vehicle of this homage and of his powers of self-dramatization was Springsteen's rare gift for narration, quite different in kind from most rockers' spiels ('Here's one off the new album'), even other demi-gods'. During the raps, the house hushed. In the hymns, they chanted along. It was a true communion; Springsteen's rapport with his flock was very real. The traumas of his own life mattered little beside the force and immediacy of the passions, the intensity of the pity and the sheer joy conveyed by his voice. Another sentence from Father Greeley sums it up: 'Springsteen sings of religious realities – sin, temptation, forgiveness, life, death, hope – in images that come (implicitly perhaps) from his Catholic childhood, images that appeal to the whole person, not just the head, and that will be absorbed by far more Americans than those who listen to the Pope.'

Springsteen's adolescent dreamworld began at fourteen. He found sex. He gave up baseball. And he got the guitar. His investment of all his hopes and fantasies in rock bore dramatic fruit. He devoted literally every non-school waking hour to the Fender. Adele was polite, if puzzled. Doug waged war against what he called the 'goddam thing'. Bruce absorbed her confidence that he'd prove to be 'someone big' (she hoped an author) who'd do great things; from his father he acquired a drive – both fleeing from some inner sense of deficiency that, at root, was pitiable – and a hate of authority. This one-two punch was to prove a potent legacy.

For any take on the turning-point, 1964 was the year. He'd finally woken up to what was inside him – and the shock would last him a lifetime. That summer, Bruce listened nonstop to the Stones and drew a bead from them to gurus like Chuck Berry and the horn-happy sounds of Stax. Rufus, Otis, Percy, Sam and Dave – these were the names that came through, trebly and static-ridden, on the Motorola. It was the long summer when civil-rights workers were slain in Mississippi; the Vietcong inflicted heavy losses on Saigon; and the Democrats met in Atlantic City, downstate from Freehold. But on South Street, Bruce fretted over scales and the two-note solo on 'It's All Over Now'. Playing the Fender six hours a day, his timbre soon ripened into technique. As if in illustration, he also hammed up his latinized, 'guinea' looks. By autumn he was a staple at Caiazzo's Music Store. He spent whole days talking shop there with fellow greasers. Now a neo-hood who wore black jeans and white T-shirts, Bruce joined his first band, the Rogues. Motive had met with opportunity.

Though they failed to come up with the Great American Single, the group's guitarist was starry-eyed even at working the Elks Club or the odd bar mitzvah. Also, he knew he was improving all the time. The rote student of Shakespeare was matched by the deft impersonator of the Temps and Tops. He was an arch-copyist, forever digging and deconstructing until he could get off a note-by-note clone. Fans would later attribute the famous Springsteen style and momentum to a God-given gift and the fact that he 'meant it'. Both of those were true, but they hid a third X-factor. He was a mimic: especially of the point-man stars of his day. Bruce's hankering for 'real' music went back to a rare row with Adele, when he'd insisted that Dylan had the 'coolest voice', whereas his mother said, 'That guy can't sing.' Within a week, Bruce was teaching the Rogues the early chords of 'Like A Rolling Stone'. ('The first time I heard it,' he said twenty years later, 'on came that snare shot that sounded like somebody'd kicked open the door . . . The way that Elvis freed your body, Bob freed your mind.') The band's own turf was staked by a fixation with the doo-wop and girl groups (whose lyrics Bruce quoted by the acre), Berry's dry colloquialisms and the free-form wordplay of *Highway 61 Revisited*. He loved Sinatra as well as rock 'clowns' already past their 1950s grandeur, like Jerry Lee Lewis. The result was a kind of devil's brew of Hit Parade styles. At sixteen, Bruce covered the waterfront from folk to boogaloo with hairbrained Catholicism. The 'key to the highway', as he called the Fender, went everywhere with him: on the bus, downtown, and sitting home, with his pa hollering upstairs. His floor was Doug's ceiling.

Meanwhile, in another grey duplex on Center Street, a second teen band was raising the roof and the hackles of their neighbour, a 35-year-old mill hand named Tex Vinyard. (He happened to be home on strike at the time.) After the shouting had died down, Vinyard listened to the group – named the Castiles, after the soap – and 'kinda' liked them. Within weeks, he was working as their cook, driver, banker and *de facto* manager, offering homespun advice and touches of 'girl-problem' help. In this last context, one Castile, the singer George Theiss, was dating Ginny Springsteen. Word, in time, passed down to South Street. One night when, in Vinyard's

words, 'it was rainin' like a cow pissin' on a rock', a punk in scuffed
dark pants and draggled hair came banging on the porch door.

'Hi,' he said. 'Name's Bruce. I hear you're looking for a guitar
guy.'

There was no lightning, no peal of thunder. Vinyard himself
'wasn't knocked out' by the first night's audition. Years later, he
remembered telling the morbidly shy boy to 'go listen to the radio'.
The very next night, Springsteen (now dressed entirely in black)
knocked again at the screen door. He coughed. Then he tuned the
guitar. Next he played three songs, note-perfect, back to back, and
absent-mindedly ripped off two more as an encore. There was a
long pause, broken by Vinyard saying Yep, he could join the band.
Bruce was quiet and, without a guitar in his hands, totally stum – 'a
cold kid', says Grice; a loner and James Dean type, according to
Kern; in Hentz's words, a 'vineyard-bottled nerd' who boasted he
had fist-fights with Doug. He was prone to crying jags. But once he
strapped on the Fender (or his borrowed blue Epiphone) it was like
the makeover scene in *The Nutty Professor*.

By 1966 the Castiles were a local fixture on the roller-rink and
pizza-hall run, churning out a relentless diet of Motown, Stones
and Who hits – and, at Vinyard's insistence, a brassily melodramatic 'In The Mood' – for $35 a night. Springsteen, in the
semi-pro and narrowly parochial sense, had arrived. By now he
was so good that, when he rehearsed in Vinyard's den, the black
and Appalachian kids would stand on beer-crates outside the
window, just to watch.

The jump from 'zero' to guitar-god, from 'nut' to local hero,
came just as other Gibraltars crumbled, ex-truths were ditched and
even Freehold – where, as Grice says, an 'alternative lifestyle meant
bowling every other Friday' – was set on its ear. Springsteen was a
gifted musician with real flair. But he could never have carried off
his tainted gains in a world of pre-1966 innocence. His very life was
being taken over by putsch. The fall-out of civic, local and family
feuds made for a creative wet-dream. Springsteen himself, emerging suddenly at a time when people were in an ugly mood, framing
his act for an audience of troubled Boomers, helped to lead a Great

Awakening which swept away much of Doug's own values. In a very real sense, he was both godfather and a child of his age.

On the national front, the Great Society prank pumped billions of dollars into state action plans, in turn funnelling funds to help towns like Freehold to their own grass-roots 'solutions'. Soon enough, the Appalachian slums were being squeezed by rising new construction, the Raceway Mall and I-33 only the most visible fruits of a whole battery of schemes, from Head Start to the Job Corps. Not coincidentally, America erupted in race riots. Unable to segregate themselves as the hated 'pointy-heads' did, working-class whites increasingly chafed at the affirmative-action and 'quotas' afforded their black neighbours – who, in their own ethnic backlash, looted Newark and dozens of other cities. Springsteen would work this strife into his 1984 'My Hometown'. Meantime, his own defiance swelled in reply to paternal rants about the 'goddamn' Fender, poor grades and lack of drive. By 1966, Bruce and Doug were at swords' points. 'When I was growing up,' the former said, 'there were two things that were unpopular in my house. One was me, and the other was my guitar.' Some of the wilder stories of the father 'smoking out' the son with gas-jets and grousing 'Wait'll the Gooks get you' are in the realm of myth; but it's clear that Doug personified a dark omen of the world of jobs and responsibility; that he and Bruce fought like ferrets in a sack; and that the latter rightly said, 'There ain't a note I play on stage that can't be traced back to my mother and father.'

At seventeen, he'd grown into a semi-hulk, 5′ 10″ and 150 pounds of classic rock-star build: hipless, with pipe-stem legs and a big head. After a motorbike wreck, Bruce would walk with a slight drag. His voice was a dry rasp, with the odd startling swoop of a laugh – what a friend calls his 'Muttley smirk'. Gap-toothed, he was clean-shaven and long-haired (another running war with Doug). Bruce's half-formed intellect found expression in wild, curly handwriting. He never read. His anthem was 'It's My Life' and his trademark a denim and leather confection that screamed 'punk'. In the few hours he wasn't practising or playing the guitar, he was off panhandling in Asbury Park or trawling the strip-joints of Manhattan – someone, even before he could drink or vote, whose type was cast.

In most ways he emerged as the classic Jersey low-life. In few but vital ones, he didn't. Even as Bruce's moods darkened, his tastes became increasingly vanilla. Amid the Who and Animals, he loved surfers like the Beach Boys. He raved about Sam the Sham's 'Wooly Bully'. He even owned a madras shirt. Springsteen was among the last of his age group to pass his driver's test. Football and team sports left him, he said, 'dead'. Yet, if he got less exercise than the dreaded Freehold 'rah-rahs', he still liked to swim and run, and bulk up in the gym. Instead of drink or dope, he was infatuated with the idea of a revolution in the head. The guitar became an extension of his nervous system.

Whatever his shin-guard flaws, they were more than matched by his academic scrapes. Bruce was strictly a C and D student. He was brought down from his self-styled 'month-long vacations in the stratosphere' by abject grades. There was even talk about whether he'd graduate. 'He was always the one least-likely-to,' says Grice. For most of the winter of 1966–67, Bruce's odds-on fate was a swift exit into Bartending School or the Engine City Technical Institute (trading in diesel and truck mechanics). Doug lobbied hard for the army. These twin horrors triggered a last orgy of cramming. Even then, school-leaving wasn't ever a good, or done deal. First, Bruce planned to hitch-hike to the Monterey Pop Festival rather than take his diploma. When that fell through, he did a bolt for New York. Adele had to follow and talk him home by promising there wouldn't be a row with Doug. Once there, however, father began raving at son, physically throwing him into his room. Unscrewing the sole light bulb, Doug then left Bruce alone in the dark, whimpering in long, shuddering sobs and vowing revenge.

Springsteen left Freehold High on 19 June 1967. He never escaped it. Teachers duly joined nuns and fathers as thematic and personal hates. He completely disowned the school 'bennies' (the ones after a 'beneficial' education) and ran with the Sharks, who wore shoulder-strap vests and raced black Trans Ams down Main

Street. Later that Summer of Love, Bruce spent a night in jail in Wildwood, down the shore, for vagrancy. The Castiles themselves fell foul of what he calls the 'first dope bust there ever was in Freehold'. He then beat a morals rap involving two Asbury girls by leaving town, fast.

It was a strange year. Pop folklore has it as an Arcadia of Monterey, Hendrix and *Sergeant Pepper*. But it was also the time of anti-war rallies and race riots in Detroit, Boston and, finally, Newark. That night of 12 July, gangs looted shops and offices and set fire to the Jersey College of Medicine. On the 13th, the National Guard went in. Mayor Addonizio blamed the gunfire and firebombing on 'Negro mayhem'. The triangle of Broad and Market streets in the heart of Newark was a war zone. When the body-count was added up, twenty-five were dead and over 600 hurt; a thousand under arrest. Lesser acts of arson and pillage broke out in Freehold. A curfew was imposed. From his window in South Street, where he lay with the radio, Bruce could see the glow of burning rubble.

Like civil disorder, the saga of Vietnam had a long fuse, starting for the US with Washington's doomed veto of the return of French rule after the Japanese occupation. In the post-war years, more Marshall Aid had gone to Saigon than to Britain. Food was followed, in turn, by 'advisers'. Troops went in. By 1967, the total ground force would reach half a million. Stark footage of those who came home not on VIP jets but in body-bags was aired nightly on TV. It may be, as Springsteen says, that 'there wasn't any kind of political consciousness down in Freehold in the late '60s'. But he was well aware of the storm clouds over south-east Asia, and of the prospects opening up there for young graduates. Eighteen- and nineteen-year-olds were enlisting every day. The drummer from the Castiles signed up and was killed. Bruce had no strong ideological take on Vietnam: that came years later. He was, however, laser-sharp about his own involvement there. He was against it. In a draft-dodging feint being made by thousands – including a future vice-president and president of the US – he did an unlikely bunk to higher education. That autumn, the Jersey Selective Service Board were told that 'Mr Springstein [*sic*] is enrolled in a liberal arts course at Ocean County College' in Toms River, thirty miles down Highway 9 from Freehold.

He lasted a year there. Bruce dropped out in 1968, after – says the writer Dave Marsh – 'fellow students petitioned for his dismissal on grounds of unacceptable weirdness'. It's true, one ex-friend notes, 'the only BA ever linked with Bruce stood for Bad-Ass'; his tousled, 'hound' look still raised hackles among young and old alike. But the key issue was that he slept through class, didn't drink or do drugs, and played the Fender nonstop. A cruel and skewed characterization, 'weirdness' underscores the split personality who, simply by being one, was nailed as 'sicko'. There were really two of him – the sweaty R & B merchant and the sleep-walker on permanent audition for the dormouse role in *Alice in Wonderland*. 'Schizophrenia,' says Grice. 'Knowledge is death,' Springsteen told him, and then he was gone.

His night job, unlike his education, was booming. Springsteen saw the Stones in Asbury Park. He discovered Roy Orbison and Marvin Gaye. Hendrix, he said, 'showed us there was a deep ecstasy to be had'. Bruce's own ear for music – his rare gift for learning any chord structure inside twenty minutes – had already led him to writing: two numbers were cut by the Castiles in a booth at the Brick Mall shopping centre. These prehistoric recordings were matched by the germ of a stage act. On Vinyard's orders, the band all dressed alike in their snakeskin vests and pants, lurching from side to side with their guitars in tandem. They toyed with smoke-bombs and dragged a ladder onstage, which Bruce sat on to start the set. Within a year, constant practice and tireless press-agentry had jockeyed them into the Café Wha? in Manhattan.

Springsteen wasn't, though, just spit-shining his style. He was also doing something that few Jerseyans of the time considered a serious option: he made his own career, set his own agenda and consciously sought an audience. Bruce's long stigmatization as a 'nut' had given him a link to fellow loners. His talent, he often said, flowed 'straight from hell'. Behind this boast lay a broad streak of self-pity; but it gave him a charter and starring role in the transition of '70s cock-rock back to a loftier tone.

A strong sub-text was Springsteen's public bid to rationalize his feelings about Doug. Here at least, for a year or two, relations were stable. They hated each other. In one epic scene, Bruce's motorbike was hit by a car; he hurt a knee. While he was convalescing in bed, Doug brought the barber in to crop his hair. This, too, ended in a fight. Most of these rows circled from the specific to the general, always or usually fixing on money. 'My father was obsessed with it,' says Springsteen. There was no let-up. Even on the raw mornings when he'd trudged off to school, the twin street names DOUGLAS and DUTCH glared down on to Broadway: another distressingly visible sign of his heritage. A third alley read ALE. At night, Doug slumped woozily in front of *Get Smart* or *Bewitched*. 'We never talked,' says Bruce. But that's to woefully neglect the yelling jags about finding a job or joining up, or the joint threats of a kicking.

Soon enough, each album and gig was salted with folk tales of fathers and sons, like a shadowy presence of things Bruce couldn't speak of openly. There was nothing that barbed about these digs: just a bazooka blast of teen retribution. He often called his Doug-fixated yarns his 'guts'. In later years, he'd say that the sagas were meant to be 'universal', offering fans a fund of public confession. It was mutual therapy.

Bruce grew warmer to Doug as he got nearer him in experience. By the 1980s their blood feud was over, and once or twice they punched through each other's crust. Springsteen was more apt to see his father as a victim. 'He'd been so disappointed, had so much stuff beaten out of him . . . he just couldn't accept the idea that I had a dream.' He even allowed himself some fond memories of going along with Doug on his haulage job and helping load his truck. Finally, on 'Independence Day', he reached the tentative conclusion, 'I guess that we were just too much of the same kind.' From this thematic breakthrough, Bruce evolved a more benign, broth-erhood-of-man ethic which swapped 'guts' for grace.

In short, Springsteen matured. His policy on 'straights' shifted slowly yet strongly. The kneejerk angst became a more adult empathy. He saw his father up close and realized he wasn't only an icy, Olympian presence but also a fallible 'real dude'. An aunt gave Bruce a snap of Doug fresh from the army. 'He looked like John Garfield, in this great suit, he looked like he was gonna eat the photographer's head off . . . I used to wonder what happened to all that pride, how it turned into such bitterness. He'd . . . had so much stuff beaten out of him.' Doug himself would duly enlighten his family with the news that 'life's shit'. Bruce wasn't comforted.

So, for a year more, it went. According to Kern, life in South Street was like 'DefCon 2 mode'. A second friend confirms it as 'just fuckin' heavy'. The Springsteen *ménage* continued only formally – and in thrall to Adele's religion – after Pam's birth. Bruce himself would speak of being drawn unwittingly into the corrosive spat between his parents. Adele lived for the 9.45 a.m. Sunday mass and the sound of wedding bells at St Rose; Doug didn't. He'd enjoy a six-pack. She wouldn't. Their few talks, hissed through carious teeth, soon left the foreshore of debate for the choppy seas of 'screw you'. The personality clash at the heart of the Springsteens' marriage extended to a row over their guitar-happy son. At career-plan level, this came down to a surreal choice between his being an author (Adele) or a lawyer (Doug). Selective Service, meanwhile, loomed.

After the Castiles imploded, Springsteen went on to cut a tune called 'American Song', fêted by the *San Francisco Examiner* as a cycle of 'political-military observations, from Concord Bridge to the present'. Actually, 'issues' normally caused him simply to step aside, though he'd make a point of announcing his sidestep. Bruce was no anti-war fanatic. His spin on Vietnam was purely pragmatic. And personal: that summer of 1969 he was bussed to a conscription exam in Trenton. In Marsh's take, 'Bruce beat the draft in classic '60s fashion. "They gave me the forms and I checked everything. Even said I was a homo, and all that. Then this guy calls me into his office, talks to me for about three minutes and tells me to go home."' Springsteen himself would speak of 'scamming' the army, though that was to give him credit for more duplicity than luck. According to the archive, he was rejected because he was

graded 4-F. The notion of Springsteen as physically decrepit takes
getting used to, but the file, number 283349100, lists him as 'unfit'
due to his motorbike wreck. When Bruce went home to South
Street and admitted he'd failed the induction, Doug said simply,
'Good.'

His father's second, listless pronouncement was that the
Springsteens were moving. Bruce wasn't just shocked at the
news – he was stupefied. The decision was, he said, so 'drop-dead'
it left him with the undertow of the 'big hate' still surging, and no
one to flog with it. Now, for the first time, he was alone. In search
of eternal sunshine – and, not least, work – the family withdrew
their nest-egg of $3,000 and headed west, settling at 170 16th
Street in San Mateo, south of San Francisco. As well as the cash,
they took the stereo with them. Bruce himself stayed on. In the
newly altered acoustics of South Street, he played his Fender and
began hitch-hiking to Asbury Park. (He'd later recall how local
truckers, seeing his long hair, tried to run him off the road.) The
faded-but-funky bar scene was the staging post for his next few
bands: Earth gave way to Child, and in turn Steel Mill. Most of
Springsteen's tricks of style dated from this era. The bluesy snap
of his writing (now done on a new Gibson) joined with naturalistic sagas of girls and cars. 'Garden State Parkway Blues' doffed its
cap to *Sergeant Pepper*'s 'A Day In The Life'; while the starting
point for 'The Wind And Rain' was Scott Walker via the Bee
Gees. Springsteen began to stud his lyrics with highway
metaphors and words like 'hubcap'. The family's defection may
have been a low, but it jolted him to new transports of creativity.
From within and without, he compounded the themes that made
him great. 'Cutting the cord', he later admitted, left him dazed,
gutted and glad to be free.

That just left the problem of sustenance. Springsteen's plans to
live on in South Street were steadily and inexorably balked by lack
of cash. Eviction came. He was twenty, a high-school graduate and
college drop-out, shot of the army, and slowly winning fame as the
nimblest fingers and best 'ear' working the beach. That winter,
Springsteen left the airless house and teenage wasteland forever.

Home now became an attic over a surfboard factory at 610 Seventh Avenue in Asbury.

It wasn't so much a park as a series of dives, haunted by trippers and psychiatric patients – never mutually biased against spas – and a rollicking pub scene. Old, sprawling churches lurked beneath a tangle of bushes and weeds alongside clapboard villas and seedy pink cottages. The juke-joints rose from lines of hovels built of overlapping boards covered with milky whitewash. Asbury's spine was a leprous arcade of hotels, honky-tonks, miniature golf courses, pokerino machines and gypsy booths. A Ferris wheel looped over the Atlantic. Below the boardwalk, the fine-grain beach rounded into a flat bay. The climate was dry. No fog rolled in, no pollution. This was the place, full of heat, noise and the stench of Hawaiian Tropic Cream, that Springsteen made his own.

Thirty years ago, Asbury had been the talk of the north Jersey shore. Behind the boardwalk lay an imposing chaos of gilded Victorian manses, music halls ringed with bands of puce-red tiles, glitzy promenades, gingerbread spires and neon. On 4 July, acts like Glenn Miller and Harry James had filled the Convention Hall while fireworks thumped overhead. The picture postcard and salt-water taffy made their débuts here. Beauty pageants and fringe sport like kangaroo boxing all tricked out the season. An annual Asbury baby show drew 50,000 fans. Yet, by the time Springsteen hit town, there were signs the party was winding down. The glossy façade of the 'front' hotels concealed abject sleaze in the blocks behind. Old businesses were folding. Even the wise-guys and carnival hucksters had moved on. The carousel horses were rusted up. Neglect, competition and a trend for more worldly entertainment produced a pattern of genteel, cosy decay. What remained wasn't so much a beach as a desert. The place had a certain bawdy charm, but, resort-wise, Asbury was on the way down not the way up. Finally, race riots in 1970 and the collapse of stores due to the glut of suburban malls nearby made it official. The boom had become a bust.

The flagging shore town was, though, the seasonal rock mecca. In the 1960s, Asbury boasted mid-Jersey's only halls catering to the likes of the Who, the Stones and the Doors. The Paramount crowded against the Palace funhouse. A wilted Berkeley Carteret hotel, at the end of the boardwalk, served up an unlikely bag of James Brown revues and Methodist rallies. Down by Wesley Lake, meantime, the Upstage opened in 1968 over a shoe-shop on Cookman Avenue. It soon turned into an asylum-cum-all-hours club. A couple called Tom and Margaret Potter ran it as a sort of safe house for aspirant greasers. She remembers the first night Springsteen ambled in: 'He came up very politely and said, "Excuse me, but would you mind very much if I borrowed your guitar?" . . . He played some blues thing . . . I said, "Oh, Lord," and [told the other] guys, "There's some kid up there who can really play."' The Pandemonium, the Student Prince and the Sunshine Inn also all indulged Springsteen's new craze for breakneck solos and heavy, Cream-like riffs. Over the road, past the wooden-shack B & Bs and taffy stands, was a low, white-walled bar called the Stone Pony. It, too, became a drop-in and hang-out. Taken together they formed a spiritual home of sorts. In Asbury, far from Doug's rages, Springsteen could lap up a happy mix of soft, pliable father-figures – Potter taking over from Vinyard – late nights and long days in the surf. Despite the dogged sun worship, the music was, however, still being polished to a gloss. Steel Mill frequently revved up with three- and four-hour rehearsals. Appraising his leader's basilisk stare and downturned lip (plus the fact that he paid the wages), a friend duly coined the name Boss. It stuck. In Asbury, in those days, it was positively uncouth to be without an alias. The demand for exotic, show-band personae soon produced Big Bones, Southside Johnny and Miami Steve. Springsteen's new drummer answered to Mad Dog Lopez.

To the scouts and sinister 'market penetration' men from Manhattan, Asbury wasn't good enough: hopelessly downmarket, randy, naff, shady and stinking of greasy pizza. It was all these things. It was also much more. Amidst the plastic-lettered, overlit casino and Madame Marie's, clubs like the Upstage vaunted their end-of-the-line vulgarity by toasting style icons set not in London or New York but the ghettoes of Memphis and Detroit. It was a true 'scene', colourful, lewd and basic. Venues were stark, with whole rooms covered in speakers and the beat careening off the walls: auditions were equally crude; try-outs were welcome; people wandered in and set up a lurching, jolting vamp while a house pro like Springsteen sat in. His own essay on the Upstage gives the feel of it: 'Everybody went there 'cause it was open later than the regular clubs and because between one and five in the morning, you could play pretty much whatever . . . You could work it out so you'd never have to go home, 'cause by the time you got out it was dawn and you could just flop on the beach all day, or you could run home before it got too light, nail the blankets over the windows and just sleep straight through till the night.'

It was all a fair way from the nuns.

For Springsteen's songs, however, hope was a kind of sacrament that wasn't shed lightly. Many of his own lyrics set up a lay, holy covenant between artist and audience. For him, issues like love, truth and self-respect weren't just personal: they were human. The snap of these themes was achieved through constant revision and reworking of hoary rock clichés into something fresh, if not new. After straggling back to the surf shop at dawn, Springsteen would often retire again to the car. Sitting in the back seat, in his private mobile studio, he'd jot down the raw verses of 'I Remember' or 'Coming Home'. Not all the band were as sure as he was about these tarted-up Dylan spoofs, but they trusted his star. Springsteen worked hard to incorporate new hues into his already vivid palette. At their best, the songs were full of life, the stories alive and moving beneath their coating of heavy riffs, unfeasibly catchy and there to be savoured.

Above all, for Springsteen playing was the thing. Other rockers 'brought' the music, but, to them, it was a means to an end. He looked on it like a jihad. 'Every time you get on stage, you have to prove something,' he said. And: 'It has to be like life or death . . . I want to be able to go home and say I went all the way tonight – and then I went further.' Even these early gigs would help recharge a genre long numbed by drones like Yes and ELP. Springsteen's shows were a rare mix of high aim and pure ham. The shaggy-dog yarns and props were matched by his clenched-teeth vocals, howled over the clanging rhythm. As a player, Springsteen brought snappy instrumental fills and jackhammer-beat precision to such feral ravers as 'Dancing In The Street'. He was the 'great accumulator', effortlessly recycling a thousand pop-guitar licks. Many of his fiery Steel Mill workouts traced their DNA back to the Clapton–Page school. He could spray notes around like Alvin Lee. Springsteen would later say he meant to be 'just like the Stones'. Another more conceptually elevated template was Hendrix's pyrotechnics. All in all, it was music for the mind and feet. Those loud, teeming, sweaty nights in Asbury, where the steam rose, girls rushed the stage and Springsteen spent whole sets horizontal, were like the mob scenes in *Strange Days*, half-paradise, half-Hades, and no one who survived forgot them.

It truly was happening, though Springsteen himself fell off the pace set by his music. He was still two people. The 'baby' ribbed by the Castiles for neither smoking nor doping had become the 'boss' who rode herd on the band, slugged beer and played pinball like a war. Passive aggression was often his native tongue, and he used the word 'fuck' as if it were a comma. If no Priapus, nor was he monk-of-the-month. At least one colleague remembers his 'screwing most of our own chicks [like a] top dog marking his turf'. On their common ground, '60s hits and the whole history of pop, Springsteen knew he was incomparably smarter than his band. Nor did he have any doubts that as a writer he was in a different class from Miami, Southside and the rest. Behind the mask of his 'good rockin'' charisma, the one-for-all ethic gave way to a dour insistence on his 'own thing'.

The boys-in-the-band were the brothers Springsteen never had. Girls he handled as sisters – he knew about them – when he wasn't trying to maul them in other ways. Though he'd been late learning to drive, and still didn't smoke or do drugs, he was famously well slept. Many or most of Springsteen's gods, of course, had lived lives whose morals were proverbial. 'Shagging [was] in the game-plan' from the first.

'I know this is idealistic,' he once said. 'But, before I started playing, I . . . couldn't relate. One of the reasons I picked up the guitar was that I wanted to be part of something. And I practised and I studied and I worked hard to do that.' In time, this passionate need for connection fairly forced Springsteen to 'relate' to his fans, not least the young, female ones. 'We wanted to play because we wanted to meet girls, we wanted to make a ton of dough,' he told *Rolling Stone*. Even in the mid-1960s, Bruce would cut out from South Street and spend whole evenings wedged in a phone box, where, he said, 'I used to stand and call my girl and get her to call me back, and then talk to her all night.'

By 1970, the new *chutzpah* onstage tallied with a sorry moral slump off it. Before going on at the Stone Pony or Pandemonium, Springsteen would keep company with a groupie in an old Chevy in the back lot. There were groundlings called Mary and Sandy, also a beauty queen known only as J. Later he hooked up with a local named Joyce Moore. This Monmouth College senior was comely, funny, erratic and 'really loved' him. Moore 'dug Bruce big-time', but she pulled back from committing to anyone. When a close mutual friend, Jim Cobanis, came looking and found them alone together, a merry row ensued, the two men ending up bouncing around a bar, off a wall, debating the matter. That was the end of Springsteen and Moore. (She then had a bad auto wreck while still getting over the break-up.) A quote from Curt Fluhr, the Castiles' bassist, sums up the cheerfully loose ethos: 'Even then, I'd have to say Bruce [was] the most heterosexual person I ever met.' A year or two later, Springsteen would sing of 'Chasin' the factory girls underneath the boardwalk/where they promise to unsnap their jeans.' Once or twice, his life of blithe promiscuity was cut short by his proposing to a lover. Somehow these bouts of 'going steady' never converted. At least one woman thinks 'the sick vibe of his parents' life' was too strong to let him move from the thought of marriage to the reality.

Writ large, it was the Jekyll–Hyde complex. Springsteen may have been, as Toni Hentz says, 'sort of dorky' as a boy. But all that changed when he plugged in the Gibson. In the words of his future manager, Mike Appel, 'Bruce got women in his life the day he first strapped on a guitar in public.' Aside from Joyce Moore, there was

Diane Lozito, sundry waitresses and students, and, later, Karen Darvin, Lynn Goldsmith and Joyce Hyser.

In short, the Freehold greaser with the mane of curly hair and a wardrobe apparently filched from a thrift store was but a chord away from the local *capo*. Like a good method actor, Springsteen so grew into and enjoyed a role – Boss of bosses – that he became the very thing he'd only dreamed of. It was more than mere fancy. By his twenty-first birthday, he was already heavyweight champion of Asbury, whose only other contenders gamely tagged along. A rat-pack grew up around him. Southside, Miami and Mad Dog were joined in turn by Fast Eddie, Black Tiny, Weak Knees and Jack the Rabbit. Springsteen effortlessly slid home his leadership of the gang (forerunner of the E Streeters) – the man of genius yoked with the men of talent, relationships that not only served all parties but also ran on genuine warmth. Aside from his obvious flair, there was the fact that Springsteen never worked a day job. Languidly sanding a surfboard was as close as he came. The sheer intensity of his professional zoom (compared by his drummer to a 'Cruise missile in flight') set him off. People talked. Symptomatic of Springsteen's popular status is Grice's quip that 'he just fucked and sang, not necessarily in that order'. A local musician called Ken Viola, talking to writer Marc Eliot, would remember him 'always saying he was going to make it, that was his big thing. "I'm going to make it, I'm going to make it . . ."'

Springsteen found his true voice in the years crawling the coastal bars. Different ingredients went into it, but the combination was unique. There was the love of primal rock and jangly pop, key to his sound, and a growing affection for soul. Dylan was an obvious grid reference. Springsteen, too, 'drooled over' *Electric Ladyland*. In 1969, Creedence Clearwater's *Bayou Country* joined the list. It was the best music of the year, Springsteen felt, with the paramount virtue he wanted for his own: it was 'real'. His slap-happy eclecticism ('they wouldn't let me in some [clubs],' he said, 'because I didn't do Top 40') was mated to a guitar style where acoustic strum did battle with Clapton-esque bombast. The rock critic and musician Lenny Kaye remembers meeting Springsteen in Asbury. 'He took me upstairs,

where we stood in a tiny room and jammed. Bruce played the shit
out of a song called "Season Of The Witch", just winged it . . . He
blew me away.' Springsteen's virtuosity was the unifying link for
tunes as far-flung as the chugging 'Why'd You Do That?' and 'Sister
Theresa', all brushes and flute. One cut from those days, 'The Train
Song', has worn well as a slab of twangy riff-rock. Less successful
were Springsteen's outings into Van Morrison-land. At this stage,
lullabies still followed belters in a hopscotch between mismatched
sounds; in manner as well as matter, the effect was of a hazy summer
night on the beach – warm, but fitful.

The surf factory on Seventh Avenue was owned by one Carl
'Tinker' West, following down a line from Vinyard and Potter as a
stock sugar-daddy. Like them, he provided Springsteen with work,
as well as room and board. In time West's role grew to include *ad
hoc* management of Steel Mill. Early in the new decade, he took the
band on a cut-rate, flat-bed tour of California. Other than a
doomed audition at the Family Dogg, a rave in the *Examiner* ('The
group deserve and demand attention') and a brief rant from Bill
Graham, they returned empty-handed – 'broke and buggered' as
one of them puts it – though there was a home detour for
Springsteen. While in San Mateo, he called at his parents' new
house. In a typical peacemaking move, Adele insisted the family
spend a weekend together on the road. Right away, the old duel
resumed. 'We got in the car,' says Springsteen, 'and drove . . . arguing all the way. First I drove and my dad yelled at me, and then he
drove and I yelled at him.' According to his colleague, 'he was
cussing Doug for weeks later in Jersey'.

Springsteen returned to a full-scale riot. On 4 July 1970, rock-
throwing and bombs joined the traditional fireworks in Asbury.
For five nights, the West Side ghetto rang to the noise of gunplay
and the loud wail of sirens; on the sixth, the army went in. No one
cause was ever given, but among the fruitcakery the words of Tony
Maples, head of the United Black Brothers, struck a nerve. 'This is
a resort town and when you go over and look at the beach, everything is beautiful and shining and it's like heaven, and when you
come out [west], all you can see is hell.'

As 'Miami Steve' Van Zandt says, the town went down the tubes and 'we went right down with it'. Steel Mill had exactly seven paying gigs the rest of that year. The band's ripped-to-ribbons faces matched even Springsteen's scowl. Panoramic pop lore, ambition and a slashing guitar style had pegged him for the top ever since he'd discovered Elvis a decade ago. With each blossoming, though, came a sudden frost. Springsteen's few highs had spread themselves thinly over five years. There was no national breakout, no smash hits. He was a showman, true, but the boom and smoke were still seen and heard only in a few seaside dives. As Lenny Kaye says, 'Bruce had a real *coastal* mindset. He lived in a surf factory, after all.' On his turf, staked out by Manhattan to the north and Richmond below, Springsteen was a star. He wrote, begged, lobbied and played like a dog fresh off the leash. A local booker named Jim Mahlmann remembers those Asbury nights as 'just drop-dead . . . Bruce had a huge sound and the stages in those cheesy dumps used to bounce up and down on the beat.' Kaye confirms that, when Springsteen hit the sweet spot and the drums booted in, the music took on a 'fat, brute life', like, say, an elephant running. *They* were glory days. But Springsteen made a defect of his merits. His provincialism – the very thing that won over Miami Steve and the gang – was a damper to the record scouts. The loon-panted moguls reserved their loftiest contempt for Jersey greasers. They treated them like a disease. While Springsteen's core audience was loyal, he wasn't making any new fans. Managing him, West found himself in a state of mingled awe and exasperation. 'Bruce hit his local prime,' but the roll-out didn't come.

The truth was that Springsteen, as Kaye says, 'was still trying to figure out if he'd cut it'. Or how. He was justifiably proud of how far he'd come, without losing track of his roots or contact with those who shared them. At first glance, there was nothing epic about Springsteen. He was neither mystic, seer nor prophet, neither chaotic nor profound. His universe was rational, his lyrics human. But kindred souls loved the human-jukebox quality of his work. To them, regardless of time, scene and changing fads, he was the inheritor of a tough, yet joyful tradition. In it, Jerseyans found an eternal image of their land – the simple line of the coast, the flight of Chevys and Fords over back roads, the belch of mills, the stink of smoke and Chuck Berry's irreducible riffs. Springsteen stood alone as the embodiment of a proud culture. Even the evolution of his nickname showed Jersey's love of a native son and his evocation of their soil. By 1970, he'd moved steadily from 'Baby' to 'Gut-rock' (for his junk diet), to 'Doc' and then 'God', Springsteen's soaring vocals showing why they got religion. Eventually, clubland settled on 'Boss'.

To some, the tag seemed to go against the grain. It was a radical swerve away from egalitarian, beach-bar *mores*. In Kern's words, 'a lot of folks wondered at a working-class hero with that handle'. Springsteen himself joined the consensus. 'I hate being called Boss,' he said. It made him sound like a mafia Don. He clearly was, though, player-manager of Steel Mill, if not their gaffer. Springsteen was already providing a slim living for the other band members. One of the great anomalies is his image as a Hamlet type that emerged from the 'extraneous bull' (his words) he tended to enjoy in the studio. In fact, Springsteen was quick to give vent to what irked him. But it was more complex than that. As a worrier, he liked to pick over different sides of an issue before holding forth. The snag was that he did so aloud, without heed to who was listening; in fact, he'd often state positions just to get a rise. But there's not a man who knew him in Asbury who'll tolerate the idea he was weak, let alone wimpy. Springsteen 'learned some hard-nut tactics on the way up', says Mahlmann. 'He *was* the boss: he knew it, we knew it, he knew we knew it. Bruce was the goods.'

Steel Mill wove on, casually adding or sacking a member, before meeting the universal fate of all Cream-inflected bar bands.* The group finally self-destructed in February 1971. Towards the end, the musicians were so poor they were travelling in by public transport. They'd been poorer. Once the band had to trek three miles to reach their gig, and arrived there white-faced and wheezing; the

---

*Among those auditioning was a seventeen-year-old high-school senior, Patti Scialfa. Springsteen turned her down as too young.

show was over before the horn player got his wind. A break, on those dire terms, was inevitable. Still, the actual split was a surprise, not to say shock. (The final rip had to do with a police raid at a teen-club gig in Middletown, a few miles north from Asbury.) While the others skulked off into construction jobs or music tuition, Springsteen faced a demoralising crisis. By then, his non-playing life consisted of pinball and Monopoly, or long hours' sunbathing. There was his run-down Ford. And there were girls. As for books or news, he 'could give a shit'. Unsurprisingly, Springsteen soon bored of his month of littoral decay: his response was a showband, Dr Zoom and the Sonic Boom, a situationist lark that lasted three nights. It featured a board game set up on stage. 'That was to give the people who didn't play anything a chance,' Springsteen told Dave Marsh. 'You know, so they could say, "Yeah, I'm in Dr Zoom. I play Monopoly."'

If musical eras are judged by the breaks they offer the talented to rise from the ranks, the one during which Springsteen apprenticed was among the greatest. There were quite different reasons for the identity crisis. In 1971, when he was just 'Boss' in Asbury, he chose to create in the Bruce persona the hint of someone dark, edgy, and, as Van Zandt says, 'kinda mysterious . . . people were afraid of him'. That daunting mask served as a protective mechanism – something like Eric Clapton's – against others crowding him. Again like Clapton, Springsteen was a chameleon. He'd change look – new haircut, gain or lose weight – every few weeks; he grew a beard. It was all but osmosis between the two men. Finally, the Asbury 'god' went to worship the one who'd worn the title since dragging the guitar out of its mewling years on *Blues Breakers*. Clapton's own pedestal had made a precarious perch. That August, broke and hooked, he was guesting at George Harrison's all-star Concert for Bangladesh in New York. Springsteen hitched to Manhattan the night before and checked into a motel. In the next room happened to be John Entwistle of the Who. All he could hear was 'Bruce playing tape after tape of his own songs, at top volume, through the wall . . . He was either re-assessing himself, or he had an ego the size of Wembley.' Next day, Springsteen watched the show from the bleachers. Then he thumbed his way back down I-95 to Asbury. As soon as he hit the Upstage he began holding auditions for a new group, this one with the blunt title, The Bruce Springsteen Band.

Like Clapton's own flirtation with Delaney and Bonnie Bramlett, it was an engaging mix of gospel, rock, pop and blue-eyed soul. Where Steel Mill had delved in bottom-heavy riffing, the new line-up ducked through the swing doors of a Memphis saloon with their saxes, trumpets and girlie chorus. To the native tradition of Muddy Waters and Chuck Berry were added touches of rockabilly, country and blues, even of prototype rap and disco (both of which rely on the mood and tempo swings Springsteen, and Clapton, flaunted). In the event, the horns and girls did one gig. The survivors – men like Van Zandt, the bassist Garry Tallent, keyboardists Davy Sancious and Danny Federici and the 270-pound self-styled 'solar eclipse' Clarence Clemons (who hove out of the fog in a white suit, tooting a sax, and was promptly hired) – would become the nub of the E Street Band. They cut their teeth that winter on the college and swim-club run, splitting door money six ways. Yet again, Springsteen would know the consolatory side of art. 'I wrote like a madman,' he says of the period. 'Had no dough, nowhere to go, nothing to do. Didn't know too many people. It was cold and I wrote a lot. And I got to feeling guilty if I didn't. Terrible guilt feelings. Like it was masturbation. That bad!'

At twenty-two, an age when Springsteen's peers were plying their trades as salesmen or petty magnates, he might have been well satisfied but for the scope of his dreams. The grubby struggle for survival was over. 'Had no dough' was to dramatize Springsteen's straits. He was making $100 a week – an impressive sum in Asbury. But cash was only part of the goal. He had 'stuff to say', and needed a bigger stage than Jersey from which to say it. After their *n*th row over the 'vision thing', Springsteen approached West one day while the latter was fixing the band's truck. 'I came by and told him [I] didn't want him to manage us anymore. He said okay, and that was it.' Springsteen's restiveness didn't, however, extend to his leaving the surfboard shop. Friends agree he wouldn't have pulled off a moiety of his strokes without affable landlords like Potter and West. Springsteen knew, too, that other patrons would follow; anyone of his combined skill, charm and sheer brass was, he rightly figured, 'waiting on the man'. That winter, he duly found him.

Mike Appel was then a lapsed musician and astute showbiz hustler. His own creativity had swung to a giddy high co-writing Paul Anka's 'Midnight Angel' and sundry smashes by David Cassidy. A college graduate and ex-marine, Appel and a composer named Jim Cretecos were then employed by a New York hit-factory, the Farrell Organization, to turn out jingles and ditties. Their idea of a 'hip performer' was Cat Stevens. As well as working all hours, scrawling lyrics, shouting epigrams, pouring energy into tiffs with his partner and generally being hyperactive, Appel was aquiver for new talent. Among the novelties filling out Farrell's roster were Tumbleweed, a country-rock act loosely managed by Tinker West. In a parting nod, West in turn mentioned a young singer-guitarist still scuffling for work on the Jersey shore. Appel, who was then twenty-nine and struggling for a role himself, said to send him up.

The man whom West brought to the Farrell office in November 1971 might easily have been just another Asbury *putz* on a trek to the city. Dressed in torn jeans and a T-shirt, Springsteen was coy about everything but self-promotion. His opening words were the very last kind of hype Appel needed: 'I'm tired of being a big fish in a little pond.' Nor could the two tunes Springsteen played at the piano have left a worse smell. 'The first was the most boring thing I'd ever heard,' Appel told Marc Eliot. 'The second . . . was about dancing with a girl who was deaf, dumb and blind* . . . I told him they were the worst songs I ever heard, utterly devoid of any pop potential.'

On that note, Springsteen took off for three months in San Mateo. While there he was shaken by more rows with Doug, and by several flubbed bids to relaunch himself as a California rocker.

---

*The Who's *Tommy* had been a hit during Springsteen's first summer in Asbury.

He straggled back to Madison Avenue one wet February night. A friend who met him there remembers him 'hunched up, no bread, no instrument case, looking whipped like a dog'. He was lugging his guitar. Christmas at home had, whatever else, unblocked the strange physiology of Springsteen's art, the glow and flash of new tunes and the steady drone of phrases he scrawled in his black notebook. In a virtual rerun of his second audition for Vinyard, he now reeled off seven songs with the 'most poetic, potent and powerful lyrics' Appel had heard. It was a heady moment. They were an odd couple, the Jersey dude and the Brill Building spiv in the snapbrim hat. Appel doesn't always cut a sympathetic dash in Springsteen biographies. As Mahlmann says, 'deal-wise, he was a thug'. But, under the drill-sergeant snarl, he could also be softspoken and avuncular, his client's fourth such patron in as many years. 'As well as dough, Mike virtually gave Bruce a second childhood,' says Grice. (Moreover, he neatly restored a touchstone – as in Appel Farm – in Springsteen's life.) The two signed three separate contracts, including one doodled on a car roof in an unlit parking lot; apparently it was too dark for Springsteen to read the fine print, which gave Appel and Cretecos twice his own royalty rate.

Moving rapidly in his smoky glasses and hip-hugging flares, Appel then browbeat his way into the office of John Hammond, the A&R boss and *éminence grise* at CBS. Ten years ago, Hammond had brought Bob Dylan to the label. Efforts to repeat this coup would see him sign names like Bruce Murdoch and Loudon Wainwright, men whose careers, to put it kindly, remained in stasis. The urbane, 61-year-old Hammond 'hated' the titanically pushy Appel. But he loved the piano-based songs, full of hooks and melodies, that Springsteen played him. After hearing 'It's Hard To Be A Saint In The City', 'Jazz Musician', 'Arabian Nights' and the other sagas of icy yet shrewd self-doubt, Hammond put out his hand. 'Consider yourself on Columbia Records.' It was 2 May 1972.

That same night, Springsteen played a solo set at the Gaslight Club in Greenwich Village. Lenny Kaye, one of 'twenty or so freaks' in the audience, remembers being dismayed that 'Bruce had gone from this ethnic rocker to a folkie . . . He seemed like a split personality.' Kaye's diagnosis was on the money. A nagging schizophrenia would goad Springsteen, and gall his critics for years to come. That lay ahead. In New York, that spring, things moved at a wild pace. On the 3rd, Springsteen cut fourteen songs at CBS, demos that re-emerged on both *Prodigal Son* and *Tracks*, the former under a salvo of writs, decades later. He signed with Columbia for a lump sum of $65,000 – $25,000 against royalties and $40,000 for production of his first album. And he bought a Harley. After the party had died down, he rang his mother and father with the news.

'Want a stage name?' barked Doug. 'I got a doozy. Johnny Superstar.'

Springsteen declined the offer.

3

The Shine

Springsteen's disastrous success made rock history. Just over three years later, when he was plastered over *Time* and *Newsweek*, the 'Newarky' punk would trade on level PR terms with the likes of the Kennedys and Kissinger. People who'd never bought an LP suddenly knew the face, and, above all, nickname 'the Boss'. The winning formula (equal parts of raw talent, hype and Appel's manic entrepreneurship) spawned an epic romantic song, three albums and hundreds of ecstatically received gigs. Springsteen made it. He played for adoring fans and built up a slavish cult in the press. He beat what he termed the 'death trap' of Freehold. He even got to dance with Adele and tongue-lash Doug from onstage. In every way, Springsteen's private war was won by the time he set first New York, then America afire in August 1975. It made him, he said, 'want to puke'.

Part of Springsteen's ballistic rise played out as a stock morality tale. As his craving for acceptance was spoon-fed until he was sick of 'kids tossing their panties at me', he declared that stigma of the creative soul, an artistic crisis. On top of that came legal and personal crises. Through it all, to his credit, he took a hard look at his fame and wondered if the game was worth the candle. He also stuck to the job at hand. Even at his leaden nadir in 1976, Springsteen preferred writing new songs to a life of sun, sea, women and industrial-strength dope. When he eventually moved, it was to a few miles up the coast from Asbury. Above all, Springsteen had an unusually sharp internal gyroscope, a fixed ethical centre. 'You ride a limousine for the first time, it's a thrill,' he said. 'After that, it's just a dumb car.'

There'd always be a part of him, inside and out of reach, that would look on the perks, and his own myth, as 'dumb'. This refreshing outbreak of sanity was offset by a mind that, in 1972, was weak and half-formed. Springsteen was still hooked on junk TV. When he went to the bookstore, it was to score a comic like *Batman*. He decorated his wall with posters of Wendy from *Peter Pan*. Rumours that he slept in sheets decked out with train engines are a slur, but convey an image people had of him. As Kern says, 'emotionally, Bruce was still the lonely kid on South Street'. He 'wasn't there yet', adds Kaye. Lynn Goldsmith calls him 'overawed' at their first meeting that April. It was a particular hallmark of Springsteen's life that he showed virtually no flair for power. As a rocker he had stunning leadership skills. But in most other respects he was cruelly handicapped. Later in the 1980s, 'agit' titles like *The Source* would make bizarre claims for 'Bruce [as] pop's crypto-syndicalist'. In fact, his zeal for pure politics – for that matter, current affairs – was nil. As late as *Born in the USA*, Springsteen hazily recalled having voted only once in his life, fully twelve years before. When *Rolling Stone* asked him his view of Ronald Reagan, *bête noire* of the free-thinking left, he replied: 'Well, I don't *know* him. I think he represents a very mythic, very seductive image, and it's an image that people want to believe in. I don't know if he's a bad man.' If anything, Springsteen, like Reagan, was a 'good conservative', holding to archaic values of hard work and grit. He was no syndicalist.

Financially, Springsteen should have been in better shape in 1972. He had his $65,000 advance and higher performance fees. Somehow, even this vastly healthier income would prove sadly wanting. That June, Springsteen promptly rehired most of his

Asbury mob to help cut his first album. He was exceptionally loyal. The band's wages came out of the $40,000. Appel and Cretecos, meanwhile, took their own hefty wedge of the pie. The management contracts Springsteen signed between March and May would later be slated by CBS as a 'slavery deal'. Writ large, it was the old story: the grinning *ingénu* slogging his way to glory on any terms. Springsteen's dream to beat the 'death trap' was sane enough. But his lack of business grasp was, even by pop-tyro standards, breathtaking. As Hammond said at the time, 'In all my years in [music], he's the only person I've met who cares absolutely nothing about money.' Springsteen never bothered to have his recording, publishing or production deals read by a lawyer. His 'give-a-shit' laxity would soon haunt him.

For a few years, at least, he was one rocker who enjoyed answered prayers. One of the rare books Springsteen admitted to having read in 1972 was Tony Scaduto's life of Dylan; in it, he recalled, the young singer had auditioned for John Hammond. Now he, Springsteen, had been there, done that. It was becoming a reality-warping hall of mirrors, a looking-glass universe where fantasy became fact. Suddenly, Springsteen was paper-rich. He was living in his own flat in Asbury. Although vastly greater fame and fortune would throw him off track, leading to long fits of silence and self-doubt broken by stylistic U-turns, Springsteen's first breakthrough was, he rightly sang, 'real cool'. Even as he struggled with the snags a record deal threw up – was he, in fact, a rocker or a folkie? – he also looted himself to draw on hidden depths of willpower and sheer *joie de vivre* by means of self-intoxification. The gleeful hoot of 'Rosalita' would say it all.

Still, even in that long hot summer Springsteen was never well-off. The fact was that he'd sold out to a famously alert shark, who, with a reverse-alchemist's knack, never quite turned creative touch into commercial triumph. Nothing could avail against that hard truth. Springsteen was still a bearded, unkempt soul who apparently owned only one set of clothes. His new digs were a studio over a drugstore and a failed salon; there, on a tack piano bought by his aunt, he wrote day and night. Nor, after Appel, Cretecos, the group and tax had all taken their bites, was the cash flow that golden. Astoundingly, Springsteen even toyed with a move back to his parents' house in California. He showed their address on his new driver's licence and passport. Adele would lobby him for years to come to wrap his degree and 'get a job'. Doug was unfazed by even the *Time* and *Newsweek* covers. Bruce's own self-image as a local rebel was, as always, balanced by a need for roots and domesticity. The special gist of his nostalgia, in the light of which Springsteen wrote even *Nebraska* and *Tom Joad*, was that of sound, traditional values. He missed his family.

He was 'saved from himself', as one of them witlessly says, by seven men. They in turn acted out of several motives, all beneficial. At CBS there was Hammond and two young publicists, Peter Philbin and Ron Oberman. An agent named Sam McKeith would begin to book Springsteen on the north-east club circuit for a dizzy $1,500 a night. At executive level, a new hand, Bob Spitz, filled out Cretecos' and Appel's empire, now incorporated as Laurel Canyon. The firm took offices at 75 East 55th Street, New York, not incidentally the same building as Dylan's old nerve-centre; CBS's 'Black Rock' headquarters was on 52nd. Late summer and fall of 1972 saw the start of a concerted 'Boss cult', his promotion the one fixed point between management and label. Hammond and Appel scrapped like polecats. But, if Springsteen's guru drove a 'slavery deal', he flogged himself, too, in his client's cause. The power of the cult derived precisely from the fact that it was a mix of raw skill and round-the-clock manipulation. Appel thought nothing of suing for Springsteen to sing at the Super Bowl, screaming down phones, witticizing at Hammond's expense, spending $12,000 on new furniture at Macy's and, of course, concentrating on the job at hand, virtually in the same breath. But no one took the cult more seriously than Springsteen himself. Beneath his foggy veneer, he played his 'rock-destiny' part to the hilt. By late autumn he'd added a hot new stage act to the icy calculations blasting from 55th Street. It was a smash formula.

Springsteen archive-rats and completists would come to see 1972 as a kind of *annus mirabilis*, the year he 'got it together' with both a record deal and a manager. Dave Marsh wasn't the first to convince himself of dubious conclusions by the neat ruse of automatic self-confirmation, excluding all doubts and contrary data. The truth was less rosy. Springsteen re-signed his band late that spring. Together, Lopez, Clemons, Tallent and the session gun Harold Wheeler – Van Zandt had briefly decamped – were a hard nut. The combination of big guitars, bouncy tunes and touch-of-funk vocals was equally potent. It's been said to the group's credit that they were exactly the kind of raffish souls Springsteen's street poetry needed; it can also be said that, on record, they tended to anonymously bring the music rather than goosing the tunes with bravura solos. The one stand-out instrumentalist of the lot was Davy Sancious. Springsteen himself hoped this keyboardist-guitarist, with his jazz-rock stylings, would become a 'second Hendrix'. He still might. Sancious' cycle of brilliance and burn-out would continue through long stints with Peter Gabriel and Sting. Along the way, he made one lasting mark on Springsteen mythology. Early that summer, rehearsals took place in sundry bars and practice dens in Asbury, downshore at Point Pleasant, and in Sancious' home in Belmar. Outside the last was a faded green sign saying E STREET. It stuck.*

Springsteen, for one, wasn't set on voguish art-rock, on mapping a given work and its specific world on to an axis of abstract ideas. He stressed the particularity and sensitivity of the mind: if 'kids [could] see and smell and taste' the characters in the tunes, he'd done his job. His music was, above all, *physical*, both sonically and in the vivid portrayal of the doomed heroes, greasers and Asburyites who filled out the lyrics. Bluntly applied, it was Byron-with-a-backbeat. In real life, Springsteen might have been a shy, tongue-tied 'dork', but in his songs the Boss's intuitive grasp of tone and colour made him the perfect antidote to glam, glitz and the dire, on-with-the-show *shtick* of the supergroups.

Springsteen inked his CBS deal on 9 June 1972. This time he

---

*The band were first so billed on 12 November 1972.

listed his 'permanent' address as care of Jim Cretecos, whom he told, 'I'm moving around a lot.' Laurel Canyon then booked him into 914 Studios in Blauvelt – the word, meaning 'bliss', was out of the ironic-name school – thirty miles north of Manhattan. But for the booth at Brick Mall, a brief stab under Bill Graham's baton and the CBS demo, it was Springsteen's first shot at recording. A bad case of nerves, a cramped capacity for 'winging it', tortured and stunted the whole band. While cynics thought the results showed a loss of both vision and artistic cool, he did his best; this and the next one were his 'shoestring albums', eked out for the sort of money others blew on their amyl-nitrate budget. Not surprisingly, Springsteen's early work didn't catch the public eye. But a dozen years later a resurgence was in full flow, and these prime cuts were discovered as the best of their time, and some of the best of all times.

The studio itself was low-rent, a grey, tar-paper bunker just off the highway. Facilities were crude. When it rained, which it did nonstop that month, water leaked through the popcorn ceiling. Technically, 914 was a lo-fi slum. The acoustics made the rhythm tracks sound like they'd been taped in a matchbox. Appel would always insist 'there was nothing we were doing that needed the excellence of an [upmarket] studio'. It's true that Springsteen's semi-shaped melodies and blurted lyrics didn't cry out for the kind of sophistry that came later. Even so, Appel's tongue can't have been far from his cheek when he told Marc Eliot, '914 was a top-notch facility.' It wasn't: Springsteen's own aside about it being 'a crapper' was spot-on. Laurel Canyon hit on the place, pure and simple, because they knew the owner. It came cheap. The two-week session cost a paltry $11,000. One consequence was that Appel pumped back the funds saved on esoteric knobs and dials into keeping himself and Springsteen fed. Another result was that the actual album sounded clunky and cut-rate.

'Mike', as Springsteen said, was 'close with a buck'. The bottom line ruled. Appel carried a book around in which he kept debits and credits; in policy, if not always practice, he preached thrift at every turn. Most pressing of all was the unceasing demand to pay homage to bailiffs and skip-tracers. For most of 1972, it was all Laurel Canyon could do to foot the bills for rent and the occasional luxury of a Days Inn. Later, Appel mocked himself by describing how he'd 'strategized a conceptual three-tab deal' with the East 55th Street landlord. More seriously, to friends, he'd ask if unwelcome 'shit' like hire purchase really rated 'so much attention from a guy trying to launch a megastar. I mean, what do they *want*?' It's true that Appel did literally everything for his client it wasn't vital he do himself. By late 1972, he kept Springsteen's diary, made his dates, dealt with the 'suits' and, increasingly, bailed out the band – Clemons' child-support arrears were just one item set against the advance. Meanwhile, Appel was in hands-on mode in and out of the studio. He co-produced the first album, scouted gigs, engaged in wild ideological yelling matches and did *ad hoc* PR. (It was his iconic leather jacket Springsteen later wore on the cover of *Born to Run*.) Added to that, Appel, as he rightly and loudly told nay-sayers, had had 'ears to hear'. As even his successor put it, 'Mike [was] the only one who saw what Bruce was about.' He was loyal, tough, always ready for a war, and didn't lack the courage of his convictions. Contrary to myth, Appel didn't hold to a secret agenda, but rather a steely sense of mission. He stood above most managers, an unflagging Boanerges devoted to his 'kid's' good, and a custodian of the brute values without which Springsteen couldn't do his destined turn as 'rock and roll future'.

The same couldn't be said of CBS. Hammond's boss Clive Davis was appalled when he heard the rough tapes from Blauvelt. 'I listened for a breakthrough radio cut and didn't hear one' woefully underplays the hysterical crunch meeting at Black Rock, where, according to one witness, 'steel chairs were thrown'. Davis – who then steered Springsteen back to the studio for the elusive hits – stood firm. Hammond himself was on side. (They even approved, at a nod, the LP's gaudy postcard-art cover.) Beneath these two, though, were men of thin lips, hard hearts and narrow minds. Springsteen wasn't *their* protégé. When the retooled album was delivered in September, it was held up behind the latest Johnny Mathis and Andy Williams discs. Unlike theirs, it missed out on a Christmas release, and thus on tens of thousands of potential sales.

Springsteen erupted. He hadn't 'hauled ass to [the] Siberia' of 914 just to be frozen out by his label. There was truth behind his rants at the market-penetration men and denim tycoons. His first album's fate reflected in miniature the in-house squabble over his 'vision thing'. On one hand, Springsteen's musical ecumenism was clearly a plus. On another level, the sheer profusion of his gifts – already blamed for forays into soul, blues, gospel, country and heavy metal – led to charges that he was, at best, a brilliant magpie; at worst, unsaleable. As the *New York Times* said, 'Springsteen can do anything he chooses, and it's sometimes been difficult for him to decide what that should be.' In time, chronic corporate confusion saw him saddled with the dread 'new Dylan' tag. Hammond himself didn't actively deny it. For years, he clung to the idea that 'pure', acoustic folk was Springsteen's native coin. Davis, meanwhile, in Appel's words, 'wanted something palatable to radio's mass audience'. The fingerprints of this boardroom power-duel were all over the Blauvelt tapes. Between the creative tug-of-war and 914's scuzzy aura, it was amazing Springsteen cut an album at all, let alone one as good as *Greetings from Asbury Park*.

A driven man ambivalent about his own unruly dreams, Springsteen lobbied hard for work. In late August the band played Max's Kansas City in New York; a set on the 30th was aired on the *King Biscuit Hour*, their radio début. He moonlighted with some of the other postfolkie types gravitating to Max's, including Jackson Browne and David Blue. (Blue remembered him as '*scary* about making it . . . Bruce had that kind of "winter spirit". Very dark.') Springsteen was writing, on average, a song a day. As well as the nine to make the cut on *Greetings*, the Hammond tapes and sundry out-takes and demos, he did an entire album's worth to be hawked around the London ghetto, bordering Denmark and Flitcroft streets, known as Tin Pan Alley. Some of these tunes landed on the desks of song-pluggers like Dick James. James began to rave about a hymn called 'Song For The Orphans' and mentioned Springsteen to a young colleague, Adrian Rudge. Rudge in turn took 'If I Was

The Priest' to his client Allan Clarke – then in the throes of quitting the Hollies – who recorded it. The single bombed, but Springsteen had the start of a British sub-cult. James would later say 'Bruce's publishing business ticked over nicely for three years', at which point it promptly exploded.

Until then, Springsteen wasn't, in fact, doing more than treading water, but from the foothills of Black Rock and Soho was, now and then, wafted the heady, aromatic scent of gold. As Allan Clarke says, 'Even those first demos had a raw edge that came through. No one put over a song like Bruce. It was a cert he was going to make it.' They were still lean times for the newly minted Boss. Of his then $1,500 concert fee, he'd see exactly a tenth. The balance was ploughed back into rent, food, fuel and the band's wages. For more than a year he made $100 a week, or twice that when he was gigging, which in 1972 wasn't often. A plea to Sam McKeith, says Appel, 'got us shows that barely kept us alive . . . He's the one who saved our asses.' The front of a 'working band' was maintained. But only just.

And at a terrible cost. Things could easily have unravelled that long, cold winter. McKeith worked all hours, but was cruelly hamstrung by the 'new Dylan' cross Springsteen lugged around. More than one booker slammed down the phone at that line. CBS's ditsy PR swung to a zenith in the months ahead. If his worst enemies had met to devise the most exquisite torture possible for Springsteen, being simultaneously underpaid and overhyped might have been it. He went 'fucking wacko' when Hammond leant on him to busk a series of solo gigs over Christmas. Springsteen's response was to ply the rounds of the college and chitlin run, an odyssey that took him from Pennsylvania to Ohio. On Pearl Harbor day, 7 December, he played gratis at a New York prison. Springsteen owed Appel and McKeith (then the sole black – or, as he put it, 'house nigger' – in the William Morris agency) his day-to-day survival on a steady diet of corn-dogs and cold hope. He spent weeks writing, playing, yawning, sleeping, driving, drinking and whiling away the nights with the band or whatever 'tail' padded the aeon between gigs. He shuffled in and out of New York, occasionally settling on to a chair at the Gaslight or Café Wha? to clock the talent. A singer named Dave Motz saw Springsteen in a club only recalled as 'not a million miles off Bleecker'. He radiated something 'hard and stony', says Motz. 'Bruce told me he couldn't ever relax – song ideas kept zinging him. He used the word zinging.' Springsteen cited one occasion when he was in bed, just about to have sex, and suddenly dreamt up a new tune. He had to excuse himself and run downstairs and play it on the piano. At the end of the evening, he told Motz he was 'living like a cur, while the suits are eating salmon at the Plaza'. When all the figures were added up, Springsteen's total 1972 road money came to $2,250.

On 3 January 1973 he began a tour that ran on-and-off until Christmas. Having played seventy-seven dates in twelve months, Springsteen grossed a total of $102,246, or an average of $288 a day. He only saw a crumb of that. Appel gives Springsteen's net income for the year as $5,000. As Motz says, there must have been 'hard, stony' moments. But there were boons, too. In the winter Springsteen often rose late, bolted his pet junk-food and spent long off-duty hours gazing at TV. Then he'd stroll out to his Chevy with his girl and drive to a club or movie. (Motz again sat next to Springsteen at a showing of *Last Tango in Paris*.) Or he'd bus in with the band to Hampton or Boston, playing as a sacrificial warm-up to acts like Chicago. It was a dingy, mean, abject life. But it beat the alternatives. Some wintry days, Springsteen would walk around in his pea-coat and scarf 'liver than they'll ever be [in California]'. This sense of escape from the 'death trap' embodied by Doug (now driving a San Mateo bus) got him through some low times. As Springsteen says, 'It was never a down. Me and [Van Zandt] would always sit back and say, "As bad as this is, it'll never be as bad as it was before we made an album or got a break . . ." We always considered ourselves to be way in front of the whole ballgame.'

That same winter, Laurel Canyon made an exotically bold bid to leapfrog the pack and launch Springsteen to stardom. They tried to wheedle the powers-that-be into letting him sing at the Super Bowl. (After the laughter died down, it was pointed out that the job was taken. Andy Williams, ironically CBS's blue-eyed boy, duly crooned a suitably vapid national anthem.) Meanwhile, 'we made our mark on the college circuit, which kept us alive', says Appel, the half-sadist, half-seer, who, glimpsing the future, now kitted Springsteen in black leather. It was an inspired choice: one of many emanating from 55th Street. Appel was almost demonic in his work ethic and chafed against those, like CBS, he dubbed 'fuckwits'. Meeting-wise, he was out of the hard-boiled, Colonel Parker school. As to charm – he tended not to overdo it. Withal, Appel had his qualities. He could make up his mind in a snap, and no one worked harder or longer in Springsteen's corner. As an ex-colleague says, 'around '73, Mike was fighting eighteen hours a day in the trenches, strafing CBS, hustling gigs, hand-holding the band, second-guessing Bruce'; and running the risk that all this might help his career.

Smooth anticipation of Springsteen's moods was, though, only one part of what Appel called his 'executive nanny' role. He was also *de facto* lawyer, banker and head spin-doctor. For him, it wasn't enough to merely strategize on the Boss's behalf; a degree of trashing his co-sponsors went with the turf. When *Greetings* was released (or, more strictly, escaped), Appel drew up a plan for Springsteen to be plausibly touted as 'one or other, a Dylan or an Elvis'. CBS proved incapable of either, but otherwise did the album proud.

Later in his career, the joke on Springsteen was the pumped-up backbeat of aerobic classes like 'Born In The USA', but *Greetings from Asbury Park, NJ* (to give it its full title) established him as a bruiser of a different hue – a free-form wordsmith in a line from Dylan and Allen Ginsberg's *Howl*. Musically, the starting points were The Band and Van Morrison. At bottom, it was as though Springsteen had combed *Moondance* for something which might count as a tune, found one, dragged it home, dolled it up, greased its hair, added beef, smothered it in sub-*West Side Story* skits and flogged the whole thing to death. On peak form, *Greetings* soared on the back of zippy, street-smart riffs, all sax and piano, and lushed-up vocals. As the name implies, the themes were the familiar ones of Jersey dudes and girls, but Springsteen's songwriting had sharpened to touch universal truths. A song like 'Growin' Up' neatly joined the dots between the teen punk and the wily superstar. As a kick-off, *Greetings* was perfect for its purpose.

At the time, of course, most fans and almost all critics never cut through Springsteen's parochialism. As well as the LP's title and eye-bashing cover (one of his most tony, if flash touches), there was his own cheerful admission: '[The label] were pushing for this big New York thing, this big town. I said, "Wait, you guys are nuts. I'm from Asbury Park, New Jersey. Can you dig it? New Jersey."' To Jack the Rabbit, Weak Knees and the rest, *Greetings* was the crowning evocation of their down-home nostalgia: you could almost *smell* the brine. The non-stop dynamo behind the concept was Springsteen's unshaken belief that the world would be as keen as he was to avenge itself on Freehold. Old scores were settled. The child beaten by the Sisters of St Francis was father to the man who wrote a track like 'Lost In The Flood'. The shrill anti-papism, unabashed lust and raw paeans to Super Eights, Harleys and 'hubcap heaven' would all be milked by Springsteen, and his various clones, in the years ahead. (His geologic recording pace meant that he perpetually ran the risk of being lapped by the very people he kick-started.) Later still, he'd goggle at the banality and bludgeon of most of this, and the solipsism of those who ran to it.

At the heart of *Greetings*' scuffed-up, exuberant tunes was the familiar poser: was Springsteen, in fact, Dylan's hitherto lost brother? The album's troubadour v. rocker interplay produced a weird home-brew of sounds. But that was nothing compared to the word-bog of the lyrics. 'I got a lot of things out in that album,' Springsteen said. 'I let out an incredible amount at once – a million things in each song.' At best, *Greetings*' phrases tore up like Jersey bikers on a beer-run. At worst, they were verbose, prolix and obscurantist. Some of the archly turned lines of 'Flood' could look Dylan's in the eye, but, even so, ran yards long. CBS's flogging of Springsteen as the house 'Bobcat' had its merits. Both men were tow-haired singer-songwriters who played the guitar. For the pigeonholers and hypesmiths, it made a neat link. But ultimately, trying to revamp the joyous derangement of *Bringing It All Back Home* did Springsteen no favours.

Greetings, in fact, bowed with just such a crassly leaden Dylan lark – 'Madman drummers bummers and Indians in the summer with a teenage diplomat' – and then went on from there to get wordy. For all its stream-of-consciousness and derivative tune, 'Blinded By The Light' was a solid, twangy opener. (It flopped as a single.) On the gentler tip, 'Growin' Up' was a wry, vivid rite-of-passage and stage epic-to-be. 'Lost In The Flood' yawed into a cheesy, Iron Butterfly-type outro via more stun-gun verses. 'For You' was an astonishingly bold stab at the mature, character-rich vein Springsteen would mine profitably in future. It also neatly demonstrated his bent for jerking maudlin tears from bouncy dance music. The arrangement was a high-octane stew of pumping piano, organ and drums. The narrative dealt with death. 'Spirit In The Night' came on like Henry Mancini in a stylistic pile-up with Steely Dan, yet neatly turned a picaresque lyric. Springsteen stretched out on 'It's Hard To Be A Saint In The City'. Here was all the consummate, pop-collage nous and slinky wit that hooked John Hammond. *Greetings* had its clunkers, too. 'Mary Queen Of Arkansas', for one, barely scaled the creative ladder to songhood. Of 'The Angel' it's kindest to be silent. But generally it was a fluid, if free-flowing début. Springsteen, as he well knew, was no 'Bobcat'. But in thirty-seven minutes, he left spurious 'singer-songwriters' like Janis Ian and John Prine in a cloud of dust. He'd arrived.

Reviews and sales were, however, less than the hoped-for bonanza. Most notices were fair, but didn't pull up any trees. *Crawdaddy* (virtually Springsteen's bulletin-board for the next two years) and *Cashbox* were fulsome. *Stereo Review* gave *Greetings* its Record of the Year award. On the downside, there were those, like *Sounds*, who slagged Springsteen as 'precious',* while not ignoring him altogether. It's conceivable, in fact, that word about him still

---

*A claim also flung at Springsteen's street-bard PR photos, showing him ostentatiously 'thinking'.

cut deeper in the industry than in public. *Greetings* would be looted for covers, not least Manfred Mann's bubblegum hit of 'Blinded'; according to Appel, 'Bruce heard [that] and held his nose with his fingers . . . I agreed with him, I thought it stunk as well.' (They did, though, cash the cheque.) Richard Williams' rave in *Melody Maker* also worked the Dylan connection, but presciently called Springsteen the 'future of rock and roll'. *Rolling Stone*'s Lester Bangs, with his coruscating need to write 'hep', said something close: '[Rev] up yer adrenaline, kids . . . Old Bruce catarrh-mumbles his ditties in a disgruntled mushmouth . . . Sorta like Robbie Robertson on Quaaludes . . . Bold . . . cosmically surfeiting', and so on. Sales of *Greetings* were in truth thin, not to say gaunt. It shifted 11,000 copies in America, twice that globally, in a year. A hint by Springsteen that CBS adjust his royalty rate upward was, said Hammond himself, 'lunacy'.

Coldly put, both the buzz and the word-of-mouth Springsteen got in 1973 were oddly mixed. On one hand, the *Boston Globe* could hail him as a 'totally brilliant, unique, soon-to-be-giant'. *Billboard* outdid itself in moon-child exuberance for *Greetings*' sad trajectory. *Record World* puffed him as one of its 'rising stars' alongside the likes of Hall & Oates. But as Bangs told the author, he 'still occupied a weird spot in the rock Alps, raved-about and totally broke'. Thus Springsteen would take a week-long berth at Max's, where he played to overflow houses, including, quaintly, Mrs Ted Kennedy. (Also in the audience, Hammond suffered a heart attack due, his doctor said, to 'enthusiasm at the show'.) Yet, in virtually the same breath, he pulled a crowd of exactly twenty at Villanova University, Pennsylvania; bombed in Hartford; and suffered the blow of playing second bill to the Beach Boys. Real indignity befell the Atlanta gig on 11 April. Between them, headliner and support sold 2,348 of 16,093 seats and settled for $2,500 and $1,500 respectively. Springsteen took home $150. As Appel says, 'Not much money trickled in while bills kept piling up.' But that was to hugely soft-pedal the swelling cash crisis. Springsteen himself told *ZigZag*, 'I'd like to get out of this situation where I haven't gotten paid in three weeks. We're at the lowest we've ever been right now . . . We've just come off the road and the guys are getting thrown out of their houses.' More than once, he stumped up loans to them out of his own funds. Every 'next big thing' should be this candid and this worthy of the shot.

There were a number of reasons for his mercurial fate. So many bar bands had gushed up since 1964 that fans were sated. Tastes, too, had changed. With the new spate of glam rock, Bowie and company walked a knife-edge between AOR and the teenybop ravings of David Cassidy. Springsteen, with his twin lodestars of Elvis and Dylan, was badly at odds with his times. That was his great strength. Localizing the eternal virtues of danceable, intelligent pop struck a chord with a fan-base who'd gone into mourning around the time of the Beatles' crackup. From the start, Springsteen aimed himself at nostalgists, hoisting his colours with *Greetings* and setting up an elite of like-minded souls recruited around an idea. Its corporate cheerleader was Clive Davis. On a local, almost block level, small but loyal cells hawking him and his gaudily anachronistic band surfaced in New England and California. (The Jersey shore had long been a lock.) The word also went deep, if not yet wide, in Britain. Springsteen did a second demo for Intersong, his London music plugger, that spring. Adrian Rudge's missionary work would reach not only Allan Clarke and Manfred Mann, but Bowie himself, then due to record *Pin-Ups* at Château d'Hérouville in France. The first track he covered was 'Growin' Up'. It didn't make the cut, but that one endorsement was akin to a royal warrant.

Bowie's acclaim was, however, a non-event alongside Appel's standing ovation. 'Remember,' he told McKeith, 'Bruce Springsteen isn't a rock act. He's a religion.' He took the analogy further. 'I always thought of myself as John the Baptist, heralding Bruce's Coming,' he says. The contrast between this and CBS's 'schizo' support, flitting between hyper and comatose, reflected more than a mere quirk. It was vital to Appel's management concept that he take day-to-day control of 'the talent', only devolving the most esoteric 'shit' to Black Rock. This was the hands-on style that led even Hammond (who hated him) to allow, 'Mike's utterly selfless in his devotion to Bruce.' Jim Mahlmann confirms it: 'Springsteen owed him the *lot*.'

Appel was quite shrewd enough to see that constant gigging (however cut-rate), and the pumping of key markets, would build demand until Springsteen could automatically fill the largest 'sheds'. A year or two on, and Laurel Canyon's books would go from thousands of dollars in red ink to millions in the black. Many of Springsteen's army in 1973 were lured by the emotional buzz of belonging to a platoon (Appel's word) of shock troops, who, while rejecting the fatuous overkill of a Bowie, later took advantage of it to flog the Boss.

Meanwhile, Springsteen continued his knock-down progression through the cold backstage rooms of gyms and Eagles halls. A star wasn't born. On 4 March he pulled out of third-billing at a hootenanny with Better Days in Seattle. The scene then shifted to Kenny's Castaways, New York. Without, Springsteen found his name misspelt on the marquee. Within, a dozen paying customers chatted and spun frisbees. It was that kind of tour. The gigs had all the pathos of slumming, with the added bonus of meeting his idols. Springsteen opened for Jerry Lee Lewis. He backed Freddie King and Paul Butterfield. And he played 'ass-wipe' to Chuck Berry. The last, a relatively rare brush between Springsteen and a childhood hero, took place in Maryland. It was a striking example of the gulf between the rock votary and his gods. (The first hint of trouble came when Berry refused to go on without being paid in cash. He then hired the E Streeters, at a second's notice, as his scratch band.) In May, Springsteen played the Ahmanson Theatre, Los Angeles, as a favour to Davis, who asked him, 'Can you make use of this huge stage?' The reply was blunt: 'I'm not interested in using it.' CBS's president left the label in a boardroom coup later that month. With Davis gone and Hammond hospitalized, Springsteen's home-office clique shrivelled to a hard-core in the PR department, while the collective muscle got behind yet another 'Bobcat', Billy Joel.

Frantic lobbying by Appel and McKeith next landed Springsteen an unlikely slot on an arena tour by Chicago, whose faintly tedious jazz-pop noodlings lumbered to an apogee that summer. His first contact with stadium rock came as a jolt. Springsteen broke under pressure from the compulsions that so nagged him. He did, true, get through the Hampton and Baltimore gigs. But things soured in Philadelphia. The smooth-listening fans rebelled at *Greetings*' pastiche of soul, R & B licks and honks of Clemons' sax. 'Kids were throwing rolls of toilet paper,' says Appel. A fan bounced a basket ball off Springsteen's piano. 'They're not paying attention to me' was his wild understatement to his manager. Something similar, or worse, happened at Madison Square Garden. Chicago's lyricist Robert Lamm recalls his warm-up as a 'very nice fellow, very committed . . . very intense', though that, too, downplays the hot fires that burned barely below the surface. Springsteen ran offstage in New York, announced he was quitting, 'shrieked like a beast' at Appel, and burst into tears. After the recriminations had died down, he vowed he'd never play another 'shed' and '*never* as someone's butt-fuck'. 'I told Bruce, okay, no more big venues,' says Appel, a policy soon enshrined in principle. To stress the point, Springsteen slammed his fist into a brick wall. Then he ran off down Eighth Avenue and made an abrupt, lurching stop in front of a bar. That was the last anyone saw of him for the night.

At this stage things, already apparently at their darkest, turned black. Not a single CBS staffer crossed the street to see Springsteen in Nashville during a company hoedown there. Davis left under a cloud. Certain promised ad-spend cash never materialized. Finally, Springsteen did an abject set at the firm's annual summit, after which even Hammond said, 'Bruce, you blew it. What in God's name were you *doing*?' They were dire times. Hopelessly adrift from his label, at breaking point with his band, Springsteen sloughed off to the clubs. 'The answer's simple,' he told Appel. 'We'll start from zero.' That only raised more questions. How could he be satisfied by faded, pocket-size Asbury when the colossal architecture of New York and LA had stared him in the face, and his ambition howled to be fed? How could he prefer a bland, anonymous dryad to the girls he'd seen surging from their tip-ups in the Garden? Back in his room, with his tinny stereo and guitar, the heavy shades of the last year began to crowd his dreams, and, from there, his notebook. Springsteen knew, he said, it was all down to 'one last toss', an all-or-nothing roll of the dice. Waking one morning with a jerk, he inked in the title BORN TO RUN.

His survival over the next two years owed much to luck, bloody-mindedness – and the band. Between them, they rattled with a spirit of impish glee and grandstanding that was as much *Showtime at the Apollo* as punk's big brother. As one of them says, the E Streeters were 'midway between fun-hogs and the Mob'. The Mafia connection might be a stretch, but, schlepping their gear, unshaven, they could do a fair, if baroque spoof of the thug-chorus of *Some Like It Hot*. Each had his own nickname and hood persona. Extending camp, ham and cod-menace into arty absurdism wasn't, however, their sole asset. They were a *band*. There was a palpable, Asbury-grounded ripple around the room whenever they showed, let alone played. It was the same 'telepathic vibe' Keith Richards touts in the Stones, or John Sayles later caricatured in the film *Baby, It's You*. Not that the group were all edgy interactions and free-form jamming. They worked as a team, tight as a liege lord and his samurai. As their drummer says, 'It wasn't U2 – nor was it Rod and his latest backing band.' The mutual loyalty (which saw Springsteen keep on even Dr Zoom's Danny Gallagher as his roadie) played its own part in setting a mood. The result was a true and time-tested classic. In the '60s, most acts' fame had been based on the old pop virtue of one-for-all cohesion, among cranky sub-personalities, for the joint good. The E Street Band delivered that quality once again.

   In fact, watching them at work was much like seeing one of those early, British Invasion draws. 'Mad Dog' Lopez was a feral, Keith Moon-style drummer. The moniker came from his bur-geoning career as a hell-raiser. Any scene involving Lopez carried a brawl guarantee. On bass, Garry Tallent was in the 'quiet-one' mould of John Entwistle. Together, Springsteen's rhythm section clung to the classic Who prototype: the one buttoned-up, veiled, going through social motions; the other (as an ex says) 'a fuckin' hog'. Personally, they were playing for time and full of life for the moment, respectively. Musically, Lopez and Tallent were the band's lethal secret weapon. They anchored the sometimes unwieldy front line without weighing it down. Slash-and-burn riffs were never explored at the cost of harmony and texture. Covering the field from blues to rockabilly, Tallent, in particular, had a near-morbid aversion to rock formula; his was the one hand which wasn't noticeably pop-picking, and better for it.

Back then, Clarence Clemons was E Street's undisputed 'Big Man'. Perhaps because he was built like the Albert Hall, he suffered a tad less raillery than the others. This ex-football star and King Curtis soundalike was, with Lopez, rock unleashed: rhythmically – and physically – muscular, but ingeniously melodic; a loud, all-hours sort with a soft, unfailingly generous streak. There was a sunny purity to his coarseness. Clemons was Springsteen's onstage foil and the rich end of a band sound that frequently had an inert organ tone at its core. Like his sobriquet, Danny 'Phantom' Federici's keyboards could (those days) be self-effacing, spectral whack. But he fitted. Raised in north Jersey – almost ET status among Asburyites – he was a public Jekyll and private Hyde. No one enjoyed a party more than him, unless it was Clemons and Lopez. Of Davy Sancious, meantime, Springsteen said, 'He was a real wild man. He had the rock 'n' roll thing in him – it always seemed like he'd be the next Jimi.' It didn't happen, but Sancious's piano-guitar weave could jump the tracks to *maestoso*-played sheets of noise. What's more, when he bared some fang, there *was* a touch of Hendrix, as well as Charlie Mingus. Rounding out the band (though still on furlough), 'Miami Steve' Van Zandt – he hated snow – was as close as Springsteen came to a soul-brother. While outwardly the most they ever did was to grub along the Jersey bars, with less idea than ever of how they'd hack it, the very fact they hung on for seven lean years shows both their latent grit and mutual bond. Van Zandt, his Op-Art shirt and toque would return. Other strong, if silent, E Street denizens included Bob Spitz, CBS's Philbin and Oberman and a new young agent, Barry Bell. The last would be a key figure in the unfolding drama of life on the road.

Showmanship was the concept that held the sprawling act together. The band were all crack musicians, but the instrument they played best – which Springsteen himself rang like a bell – was the house. Between them, Mad Dog, Phantom and the rest made for brazen street theatre. Gradually, over 1973–74, they became a showband as well as a bar-band. Still, for all their bug-eyed posing, the sidemen remained just that. You looked at them for five seconds, their idiosyncrasy blurred by camping, then ogled Springsteen. Offstage, he was still the same narcoleptic loner. But once on the boards, it was like a case of possession: he was a dazzling physical presence, a comic delight, an imaginative treat, a raconteur, wit, and, above all, vivid embodiment of the music. Springsteen's introductory raps went several miles beyond 'How ya doin', Paducah?' They were at once dark, funny and delivered with a heart that suggested many of the yarns stemmed from deep source material. Those still thin audiences soon learned a brand-new thing about the Boss: he was a born storyteller, whose narrative gifts came from his New York–Italian grandparents. (He also, says Lynn Goldsmith, practised them nonstop in front of a mirror.) The miracle of it was that at the core of the act in which every pun and gag seemed radiant with *joie de vivre* lay the grisly saga of Springsteen's childhood. Out of that dark pit he created the resplendent twin peaks of faith and hope.

Not his only peaks, it turned out. Springsteen's authorial clout was also at work in the lyrics. Combined with the scene-setting links, they set up what Bangs called 'an integrated Wonderland . . . half Elvis and half campy Conan Doyle'. This mutant crossbreed of, so to speak, 'Hound Dog' and *Hound of the Baskervilles* would become Springsteen's forte. No one did it better. If the raw music granted hints of immortality and a freedom from the confines of time and place, the blarney gave a chance to slip oneself. As fans wove to the beat, they shared in the delighted generosity of a man whose wry spiels raised not only his own profile, but belly-laughs. As Spitz said, 'When Bruce got on stage, [Appel] and I would sit there and say, "Where are all these stories coming from?" Bruce didn't get onstage and kick ass – Bruce got onstage and was *funny*.

He'd intro a song for five minutes. People would roll in the aisles, then he'd play . . . Underneath that reticence was a guy who really had a good grasp of where he wanted to go.'

Late that summer Springsteen went back to Max's. Here both ids – the funky-butt rocker and the folkie – were on hand. After a solo acoustic spot, the gigs turned anthemic on Clemons' arrival. Though the full-bore sets seemed to contradict the venue's stamp-sized stage, the crowd didn't care as Springsteen delivered an hour of sweaty, fist-pumping choruses and seat-shaking ravers. A show at Roslyn became a near-riot. He played hometown gigs in Asbury. Along the way, Springsteen drilled, practised and polished the new songs to a gloss. 'My faith's unbroke,' he wrote his girlfriend, in the stilted tone his letters took. He told her more. Now and then he 'tossed off a tune', he said. 'It's a gasser to write when you're in love, no shit.'

But shit wasn't long in coming. In July Springsteen made the return trek to Blauvelt and the cinder-block tip off Route 303. By now his technique had crystallized and the songs were the full artistic expression of a clear mind. His direction of the band was masterly. He usually had them rehearse their parts separately. After listening to a sax solo, Springsteen might mumble, 'Too blue,' or 'Go Rio,' his gnomic quip the equivalent of a thumb twisted up or down. Or he'd play the bass or piano himself, to show what he wanted. (The actual recording struck the core of a vinyl nut: how to dovetail all the songs inside forty minutes.) Then, after a take, he'd huddle with Appel and the engineer Louis Lahav. A musician recalls him taking two straight nights mixing 'Rosalita' down to the bone. Springsteen next 'tried it out on the dog', playing a tape to two or three friends in Asbury. If a sequence missed fire, or fingers didn't pop at the expected place, retakes were in order.

Springsteen's visionary talent and newfound concision still jarred with his surroundings. 'It was more like Hitler's bunker than a studio,' says a man who would know. What's more, in a vital gesture to economy, Appel now booked only the graveyard shift. Vampire's hours suited Springsteen to the ground, but left their mark on the band. More than once, Tallent or Sancious nodded off in their booths. That was nothing compared to the ennui at CBS. One August night, the new A&R guru Charlie Koppelman drove to Blauvelt. After hearing the rough edit, he drew Appel and Spitz aside. 'Fellas, we may have run to the end of our days. This isn't an album we're going to put out.' Springsteen promptly remixed the tapes, smoothing the edges and sweetening the centre. The astonishing result of his ploy worked wonders. 'He finished the songs and got rid of the filler,' Spitz told the author Fred Goodman. After a second run-through, Koppelman relented. 'You know,' he said, 'Bruce's only real rival is the Archies.' His crazy dystopian 'slum operas', a memo added, were 'pure soap'. When Springsteen was told he was wrong by Appel, by Black Rock and William Morris, by the band and even by his girl, there was only one conclusion to be drawn. He knew he was right.

The Wild, the Innocent and the E Street Shuffle appeared that autumn, the season of the Carpenters, Slade and Bowie's *Pin-Ups*. It finally merged the twin hemispheres of Springsteen's brain. Though still low-fi,* *The Wild* was anything but unvarnished: the second half, in particular, ran as a lush three-part suite for the street, with 'August' burnt all over it. There was a massive progression not only from *Greetings*, but across the album itself. The mini-sonatas like 'Kitty's Back' freighted mood and character with a bossy chorus; '4th of July, Asbury Park (Sandy)' hung together as an ode to the boardwalk. 'Serenade' read like a smoochy Baedeker tour. Better yet, 'Rosalita', with its multiple fake climaxes, was the showstopper Springsteen had been threatening for years. Before this, he was a lyricist who happened to write music; afterwards, he was a composer of Spector-like 'symphonies for the kids'. *The Wild* had both sides covered. Most reviews were good enough, but Springsteen was struck even more, in time, by the album's wallop on his peers. *The Wild* was a potent and rich start-up for the likes of Mink DeVille and Dire Straits. In an epic volte-face, it graced, or at least underlay, Morrison's *Veedon Fleece*. Even Elton John cultivated

---

*Hear the clunking piano-pedals on 'Incident On 57th Street' and 'New York City Serenade'.

a rhapsodic, latinized mode before darting back to the schmaltz of *Captain Fantastic*.

The Wild started out like a New Orleans funeral and wound up the jazz-funky epitome of Harlem. Springsteen filled the gaps between with soul singing, scatting, whoops and mutters – and, on the title tune, a lift from Major Lance's 1963 'Monkey Time' – while the band laid down their quirky slabs of tuba, accordion and wobble-board. It was that wiggy. 'Sandy' crackled with sunny energy and a teeming cast of doomed lovers, fortune-tellers and cops; the sort of song Lou Reed might have written on his summer holiday. In 'Kitty's Back', Doobie Bros-type grooves tapered into a Louis Jordan, jumpin'-jive outro. Spectorish production added just the right tone to 'Incident', a shady, riveting safari down the alleys of New York. 'Rosalita' simply became part of the atmosphere. (The name was no fluke: 'Rosie' was everywhere in Freehold, as well as on a beam over Route 33.) It would also be Springsteen's first watchable video. The gaudy scales of 'Serenade', finally, bobbed and wove without ever quite attaining lift-off, or rising above its working title of 'Vibes Man'. This shouldn't have added up to a great album, but that came from the lyrical skeins (now yoked to the music) and the rich, brassy textures. The riffs strained some of the songs' shaky melodies, yet somehow kept them aloft: they worked.

Springsteen's street-level research and long hours in Blauvelt paid off. *The Wild*, like *Greetings*, died commercially (though cash rained down for it in later years). But the critics sat up. For *Rolling Stone*, 'having released two fine LPs in less than a year, Springsteen is obviously a considerable new talent'. Even better was Bruce Pollock's rave in the *New York Times*: 'A stone, howling, joyous monster of a record . . . a word virtuoso . . . Swatches of local color . . . images of hustlers in leather and their dungaree molls . . . a wild, brawling bash, a precise and exuberant picture of teenage romance in the '70s'; and on over four columns. Such PR couldn't have been bought, particularly for an artist at the crossroads of rock, funk, folk, soul and salsa with two flop albums.

Springsteen put in long hours, still blitzing clubland and writing in the off-days between gigs. He ended 1973 where he began it, onstage at the Main Point in Bryn Mawr. It was a mongrel year. The two albums were offset by the twin duds of the Chicago tour and the CBS meet. He was $5,000 richer. But even non-stop yomping and Appel's all-hours hype barely covered costs. Springsteen finally wrote his mother a rope's-end note, which he hoped would lead to a loan. He said he'd slumped into a 'sad-sack mood', doubtless hereditary in origin. He calculated right. Adele firmly rejected the imputation of any genetic slur, but came through with the cash. It 'kept me alive', he said.

Compounding Springsteen's problem, that winter, was the weather. It was the coldest Christmas in living memory. There was an oil crisis. When he had gas in his car, he shuttled in and out of Boston, Richmond or the office on 55th Street. Laurel Canyon's mini-Kremlin, already in hock to its landlord, was faced with bankruptcy until *The Wild* took off, and would find it hard, even then, to hold things together. Early in 1974, Jim Cretecos baled out. That same month, Lopez was fired, replaced by Sancious' friend Ernest 'Boom' Carter. It was the darkest low in an apprenticeship not untouched by angst. The band were anarchic and, financially, things were at meltdown. As Appel says, 'I seriously considered . . . turning all my contracts over to Bruce and saying, "Here's the contracts, these big contracts that are worth exactly nothing. Good luck. I'm going back to writing commercials. At least I can earn a living."'

Despite, or because of, the crisis, Springsteen's show continued to operate at full throttle. Still trudging the bar and college run, he doggedly honed the gigs offstage and on. Gradually, over the first quarter of 1974, he glossed his set into a minutely rehearsed, blocked routine that was as much Broadway as boardwalk. He hired Louis Lahav on sound and the lighting magus Marc Brickman. They presented the concerts as a theatrical tapestry: it was the 'spectacle' that brought the production to life. Springsteen himself was all-action. Some nights it was as if they'd brought him in in a cage. He not only flaunted his love of melodramatic soul-revue splits and slides; in a true James Brown touch, he'd even swoon to the stage. It all followed in the exalted tradition of the Apollo: raunchy, horn-heavy riffs buoyed by the breathy vocals of a sweaty frontman. Not too many whistlestopped armouries and gyms had had their roofs raised as they were by 'Rosalita' or its twin, 'Thundercrack'. By now, Springsteen had a hard-nut cult in Jersey, New York, Philadelphia and Boston. After two rabid nights that Easter, Phoenix, too, joined the roll-out. Part salty pro, part raw tiro, he was a dynamic, guitar-slashing presence, strutting, chuckling, rapping, stinking of Ben-gay, a twitchy figure in jeans and form-fitting shirt *en route* to becoming a working-class hero. Live, Springsteen had arrived.

Onstage, he had the aura that surrounds the truly gifted – what Keith Richards calls 'The Shine'. Thematically, Springsteen was of no fixed abode. Professionally, he had definite set values. His gigs were, foremost, *fun*: dirty, all-night affairs full of buzz-saw riffs and jamboree singalongs. The E Streeters had long gelled into a band. Springsteen himself could play blistering guitar and always sang at the top of his range. His material was getting ever better. Listening to his new fare was akin to snooping on a private, if shrill conversation; yet, like films, 'Rosalita' and the rest unfurled vast emotional canvases on to which fans flung their own lives. Much as it was a feat in itself to write such tunes, at least part of the appeal was symbolic. Springsteen was the reincarnation of rock's lost innocence. His synthesis of late '50s and '60s hits won him an adoring press, trying, bluntly, to relive its youth. 'We projected,' said Bangs. Springsteen's reputation as a folklorist stood high. Pop archivists took him as their own. In London, Richard Williams had quite rightly branded him the 'future of rock and roll'. Neal Vitale of the *Boston Globe* and *Crawdaddy*'s Peter Knobler soon chimed in. Bruce Pollock, *Rolling Stone*'s Dave Marsh and the critic Jim Isaacs all joined the chorus, at once wistful yet whipped-up, until buried under the weight of Jon Landau's epic hype. Also rooting for Springsteen were a swelling number of 'real dudes', as opposed to nostalgists and the hacks in magazines. They, too, were fanatically loyal. When the Detroit rocker Mitch Ryder made some flip asides about it being 'dark and mean' of Springsteen to cover his, Ryder's, work, he came under a salvo of hate mail. 'I got death threats,' he says today.

Predictably, there was a backlash. Bangs best caught it when he said, 'It was mad for about a year, at which tick it went yoyo.' (As John Entwistle adds, 'I always believe that "future of rock" crap whenever I hear it.') The poet, drug activist and ex-MC5 manager John Sinclair later slagged Landau and Marsh as co-plotters of a 'shillfest' for Springsteen, whom he called a 'decent, fourth-wave rocker'. The actual songs, he wrote, were 'tales of a mythic urban grease scene which, taken together, form a script for a third-rate TV treatment . . . hollow . . . inane . . . fantastic.'(Sinclair's oral blast was more colourful.) In time, Springsteen himself mutinied. Gazing at his mugshot on the covers of *Time* and *Newsweek*, he told Ray Coleman, 'Who cares about that! Just a lot of jive, a lot of jive.' He later mauled his own CBS-bred 'bull': 'One of the bad things about all the [PR] was that it made me look like I'd come up from nowhere.' By then, he rued, his hard-won freedom had become a straitjacket. 'I felt like I lost a certain control of myself . . . I felt the thing I wanted most in my life – my music – being swept away, and I didn't know if I could do anything about it. I remember during that period someone* wrote, "If Bruce Springsteen didn't exist, rock critics would invent him." That bothered me a lot.'

Invent what? In most takes, Springsteen was a one-off, singly free of pop shysterism, so virginal and pure that, as Bangs said, 'you'd be proud to quaff his bath-water'. He was certainly naïve. A *Globe* write-up spoke of him as 'downright boyish, like a kid grown big'. At twenty-four, Springsteen was fey, wiry, waiflike – his clothes always seemed to swallow him – rail-thin and, says Motz, resembling a wet rag. Some of his ingenuous charm came through in a quote to *Rolling Stone*. 'When our band goes into a Holiday Inn, we step up in the world. The beds are nice. They got color TV. I love them places.' A friend puts Springsteen's emotional age at 'around seventeen: stump-dumb with an attitude'. Grice says, 'Bruce was bright, but not very broad or deep. And he was uptight – there was

---

*The *New York Times*'s Henry Edwards.

the hint of a big-time inferiority chip.' That chimes with a colleague's view of him as 'always the crowd-pleaser . . . he never liked to say "no" to your face'. His greenness showed both at home and on the road. Springsteen still bunked down like a high-school student with *Peter Pan* posters on his wall. His domestic arrangements offered few challenges beyond tuning his radio. While other tycoons like Jagger micro-managed their empires down to the dime, Springsteen told a lawyer in 1976, 'I never look. That's my problem. I never looked at Mike Appel, and I found out that I don't own a fucking thing . . . That's me. I don't look.' His hobbies were the engaging ones of sex, surfing and junk food. Yet, to Marsh and the pack, no other rocker ever commanded such eggshell-treading respect. Even Springsteen's latter-day nickname had the nervy double-edge of gaffer, or Mafia Don.

Springsteen, to his credit, always passed on drugs (once using the rubric about being 'high on life'). A man hired by him for eight years – who, like most friends, prefers anonymity – 'never once saw him do more than aspirin'. He was blushingly frugal compared to other pop gods. There was a similar simplicity, and intensity, in Springsteen's love life. Here his policy was of safety in numbers. He may have shunned dope, but he was notably keen on both rock and roll and sex. Grice calls him 'hornier than a brass band'. Slurs that he was 'bent' – a warped reflection of his relationship with Adele – also did the rounds. One of the songs Springsteen cut for his original CBS demo was called 'Street Queen'. In later years, he wasn't above the odd homoerotic live bump-and-grind. But those (and his occasional soul-kissing of Clemons) were mere hobbyism. An ex-lover assures us he was 'all man'; a veritable Alan Clark on Viagra. Looking for something to give his life meaning, he lurched from girl to girl until, in New York, he met one Karen Darvin. There the bouffant blonde made the closer acquaintance of the leather-clad rocker. Springsteen raved about her 'poetic beauty', her shining soul, her clever, realistic sense of life, and, yes, her 'great ass'. He sometimes played with a pair of her panties stuffed in his pocket.

Springsteen, says Motz, was 'fast becoming, in the nicest way, a cadger and sponge'. He could give as well as take it. Late at night, he liked to jawbone for hours on his pet riffs, screeds in which his listener was drummed and hooted off stage. Among his texts were the Founding Fathers, Malcolm X, Walt Disney, Watergate, Nixon, Kojak and John Wayne. He moved easily from there to pop icons like Elvis and Jackie Wilson. He was filled with guff as well as musical theory. It all rained down, along with paeans to Lennon, Jagger, The Band, Stax, James Brown, Al Green; sex, Chevys, fries, the Pope, Jackie and Ari, baseball and Les Paul. There was nothing sham about Springsteen's vaunted shyness. He once locked himself in a bathroom when a friend of Darvin's came to call. But he could, and did, talk the legs off his peers, even those able to hold their own in the field. By now, he was influencing some of his heroes, like Dylan and (striking a lower chord) Manfred Mann. That August, Springsteen made the trek to Sigma Sound in Philadelphia. He was rewarded by an audience with David Bowie. The drugs, of course, were a problem. So was the retooled 'Growin' Up'. But because, in his words, 'me an' Dave should be tight', he went on acting as though they were, and the stranger Bowie got, the more defiantly Springsteen kept smiling. The two men's mutual admiration club was in constant session from then on.

   This was the Springsteen who now stepped up for his life-or-death shot at fame. The lyrics he wrote that spring and summer were rife with last-ditch imagery, lines about 'hiding on the backstreets', his 'back to the wall' in a 'death trap/suicide rap' mingling edgily with the brittle hopes of a man nearing the end of his long tether. What Springsteen was doing wasn't so much composing as clawing the bars of his sanity. 'He could seem dozy,' says Motz. 'But underneath there was a fire, a coiled spring. It was very weird – *Bruce* was very weird.' That whole year, he was at his notebooks twelve hours a day; 'a ticking bomb', in Dick James's phrase. Everything, however trite, was grist to Springsteen's artistic mill. One of the E Streeters saw him 'pick up a candy wrapper, hold it out, X-ray the label, then shove it in his file'. Watching, it was easy to imagine his antennae quivering, that, even in trivia, 'Bruce always found some riff'. All experience was put in service of the songs. One of Springsteen's new verses spoke of being 'sprung from cages out on Highway 9'; Ocean College's address. Some of the cast of *Greetings* and *The Wild* also made comebacks. Predictably, he had trouble lightening the mood around his creative hothouse. Springsteen's head and hands were in perpetual frenzy. To friends, he always seemed lonely, even though his frenetic gigging and home life meant he was rarely alone. That long season, he and his girl were 'going nuts . . . we were in this room and it just went on and on'. As the pressure gauge hit red, Springsteen told her, too, it was all or nothing – 'If I fuck up now, it's over' – road's end, with nowhere to go.

He didn't fuck up. Springsteen was making dramatic gains as an architect, not just author, of songs. Most of the cuts on *The Wild* had hovered around the seven-minute mark. His third album would be FM-friendlier, and united round a key theme (if not the dread 'concept'). Springsteen defined his MO to *Rolling Stone*: 'My job is I search for the human things in myself, and I turn them into notes and words, and then in some fashion, I help people hold on to their own humanity.' In practice, he said, that meant most of his characters were 'always in transit'. Their very mobility fed the barb that, at core, Springsteen's songs were the aural equivalent of road movies. Cars and speed had been his factual way out of small-town Jersey. So were they in his fiction. But Springsteen was doing more than just adapting 'Sandy' or 'Rosalita' for the freeway. He'd also learned to write cinematically. 'There's no settling down, no fixed action,' he said. 'The songs don't have particular beginnings and they don't have endings. The camera pans in and then out.' In 1974, he came out of the gate as an *auteur* – someone who sought (as Appel points out) to be a vagabond with a moral centre, a contradiction in terms that spelt genius.

The fruit of all this was a song Springsteen wrote, perched on his bed in Long Branch, an imagistic saga of 'suicide machines', rims, engines, rear-view mirrors and roads 'jammed with broken heroes'. The words stewed in an equally lush, rich arrangement. With its synthesized intro, multilayered dubs – guitar over guitar – strings and Spectorish bells, it was all a long way from Steel Mill, let alone the Castiles. That May, Springsteen came onstage at Cambridge,

Massachusetts, grinned and, for the first time, cued in the riff of
'Born To Run'. 'I remember it well,' says Grice. 'I actually *did* break
out in a cold sweat.'

As a job, being a 'recording artist' is notoriously free-form in
accommodating varying modes of behaviour. There are those (like
Bowie) who work fast; and others, serenely unruffled by deadlines,
who spend days fine-tuning the right click or bonk for each beat.
But even the rococo fidgetings of a Yes or ELP paled next to the
doodlings on 'Born To Run'. Springsteen cut his signature song
over four full months that spring. The stucco shanty in Blauvelt
became a lab for edgy experiments in drones, dubs and overlays; a
Lilliputian saga of whits and wonks that Springsteen compared to
root-canal work. Like its warm-up track 'The Fever', 'Born To
Run' became a statue to itself, a teen-angst hymn buffed against a
million airplays. Never had the Wall of Sound been in such sleek
context. As early as 1971, Springsteen told Ken Viola, 'I've worked
[out] how Phil Spector makes records.' For his part, Motz 'heard
Bruce virtually have orgasms over Les Paul'. He went on from
there to turn his side interest in echo and tape-loops into a full-
blown fad. 'Born To Run' featured some sly *à la* Philles touches,
not least the song's Ronettes-meet-Glitter Band intro. But generally Springsteen aimed for a 'block' mix, where creamy
embellishment ruled over solo effects. The once-rigid dividing
line between 'waffly' pop and 'heavy' soul broke down. The result
was a treacly confection of noise, where every roar was matched by
a rippling counterpoint and a yahoo chorus. Springsteen had no
doubt of the tune's commercial potential. After playing *Crawdaddy*
a tape of 'Born To Run', he punched the air and yelled '*WABC!*',
the New York Top 40 station. Then he began cutting the rest of his
album. Springsteen would say he was 'born, grew old and died'
making the record, recycling all the house-sounds he loved – from
Sun to Stax – and processing them into something new. Somehow,
set against the bazooka blast of the sax and Springsteen's vocals, it
worked.

   Some of the same fat production values were at work live. The

E Street Band had a love of black music – as well as, briefly, three black members – and a palette including jazz, funk and even gospel (in the Ray Charles-tinged 'Fever'). It made for a heady set. As David Blue said, 'it was right out of [*God's Trombones*], a big revue-type show that was more brass than improv'. As well as Brickman's lights, there was the married team of Louis and Suki Lahav, the one doing sound, the other bringing violin, and a dramatic flair, to the mix. The early *Born to Run* cuts Springsteen débuted in 1974 leant heavily on soul-train riffing, specifically the bond of the strings and sax to the vocals. Raw power stood in for song-thrush virtuosity. Along with the whomp of the band and the stagecraft, sheer roadwork – he played over ninety gigs that year – was making Springsteen a living. But only just. The booker Jim Mahlmann recalls 'do[ing] two dates with Bruce for a total of $1,500, scrawling it all down on a napkin' – funnelling the cash to Laurel Canyon, though Springsteen's agent was still, technically, Sam McKeith. Punters at another club in Austin, that March, paid $1 each to see the 'New Jersey wailer'. Springsteen travelled in to the gig by train. He stayed at a Val-U Inn. After paying Appel's commission, the band and treating himself to pizza and a movie, he netted exactly $80.

Through it all, Springsteen's inner life remained a mystery, even to his clique. When trouble struck a friend or stranger, he was a consoling force who managed to find the right words. But people also saw that he kept his distance. He rarely pumped Appel about the 'big picture', but zeroed in on each night's gig as a self-contained biodome. Two bookings that year stood out: spring dates at Charlie's Bar and Harvard Square Theatre in Cambridge, and a summer night opening for Anne Murray in Central Park. After he left the stage in New York, several thousand Springsteen fans likewise exited.

At this pivotal rip, rich in kudos but near broke in pocket, he met the man rightly called his svengali. On a raw April evening, Springsteen was reading a review of *The Wild* taped to the window of Charlie's, the lights of which, a neon profusion, spelled out his own name. Dressed in regulation jeans and T-shirt, he was jumping up and down, half from cold, half with glee. The piece's author walked up to meet him. 'Loved the album,' said Jon Landau. 'Not the production.' Two hours later, Landau left the club glazed-eyed and grinning, 'a stone fan' he told friends around town. Next month, he saw Springsteen second-bill for Bonnie Raitt at Harvard Square Theatre. This time, he went home, typed up a storm and filed it with Boston's *The Real Paper*. The strap-line would be quoted (and misquoted) the world over. 'Last Thursday . . . I saw my rock 'n' roll past flash before my eyes. And I saw something else: I saw rock and roll future and its name is Bruce Springsteen.' It may have been the most significant single arts review of the 1970s. It certainly was for Springsteen and Landau.

He was then twenty-seven, and had been writing for eight years. While reading history at Boston's Brandeis University, Landau began reviewing for *Crawdaddy*, before graduating to the newly coined *Rolling Stone*. His savage pan there of a Cream gig caused Eric Clapton to black out. He also played guitar, and produced. Low-fi gems such as *Back in the USA* mingled with columns in weeklies like *The Phoenix* and its successor, *The Real Paper*. To this staggeringly eclectic CV, he added film work and a greatest-hits book, *It's Too Late to Stop Now*. As a critic, Landau was a mixture of ambition, talent, neck, charm, ego and sheer comic lack of self-awareness. Hardened and trained by a long fight with his own insecurity, he was a master butcher of the weak and waffly. More than one group, including Cream, never quite came round from his knife.

Tall, thin, bespectacled, Landau was both going through a divorce and suffering from Crohn's, a gut spasm that often left him in crippling pain. Personally and professionally, he was in flux. Fate had given him neither the constitution nor the physique to be a pop star, as he'd once dreamt. It had, however, superbly equipped him for the strong-arm world of rock management. Landau's devotion to the grail of Bruce Springsteen was kindled by a mutual adolescent love of men like Elvis and Sam Cooke. In theory, he first befriended the 'Jersey wailer' as a co-fan of such dirty-faced icons. In practice, Landau would come to be strategist, mentor and gatekeeper, the heavy hitter in a triumvirate with CBS and Laurel Canyon. So stuck was he on 'Born To Run', he listened to it nonstop in bed while recovering from bowel surgery. 'As good as the King,' he said. In time, he duly morphed into Colonel Parker, with minders and flaks of his own. The author and DJ Charlie Gillett knew Landau in 1972–73, when he was a 'kindred spirit, against million-notes-a-minute guitar solos and all in favour of good, funky R & B'. A few years later, Gillett tried to re-establish touch and found only 'a shit'.*

Nor did *The Real Paper* rave exactly come about in a void. It followed in a line from CBS's 'Bobcat' effusions and the missionary zeal of a Bruce Pollock. There was also the fact that Richard Williams had seen the 'future of rock and roll' more than a year before. Several New York- and Boston-area critics could also lay claim to the phrase 'Bossmania'. Appel, too, had long had an idealistic vision of Springsteen's career, if not the charm or cash-flow to milk it. But none of this advance work would crystallize opinion as much as Landau's. Virtually overnight, it quashed CBS's doubts about funding, still less plugging a third album, shaming them into budgets of, respectively, $50,000 and $250,000 on *Born*. For this titanic coup alone, the twin Zeppelins of 'jive' and 'bull' were worth it.

Springsteen's triumph, aside from his raw skill and iron will, was due in part to the sheer loyalty he got from fellow pros, friends and management, as well as the 'real dudes' who packed the beer- and cigarette-stained dives around Boston and New York. In this, first Appel and then Landau and Dave Marsh resembled a medieval religious or military order, like the Knights Templar of the Crusades. These various failed musicians or ex-White Panthers joined in like-minded alliance around an abstract, rock, and a flesh-and-blood archetype, Springsteen. And like the Lionheart, he was the voice of deepest principle. His proven commitment to live up to

---

*Although Springsteen met a real need for Landau, it was mutual. That March, Jim Mahlmann had watched 'Bruce wig out with Appel . . . Everyone, especially CBS, wanted him to change shop.'

pop's holy covenant won him his spurs. In a corrupt business under the glam and megaband heel, Springsteen represented the values of grit, ethnicity and fun – and he was trusted because of his impressive spunk and willingness to go toe-to-toe with the suits. Marsh himself would analyse the sect, of which he was both diarist and paid-up member, when he wrote, 'Springsteen has a tendency to inspire messianic regard in his fans. This isn't so much because he's regarded as a savior . . . but because he fulfils the rock tradition.' John Rockwell's equally spot-on quip was that 'he awakens ageing writers' long-lost memories of when they were young'. Romantic hope like that, of course, took an innocent and unshakeable faith that Springsteen was Everyman, or at least every American. Those, like Marsh, who sought to keep alive Elvis's flame now got behind their consensus, a man who enjoyed collecting sounds as much as playing them. If Springsteen meant freedom, it was that of the specimen jar for the bug; if Marsh's was the way to celebrate rock and roll, it was the toast of the history club. 'Bruce was the hacks' emotional, as much as musical saviour,' in one arch view; a 'cool choice' also noted by Paul Jones, singer of one of Springsteen's pet hits, 'Pretty Flamingo'. 'Bruce's gift is to listen to bands like the Stones, basically aping Chuck Berry, and songs like "Flamingo", all Sam Cooke and Percy Sledge phrasing, and act as both receiver and transmitter. He's hip enough to hear the original black roots, and shrewd enough to translate and smooth them out for the masses. Ry Cooder does something similar. It's very subtle.' This walk down rock's mirror-hall and tenement blocks would take a firm sense of one's own bearings. As a pop folklorist and historian himself, Landau was Springsteen's perfect guide.

Aside from pure nostalgia, Springsteen won through on the basis of human empathy. An immensely 'real' and contagiously frank man, he was an unmatched find. When Landau and Marsh came to probe his background – with its classic Boomer core of an angry father and a bolshie, guitar-wielding son – that, too, spoke their language. Another starring trait was his Jersey past. With its brassy boardwalk, bar and beach culture, Asbury was the ancestral home of the attitudinal rocker. In later years, tourists and critics alike would find it hard to resist turning Springsteen into a symbol – or Identikit, in *Sounds'* dig – of his time and place.

Springsteen met Landau's fixation with friendship. It was a true relationship, serving both parties. Landau would introduce his protégé to a world of classic books and films which, inevitably, came to shade the music. He played something of the role of cultural tutor to Springsteen. Landau also knew that the screenplay of his own life, however complex on the margins, was rooted in the fundamental theme of serving his 'boy'. Springsteen, for instance, lived in fear of the press. He was innocent of the dark arts of PR, let alone 'market penetration' and 'positioning'. Landau smoothly brought his accumulated smarts to bear. He brilliantly grasped that the emotional wall Springsteen built round him was shaped by his reaction to Doug's rages, by the hurt and isolation of life in Freehold and by the dingy houses where the young Bruce had learned the art of living without friends. Landau, in short, became a composite father–brother type. This dual rapport was at the root of a uniquely tight bond. Its rewards were vast. Landau grew Midas wealthy. The crack that he was like 'a pig in shit' on finding Springsteen was obviously a wicked one, but conveyed a view people had of him. 'Jon looked at Bruce and saw . . . zang, the bucks,' says an exfriend. Another account has him bearing down 'with all the finesse of a Mack truck'. Gradually, over the winter of 1974–75, the axis shifted. Within eighteen months, Landau would oust Appel as Springsteen's confidant, producer and, last, manager. The frail and fed-up man who'd wandered into the Harvard theatre at a low ebb was *en route* to becoming a rich and revered plutocrat.

The hard slog of recording, meanwhile, ground on randomly all year. Springsteen had cut 'Born To Run' by midsummer. He was in agonies about its follow-ups. Some of his Libra streak – his 'long time before moving' spied in the pram – came out at Blauvelt. Springsteen wasn't afraid to go it alone against the band. What he was loath to do was side openly with one highly prized 'bud' against another, especially Appel and Landau, reflex foes who ruffled easily at real or imagined snubs. Springsteen was sensitive – too sensitive – to their feelings and ever keen to tout a façade of unity. His unwillingness, as he said, to 'whip butt' cost him dear. Cutting losses, hitting marks, making schedules – such things weren't within his ken. Springsteen went back to his piano. After 'Born' was in the can, he slaved over songs like 'Jungleland' and the (unreleased) 'A Love So Fine'; a stripped-down, acoustic 'Thunder Road' (with a different girl's name on the guide vocal) was eked out that fall. Even at this stage, *Born to Run* was destined to be compared with its two predecessors. Many of the same types reappeared from *Greetings* and *The Wild*, though, this time round, less doom-struck and anchored to sheer, slick songs about sun, sex and, above all, flight. As always with Springsteen, the actual tunes came in a flash. Recording them was another matter. From 'Born' on, the Teen Tycoon steered his course – he was the Spector riding shotgun as Springsteen lurched back and forth to Blauvelt. While everyone worked to the bone, the hard truth was that 914, with its leaky roof and out-of-whack piano, wasn't best placed to re-create the 'kids' symphonies' of the Philles' salad days. The band, too, groused at the long nightly haul up Route 303. Too often, the sessions broke down in tears. The job ground up Louis Lahav, drove Sancious and Carter to despair and out of the fold, and fixed Appel, who'd pay for his attempts to exercise power in a vacuum.

'We're fucked,' Springsteen would say daily. This acknowledgement of studio life seemed to be *Born*'s roundabout way of reaching for new depths of realism. The Berlin Wall between the blustery, technicolour music and its grainy, *film noir* setting was just one of the album's stresses. There was the problem of survival. Strapped for cash, Springsteen was still doggedly trucking between club, bar and festival gigs to pay the bills. Of the last, his upstaging of Anne Murray was a zenith. The nadir came in the dank, smoky gyms and swim-meets where – in those pre-video days – a band sweated up a name. In a bid to raise both hopes and funds, Appel promptly fired off a tape of the new single to Black Rock. He followed it up by a meeting with Irwin Segelstein, president of CBS's home division. Anticipating a coup, Appel upped the odds by telling Springsteen he meant to 'kick butt', hard and wholesale, round the label. But the encounter took a rather different turn. A blasé Segelstein

yawned when he first heard 'Born To Run'. At four and a half minutes, it was 'too long' for Top 40 radio; more like 'born to crawl',
added a cipher dutifully.

The song would have died in the crib but for Segelstein's son. A
senior at Rhode Island's Brown University, he read an interview
Springsteen gave the campus paper that May. In it he was asked
about the current 'vibes' at CBS. 'They've been treating us pretty
bad,' was the stark reply. In Appel's words, 'The kid must have read
his father the riot act, because next thing I know, Irwin gets me on
the phone . . . He wound up inviting me to lunch. And that
moment became something of a turning point for Bruce, the precise moment when CBS began to change its attitude.' Appel still
sent tapes of the song to game DJs in key towns blitzed by
Springsteen. Most also got a home pressing of 'Jungleland' or 'A
Love So Fine'. The gratifying fruit of this legal bootlegging was
heavy airplay around Cleveland and Philadelphia, a tribute, first, to
Springsteen's hard work, but also to his manager's pit-bull gump-
tion. Appel's *ad hoc* PR paid off. While stations like WMMR got
behind 'Born To Run', CBS finally rekindled some of its pro-
Springsteen fire. The tag-line for this second-wave crusade was
Landau's blurb. Whole chunks of it were lifted from their original
copy. I SAW ROCK AND ROLL FUTURE ran as a bold, block-capital ad in
Rolling Stone and elsewhere in July 1974. Springsteen himself rang
Landau to thank him. He still needed all the help he could get. It
was another year before he resumed his old beef at being hyped.
'The whole episode [was] a big drag for me . . . I mean, who wants
to come onstage and be the future every night? Not me. Let the
guy who thought [it] up come out and do it . . . See how he likes it.'

In August Carter and Sancious left for their own star-crossed
band, Tone. Their replacements, signed via a *Village Voice* ad and
open auditions, were, respectively, 'Mighty' Max Weinberg and
Roy 'Professor' Bittan.* The former got the job by passing a test
Springsteen set every drummer, 'where they'd be playing this
straight-ahead rocker, and he'd stop the band . . . He'd pause, then

---

*Also on call, though rejected again, was the singer Patti Scialfa.

suddenly thrust his hand up in the air. I was the only one who hit a rim-shot when he did that.' Weinberg's dramatic flair was matched by Bittan's. The pianist tempered his rollicking, Fats Domino fills with theatrical nous befitting his pit days on Broadway. Both men were finds. Between them, they'd help reinvent the band without tossing the full-blooded riffs and rhythms at its core. Meanwhile, Springsteen was forced off the road. Yet again, recording broke down. There was no money. He was 'fucked'. It was at this dire strait that he sought out Landau, after another Boston gig in October. Over the past six months, the critic had both divorced and had bile surgery. He lost so much weight from these twin blows that Springsteen didn't recognize him.

Despite his own lofty role, Landau – like almost everyone else who loved primal rock – was in awe of Springsteen, while simultaneously responding to his frank, if fey personality. Meantime, says Grice, 'he used Bruce just as Bruce used him'. The two men became close that winter, Springsteen often crashing at Landau's New York apartment rather than driving home to Jersey. They bonded over old 45s. As Landau said, 'We stayed up all night just talking about everything in the world . . . We played records for each other all the time. He'd come over and say, "Have you heard this or that?" We'd turn [each other] on to things.' This mutual love of pop lore and historiography – from 'Louie, Louie' through Landau's own work – made for more give-and-take in three months than Springsteen managed with Appel in three years. For the first time, he had a sounding-board and official best friend. Virtually from the cot, he'd been afflicted with an impersonal fear not just of parents – he was too democratic for that – but of all adults. (Springsteen, by and large, 'dug kids'.) Deadly in earnest, rigid, self-exacting, he never opened up, even to Darvin, offstage. Rather, he projected his need for love into the stalls. Now, at twenty-five, he found his mate. It was like, he wrote, 'I was the only ET on earth, and then here was the other one.' That bad. 'Bruce went quietly nuts for Jon,' notes a CBS staffer. Slowly, Landau began to annex one after another of Appel's duties. He wasn't the first critic to dabble in the arcane realm of 'brand positioning'. But, unlike other Olympian pundits, Landau actually knew his stuff. He had ears. As Springsteen says, 'Jon taught my drummer . . . I'm sitting there during all these sessions, and you know one of the problems with my records was, like, the drummer was, like, you know, he wasn't there. I didn't pick it up and Mike didn't pick it up.' By February 1975, Landau felt bold enough to suggest Appel's presence be more sparingly required at Blauvelt. From then on, it was war.

Landau liked victories. It's often said that he presented minor wins and sometimes losses as major feats. What's less often said, but also true, he did so not to kid others, but to convince himself that tactical gains would boot up strategic triumphs. His first battleground with Appel was the studio. That March, he engineered a move from Blauvelt to the Record Plant in Manhattan. Landau was enough of a true believer to both rationalize and humanize his principles. First, he flattered the principal. As Springsteen says, 'We didn't go [to New York] until Jon said, "Hey, man, you're first-rate, and you're in there in second-rate bullshit. You're first-rate. Man, go first-rate."' Next, he proved his mastery of logistics and detail by personally closing the deal. Landau's vigilance never slept; it was his 'fuckin'-near military' grasp that so struck Springsteen, with his famously lax eye on things like time and money. They gelled. Unlike Appel, Landau lived for work, spending long hours every day at his desk, reading a constant flow of memos and bills, which he annotated with minute, spidery notes. One result of this micro-management was a smooth transfer to the front room at the Record Plant. Once there, Landau promptly hired the engineer Jimmy Iovine (veteran of Lennon's Spector-produced *Rock 'n' Roll*). Another was that, as from 13 April 1975, he officially took a cut of the action, 2 per cent of *Born*'s retail sales. Landau's share came half from CBS and half from Appel.

The old saw about a miserable life making for great art – or music booming when the musicians don't – was stood on its ear in *Born to Run*. Until then, Springsteen hadn't really known what a producer did. What he most often asked for was that they 'fix it' by finding a middle road where none existed between the arrangements and the time limits of cutting on vinyl; in short, an editor. For both technical and personal reasons, working in Blauvelt had been a Goyaesque nightmare of late-night waffle. That all ended. In just one example, Springsteen, Appel and Louis Lahav had fretted for weeks over a sax solo that, though tuneful, was grounded firmly in the wiry funk and idiomatic soul of, as Clemons said, 'another bag'. The track was then called 'Wings for Wheels'. Landau listened to the tape, slid a knob or two on the desk and muttered, 'Gotcha.' The break became the outro and the song became 'Thunder Road'.

That was the very moment, says Springsteen, 'it clicked . . . Jon just made me aware, like . . . that I could do better, that I could be better.' Landau also gave full rein to the supporting cast. With Sancious, the E Streeters had lost their sole virtuoso; but Clemons, Tallent, Federici, Weinberg and Bittan (the last two earning $75 per week apiece) were both sweaty yet ingeniously melodic, a formula other, better-heeled supergroups could only feebly crib. Though they coalesced around Springsteen, they were never just a choral society. As the promoter John Scher told *Backstreets*, 'The [band] worked on all cylinders . . . It was a finely tuned machine.' That was true, but Springsteen was still squarely behind the wheel. 'It's definitely me, I'm a solo act, y'know,' he'd say in 1978. Even Dave Marsh came away with the scoop that 'Bruce stands distinctly outside [the] group . . . There is a sense in which he doesn't mesh in any society.' To Grice, there was 'always the hermit' about him, as well as the monk.

On one level, Springsteen's simplicity was very real. While CBS's 'rock and roll future' ad was shifting thousands of units of *The Wild* and even *Greetings*, little of it came his way. By mid-1975, he kept twenty-two people on his payroll: as well as the band, there was Appel, two minders, sundry roadies and guitar techs and a full-time cameraman, all signing 'Laurel Canyon' on tabs charged to his account. Springsteen himself grossed $12,500 in royalties and $8,500 in tour fees in 1974. Residuals may have upped his pre-tax income to $25,000, roughly the same as a blue-collar worker. He lived in a bungalow at 7½ West End Court, Long Branch, less than twenty miles from Freehold. Its centrepiece was a moth-eaten sofa salvaged from the alley. The rest of the furniture looked as though it had been condemned. When he had car trouble, which was often, Springsteen took the bus in to Manhattan. He still seemed to own only one T-shirt, and favoured broilers where he could chug junk-food and no one bothered with cutlery. Landau would recall sitting with Springsteen poring over the *Born to Run* sessions. 'He said he had problems . . . There were sounds in his head, or ideas in his head, he [couldn't] capture on tape.' Typically, this late-night artistic review took place at a burger stand.

There was, of course, more to him than the bluff, good-rockin' persona touted by the likes of Marsh. Springsteen hit 1975 as a mixed bag: a rare talent, a man to be relied on, but also a hard man to work with, who 'personalized everything'. As Landau himself said, 'underneath his shyness is the strongest will I've ever encountered. If there's something he doesn't want to do, he won't.' (Springsteen's first line of resistance, as far as live gigs went, was against 'sheds'.) This obduracy was also on hand in the studio. The 'cult of personality' increasingly cast Springsteen as more than mere Boss; he got his way because, as one of them says, 'all the band were in awe of him'. He seemed to 'take it more seriously' than them. 'We played to live – he lived to play.' Like, say, Andy Warhol, Springsteen was an extraordinary ordinary man. His final success came from both genius and a dour-as-does-it willpower. He was at the Record Plant from 3 p.m. to 6 a.m. every day, cutting the album *Sounds* would call 'rough 'n ready'.

In the studio, Springsteen was a perfectionist to the point of pedantry. He spent hours correcting and editing his lyrics in a maze of inserts, arrows, zig-zags and fussily infinitesimal revisions. That was for starters. He calibrated his songs all year. Some of them went through thirty, forty, and, in one case, fifty-six drafts. But the words came out turbo-charged next to the music. The first *Born to Run* session was in April 1974; the plug was pulled in July 1975, and even then he wanted to start over. For anyone else, working fifteen hours a day for fifteen months would do. But, on many of those days, Springsteen was also on the road, huddled with Appel and Landau, playing, rehearsing, auditioning, giving interviews or off with Karen Darvin. With friends like her, this great solitary man would become a 'warm, loving guy'. As success came, he unwound; though, even then, he relaxed flat-out. 'BS went everywhere, did everything,' says Motz. Springsteen's 'go-go side' extended to dancing, tooling up and down the turnpike, pinball, softball and long walks on the beach. Here, in Asbury, the Boss became Bruce again. He'd stroll down the boardwalk enjoying a bite or sit in a bar for an hour with his fans. A local named Joey Mazo met Springsteen in 1975. 'Provided you respected his space, he was the nicest guy ever. Bruce wasn't acting being one of us. He just was.' It would be trite but true to say he 'never forgot where he came from'. As he put it, 'I'm not into people screaming at me . . . Once they do, it's over.'

For all the populist charm, there was also a core darkness about him; he was too steeped in Freehold. Like Doug, he learned to deep-six his feelings with a skill in dissimulation that became second nature. Offstage, he was warmth itself to his press and fan club. He rarely met a court he didn't like. Springsteen was less good one-on-one. Onstage his knack was precisely to home in on a single member of the crowd without snubbing the other two or three thousand; pageantry *with* intimacy – no mean feat. Springsteen wasn't after mere ego validation. The gigs, even the patently barmy ones like church services, went both ways: he learnt how to find love and how to give it. As Landau said, 'Bruce wants it all . . . he always wants it all.'

Springsteen spent the first quarter of 1975 on the road. He gave Appel firm orders about what kind of gigs he wanted to play. As well as his long-term veto of sheds, he banned buttons, badges, posters and T-shirts – the very logoed goods and relics other rockers used as a nightly fix of immortality. But that was his one and only major inhibition. The shows that spring were a riot of songs ancient and new. Springsteen also neatly resurrected the spirit of his mentors, with classic renditions of Chuck Berry, Little Richard and Animals hits; the Detroit Medley would début on his birthday. A set on 5 February, meanwhile, yielded the legendary bootleg *The Saint*, *the Incident & the Main Point Shuffle*. It became one of literally dozens of spurious tapes and knock-offs to do the rounds until, finally, CBS went to law. In a separate move later that week, Suki Lahav left the fold. Springsteen, Landau and the band then took up residence in their album. These all-night shifts at the Record Plant went on for four months. Springsteen seemed to emerge once, for a radio talk with, bizarrely, a Catholic priest, but that was to give him less credit for steely application in the studio than fair. The interview had actually been taped in 1974.

'I want to get girls into the group,' Springsteen said, 'because I've got some good ideas which add up to more than just background vocals. But right now I don't have the money.' Ironically, just as the band's token woman walked out the door, an old hand walked in. 'Miami Steve' Van Zandt also arrived at the very moment production broke down. For the third time that night, 'Tenth Avenue Freeze-Out' crashed in a heap of mangled sax and chugging trombone. The jazz trumpeter Randy Brecker recalls 'sitting with the meter ticking' while the horn section 'interminably' argued the toss. 'Miami blew in like a tornado . . . There we were, the New York pros, and this wild-looking gypsy guy tears up the charts and *sings* the lick. From then on, things took off.' It was now, after Van Zandt rejoined, that *Born* caught fire. More than that, the way he and Springsteen worked two guitars became a signature sound, full of warped soul breaks and hefty, production-type riffing. A photographer named Joel Bernstein* would work with the band later in the seventies. 'Steve fitted in as the piratical first-mate and bosun. He was no song-bird, but he had a great ear for arrangements.' According to a second source, 'basically, he acted as a midwife to the tunes in Bruce's head'. Van Zandt took his handle from a love of Florida, the sun, and, by extension, thermal surf and soul hits. The other late recruits' names were equally well coined. Weinberg was a mighty, yet never metronomic presence on drums; Bittan, professorial in both looks and the esoteric world of codas, cadenzas and discordant arpeggios – a Van Zandt with formal

---

*Responsible for, among other shots, the cover of 'Hungry Heart'.

training. This magnificent seven finally wrapped *Born to Run* on 19 July 1975. Four hours later, they were rehearsing for the tour that made Springsteen a star.

Those titanic concerts that summer and fall became lore. Springsteen's albums may have been on the short side, but, at three hours, the gigs never were: atavistic rave-ups that flouted the laws of nature long before chaos theory had a name. As Jim Mahlmann says, 'some nights, whole rows of chairs would be literally bouncing up and down on their legs by the encore'. Or encores: there were three or four of them. Somewhere around 1 a.m., the band would drag Springsteen off and throw iced-water over him while he lay, steamy and happy, on the dressing-room floor. It was ever thus. While there was no lack of flesh in tow, the audience became his real love, the one he lived and died for nightly. Time after time, he opened a vein for them, belting his new songs alongside the feral covers of R&B oldies. He may have been no great singer or soloist. Springsteen was, though, a great rock and roller, for whom the stage was a 'day at the beach' after the 'shit' of the studio. A strange personality for a pop icon, on one level. And yet not so strange: for with masses Springsteen was wryly articulate, and in public often got the sense of communion, if not affection, he so missed in private.

In this theatrical context, his act became a living model of 1970s 'nowness'. Springsteen's human-jukebox trait concealed a long apprenticeship. Already a stage veteran, he hit his mark with both his prodigy and power still intact. (Though to a few credulous types he seemed to have emerged from the ether, it was actually his tenth year on the boards.) As always, his hypnotic effect on the house came half from the music, half from his soul connection with fans and grizzled hacks alike. Springsteen's raps were semi-sunny, semi-dark, part cornball charm, part voyages round his father, but both sides had this in common: they were more heartfelt, more vivid and above all more real than the vacuous 'Hi, y'all' clichés of the mega-bands. In what seemed an instant – but was actually a decade – this grease-haired Byron conquered Olympus.

The actual moment came in August. Appel had wanted to book

Madison Square Garden to usher in *Born to Run*. With memories of his 1973 bomb there and later arena-dread, Springsteen plumped for a five-night stand at New York's Bottom Line. He didn't disappoint. To Dave Marsh in *Rolling Stone*, 'Not since Elton John's initial Troubadour appearances has an artist leapt so visibly and rapidly from cult fanaticism to mass acceptance . . . It was a time to hail from Jersey with pride.' The *New York Times* splashed its review over eight columns. Their verdict: 'The shows will rank among the great rock experiences of those lucky enough to get in. Mr Springsteen has it all – he is a great lyricist, a wonderful singer, guitarist and piano player, has one of the best bands anybody has ever heard, and he's as charismatic a stage figure as pop has produced.' From then on, the media chorus became a giant band playing but one tune. A star was born.

Springsteen, to his credit, stood largely aloof from the hype. It was just one of the elements of that epic misunderstanding that began with the 'Bobcat' tag. From then on, it seemed, the CBS PR machine had had only two gears – reverse and overdrive. Of the five thousand punters who passed through the doors of the Bottom Line, fully a quarter were record company managers, salesmen, liggers and DJs hosted by the label. The rest of the $250,000 budget went on a fit that, six months ago, would have left Springsteen – who still wore his anti-materialism as a halo – toe-curlingly embarrassed. As well as the freebies, back-handers and goody-bags, there were T-shirts, key-chains, photos and three different kinds of poster doing the rounds. Appel, meanwhile, in a spurt of his own entrepreneurial genius, was hustling for a *Playboy* cover story. Many of the media took the opportunity not only to fawn over Springsteen, but to back-scratch and log-roll for each other. Earlier in the year, Dave Marsh had joined the inner circle by way of his friendship with Landau; he, John Rockwell, Robert Hilburn and a small but elite corps soon began writing critical Valentine's cards. It became part of the Summer of Springsteen. When the BBC's Bob Harris arrived in October, he found 'all the hoardings plastered with Bruce's name. It was incredible . . . like a huge switch had been thrown.'

On one level, the PR and promotional frenzy did Springsteen no good. In focusing on an image of him as a pop messiah (or, later, a guitar-toting Rambo) fans avoided having to think about the songs and the guts and hard work it took to play like him night after night. It demeaned the music. In time, the buzz about his hype became one of the incestuous sub-plots of Springsteen's career. Even some of his old gang like the DJ Denny Sanders rued the overkill. 'Because the rock 'n' roll well is really dry, [CBS] are going crazy for Springsteen.' According to this view, he was a fad, not a passion, something flashy, thrilling but ultimately throwaway, like the 'Bolan Boogie' of 1972–73. As Stephen Stills said, 'Bruce is good, but he's not that different from a lot of people . . . He's nowhere near as good as his hype.' Yet, despite it all, Springsteen would survive the low-radius cycle of trendiness that ruined Bolan. As well as Landau's savvy, he had the one thing going for him – raw, unadorned talent – that generally does for fashion. Every 'rock sensation' should be as brazenly outdated and mint-new.

The British press, meanwhile, stroked their collective stubble over this latest mythologized slab of American art. Via his Intersong demos and Adrian Rudge, Springsteen had long had his fans in London. Tireless plugging by Polydor would lead to the Hollies' cover of 'Sandy' grazing the chart in 1975. A second, uncut lyric, 'Marie', got constant pirate airplay. In the print press, Richard Williams and a tiny but well-placed clan had been praising Springsteen to the sky since *Greetings*. To them, he was the authentic voice of a counter-coup against 'old farts' and MOR worthies like the Carpenters. British rock, on the whole, was in a state of fledgling revolution. As Williams says, 'In '75, the scene was stale and self-parodying. Bruce was a raw talent who didn't stoop to industrial tricks like merchandising or hit-mongery'; in those turbid, pre-punk days, said Bangs, 'the Limeys had been antsy for a Springsteen since the Stones first caved on *Goat's Head Soup*'. Soon radio and TV types like Mike Appleton, Bob Harris, Paul Gambaccini, Tony Wilson and Andy Peebles were weighing in with their own encomiums. Corporate back-up duly followed. CBS in Soho Square launched a crusade that made the head office's look woefully laid-back. By August, it seemed almost a churlish technicality to point out that Springsteen's 'global tour' still hadn't left America. It hardly mattered. Thanks to the PR, he was no longer a comer, but a star who'd arrived.

Yet again, there was a backlash. David Sinclair was one young writer who gagged at being force-fed a diet of 'Bossmania'; there were others. Springsteen's reputation, deserved, was of a hard-working, hard-playing pro. It was nothing personal – just that the verbiage from Soho could go both ways. As *Mojo* said, 'It caused you to think the boy from Jersey might not only have made a good record, but made the lame to walk and the blind to see.' It was 'fuckin' heavy', says Keith Richards.

In brief, the eastern front of the campaign involved: billboard, press and radio spots, all flogging the 'rock and roll future' tag; topping even this, a foam-flecked ad reading FINALLY THE WORLD IS READY FOR BRUCE SPRINGSTEEN; and critics jetting to New York to catch the act. By late summer, the machinery was running at full bore on both sides of the Atlantic. For more than three years, Appel had been touting Springsteen as a sure bet, and now his coverage also ran on predictable lines. It followed down one of two tracks. While *Rolling Stone* named him 'artist of the year', *Sounds* slated Springsteen as the 'jive of '75'. With a few shining exceptions, the UK press generally occupied itself with treadmill praise or the reflex pricking of the hype. Either way, he became one of the most polarizing names in rock. In Britain, that autumn, you either loved Springsteen or you hated him. What nobody did was ignore him. Such controversy couldn't have been bought, especially for a man who hadn't yet got on the plane.

In that huge kriegspiel that became Springsteen's life, he seemed to live between two exiles: to be the 'coming man', but also one who'd, in a flash, pull back, freeing 'the Boss' from the rabble and becoming Bruce again. Despite the Brandoesque swagger* he was essentially quiet and even tongue-tied, an 'ultracoy kid', in one

---

*Springsteen would later be asked to star in a musical remake of *The Wild One*. He didn't.

view, who preferred TV to partying. Typically, after playing into the early hours, Springsteen would wolf down his Big Macs and sit up all night. Dawn would find him still slumped with his hands on a guitar, his notebook or, as one of them says, 'some model's ass'. He was the epitome of a certain kind of American male. The unchanging roundelay was that he was 'real'. Plaudits teemed down. Bob Harris, who met Springsteen that autumn, thought him 'sweet'; to Allan Clarke, he was a 'down-to-earth guy'. A man calling himself Doc similarly ran into his hero in the Eatontown, Jersey, mall. 'He talked to me for a while about writing the songs on *Born to Run*, real shy, real civil . . . not like other hot-shots.' Despite the fey, mousy affect, Springsteen could be wry and witty. 'Someday we'll look back on this/and it will all seem funny' he'd sung on 'Rosalita', proving he was less star-struck than some of the fans. When the CBS suits arrived to hear the final cut of *Born*, Karen Darvin says, 'he and I laid on the floor of the studio and laughed at how seriously everyone was taking it'. Springsteen, in short, was at once credible and incredible – a 'down-to-earth guy' who took wing onstage.

Darvin was a fixture that year. The freckled, ash-blonde model, in whom a wisecrack floated behind a warm smile and a yoga body-glow, had migrated up from Texas. It was, all sides agree, a case of true love. Springsteen was faithful to her in his fashion. He still rooted around in bed for what he'd lost in childhood, but the groupies and one-nighters never lasted. Within a day or two, he'd be back with the woman he called 'Hon'. Home for them was the green-painted house (with Springsteen's yellow '57 Chevy outside) near the beach in Long Branch: ex-resort of presidents, now, like Asbury, sadly slumped. On a rare night out, they might walk down Ocean Boulevard for a tube-steak at Max's, or catch *Jaws* at the Roxy. Springsteen and Darvin's routine was upended that June and July, which they spent in room 206 of New York's Holiday Inn. This purdah, for the final leg of the *Born* sessions, nearly did for both parties. 'It was the heaviest,' he said. 'I told [Darvin] I understood exactly how she felt; she was in this hotel room for hours and she was seeing me only at night . . . She didn't know anybody else, so of course she'd get mad at me. So that got insane, the whole thing, it was really, like, freak-out time.'

Sexual problems were matched by hassles with the band and management. Springsteen's unity with his coalface colleagues broke down around the nineteenth take of 'She's The One'. His good mood returned in time to sour again in a tiff about money. According to Appel, 'Bruce had decided in a moment of great magnanimity that he wanted to give away half his income from all sources to the [group].' That whim was scrapped overnight. The fallout from this U-turn – and a sub-plot about the E Streeters signing their own CBS deal – soon paled by comparison. Around Independence Day, Landau and Appel's feud curdled into 'fuck you' vernacular. In one stunning scene, they had to be pulled off each other on the Record Plant roof. The exact pretext for the row was an 'artistic dispute' (mainly over whether or not Springsteen should do a live album), but for months both men had slipped, at odd moments, into the snarling peals of a dogfight. Thus, with the management team at blows, the band mute and Darvin pacing the floor, *Born to Run* went to bed. Springsteen was up at eight the next morning. He had a gig that night at the Palace, in Providence.

In the beginning pop music was about singers telling compressed stories over a dance-hall beat. Somehow, in the half-century between Rudy Vallee and Vangelis, that mission statement got lost in a fad for clever-dick tunes, brilliant and dazzling, but no heat. *Born to Run* was Springsteen's back-to-basics shot, full of monologues (with the accent on *mono*), 'kids' symphonies' with a looming-middle-age subplot. *Rolling Stone*'s Greil Marcus suggested that the title's source was the '50s arch-punk motto 'born to lose'. Springsteen's characters were, sure enough, on the lam, weaving down youth's symbolic highway – about as long as an old 45 – where 'girls comb their hair in rear-view mirrors/and the boys try to look so hard'. Their stories were told in a breezy (and, at bottom, windy) epic that established the Big Three themes: sex, escape and the redeeming power of music – the randy rocker's combination plate. What Springsteen added to the mix was an encyclopaedic command of pop lore, sopped up over seventeen years, and a cocked ear for the beating of time's wings. At their best, *Born*'s songs transcended nostalgia and took their dramatic snap from a dirge-like sense of loss, of life closing down. Their inner tension wove the same teary spell as Thomas Bayly's *Long, Long Ago* or the Flanders Field poets. The ruefulness of the lyrics gave the late-summer images a whiff of death. (At worst, they played for laughs.) Springsteen himself had clear ideas about the key text: 'In *Born to Run*, there's that searchin' thing.' And tone: 'The only concept was I needed to make a big record . . . Just like a car, zoom, straight ahead, that when the sucker comes on it's *wide* open. No holds barred!'

That said it for the production. As Bittan confided, 'Bruce wanted a record where the singing sounded like Roy Orbison and the music sounded like Phil Spector.' In practice, this one-two punch translated into a baroque, kitchen-sink collage of layered riffs, bells, strings and exaggeratedly low vocals belted at the top of their range. Between them, Springsteen, Landau and Iovine cloned the *bona fide* 1962 strains of Darlene Love, as well as an authenti-cally dire mix. (Springsteen disgustedly threw one master tape out of his hotel window.) A heavy echo set the guitar into a Duane Eddy-like twang. By and large the sound came over as clunky and ornate, full of scrollwork that was self-consciously florid rather than in thrall to the music. 'Weirdly pumped-up', says the lyricist Tim Rice. Charlie Gillett equates *Born* to 'Elvis meeting the Ronettes in an echo-tank'. One wry and plausible explanation comes from a man also bidding for fame in 1975, John Entwistle. 'That over-the-top shit often happens on a last-ditch album. It's like, "I'll show you, you buggers . . . Here I come!" I tried it on *Mad Dog*. Of course, unlike me, Bruce had the tunes.'

'I hated it,' Springsteen said of *Born to Run*. 'I thought it was the worst piece of garbage I'd ever heard.' The account of him whooping and yelling after cutting the title track hardly supports this claim, though it's true he was his own biggest fan and worst enemy. Third-party critics divided roughly down two lines. There were those, like Gillett, who thought it 'hollow' – poor fare, pretentiously wrapped – music that revelled in its insularity. 'For me, it didn't work, period. That production would have done better on a Meat Loaf album.' The charge here was that Springsteen had betrayed the left-field charm of *Greetings* and *The Wild*, as if by overplaying, and thus by inference 'selling out', he'd in some way impoverished his gifts. 'Inner vacuousness' was *Time Out*'s fell phrase. 'The record's as stiff as a frozen mackerel. Most of the songs are weak, as if he wrote them to suit the sound . . . hideous . . . the strength, spontaneity and visceral rush of the early music is gone.' This was a theory heard frequently among first-wave fans, who saw the masses coming up behind, fast.

The consensus, though, was that *Born*, emerging from the anaemic pack of cod-soul, MOR and ditties by Max Boyce, was both retrograde and a catalytic blast of loud, electric rock. It stamped Springsteen as a synthesist as much as an original. Not that he was just welding golden-guitar riffs to rouse-the-house melodies. Springsteen's best songs, like 'Thunder Road', had a self-effacing yet raw power, combining pop hooks with a subtlety of phrasing beyond even Elvis, let alone Meat Loaf. As Richard Williams says, 'Bruce actually used punctuation.' He sang as people thought and spoke, with an imposed delivery that allowed for commas and brackets and question marks. More than once he communicated in a semi-colon. *Born to Run* rightly won fame as the dead-ahead rock album of its time. As Greil Marcus wrote, 'Magnificent . . . a '57 Chevy running on melted-down Crystals records that shuts down every claim that's been made. And it should crack his future wide open.' It did, but Springsteen was about much more than dementedly chirpy licks with a big beat. Virtually all the spare, folkie syncopation of *Nebraska* could be found on *Born*, making it that rare gem – a work that gently deflated expectations, but delivered.

For an LP best known for crunching blues changes, *Born to Run* bowed with a folk-bard soliloquy. 'Wings For Wheels' was to have been the kick-off for a conceptual, Joycean ramble around 'Bruceday'; under Landau's helm it evolved through a thematic make-over and a title change into 'Thunder Road', the name of a

Jersey drag strip. From a hobo's harp, the song accelerated (more like a Coupe than a '57 Chevy) via neo-classical arpeggioed piano rolls and a heavy, prairie-Stones beat until Springsteen's parting salvo at Freehold: 'It's a town full of losers . . . And I'm pulling outta here to win'. Thanks to the punch of the horns and the ruse of writing half in the third person (making it a running gag, a sort of 'Changes'-cum-*American Graffiti*), 'Tenth Avenue Freeze-Out' re-proved itself again in the mould of 'Spirit In The Night'. The other tracks held their own pleasures: 'Backstreets' conjured just the dying-light and living-hell aesthetic that gave *Born* its edgy undertone. The languid pop-soul rhapsody brilliantly suited the narrative tug (only slightly spoilt by Springsteen singing the same line eighteen straight times). 'She's The One' was an elaborate excuse for a Bo Diddley stomp. Appel, in a rare show of artistic muscle, had lobbied hard for 'Meeting Across The River'. Springsteen would remember writing it in 'about an hour', its *film noir* shtick only saved by the lyrical trumpet fill (also, says Brecker, done in a trice). Just the opposite went for the switchblade hop of 'Jungleland'. It had the lot – a violin, cocktail piano, the guitar solo that virtually gave Boston's Tom Scholz his braggadocio sound, and Springsteen's roaring vocal – a masterly slab of street theatre with the grip of a hangman's noose.

The title track simply became part of the ozone. Musically, it exploited Springsteen's early '60s yen by way of the 'Telstar' riff, so cocky and elastic that it stood being wound down chromatically until the wild count-in to the end. Lyrically, it established Springsteen as the bridge between the Beat Generation and Generation X. 'Born' pulled off the feat of being both starry-eyed and downright horny ('Just wrap your legs round these velvet rims/And strap your hands across my engines'). As Springsteen told Dave Marsh, 'The most important thing is the question "I wanna know if love is real." And the answer is yes.' It was a stunning four and a half minutes of bullet-train rhythm, high-tension guitar and not so much a wall as a full house-of-sound. But it was more. However loose 'Born' hung as a bawdy, knees-up rocker, it was also one of those songs that works its way under the skin, shedding spin-offs and a slew of re-releases and covers, until it stopped being a hit and turned into an industry. In chronological order, it gave Springsteen his album title (beating out 'American Summer', 'The Legend of Zero and Blind Terry' and 'War & Roses'), rose to nineteen on the *Billboard* chart, survived being cut by everyone from Allan Clarke to Frankie Goes to Hollywood, got itself adopted as Jersey's 'youth ode' – apt for the state's street-poet laureate – and made into two videos before being re-tooled entirely as a half-fond, half-melancholy ballad and, finally, voted the 'greatest song ever' – certainly as a turnpike romp – by a blue-riband panel of *The Times* and Radio One. Along the way, 'Born To Run' became a vivid presence in the world's imagination. Critics hailed it as equal to, in 'some ways better than' – or as souped-up as – 'Bohemian Rhapsody', the other epic pop yardstick that fall. Here and there the reviewers got tetchy, making it a point of honour to show their independence by carping. To Gillett, for one, it was 'about as exciting as a night storage heater'. But the few rants were buried under the full weight of the raves. 'Born To Run' was destined to be one of the few universal smashes of its time.

With its sassy black-and-white cover shot of Springsteen nuzzling Clemons, the album, too, in the teeth of a PR storm, floated serenely into the cultural stratosphere. *Everyone* either had it or knew someone who did. *Born to Run* wasn't just a creative milestone. It was a commercial boon, too. On both sides of the Atlantic, virtues were discovered in Springsteen that had somehow previously failed to surface. *Born*'s title took on new meaning in the weeks and years ahead as cash rained down on record stores. Within three months, it had sold more than a million copies in America. It spent a straight year on the British chart. For acting as a catalyst and contrast-gainer, Landau earned an initial $100,000, the first wedge of what became a stipend. (Springsteen himself made four or five times that.) Financially, the scene was suddenly golden. But the royalty cheques churning out of Black Rock were only one sign of the decades-long, global bonanza. The cognoscenti now got behind Springsteen as for no other rock star since Dylan. He'd started 1975 with his hard-earned pockets of fans, but no real mainstream base. He ended it rich and famous. All-round prowess, hype and hard work each played its part. But what really did it for Springsteen were those forty bittersweet minutes of vinyl. Precious few other albums better dramatized what it was actually like to be alive as the century hit its fourth quarter – to keep boredom and obsolescence at bay by wearing an LP's grooves down to thin air. It was that good.

4

Follow That Dream

On 6 September 1975, Springsteen gave up his old house, his car, his free time and his life. The tour that opened that night – along with the platinum smash of *Born* – turned him from a regional love into a popular and critical darling. He worked hard for it. Those nonstop, raise-the-roof shows were a two-way street. The audience not only bayed for Springsteen, but got back a jolt of confidence and confirmation of their own. In one sense the myth was as much the wish of the fans – the embodiment of their unconscious needs – as foisted on them by the hype. For their five bucks, they got fifteen songs and an encore that lasted half as long again. Sound and lights were both exemplary, the band revelled in their fraternal weave, and nobody needed binoculars. Springsteen's act was intimate and real, rendered with a kind of Jerseyan wit that lingered long after the last note. These were some of the most consistently hot, yet coolest sets of the 1970s.

Springsteen turned twenty-six that month. He celebrated onstage at the University of Michigan, turning a two-hour gig into a four-hour party, hitting its climax simultaneously with a cake, a zap of Brickman's lights and a five-song medley of '60s hits. On 8 October, *Born* officially went gold. It dragged the first two albums with it. Technically, at least, Springsteen ended 1975 $191,779 better off, though the months ahead would prove the difference between being paper-rich and liquid. The actual cash came later, and even then it was a struggle. Springsteen 'broke', and he was broke. His most tangible asset from *Born* was a 1960 Corvette, one of a stable of hot-rods he owned. The next week he opened a four-night stand in the Roxy, Los Angeles, duplicating his coup at the Bottom Line. *Le tout* Hollywood was at the club: Robert De Niro, Jack Nicholson, Warren Beatty and local pranksters from Phil Spector to Jimmy Connors. Bob Harris flew in for the BBC. 'The first night I looked over and there were Bowie and George Harrison sitting with their arms folded, talking through the first number. Three songs in they were hooting and hollering along. By the time "Pretty Flamingo" came round, there wasn't a dry seat in the house. As far as I was concerned, Bruce left that gig a superstar. We knew it, he knew it and, from their faces, Bowie and Harrison knew it too. It rubber-stamped him with the shakers.'

From then on every public act by Springsteen, however trite, did the rounds. As well as his managers, apparatchiks and yes-men, he made fans of the industry. Dylan was said to 'dig' *Born to Run*. Jagger 'loved' it. Even Spector paid court. The personality cult was high enough until the *Time* and *Newsweek* covers, at which point it went astral. By late 1975, Springsteen was happening like war happens. It was a blitz. Thanks to CBS and Appel, the tour was plotted as a campaign, and the band and its joy division bore down in an army. Everywhere they drew wild, capacity crowds. The nightly rallies were stoked by a mixture of myth, heat, light and the all-embracing 'togetherness' of the show, directed by Springsteen and honed by Van Zandt in the service of an act. Little or nothing was left to fate. Anyone thinking that Springsteen's breakthrough was an accident, a kind of listless fluke – or that he met the E Streeters on equal terms – should have tuned in the interview he gave Swedish radio. 'All the Stax stuff and Atlantic stuff, I'm very into that . . . The band has moments when it's based a lot on those R&B bands, especially in the way I use the band. I use the band in a very similar way: if you see Otis Redding in *Monterey Pop*, the way he uses his band; the way James Brown uses his band . . . The best band leaders of the last ten, twenty years, from what I've listened to, have been your soul band leaders. They whip them bands into shape. I tend to use mine that way.'

If Springsteen and Van Zandt's choreography of the shows never stooped to that faintly dreary tool, the fog machine, no such restraint was embraced by CBS. Plenty of smoke was being blown offstage. Heavyweight critics like John Rockwell and Robert Christgau were suddenly rung person-to-person and chauffeured to gigs. Peter Knobler, Robert Hilburn and Dave Marsh all filed their eulogistic copy. Even Landau, in a professional dead-zone between management and journalism, continued to edit *Rolling Stone*'s album reviews through that midsummer. Nor were the niche titles ignored. *New Times* duly weighed in with a piece calling Springsteen 'one of America's heroes'. *Village Voice*, *Newsday* and *Playboy* all variously crawled on the bandwagon. *Business Week* did a 'colour piece' – as it happened, wholly lacking in colour – on 'The Merchandising of a Superstar'. Within a few months, there was a kind of print consensus about Springsteen, just as, on other fronts, there would be on Steve Martin or *Star Wars*. Critics had their agenda and pursued it, and fulfilled their dreams in his triumph.

Conventional wisdom, for most, offered a choice between merely serving the hype or living off it. By the time *Born* went platinum, a pack of ambitious writers was halfway to colonizing Springsteen and his work. In the turf war between the dailies, trades and broadcast media, a few fans scrambled for the no-man's-land of the letter pages. Typical was Steve Voorhies in *Rolling Stone*: 'It's good to see Bruce Springsteen getting the coverage he deserves in the rock press, but you guys haven't got it straight yet. He is not the New Dylan. He's not the New Elvis, either, though that's closer. Springsteen is What We've All Been Waiting For. He is Rock & Roll Reborn . . . Springsteen is the Real Thing.'

Always looking for the novel – particularly if simultaneously it allows for cap-doffing and snook-cocking at America – UK pop hacks dutifully applied themselves to the trough. They were fed a steady diet by two CBS PR men, Lewis Rogers and Colin Forsey.

Below them, a mobile sales force, reps and agents all plied their shrill trades. On 1 September, they began soliciting airplay, lobbying DJs and generally turning the press into a giant needle stuck in one groove. Within days, thanks mainly to in-house plugging by Roger Scott, 'Born' was formally a climber at Capital Radio. By late October it was enjoying 150 plays a week. *The Times* mentioned Springsteen. *NME* did a five-page spread. Virtually every biographical scrap was swept up and recycled into variants of the legend. Quotes from Springsteen were printed everywhere, including a graffiti campaign in London phone boxes.

This fun-house of hype reached its shining apogee on 27 October. Springsteen made the front of *Time* and *Newsweek* in the same day. Not even Elvis or the Beatles had done that. This twin drama, a feat of blunt solidity, was Appel's work. When the ritual gestures had been made, the courtship done, the speeches over, it all devolved to Mephistophelian nerve on his part. Appel soon won *Newsweek* by telling them 'no cover – no story'. The dual sell, up Sixth Avenue at *Time*, was a harder slog. CBS's Bob Altschuler and the PRs drove the deal, leaving Laurel Canyon to close. The actual interview, by Jay Cocks, went well enough. But *Time* chafed at being hustled, insisting that the small matter of New York going broke would, in fact, lead their next issue. Here Appel pulled his master-stroke. 'Fine,' he bawled. 'You can do the story later, and maybe *Newsweek* will do it [first], but you'll eventually have to put this guy on your cover. Right now you have a chance to be visionaries. Six months, and you're functionaries.' He hung up. Whatever mutual panic and swift research went on over the next two days, it was enough to bring both titles to heel. No other non-politician had ever received American media's ultimate accolade. This double coup not only made Springsteen a household name. It also set off an inquest as to how the arch-rivals had been two-timed by Appel. In its next edition, *Newsweek* ran an 'explanation' to its readers, denying any intrigue, though implying this icy, shrewd conglomerate had been duped by Springsteen's manager. *Time*'s editor-in-chief Henry Grunwald would duly call it the 'greatest embarrassment' of his life. It was a busy year for Springsteen, but even he must have been struck by how it ended: barnstorming North America while two of the world's wealthiest and most resourceful publications argued the toss over who'd 'discovered' him.

Not everyone fell to Springsteen's seemingly unstoppable PR offensive. His show at the Paramount, Oakland, was a misbegotten rehash of his power-chord Child days; there were pans of him in Portland; and, most famously, at London's Hammersmith Odeon, where the BBC's Jeff Griffin thought him 'a low-rent Bob Seger'. Some of his earliest disciples in the fourth estate began to recant. Literally thousands of reviews and thumbnail sketches – some so off-kilter they spelt his name wrong – appeared that winter. He heard from friends who'd not seen him in ten years. There were begging letters from Freehold and muffled calls to San Mateo. (Doug's exemplary response – 'Why *not* you in *Time*?' – was the model of what every gobsmacked father should try for.) Family, press and hangers-on all jostled together in spin-drier fashion, choosing between three lines: praising Springsteen; burying him; or ruing that he'd been 'discovered' at all, as if by going nationwide he'd lost the street-kid ethic he wore as a medal. *Rolling Stone*'s Ken Emerson was dean of this last school. There were others.

Oddly, the one person relatively unmoved was Springsteen himself. As his life became an Oz of photo-ops, sound-bites and merry rows over the *Time* and *Newsweek* saga, he sheathed the hype in a shy grin, a coy, protective shrug signifying the irony of it all. There was, even so, a downside. Totally ignored for years, to be anatomized like a frog was new. Springsteen's reaction was indifferent in public, but exorbitantly crisp in private. He loathed being typed, as *Time* said, 'as a '50s hood in James Dean' – or any other – mould. Pigeonholing sent him 'nutso'. He bridled at the very hint of the names Elvis or Dylan. Springsteen's most common tactic, though, was to turn away, embarrassed, letting the music do the talking. He took nothing for granted. 'For every night like [the Roxy], there were a hundred other nights that I played in these little bars in Jersey, and there was nobody there . . . And I was long enough there to never forget.' That same interview revealed that traits constant through the mid-1980s were already in hand. The denial of any agenda or politics, his directness, the moral commitment to the fans had all crystallized. *NME* asked Springsteen whether he drank, smoked, partied, voted or liked seeing his picture in the paper. His one-word answer, repeated five times, was 'no'.

Pop badly needed such an image. As Lennon had sung in a tart denial of the old creed, the 'dream [was] over'. It certainly was for the likes of the Beatles, Hendrix and, now, Elvis. The '60s adventure of the mind had shrunk down into mass entertainment. Most stars of the day routinely came on knock-kneed and tragic like the seedy vaudevillians of *Spinal Tap*. Studios and stages pulsed with drugs, notably cocaine. Spandex was at the height of its grim season. As for moral commitment – most rockers tended not to flog it. Almost all brought with them the accumulated quirks, bents and hang-ups of years of living under the unifying and corrosive heel of one awful nut – insecurity. Springsteen, too. For him, though, anxiety put a premium on loyalty; on the need to attach himself to fans one by one, to have fixed points in life. What he gave, he expected back. Nothing hurt him more than to see a friend turn coat. Hence, too, his dread of the distorting lens of the media. Immediately after being grilled by *Newsweek*, Springsteen rang his manager. 'He was livid,' Appel told Marc Eliot. 'It was horrendous . . . I tried to explain it to him, but he was adamant. "That's it, I'm not doing any more interviews, I hate it, I just hate it."' This particular funk hit bottom on 4 October 1975. For the first and only time yet, Springsteen refused to go on. 'There he was, coiled in the foetal position in the dressing-room,' says a first-hand source. 'I remember that his skin, oddly, wasn't white. It was grey, all grey.' Springsteen himself told Robert Hilburn, 'At that moment, I could see how people get into drink or drugs, because the one thing you want at a time like that is to be distracted – in a big way.' Van Zandt, in the end, talked him out of it. The show went on. (Springsteen, already sick of 'whoring' to the media, duly included his own barbed code in the set – the Temptations' 'Ain't Too Proud To Beg'.) The roll-out continued. There were no more tears. The fact remained that Springsteen was unsuited, genetically, for the sort of madness that hit him in 1975. The band knew it, and at that dire backstage pass, he knew it, too.

From the Roxy, Springsteen vectored up the west coast, hitting Seattle on 26 October. Bright lights outside the theatre nearly rivalled the stage kind. The functions of fame were everywhere; the very walls of the jerry-built 'Bruce Information Center' collapsed in the scrum. Springsteen himself was under stress. He went through a full day of interviews, sittings and sound-checks; in the press den he was asked more than fifty questions, from 'What do you think about Franco?' to 'Are you real?' He answered them all. The actual show was billed as the 'bop of the year' and nearly lived up to it. According to the local critic, 'If you like rock 'n' roll you can't help liking him, because he's everything good it's ever been . . . The music is an amalgam of nearly every popular trend since the beginning. It is almost pure nostalgia.' On that note, Springsteen doubled back to California, did Arizona and wove a meander to Florida. During this lull between national and global kudos, he often fretted about 'bombing in Beatle-land', as he put it. Appel tried to calm him by brandishing a veritable book of hearty UK reviews. But for someone who'd been virtually weaned on a diet of English pop, 'bombing' there wasn't just a sub-plot or footnote – it was the very headline of his career. In italics.

Springsteen landed in London on 17 November 1975. 'It was like being on Mars for us,' says Max Weinberg. 'We came in one day and played the next, so we were all messed up.' As, too, was British pop, sweating out one of its cyclical spasms of campy, *Jaws*-era scores and schmaltz. (On that Everest of pap known as the Hit Parade: Billy Connolly, Barry White, Perry Como, Peters and Lee, Demis Roussos, Mud and the Bay City Rollers; *Keep On Wombling* had just spent six weeks at the top.) For Graham Parker, an R&B shouter whose career part-shadowed Springsteen's, 'he hit at the perfect time . . . People forget how fucking *awful* it was. The charts were all either shlock, rentasongs or old farts playing guitar solos. Britain *needed* Bruce.' For Bob Harris, 'you could actually *feel* the build-up among press and fans'. The third member of the triangle, CBS, merrily jigged along. By the evening of the 18th, Rogers and

Forsey had whipped up an atmosphere of Cup Final-like frenzy, with Hammersmith awash in touts and memorabilia, and the Odeon decked out with FINALLY . . . READY FOR BRUCE SPRINGSTEEN splayed across the marquee.

Now all that remained was the show, which did not go well.

'Bruce was so mad that night in London,' Appel said. 'He went really nuts . . . He wanted that fame and glory, but I guess he wanted it on his own terms.' Springsteen's first act was to rip up several posters of himself in the foyer. This temperamental fit may well have been nerves. But yelling 'Kiss my ass!' across the dressing-room struck at least one old salt as 'loco'. By the time Springsteen hit stage, says Richard Williams, it was 'weird . . . my God, the tension'. Even later, when he became the lay guru, adept in the use of tropisms and saws, he could still dash the mood by odd bouts of churlishness – pawing Lynn Goldsmith, turning the air blue when a teenager lit a firework. Whatever the reason, Springsteen was in a foul temper that night in Hammersmith. Critics pondered whether, in fact, the all-American boy didn't travel well. Others found it hard to credit the rock legend was this quiet, bearded, uptight-looking soul with the baggy trousers and cranial tea-cosy. The sound, meanwhile, swung back unapologetically to Memphis and Harlem. It was like looking through the pinhole of a scenic souvenir charm and seeing a whole pink-suited Apollo revue: except this was England and the star, the James Brown, was wearing Levi's. And that hat. There were barbs that Springsteen seemed to patronize Clemons in 'Tenth Avenue Freeze-Out'. Next he flubbed 'Born To Run'. Then he stalked off, slammed the stage door with the word 'Fuckit!', paused to piss on the lawn of St Paul's Church and wandered into the night. After side-trips to Holland and Sweden, he was back at the Odeon on the 24th. As *Sounds* said, 'we may never know what frosted Bruce' on his British début. What's certain, though, is that he was still apologising for it – onstage, at Wembley, in May 1981 – five and a half years later.

A few critics flayed the second Hammersmith gig with equally bleak pans. A 'hollow triumph, not much there', says Charlie

Gillett. But most notices were all Springsteen could have hoped for. To Allan Clarke (whose cover of 'Born' was rush-released and died overnight), it was 'rock and roll redux'. Peter Gabriel calls it the 'second-best concert ever', after Otis Redding. In Graham Parker's words, 'That album and gig virtually kick-started a new wave of ethnic, meat-and-spud rock, instead of all-night jamming or geezers in capes playing scales. Bruce was a *song* guy. None of your back-to-the-crowd bullshit.' To a generation of British fans, that final London show became tantamount to holy writ; but what struck you at the time was the gruff rasp of the voice – reduced to station-tannoy level by the Odeon's PA – and the wild onstage zip, a potent brew of whoops, yells and piano-top jiving. All in all, it was goodbye to blind worship and autohype; hello to long-term respect, truly fixing Springsteen in the eye of the future. 'Breaking' in Britain was a sign of making it, and also gave his fans the satisfaction of emotional catharsis when few other thrills were going.

In the days ahead, the press duly bristled with essays slating the 'waffly, white pop' – whose 'jacksie', said the *Globe*, 'King Bruce' had well and truly kicked – and romanticizing the Jersey shore. Most were of course written by waffly, white authors, or those who knew as much of Asbury as they did of the Antarctic. One of the saner critics, Richard Williams, speaks of the uniquely atmospheric mix of 'expansive pop and piano balladeering'. Less constrained was the hack from *Melody Maker*. 'The truth is, [we] need Bruce Springsteen. He is a large personality in an era of small talents . . . believes in the power of songs and communication . . . touches some particularly sensitive chord, submerged deep in the rubble of the subconscious . . . I listen to Springsteen like I used to listen to Dylan, John Lennon and Chuck Berry – as though a life depended on it.'

Springsteen rounded out 1975 at home, jagging between Boston, New York and Philadelphia. By 2 December he'd added 'Santa Claus Is Comin' To Town' to his festive locker. Fame generally buffs up a performer's live act, and his was no exception. One by one, the hybridized, mongrel cuts off *Greetings* and *The Wild* gave way to the euphonic clang of *Born*. Springsteen also began to salt his gigs with more and more shaggy-dog stories starring Doug. Onstage yarns about the two of them driving silently up Route 33 joined other lyrical and allusive riffs on displacement. But these dire interludes were still outweighed by bright, chirpy raps not meant to convert fans so much as reassure them. That goal never really abated. Springsteen was at his best playing in front of a sea of undifferentiated faces; introspective biographical data was always followed by variants of '*Rockit!*' After two months he was back lobbying Appel for dates, eager to work.

Springsteen spent much of the winter with Darvin. Here, by contrast, he never quite slipped the internal anchor that for him went with living. Even the 'warm, loving guy' held back, one of half a dozen sub-personalities that tended to the dour. Quite the strangest thing about Springsteen Fever was Springsteen. Friends in Jersey talk of him as 'hooded', 'shut down', 'clenched', a 'quiet, shy guy' who seemed to be half in the real world and half out of it; as Grice says, 'scoping out Babylon'. Above all, 1975–76 were the years he grappled with what sort of rock star he'd be: the kind who toed the home imperium of sex, drugs and long limos; or one whose soul and mind ventured abroad. This pattern would be repeated throughout Springsteen's life. Any change in his professional or personal lot resulted in a mix of joy and panic. He reacted to *Born to Run* one way in public, another in private. One night at the Roxy, Springsteen sought out his fellow Jerseyan Jack Nicholson. 'I asked him how he handled the attention. He said for him, it was a long time coming and he was mostly glad to have it. I didn't quite see it that way . . . I felt control of my life was slipping away and that all the [fame] was, like, an obstacle.' A complex man, Springsteen. After telling tens of thousands of fans about his father-angst, he took a long trip to San Mateo, where a neighbour, Luis Gleick, saw 'the pair, Bruce and Doug, strolling up 16th arm-in-arm, laughing and looking like two buddies on the way to the bar'.

As well as making nice to his parents and Landau (also in California), Springsteen was doggedly writing songs on his tack piano. He began tinkering at his fourth album in January 1976. One track, 'Darkness On The Edge of Town', was already done;

demos of 'Dawn Patrol', 'Frankie', 'Drifter's Barrio' and 'You're Gonna Cry' – some good, some not so polished – were being cut as fast as he could hum them. At this early stage, Springsteen was less stuck on the tunes than the words' inner music and thematic harmony. His desk was an altar where the ideals of truth, grit and blue-collar solidarity were held sacrosanct. Every verse and every chorus was groomed like a show-dog. All this went on while Darvin flitted restively between Long Branch, Atlantic Highlands and a rented room in New York. In a bid to defuse domestic stress and simultaneously rev up the band, Springsteen began a tour that March. Originally planned as a stopgap safari of shore clubs, it ran for two months, from the spring solstice to Memorial Day, taking in uncharted parts of the South. He played no fewer than five separate towns in Tennessee. Springsteen became the first rocker to headline the Grand Ole Opry and grace the West Point military academy. Despite his having a platinum record, there were few or no bows towards luxury. Along with the band, he travelled in a converted bus. Lodgings were of the roadside-motel type. There was, however, a gradual scaling-up in halls – on 28 March Springsteen played to 6,000 students at Duke University – though, even here, his ban on T-shirts and the rest remained.*

Slated by the band as the 'chicken scratch run', their progress that spring was an odd mix of repetition and revivalism. Springsteen merely went through motions in Ohio and New York. But in Memphis people saw him for the first time, and his act, the way in which his pent-up vocals seemed almost to choke him, his thin smile showing bared teeth, his quick-witted intros and multiple encores, all became gospel to thousands of new fans. Later that same night, Springsteen, Van Zandt and the PR Glen Brunman took a taxi to Elvis's home, Graceland. It was 3 a.m. The lights were on. Springsteen wordlessly shinned up the gate, dropped down and walked towards the house. It's tempting to wonder what might have happened: whether there'd have been a symbolic, logical nod from one superstar icon to another; or if Elvis had even heard of

---

*There were, even so, posters of him in both *Playboy* and *Penthouse* that year.

him. We'll never know. Heavy hands cut Springsteen off at the door. As he said, he began 'pullin' all the cheap shots I could think of – you know, I was on *Time*, I play guitar, Elvis is my hero, all the things I never say to anybody. Because I figure I've gotta get a message through. But [the guard] just said, "Yeah, sure. You gotta get out of here."' Springsteen did. From this near-miss came 'Fire', a fan's ultimate gift, sent to Elvis the very month he died. Creatively, it might have saved him.*

The tour's mood was leavened by other itinerant pranks. After a few days on the bus, Springsteen would feel the urge for open air and to bond with the band, trading in his jeans for a white muscle-shirt and red shorts to stage softball games on the road. They were no picnics: the E Streeters had their own uniform, drills and an *ad hoc* coach bearing wisdom on trajectories and wind-speeds. The star of the line-up, offstage as well as on, was Springsteen. For most of these fixtures he was a sunny, all-action presence. Clearly, certain claims about him were rash, not to say wild. For all the 'tall talk', as William Burroughs noted, 'Bruce [was] exceedingly straight'. By temperament, he was middle-of-the-road, pragmatic and enjoyed nothing more than swinging a bat in the park. These wholesome, all-American traits were the very nub of his appeal. Musically, too, Springsteen went both forwards and back. For every new song he wrote there was a lovingly recast oldie. Many of the lawmen, hoods and arch-punks who peopled *Born* celebrated the '50s more than heralded the '80s. This twin allure, to rock and roll future and past, would serve Springsteen well, tapping into a vast, all-ages base beyond any other star, bar Elvis.

Springsteen's tour wound down with a snap show at the Stone Pony in Asbury. On 7 June he played a similarly ad-lib set at *Crawdaddy*'s tenth-anniversary party in New York. These ground-zero rave-ups were, said Burroughs (there at the latter gig), 'proof that, at twenty-six, he was heading for Grand Old Manhood. The guys in the band, and most guys generally, just loved Bruce.'

His relations with Appel weren't, though, thriving. Plainly, this

---

*The song became a hit for, among others, the Pointer Sisters.

pair's greatest potential had always been for disaster. Springsteen was an essentially decent, naïve man with no head for money. Privately, he tended to be dour and self-defensive. Nor did this cloak a wide-ranging mind. Springsteen knew his rock and roll, but neither he nor his intellect got out much. Appel, by contrast, was all warhead, little or no guidance system. He often gave the impression of being driven by an uncontrollable fire emanating from kilns deep within; of being, Burroughs said, 'sick'. There were hints, even in the dual cover-stories, that hot furnaces burned below the skin. 'The industry's at the bottom of the barrel,' Appel told *Newsweek*. 'What you've got to do is get the universal factors, to get people to move in the same three or four chords. It's the real thing! Look up America! Look up America!' By spring 1976, his feud with Landau (wrongly identified as Springsteen's manager in the same story) had become a vendetta. Now Appel also began to strafe his protégé. The man who angrily preferred to play small clubs rather than step up to sheds came under a constant barrage from Laurel Canyon to 'milk it'. In short order, Appel signed a deal for Springsteen to close out the show at the Montreal Olympics, as well as million-dollar options on a TV special and a one-day 'Jersey Bands' gala: all vetoed. That was bad enough. Then Springsteen met Landau in Gotham and things with Appel underwent a deep – and as it proved – permanent change.

The events of the next sixteen months were an ugly, protracted spat that disrupted Springsteen's album and nearly derailed his career. It began when Landau – in California producing Jackson Browne – scanned the Laurel Canyon contracts and told him to get a lawyer. A music attorney called Mike Mayer instantly saw through these, to Springsteen, raw deals. Walter Yetnikoff, the new head of CBS, also 'told me that he knew I really got a bum rap, and the per-centages . . . were ridiculous. He said that any artist that sells a million records ought to walk away with a half-million bucks, easy.' (Springsteen had $3,000 in the bank.) Finally, there was the ques-tion of the label having just paid Laurel Canyon $500,000 against future earnings. Rather than dole that out, Appel used it to try and up the odds of Springsteen signing a new contract. He succeeded only in raising hackles. Armed with an accountant named Steve Tenenbaum, Springsteen promptly audited Appel's books. This revealed 'slipshod, wasteful and neglectful' management, failure to keep 'adequate accounts . . . enormous amounts of expenses and disbursements' (denied by Appel) and, all in all, 'a classic case of the unconscionable exploitation of an unsophisticated and unrepresented performer by his manager for the manager's primary economic benefit'.

Specifically, Springsteen was banking less than a tenth of the money he made. As fast as he earned it, it was haemorrhaging out again on salaries, bills and, more pertinently, fees, cuts and commissions. For four years, he'd lived on handouts. Appel would pay his rent out of CBS funds and divvy up the balance into regular slabs of pocket money. On 14 May Laurel Canyon sent Springsteen a cheque for $67,368.78 in settlement. This seemed to keep the peace for a month. Springsteen and Mayer then turned to the half-million-dollar advance. Even that, perhaps, might have been fudged but for a zoning war between Laurel Canyon and William Morris's Barry Bell. Here some discrepancy exists between Springsteen's take ('Mike's my manager, he's my producer; I just don't want him to be my agent') and Appel's ('They screwed me'). When the dust settled on that rumbling sub-plot, the writing was on the wall. As Appel says, 'From then on, I knew I couldn't trust Bruce any more . . . I stopped hearing from him for the most part.' The fabric of compromise between manager and client had been torn apart, and there was no way to stitch it up again.

In fact, to most money-men and suits generally, Springsteen was a pesky gadfly. He rarely doubted the moral cogency of his stand. Every issue was a clash between the forces of light and dark. 'Bruce Springsteen put the BS in bullshit,' snipes one old foe. Certain critics have tried to bridge the gap between his supposed brag and bluster and his undoubted philanthropy by blaming the feud with Appel for 'warping' him. More likely, Springsteen's fits of pique were linked to his boyhood wars with Doug. They left two pervasive scars. First, Springsteen nursed a latent rage, rooted in frustration and boredom with a family increasingly mired in cultural and actual beggary. A touch of swagger seemed romantic to someone with no experience of the privation, sweat and rapid dis-illusionment of real work. Much of Springsteen's pose was strictly of the cartoon kind: supplying Robert De Niro, for example, with his classic 'You talkin' to me?' line in *Taxi Driver*. Some was plain ugly. Springsteen began one summit with Appel by saying, 'Mike, Mount Palomar couldn't detect my interest in your problems,' and went on from there to get tense. Beyond the limited scope of his stage act he was 'almost unbelievably touchy', as Motz puts it. 'Bruce sizzled like a lit rocket.'

Springsteen's second major theme was an honest, if staid insis-tence on utter probity. With him, everything had to be a square deal. Whether it was a rigidly enforced Pepsi-for-property swap in Monopoly, or line-reading credits and notes, any error in detail sent him into a funk: pedantry that, at this stage, still substituted for a world-view. Thus Appel's real transgression was to not give Springsteen a fair shake. 'It got to where I couldn't even quote my lyrics,' he said. 'I couldn't quote "Born To Run". That whole period of my life just seemed to be slipping out of my hands. That's why I started playing music in the first place – to control my life.'

He certainly ruled his band. Much as they were a gang, the E Streeters were also a firm: in rehearsal and live, there were echoes of old-fashioned deference, of middle managers fearful of familiar-ity breeding contempt, bosses who commanded undying awe. Springsteen paid the group's wages, may or may not have footed their health bills, and set a strict 'one strike' policy on drugs. 'Bruce had rules of behaviour and everyone was afraid to cross him,' notes Lynn Goldsmith. Even off the road, Springsteen drilled the band four hours a day, every day. 'You played what you wanted,' Weinberg told *The Ties That Bind*; 'and if it didn't fit, you didn't play it, because they were Bruce's songs.' He demanded untold studio retakes of most cuts, even when, as was his later habit, he'd tell the engineers to go for a 'dirty' mix to ape the *musique vérité* of the early Who. 'How'd it sound?' Springsteen would ask Jimmy Iovine. If the reply was 'real slick, Boss', he'd start over. One result was that within two years, when *Darkness* came round, the band had knit into a crack unit at the peak of its dam-busting power. Not that it was all bombastic, pre-grunge clang; there were moments of self-restraint, of 'ebb and flow', says Weinberg, meant to 'make you think'. The group's evolution coincided with Springsteen's own major artistic growth. Thus, he had the ideal vehicle for the neo-liberalism and lyrical nous that could be blunt to a fault.

The prime beneficiary of all this was neither Springsteen nor Landau. It was the fans. Many of them were as likely to seek the sublime in his four-hour shows as in a religious service. Tens or hundreds of thousands found a ritual intensity in the tours of, most notably, 1978, 1980–81 and 1984–85. By filching qualities of 'sacred music' like repetition and singalong choruses – not to say his ability to 'put a song over' – Springsteen smoothly ascended to the rock pantheon. When he played now, crowds looked to take the measure of a man widely figured as a kind of messiah. They saw a wiry, thin, shy-looking soul who, says Saul Todd, 'winced a lot, like someone swallowing bile'. Yet, when Springsteen wanted, he was always or usually friendly, down-to-earth and funny. It's hard to think of another cultural idol pulling his stunt at Graceland. (Springsteen was even able to charm Elvis's minder into merely walking him back to the gate.) He was also warm, generous and unflinchingly loyal to old friends. Springsteen never forgot his roots. For years, a sure sign he was entering one of his retro, back-to-basics incarnations would be an *ad hoc* gig in Asbury. That winter he also wrote the liner notes to Southside Johnny's first LP, *I Don't Want to Go Home*. They ended: 'It's time to speak the names of the lost soldiers, 'cause the music on this album – Johnny's music – is something that grew out of those friendships and the long summer nights when there was no particular place to go and nothing to do . . . except play.'

Springsteen, through a mix of skill, drive, prodigious songwriting and barefaced hype, had already left Southside and the other Upstage alumni standing, distant objects seen in a rearview mirror. He was still, though, only half way to Olympus – a demigod. Springsteen took home just $350 a week, the same as the band. By summer 1976 he was living in a rented farm off Telegraph Hill in Holmdel; ten miles, and several light-years, north of Freehold.

Hard by the dirt road leading to the Telstar receiving post, 'Boss Acres' was typical of its time and place: a 1930s two-storeyed home in peeling wood. The house was furnished with a large hi-fi and Springsteen's new truck out front. There was no visible woman's touch. He still saw Darvin, though the affair came increasingly to bear that stigma of the pop star–model fling, 'tempestuous'. They parted in 1976. Springsteen's look and daily life were both largely unchanged. He was studiously bored by fashion, though not above wearing a gold cross and earring. *Time*'s apt phrase was a 'glorified gutter rat'. Springsteen's black beard, splintered with red, hinted of nautical duty. His duck-walk, too, gave him the list of a man struggling into a high wind. As to diet: the 'gut bomb king' still tucked into an array of Drake's cakes, burgers and fries. Springsteen's junk-food platters only enhanced the air of severe, no-frills dignity about his leathery frame. Certainly he looked like a man on the move, a man apart. He looked like a star.

Conversely, while restating first principles, Springsteen was fast reinventing himself. After *Born* took off, he became less of a merry prankster and yet more of a troubled soul. Management jitters and a hit album left him well-off but wary. Much to his credit, Springsteen took stock and grew without swelling. As he told Dave Marsh, 'I guess that [in 1975] I kind of established a certain type of optimism. After that I felt I had to test those things to see what they were worth . . . The one thing I [felt] was a real sense of responsibility to what I was singing and to the audience . . . I decided to move into the darkness and look around.'

Such was the man who went to the mat with Appel. Springsteen's putsch took a tortuous path and more than once looked set to fail. With both sides stubbornly dug in, trades like *Variety* even mooted whether it was 'Loss for the Boss?' Among the knottier issues were: Appel's sole ownership of the songs; dour retention of the $500,000 advance; and his vetoing of Landau as producer of the fourth album. Unsaid but also salient was the fact that Springsteen had outgrown his old manager. Four and a half years had passed since he'd first stumped into Appel's office and announced he was 'tired of being a big fish in a little pond'. Their deal had always worked in close connection with the goal of Springsteen 'making it'. And now the whole saga had come full cycle. Appel had had the ears to hear Springsteen before anyone, not least Landau. He'd kept him going virtually single-handed. But as for the simple acts of grooming a star, strategizing and generally gilding Springsteen's 'vision thing', he was a loss. Truly it seemed that, with *Born*, the old friends were done as a team. The events that followed were only the reaping of the whirlwind sown in 1971–72. They can be quickly recalled.

On 27 July 1976, Springsteen formally sued Laurel Canyon. The core charges were fraud, undue influence and breach of trust. In hoary legalese, Appel was accused of 'low fiduciary tort' – failure to act in his client's best interests. He loudly denied it. The 'capital generator', Springsteen, demanded compensatory and punitive damages of a million dollars. Counter-charges duly came – suddenly.

Two days later, Appel in turn sued. Here, again, there were three separate actions: to stop Springsteen being produced by anyone but Laurel Canyon; to halt work on the new album; and specifically to dump Landau. There was no claim for money.

On 9 August, Appel's lawyer Len Marks filed a further motion to also bar Springsteen from entering a studio. It was another hammer blow. Sessions went on hold. But even here, as he sought to deep-six the career he'd helped launch, Appel revealed something of himself. As Marks said, 'Basically, Mike was interested in trying to have the relationship continue, not spending his life in court.' Several back-channel tacks were made that summer. For three months, Appel did everything he could to settle. Springsteen himself, unsurprisingly, reacted to the threats raining down on his future by firmly shunning all bids to negotiate. Meanwhile, in a separate but parallel move, he dropped his old agent Sam McKeith and signed with Barry Bell and Frank Barsalona at Premier Talent: they promptly anteed up $100,000. With the exception of Van Zandt, all Springsteen's original crew had now been purged, or, in Hammond's case, taken well-earned retirement.

The first deposition, on 16 August, proved to be not quite as civil to Springsteen as Appel had been. Marks's questioning, in particular, grated. Springsteen's replies were a performance – the man of talent jigging on the conference table like a drunk sailor to a horn-pipe, at sea in a world of notaries and stenographers. His testimony was something like his live act. 'A floor-show', one party calls it. He variously strutted, screeched, roared into song, brooded and bawled abuse at Marks. In so far as there was a theme, it was Springsteen's key one of loyalty: 'Mike told me, "Trust me, trust me," and I signed the goddamn [contract]. And the first thing he did was to go to CBS and make his deal twice as good . . . I went out and worked my ass off for four years and the money came in and [Appel] took it . . . I fired him because he lied to me, because he was dishonest with me; he betrayed my trust . . . He cheated me . . . Somebody stabs you in the heart I learn to stab them back.' (Appel denied it.) This went on until Judge Fein made Springsteen aware that his rants, liberally spiced with words like 'fuck' and 'cunt', could be read to a jury. After that, said Marks, 'Bruce was like a lamb . . . There were no more outbursts, and we continued for several more days until we finished his [evidence].'

On 15 September, Fein upheld Appel's injunction. Springsteen was now barred from plying his trade. As he told the judge, he was 'fighting for [his] life'. At this dire pass, Springsteen's mother, still working as a minimum-wage law secretary in California, sent Appel a book called *Business Problems of the Record Industry Workshop*. Adele was determined that her 'two kids' could settle their tiff. For years, she'd never missed Bruce's press cuttings or albums. But she followed them as though he had a permanent lead role in a playground drama. She never grasped the scale of the stage he starred on. Most of the media, though, gave the suit full acreage. *Rolling Stone*, *Cashbox* and *Billboard* all ran features. The *Chicago Tribune*, meanwhile, was the first to ask the fell question, 'Whatever Happened To Bruce?'

When not giving evidence, huddling with Mayer and generally being the hostile witness, Springsteen was home in Jersey. Much of the nation was gearing up for the Bicentennial that year. The date that meant more to Springsteen was 1 June, the planned start of his fourth LP, provisionally titled (again for a film) *American Madness*. Rejecting scornfully the pretty confections of *Born*, he was raring to do a '*real* album'. Every day that passed was a 'pisser' until the tapes rolled. Yet, for all the hassles, Boss Acres wasn't the worst place to take a few weeks off. As Springsteen told Dave Marsh, 'I had a truck and a motorcycle; I was living out in the farmhouse; we had a pond and a pool.' The band, Landau and Marsh himself would set up a kind of commune in Holmdel. As usual, everyone had an alias: the king, the duke and the duchess all dancing a slow sequence of gavottes revolving round the Boss. 'What I always feel,' Springsteen later told the *Tribune*, 'is I don't like to let people down who've supported me.' He meant it; what's more, he found his loyalty blighted by a long-running 'shit-storm [of a] lawsuit'.

Springsteen was certainly a good friend to the various handlers, briefs and gofers who gravitated to Boss Acres. As well as Landau and Marsh, there was Barry Bell, *Record World*'s Dave McGee, roadies like Mike Batlan and Doug Sutphin and Springsteen's valet Ron Breuer. Less lucky was Sam McKeith, the man who'd kept things afloat in 1973–74. Slowly, he found his presence no longer required; locks were changed, phone calls unanswered. He was out. Much of the real blood-letting like this went on out of Springsteen's sight, thus allowing him to credibly say he 'hadn't known'. Even so, McKeith didn't lose his job and land on the street by chance.

With his money frozen and enjoined from entering a studio, Springsteen hit the road. The tour that fall was, says Todd, a 'wits'-end punt', to humour the band and shake down much-needed cash at the turnstiles. It took its lumps from the critics, though fans loved the seventeen- and twenty-song sets that packed halls from Phoenix to New York's Palladium. Down the way, Springsteen fired Mike Mayer and hired a *de facto* manager and non-trial lawyer, Michael Tannen. Actually descending into the briar patch of litigation fell to an attorney called Peter Parcher. One courtroom foe describes fighting him as 'like trying to dislodge a Rottweiler from your nuts'. Everything changed from then on. That December, Springsteen duly petitioned Fein to allow him back to work. He included a dramatic plea for Landau. 'I enter the studio with virtually millions of scattered ideas to which he, through his unique ability to communicate with me . . . has been able to provide the focus and direction necessary to shape my thoughts. Landau's ability to communicate with me stems from the simple fact that I trust him.' Springsteen was touring again in February. As the cold winter days passed and crowds still came, what Motz calls his 'dopey nerve' seemed to stiffen. Before a gig in Boston he told Tannen, 'I'm fighting . . . If it takes another ten years, I don't care.' As if on cue, Springsteen finally won a legal battle. The ruling on 22 March allowed him, technically, to 'assert a fiduciary defense' and, practically, to re-argue the case for Landau. Appel, it now seemed, might lose a trial.

After ten months of argument and hundreds of thousands in costs, the case ended in an all-night wrangle in Marks's office. Under the terms of the deal of 28 May 1977, Appel gave up most of his publishing and all his management rights for $800,000. His production cut for the first three albums fell from 6 to 2 per cent. He claimed a moral victory. If so, it was pyrrhic. From then on, his fame for having 'screwed Springsteen' became proverbial;* and unjust. Perhaps the bitterest pill of all, though, was his selling his final share of the action for $425,000. That was in 1983. Twelve months later, when whole fortunes were made on *Born in the USA* and Springsteen's back-list went Croesan, Appel could have named his price.

The distinguished club who discover rock stars only to lose them tend to share a forlorn yen to rehash for the rest of their lives the fine nuances that stood between them and the prize – the misunderstandings over cash, or the predatory rival bearing an all-too-sweeter deal. As with Andrew Oldham, Ken Pitt and Bruce Pavitt, so with Appel: home-town scenesters ousted by artistic coup. They can be very good managers. No one could have worked harder. What they lacked was the will to expand. The reinvention of their mewling charges into nubile icons – small fry grown big – shook them cold. Appel, to be fair, came to grasp the inevitability of

---

*In a readers' poll, *Backstreets* gave 'firing Appel' as Springsteen's best-ever career move.

what he called 'shit happening'. After more than a decade's purdah, he emerged with a new agency, called Little Wonder. Springsteen loaned him $175,000. By the early 1990s Appel was speaking fondly of the old days, when everything still lay in the future. He'd made a 'few mistakes', he said. Yet he 'loved Bruce'.

Historically, apologising for himself wasn't a tactic Appel had had much use for, as others tended to pre-empt him. Most Springsteen biographers flayed him: also the fans. In their reading, Appel was a pushy yob who happened to get lucky. Undoubted devotion to his client was offset by mad chimera like having Springsteen sing at the Olympics one day, in a tent the next. There were no lack of humanizing quirks about Appel. He was the fast-talking barker with the choirboy looks, the hairshirt ascetic who liked a party, the ex-marine who hawked Springsteen around the shacks wearing his drill-sergeant's hat. Appel was always a weird crossbreed of grunt and guru. But the disparate parts gelled into one when seen from the perspective of his overriding ego. Contrary to public demonology, Appel was rabidly loyal. In deed and word, he was animated not by blandly trite boilerplate on demographics, spin-offs and crossovers; Appel had a dream. It was the very one that raced the piratical heart of his arch-foe – 'rock and roll future'. He, Landau and CBS were all trying, in their various ways, to help Springsteen nudge pop into this new age. Appel's own management creed, based on a grand – not to say grandiose – vision of himself as John the Baptist, was honed over four years. Others, meantime, made their Springsteen policy on the fly. A war was ordained, and duly came. Somewhere in all this was the metaphor of a man undone by the very thing he'd worked for. But out of Appel's Greek tragedy came an engaging sense of poise and even a taste of latter-day fame. To get a second chance, after all, you have to have taken a first one.

Springsteen would never quite get over the lawsuit. He spoke of it often on stage. Introducing a song at the Oakland Paramount in October 1976, he said that his next album would be out 'as soon as I learn my lesson in showbiz'. Appel was also on his mind during gigs in Phoenix and Williamsburg. According to the *Washington Post*, 'Springsteen has had to postpone release of his new LP and alter his schedule', which he referred to 'several times' while there. It was the same rap in New Jersey. 'I went and did my audition with ['Growin' Up']. I remember I went up to the record building, y'know . . . All them lawyers. Everybody had one but me.' Not so long ago, self-pity would have been a sentiment to slough off, its excesses mocked, its moist eye risked only in wry yarns about Freehold. But being hauled into depositions and banned from the studio was a scar that never fully healed. Although Springsteen won the suit, he felt that, in certain key ways, he'd lost.

Otherwise, he put the nightmare to good use. In August 1976 Springsteen wrote a song called 'The Promise'. Though not explicitly about Appel, its rip – 'We were gonna take it all/And throw it all away' – cut to the bone of their feud. Forced out of the Plant and on to the road, Springsteen's live act also hit fever pitch. He both enlarged and improved his shows, a feat beyond most of his highly touted peers. Before playing the Philadelphia Spectrum, Springsteen did a three-hour sound check. In order to get a feel of the hall, run down the cues, test the sight-lines and still have time to chat at the door, he appeared for an eight o'clock gig at 3 p.m. – an hour at which the Stones, for one, would have been starting breakfast. He obeyed his own law-office axiom about 'work[ing] my ass off'. Springsteen's twinned art and craft brought deservedly warm reviews in New York. 'Cocky and tireless,' wrote John Rockwell. 'He projects about the greatest ebullience of any performer around these days . . . There's an element of calculation and a surfeit of talent to guarantee a certain level of quality . . . Yet Springsteen leaves himself room for inspiration.'

He did. But Springsteen's shows were still as blocked and drilled as any showbiz carnivore's. His own 'hound' look and double-dog-dare-you scowls were a constant reminder both of his mood and new image. According to Lynn Goldsmith, 'He thought a lot about it . . . We'd go through pictures of Dylan and talk about Bob's hair, Bob's shirt, Bob's shoes. He'd buy old clothes at Trash and Vaudeville in the Village, then make them appear even more used by running over them with the car. He never wanted me to [sell] a picture of him smiling.' It's long been an article of faith for biographers that the lawsuit both hardened and buoyed him. Like a suddenly sprung convict, Springsteen felt that he ought to be doing more than he was, and that 'hammering it' was all that mattered. As well as the sound-checks, he now amped up for the gigs by a series of struts, squats and mental stretches in order to become 'the Boss' for four hours. Finally, as the curtain rose, the crackle of walkie-talkies would echo up the cold backstage gangways. 'Bruce is on his way.' 'Bruce is ready now.' To a zap of pulsar-white light, Springsteen and the band would run on, wave and count in the Stax-revue riff of 'Night'. They managed a miracle: resurrecting the paisley-jive of the Apollo while playing the field from metal to folk. As 'Jungleland' gave way to 'Rosalita', which ushered in 'Born To Run', the crowd became a congregation – ecstatic early Christians, or hadjis – going, Springsteen said, 'nutso'. Many of them, he rightly guessed, were struck with what he called 'the dread' and the need to connect. At least one concert-goer a night would rush the stage and kneel at his feet. Others, like Charles Cross, would imagine they'd been 'baptized in some alien way'. The result was the first spring-tide of Bossmania: fans wanted to touch and feel him, to share the sudden, transcendent peep of unity. Other rock gods had grown obsessed, or worse, by such worship. Springsteen's own eyes were still skyward, but he kept his feet planted fast on the ground. Not only was he, as Todd says, a 'righteous guy'. Springsteen also knew the tactical use of method-acting. Reviewing a show in 1978, *Rolling Stone*'s Paul Nelson called him an 'exuberant but dreamy montage of every pop and film star whose picture ever graced your wall: Montgomery Clift, James Dean, Elvis Presley, Al Pacino, Robert De Niro . . . the collective resemblance is uncanny'. Nelson was speaking literally, but it was a figurative sketch if ever there was one. Like Clift and the rest, Springsteen proved that real drama isn't just the stuff of posing. He was no more 'the Boss' offstage than Woody Allen was nuts or Jack Nicholson a suitable case for treatment: Somewhat.

The shows, as well as ritualistic, were both lava-hot and melodic, mixing the *Sturm und Drang* of stadium rock with touches of Christmas panto and Saturday-morning cartoons. Spoofing himself was just one of the crosses Springsteen had to bear. At times it was uneasily like pop for the theme park, not the heart or mind. The mugging with Clemons could give it a burlesque, bones-and-tambourine edge some thought racist. Yet song after song still soared out of Springsteen's locker, the fullest since the Beatles went over the hill at Candlestick Park: every number was both fresh and an old friend. At worst, they rose above their own vapid tunes, on a performance of blazing and sweaty charm. The very best tracks roared through the din as gems of feelgood soul. Voice and guitar set up a blade-sharp sound as the six hands strutted their stuff. Fads come and go, but those bottom-heavy riffs and poppy choruses were the best anthems of their day, and among the best ever. Springsteen was an infinitely subtler type than, say, Eddie Cochran, yet some of the same virtues were at work: dynamics, raw power and canny stagecraft that was almost classical, a late-fifties skit with punk undertones. Like Johnny Rotten, he brilliantly made the case for an art form in need of revival.

Not untypical was the *Chicago Tribune*'s review of a gig in February 1977. 'Springsteen put on a show of high-voltage excitement, if not exactly staggering in charisma . . . His movements often seemed contrived . . . Mildly embarrassing . . . [But] enough intrinsic [drama] to carry the audience. Despite his self-styled street punk image, Springsteen has class.'

Critics like the *Tribune* had begun trying to fix his place in history as soon as his face hit the airport newsstands in 1975. Barely had he cut *Born* before admirers predicted Springsteen would become a great – or *the* great – man of his age. Thereafter his stock jumped up and down in time with the fortunes of the industry and the bias of his would-be judges. But Springsteen amply passed the one acid test of genius. His work went both fore and aft. In practice, that meant he bent knee to the original guitar elite. By 1978, he was regularly belting covers of rock chestnuts like 'Heartbreak Hotel', 'Summertime Blues', 'Rave On', 'Sweet Little Sixteen' and 'Raise Your Hand', as well as his stock 'Devil' (a.k.a. Detroit) medley and sundry British hits. Many of his audience were witnessing such bygone, towering obelisks for the first time. In the studio, too, Springsteen went out of his way to court the various stars who'd fired him. He mingled affably with the Stones while they mixed *Love You Live* (Keith Richards remembers him as 'nice, quiet and shy – a real gent'). Springsteen sat in with Roy Buchanan and Eric Clapton. He did a brief but striking cameo on Lou Reed's *Street Hassle*. None of these *ad hoc* sessions made news. They were Springsteen pleasing himself, not his fans or label. But in breathing life into some of his idols, he amply fulfilled Richards' own wry self-epitaph. He 'passed it on'.

Genius also meant carrying forward the blood and pride to others. As Graham Parker admits, 'Bruce, for me, was a god. I was shitstruck by the guy. His idea that every track should work, no fillers . . . that was fuckin' rare in the '70s.' Parker's *Howlin' Wind*, Dr Feelgood's *Sneakin' Suspicion* and Elvis Costello's *My Aim is True* – all, in their own ways, exulted in *Born*'s glory. Meanwhile, Bob Seger and his group virtually evolved into a clone of the E Streeters. Brokered by Jimmy Iovine, Springsteen also wrote a number of songs for Patti Smith. One of these was a latinized demo of 'Because The Night'. According to Lenny Kaye, it was a true collaboration. 'Bruce did the hook, Patti the words and we [the band] gave it the cannon-blast beat . . . His lyrics tended to be within his Jersey-shore mentality, while hers roved into the night and love . . . They took it to the hilt.' Nonetheless, 'Night' showed Springsteen to be one of the genre's most versatile writers, even playing with accepted notions of what a 'pop star' should be. Few others of his ilk were as flexible or staggeringly eclectic. With his searing, sheared riffs, Beat-poet raps, preachments on the value of character and the need for good faith, Springsteen perfectly reflected his home values; on him thudded the shroud of spokesman, not for his generation, but for the American Way.

His work ethic, for instance. Post-*Born*, Springsteen shed his boyish awe of stardom, its moral vacuity, constipated egotism and apathy. Not for him the dire progression from club to club of those, like Jagger, who would have gone to the opening of a door. The deal with Appel – officially billed an 'amicable settlement of all differences . . . and discontinuation of outstanding litigation and claims' – was hammered out on a Saturday morning. Over the weekend Holmdel was a place of total frenzy. On Monday the band assembled in New York. Springsteen followed that night. At five the next evening they plugged in at Atlantic studios. It was a strange summer. As Saul Todd says, on the 'hatch, match and dispatch' front Springsteen was busy enough – giving interviews on the new whim for breakneck pop, gobbing and bondage,* shmoozing with the Stones and ruing Elvis's death – aside from the churlish technicality of CBS's plea for 'more *Born*'. He didn't ever do that. But it was still another hard year's grind on a work whose grainy riffs and scads of sub-text made it, too, an epic. Springsteen was in his element amid the controlled chaos of a studio. Working round the clock with Landau and Iovine, he began to pare a master-list of thirty demos. By early July, a dozen backing tracks were in the can. On the downside, there was a glitch with Weinberg's drums, as well as certain other housekeeping snags at Atlantic. Just as he had for *Born*, Springsteen made the move to the Record Plant. Thereafter, for the rest of the year, he was busy either rehearsing, recording or editing, when not doing low-fi gigs around Asbury.

Corporate assets like Springsteen always take record-label heat to cut three or four 'accessible' tracks per album. He had ten times that. Freed from any need but to write, he did his best work in three years. The music, says a bandmate, 'fairly flew' from him. He was that fast. Early on, Appel had got Springsteen to work up tracks for *Greetings* by asking him to hop the bus in to Manhattan. By the time he hit the Holland Tunnel, he'd have a new one ready. It was the same fifteen years later, when Van Zandt told the BBC, 'He'll say, "Oh, I wrote seven songs last night" . . . You just wanna kill him, y'know?' Springsteen's band were sometimes amused to hear him, when thinking out loud, howl a sort of whooping glissando

---

*By chance, one of the groups then flying under the punk flag, the Police, first met up early on 28 May; two '80s icons, Sting and Springsteen, were launched and relaunched on the same morning.

that roughly meant *Eureka!* He seemed to act as a kind of receiver, using some unconscious hunch for the right hook. Springsteen had a wardrobe of such hooks in his head, a whole arsenal of verses, beats, bridges, middle eights and codas. He synthesized. As always, his best songs went both to and fro. He had the knack of consolidating, pushing edges, actively mapping live frontiers as well as mining those of a dead era. When the band doled out Mob sobriquets, Springsteen wasn't in contention for E Street staples like Brains or Fingers. The consensus was ever Boss.

Even so, Landau was 'a big help to me. He helped me see things – to see *into* things – and somehow it would come out in the songs.' What Springsteen meant was that he was undergoing an 'artistic crisis'. His bawdy cast of hoods, lover-boys and leathery nomads were still on the road, though this time round, he said, 'they're going from nowhere to nowhere'. The racked lyrical soul-searching cost Springsteen months, and several torn-up notebooks. A whole day could be spent rejigging a verse and jumbling the words to find new lines created in the process. By contrast, the music came almost in real-time. Springsteen wrote a track called 'Factory' in twenty minutes. Like much of the material, it homed in on Doug. 'Adam Raised A Cain' and 'Independence Day' also dwelt on this, to Springsteen, fascinating theme. The result of his twin father-figures' pull – half nature and half nurture – was a glut of new songs, many of which never made the cut. Springsteen tossed material that others would (and did) beg for. 'Rendezvous', 'The Promise', 'Hearts Of Stone', 'Don't Look Back' and 'Fire' – Tim Rice calls the last a 'word-tripping classic' – were all left in the CBS vault. 'Independence Day' was held over. The raw recording, meanwhile, was done live in studio B, once or twice on the fly. Aside from the lyrics, what took Springsteen a full year were esoteric if vital jobs like sequencing – fixing the LP's running order to give it its optimal 'vibe' – mixing and design. He agonized for weeks over the cover art. (Springsteen personally flew to the lithographers to track the colour-printing process.) The ebb and flow of such minutiae wafted the breath of life to him, even when performing drudge work that might have been best left to roadies. If Springsteen, at no time in 1977–78, ever swept up the studio floor, that must have been the one and only chore he delegated.

As usual, the sessions charted Springsteen's romp across musical borders. But the final tracks weren't limited to pet stamping grounds like Spectorish ballads or power pop. His work's specific gravity doubled overnight. Those long months in the Plant saw a steady shift of Springsteen's sound from being predominantly open and 'up' to becoming increasingly closed and dark. This shading of his mood and music took place in the name of maturity. Yet, to his credit, Springsteen kept up his quickfire, quirky and finally life-affirming homage to the past. A typical set would see him roam the field from 'Mona' to 'Little Latin Lupe Lu'. Moreover, when Springsteen raided the Bo Diddley or Righteous Brothers archive, it wasn't from the angle of some post-modern ironist sending up 'golden greats'. He really meant it. Springsteen steered clear of the sort of hammy, gut-eroding scorn of most superstars for the music that made them big in the first place. With him, the love was there; also the notion of genre-busting catholicism. Among Springsteen's favourite albums that year were *Saturday Night Fever* and 'most anything' by Sinatra.

The professional range tended to blur the fact that Springsteen himself was the most non-specific star since the salad days of Dylan and Neil Young. He reacted to metafame, says one friend, 'as five guys named Bruce'. Just being Springsteen, a household word, gave him reason to protect what space was left. He woke up every day under a blizzard of feedback. There was gossip – the framework for the tabloids' manic riffling – as well as the kind of 'deep research' that involves sifting through dustbins and a long lens. Disgruntled ex-friends and dumped lovers suddenly found themselves rung by 'people page' editors and assigned to ghosts. Doug and Adele were doorstepped, and his sisters weren't skipped. Freehold was blitzed. At first it was a joke, Springsteen said, but after the fourth or fifth relative rang up in tears, you longed for the good old days of *Valentine* and *Jackie*.

Though the gap between the Springsteen hype and reality wasn't proved, it was tacit in nearly every speck of 'dirt', making the ambiguity at the heart of the American Dream crystal clear. Unsurprisingly, he tended to shrink from the attack. Springsteen lived and died for his fans onstage. Off it, he was a full-time under-study for the role of J. D. Salinger. Thanks to a new deal with CBS and a cash fix from Premier, he was at last starting to make real money. The Holmdel farm was no cosseted rock star's pile. But it had the major boon of being remote. Springsteen had once said he wanted to 'take a tune like [the Tornados'] "Telstar" and beam it down' to his own work. If so – and it clearly was – his new address was ironic. Boss Acres was next to Bell Labs' tracking-post for the very satellite that gave the song its name. Meanwhile, just over the Garden State Parkway, lay the Arts Center that featured in 'Jungleland'. The house itself was crowded by white dogwood blos-soms and azaleas, live oaks flanking the drive off Telegraph Hill. Inside, it was oddly empty. The place was bare, dark and, in certain visible spots, none too clean – a cave, friends called it. Here the Boss became Bruce again. 'You have to be self-contained,' he'd said. 'I eat loneliness . . . I feed off it.' Besides TV and the hi-fi, Springsteen's only other pet love was horses. A neighbour called Amy Frechett used to see him out riding in Holmdel park. He was alone. If every adult has his inner child, one age flogged a thousand ways, then Springsteen's was rooted fast in 1955, the six-year-old squatting for hours in his room, 'a kid,' he said, 'who didn't have anything to hold on to, or any connections'.

One of the reasons people were protective – at times, precious – about Springsteen wasn't hard to find. They worried about him. Instead of being sucked into the decadent lunacy of mass fame, Springsteen could seem painfully shy one-on-one. It was partly the way he looked. Without his beard, he came over as frail, fresh-faced, and, at a pinch, somewhere between seventeen and twenty. His voice, too, could swoop into little-girl register. As well as his junk food and Frosties, Springsteen typically liked to gulp iced glasses of milk. While in New York, he was apt to go to a cartoon cinema in Times Square, or watch *The Buddy Holly Story*. His idea of a good book was *Elvis: What Happened?*. As Goldsmith says, 'He was a guy who wore jeans and ate at McDonald's.' Ellie Smith, the PR girl who met him at Heathrow in November 1975, found Springsteen a 'very simple, unsophisticated person . . . He was completely in awe. We went to this restaurant that served ethnic-type food. I was sitting next to him and said, "What are you going to have?" And he said, "What are *you* going to have?" He'd never [eaten] food like that. I told him and he said, "I'll have it, too."' Whether rubbernecking in London or playing softball in New York, most of what Springsteen said and did revealed a dim, unfledged mind and an innocence that both jolted and charmed gnarled pop types. 'Bruce was really sweet back then,' Marc Brickman told the author Fred Goodman. 'He just wanted to have fun, and he wanted to make people have fun . . . I don't think there was a negative bone in his body.'

For all, too, that the new songs talked stuff about Badlands and Streets of Fire, Springsteen took as read that it was a 'gas' to be a rock and roller. He worked hard not to lose touch with the first sources of his inspiration; or the kids. Mitch Ryder calls him a 'hundred per cent, château-bottled good guy'. When Graham Parker met Springsteen backstage in New York, 'he not only flattered me by saying, "You're the only act I'd pay to see," he was genuinely down-to-earth, funny and hip'. Springsteen picked up Amy Frechett's brother, Chris, when the latter was out hitching. He was 'great'. In Todd's view, 'Bruce got about ten times smarter, and cooler' around 1977. Not that it was all vacuous good-deedery. Springsteen had obviously logged time contemplating his spot in the showbiz firmament. He wryly remarked of a town called Truth or Consequences (located near a bomb-test site in New Mexico), 'Man, I can dig that.' As Pete Seeger has it, 'He was, and still is, okay. Anyone who says, like Bruce, "a star will last as long as he can look down through the footlights and see his own face there" gets my vote. He isn't a guy abandoned to his own self-hype.'

Springsteen's overall niceness was very real. It smoothly won over men like Todd and Seeger. And yet, for others, something was missing. The search for hard-core dirt was as fruitless as that for a pat biography. Anyone in the lively arts is prone to the charge of whimsy and play-acting, but when it comes to Springsteen the stench overpowered his straight-guy image. On one occasion at Holmdel, the arrival of a noted critic was announced. Springsteen's reception of him was so icy that a CBS gofer had to 'help fill in what became an hour of mumbled "yeps", "nopes" and "dunnos". Bruce acted like a man having dental work.' When he'd done, Springsteen returned to the kitchen, wiping his brow. 'Guys,' he said with a smirk, 'give me a beer. He thinks I'm nutso.'

Some thought the self-take applied to Springsteen at work. He'd hoped *Darkness on the Edge of Town*, as it became, would be cut by mid-winter. But Christmas came and went and still the flangers, filters and tape loops kept rolling. By early January there were growing signs that the original plan was too tight. Advance orders for *Darkness* made it Springsteen's biggest album yet – bigger than *Born*. He was aware, he said, of the pressure this built; of the threat that 'as I go, so went [rock]'. When the Who or Stones or Dylan bombed, they hurt themselves and their labels; if Springsteen flopped, he ruined the dream for millions. The result was a Sisyphean slog that eventually comprised two studios, sundry engineers, tape-ops and Sherpas and a mastering lab in Los Angeles. By November, Springsteen was still doing long stints in the rehearsal factory. Recording had settled into a daily 3 p.m.-to-midnight shift in Manhattan. Here, at least, amenities took a welcome leap from the crude, four-track world of Blauvelt. Springsteen would never again sink to the kind of chicken-coop facilities of *Greetings* and *The Wild*. The Record Plant featured state-of-the-art ADT and EQ-ing boxes, as well as a kitchen, bedrooms and an exercise area. As soon as the flu season hit, Bittan and all the other gymnasts fell ill. Springsteen, who did most of his weightlifting with fork and cup, remained drolly immune. 'I get sick, I take another shot of Elvis.' Studio logs show he never missed a date.

If Springsteen failed in his mission, it lay in managing the smaller items too tightly and the larger ones too loosely, most especially in the weak, not to say woozy arrangements. 'I over-sang; we under-played' would be his own cutting verdict. So often accused of 'hammering' the band, in fact Springsteen usually declined to give direct orders or deny a Clemons or Van Zandt his head. The gauche Appel may have been constitutionally incapable of grasping his client's delicate wiring. Yet, if nothing else, he'd had a clear idea of time and budget. The results had been characteristically patchy yet earthy displays of raw musical values. Landau, for all his own smarts, tended merely to bear *Darkness'* tortuous fine-tunings with a thin smile.

They were tortuous. For ten years, Springsteen had been sold as a free spirit, someone whose work followed in the grainy, one-take tradition of a 'Sh-Boom' or 'Maybellene'. Now, that claim seemed patently false, and it was clear, as he fretted over leakage and chaired studio sub-groups on oscillation and reverb, that he no longer bought it himself. Cutting an album in ten days was a job, but it wasn't unmanageable. Rather than try, Springsteen gave up a year of his life to making forty-three minutes' music (though, it should be said, what music). As usual, some of the perfectionist yen that endeared him to fans made others cringe. There was a constant struggle to squeeze the songs on to two sides of vinyl, and no one in the Plant had any idea that, soon, they could fit twice as much on less. The great CD awakening hadn't yet come.

Darkness' due-date passed. Grey, humid days and cold nights seemed to emphasize the long saga, which made *Born* seem glib by comparison. Springsteen saw in the new year by guesting with first Patti Smith and then Southside Johnny. Bootleg video of the latter gig shows a fresh-cut figure in blue, prowling the stage, goading the crowd into manic gyrations. Though Springsteen's shtick was, for once, fuelled by green-room toping, the fans, made up mostly of drunken males, loved it. Their chant of *Br-ooose* gilded the cameo into a full-scale party.

'Anyone who works for me,' Springsteen told the *Chicago Tribune*, 'the first thing you better know is I'm gonna drive you crazy . . . I don't compromise in certain areas.' On the one hand, his constant retooling of *Darkness* was all to the good; as Landau said, proof 'he was totally committed to making a record true to his feelings'. On the other, Springsteen's nit-picking made precarious sense. The album's mixing and mastering were done by March and

May, respectively. Springsteen then not only visited the shop where the cover-proof was being set. He became the first artist in CBS history to insist on personally running the sleeve's presses. That done, he flew back to Los Angeles to overdub yet another guitar solo. Springsteen's last-gasp intervention meant the album's entire second side had to be redone. This general transition from free-form rocker to finicky product manager was one of the weirdest *chansons de geste* of its kind. It made even famously hands-on souls like Jagger seem lax. One result of Springsteen's post-Appel need for, Motz says, 'the three Cs' – control, control and control – was that *Darkness* was an odd mix of musical obscuration and fine detail. Another was that he had to start his new tour without it. When Springsteen hit the road in Buffalo on 23 May, the printers and shippers still had a full week's work to do.

The seven-month, 118-date sortie that followed not only reminded fans of why they liked Springsteen in the first place. It turned heads. When the industry came to fix on its pet son for 1978 there weren't many entries, and the verdict was quickly reached. FM radio was already blasting *Darkness* round the clock. Not just the trades but heavyweights like the *New York Times* sent their arts virtuosi to the gigs. There were still major differences in outlook and policy between him and the media, two entities who didn't exactly love one another, but who each had a mutual need – much like the two convicts shackled together in *Fled*. The tie that bound Springsteen and the press was expediency. He didn't trust them, but bowed to their numbers. Most of his gigs were in 10,000–12,000-seat halls; the *New York Times* spoke to millions. For their part, even the most hoary and sceptical pundits were won over by this pattern and exemplar of true-blue values, decent, upright, humane and – above all – 'straight'. 'Why play for so long?' the *Tribune* asked. Springsteen's reply wasn't just a mission statement that put many a hack to shame – it ended with the word that was his code and throughline. 'It's like you have to go the whole way because . . . that's what keeps it real.' An interview in *Rolling Stone* bristled with monkish vows that, for Springsteen, touring was more than a mere sales jaunt. 'There's a certain morality of the show and it's very strict . . . I play Buddy Holly every time before I go on, that keeps me honest . . . That's all I try to do – live so I can sleep at night. That's my main concern.'

Springsteen certainly ducked the on-with-the-gig inanity and witless roar of most rockers. He didn't, however, completely shun the lifestyle. 'Bruce,' as Motz says, 'was as solid as the Jersey hills.' But not quite as green.

Speaking of an era ten years before, Curt Fluhr summed up his friend: 'Even then, I'd have to say Bruce [was] the most heterosexual person I ever met.' It was a heady start, and Springsteen won a vulpine fame he never quite lost. By 1977, Darvin had joined his list of ex-lovers. She later married the 'found' noise pioneer and futurist Todd Rundgren. Springsteen then kept house with a woman called Joy Hannah; a seventeen-year-old high-school girl; a character known only as the Mass Market; and Lynn Goldsmith. Alone with a small group of mates, mainly musicians, Springsteen would say there were two reasons he was attracted to the last, one abstract and the other personal. The abstract, he said, came from Goldsmith's niche in the world of galleries, openings, theatre and non-orthogonal pop like Eno's; he wanted to be 'raised up' by her. ('I took him to the Museum of Modern Art. He taught *me* about Bo Diddley,' she says today.) In the good-guy, bad-guy formulation to which Springsteen bent, 'education' now became the holy grail. His mania for vicarious participation in high art hit its peak in the late '70s. The second, personal motivation sprang from loneliness. He 'dug pussy'.

Bluntly, Springsteen needed women to make good a crippling lack of self-confidence. Though he was rarely without a blonde or a Texan model in tow, the affairs still acted out the rites, manners and forms of language he'd learned as a boy. That meant a permanent apparatus of self-containment, and, by and large, a total absence of the ethic behind the music. Even a screaming, death-in-life row with his lover was mere grist to his mill, as when Goldsmith once complained of her being screwed 'point blank' only to hear the phrase promptly worked into a song (and, twenty years later, the sub-title of this book). Springsteen's lack of 'reality' with his partners was something he ruefully noted in 1992. 'I found I'd gotten very good at my job . . . and for some reason I thought I was capable of a lot of other things, like relationships.' Around the same time, he was apt to quip that he'd had 'lots of women – always the same problem'. It wasn't just that Springsteen, as some said, was really a 'guy's guy'. The truth is that he was better at dealing with people as groups, crowds and statistics. For years he both wanted and needed the chance to perform, the key love of his life being that between himself and the audience. It was the old story: tongue-tied boy learns he has a gift, but, offstage, would always rather be alone. As a fully engaged, individual talent, few came close to Springsteen. As a man, none did.

That begged the question. How much of Springsteen's act was apparent; how much was real? A man of substance or one who merely looked and sounded the part? There were several mysteries about the Boss, rock redux and unwitting mouthpiece for a generation: the chief one being that he seemed to be several different people. At one end, there was the mass worship and media-pack hagiography. Even as *Darkness* was belatedly flying out of the shops, a second-wave Springsteen cult was rising as from the ground. Its intensity soared like a rocket on the day of the LP's release, and hung high over American skies for weeks. To the hundreds of thousands who bought the album or watched the shows, he was a latter-day saint. At the opposite pole, Adele still lobbied for her son to 'get real'. Six years after first signing a deal and two and a half since *Time* and *Newsweek*, Springsteen, she thought, should 'settle down' and 'do a day job'. Doug's views aren't recorded. Between the two extremes were the musicians, producers, roadies and lovers for whom, one says, he was 'cute, but tough to know'. Many of the day-to-day hassles and major traumas with friends like McKeith went on behind his back, without jolting him or his self-image. Springsteen remained serene in the centre of his universe, awaiting his next performance.

He was still the unspoilt Jerseyan-made-good. Aside from the sex, Springsteen never stooped to other rock-star accessories like clothes or drugs. He drank milk, Coke or the odd brew. One glass of champagne, he said, and he was 'spaso'. People kept waiting for the rot to set in, but Springsteen just chugged on like the 'cash generator' he was. As he told *Rolling Stone*, 'The stuff I always feel closest to [is] the small-town kind of stuff, because that's the way I grew up . . . that's home stuff, you know.' He was speaking about *Darkness*, but it was the keynote of his whole life.

Springsteen did, however, grow. Prodded by Goldsmith and Landau, he was getting more 'arty' than in the reign of Appel and Darvin. As a natural corollary, he began to read. By 1978, he was deep into the works of Flannery O'Connor. He skimmed *To Kill a Mockingbird*. Springsteen was about to discover Ron Kovic's *Born on the Fourth of July*. In time his autodidactism took in photography (Robert Frank's *The Americans*) and film (*The Grapes of Wrath*, Sergio Leone); he went back over the John Ford classics. Springsteen's sonic vocabulary, meantime, remained fixed in the Hank Williams, Elvis, Dylan and jangly British hits of his youth. A bandmate swears he 'used to bob along to "I'd Like To Teach The World To Sing".' Springsteen's whole genre-tripping – his fusion of, so to speak, *The Searchers* and the Seekers – helped him work up a progressive, fast-building audience. Some of the guitar-and-sax blast of *Born* might have been lost forever; but increasingly, his songs had the smooth flow of good storytelling.

The Searchers' migrancy may have been that of border-jumping, but Landau, above all, knew that frontiers crossed weren't merely the kind drawn in dirt. His restless careerism was forever challenging the lines between pop and rock, art and commerce, the past and present, do-goodery and greed. Nineteen seventy-eight was the year he took over. Landau – smooth, hard-headed and defensive where Appel was cocky and manic – not only assumed responsibility for management and production; he suavely steered Springsteen into new playgrounds like Madison Square Garden on the basis, said CBS's Peter Philbin, 'he was letting his fans down and had to play bigger shows'. The result was a gradual but total U-turn in Springsteen's policy on 'sheds' and a lifting of his ban on T-shirts and such. As Todd says, 'Oddly enough, the Boss had always hauled off at [Appel] about not ever – this is a quote – "kissing corporate butt". Then, the moment Mike's out, Bruce is sitting down with the suits at the Garden.' The job of rationalizing the seemingly venal fell to Springsteen's mutual amanuensis. Pop history teems with Landaus, hardmen whose very toughness is a distorting prism through which their nice-guy charges look gentler. All the old ideas about chastity, community and covenants were simplified into, or devoured by, this new bond between manager and 'kid'. Around Asbury in the late '60s, Springsteen had spoken of wanting to be '*just* like the Stones'. A decade later, a full revolution had brought him in a circle. Springsteen's ballistic rise had been 'real', moral even, and often at odds with the cynical pandering of most stars. He was still a raw, ungilded celebration of rock-and-roll values, but his most precious asset – purity – died in 1978.

Landau's power-play was a *fait accompli* by midsummer. 'He kept saying he didn't want to be manager,' Brickman told Fred Goodman. 'But he'd always be around. He laid back; he calculated and watched.' The twin dramas of *Darkness* and the year's tour soon focused on the need to fill the void. With Tannen increasingly sidetracked in film work and left cold by the world of road-running – and Bill Graham vetoed by Goldsmith – Landau was a sure bet. Along with Philbin and Bell, he formed a trio of hyperactive *consiglieri* covering Springsteen's back. It was an inspired pick. Landau was the perfect man to steer him through the shark-infested waters of stardom; just as Appel had been the *ne plus ultra* of door-kickers. Springsteen always or usually chose well. On the straitened canvas of his interests, money-management and 'bullshit' had loomed as the two he loathed most. Both were Landau's pets. He was a master of logistics and negotiation, the bedrock on which Springsteen's whole career now ran. Landau not only went toe-to-toe with CBS and Premier; he happily spent weeks agonizing over arcana like the colour-tinting of *Darkness*' cover, or the sequencing of its songs – specifically, insisting that the album's first and last tracks be 'on message'. This trainspotter's attention to detail matched even his client's. (According to one woman, 'put them in a studio, and they're like two kids in a sandpit'.) Such was the co-dependent relationship Appel, and others, sniffed was 'love'.

Above all, Landau possessed the gift of seeming infinitely plausible as a friend. In the same source's words, 'Jon's like a throat lozenge – there's something soothing about him. He speaks so soft.' Landau, of course, also clung to the habit of carrying a big stick. If Freehold was the chief author of Springsteen's isolation, his manager was at least its agent and PR. No one got too close to the talent. Certain cronies, long used to an open invitation, now found their way barred backstage. The photographer Jeff Albertson, one of Springsteen's first fans, was 'warned off' before a gig in Boston. McKeith, Brickman and Van Zandt himself would all, at different times and of varying causes, feel the lash of a man whose credulity was taxed until he was quite ready to hold that 'Take a vacation, Jon' was the start of a coup, and that behind every unauthorized writer there was a thug from England with a chequebook in one hand and a hatchet in the other. Nothing Landau did was either illegal or novel in the twilight zone of pop management, whose feral ethics would have won a fond nod from Vlad the Impaler. But for that blend of entrepreneurial qualities aptly put as 'velvet on iron', he stood alone.

Of course, it wasn't as if others – say the Stones – were an effortless feat of unsculpted, free-form self-expression. All the class acts had a Landau. Where he scored over a Roger Forrester or Miles Copeland* was in coaxing his client's raspy voice and half-baked mind into something articulate, bold and quirkily radical. The old, *Born to Run* songs had tended to hot-rodder stereotypes: what John Sinclair calls the 'mythic urban grease'. Springsteen himself would admit writing in the style of the Animals' 'We Gotta Get Out Of This Place' and 'It's My Life' – the cocked snook of the exile. Though *Born* had begun as a sub-Joycean spiel and ended on an anguished, *Waste Land*-like note, 'wounded not even dead' in 'Jungleland', like all Springsteen's work its spiritual base was Jersey, *circa* 1958–63. Reviewing a show in 1975, the *Seattle Times* had grasped: 'It wasn't [about] the future, it was [about] yesterdays.' Yet within two years Springsteen was quoting O'Connor and

---

*Eric Clapton's and Sting's managers, respectively.

Steinbeck as well as Elvis and Spector. Brickman is only the most compelling witness to call Landau a 'tutor' and 'mentor'. Lenny Kaye also says 'Jon's stellar IQ and cinematic eye – he'd been a movie critic – spun Bruce a certain way . . . He recut both the man and material.' According to this take, *Darkness*' real hero was Landau, and in particular his celluloid idol John Ford. A friend once 'mentioned to Jon that a lot of Bruce's lyrics read like Westerns'. Landau at once 'seized on this like a hyena lunges for meat . . . "They *are*," he said.' Ford's films (notably *The Searchers*) now lent a thin veneer of philosophical gloss to the pervasively bitter rant of an 'It's My Life'. It's fair to credit Lynn Goldsmith with opening Springsteen's eyes culturally. But it took Landau to reach his heart and mind.

As *Darkness* came round, said Springsteen, 'I focused on this one idea: What do you do if your dream comes true? What then?' Answered prayers had jolted him. By now, the triumphal whoop of 'Rosalita' – 'The record company just gave me a big advance' – had become a *cri de coeur*. He'd seen the dark side. As Springsteen told Dave Marsh, 'I got out there – hey, the wind's whipping through your hair, you feel real good, you're the guy with the golden guitar or whatever, and all of a sudden you feel that sense of *dread* that's overwhelming.' Put otherwise, the cumulative blows of the lawsuit and creeping maturity had done for the panic of always needing to 'have a gas'. From 1977–78, Springsteen relaxed into the role of the wounded meritorious ego. He grew up. His songs scripted only a cameo part for the mythic greasers. To his and Landau's credit, he rose above the affirm-in-the-negative teen yarns of *Born*. Springsteen not only broke his emotional quarantine ('I've always been fighting between feeling real isolated and looking to make some connection'), he took up external cudgels. Traditional symbols of American materialism and glut were his points of departure. Using a pluralist text by Henry Steele Commager and Allan Nevins as a route-map, he not so much rewrote as discovered history. Springsteen fumed at Richard Nixon. His awareness of Vietnam took an upward lurch as a result of *The Deer Hunter*. He even picked up on the fag-end of the original civil rights movement, hailing Martin Luther King (murdered in 1968) as a 'guy I'd dig to meet'.

The concept of emotionalism – the theory that the artist tries to grab the world not by reason but through the medium of his passions, the tool of his cognition – was stamped in *Darkness*' grain. With a few rare exceptions, Springsteen broadened his music and deepened his lyrics. The map grids for the first were an alluring mix of old (Jimmie Rodgers, Roy Acuff) and new (Graham Parker's *Heat Treatment* informed at least half the hooks), with dashes of Otis Redding and Sam Cooke. Hank Williams' angular, touch-of-twang balladry was Springsteen's starting point. 'Rock and roll is like all sports in that when you're thirty-five you're considered an old man,' he noted in 1978. '[But] it's not true. That's why I listen to country music a lot, 'cause it allows growing up . . . You know what rock is? It's me and my band going out to the audience tonight and growing older with them.' Lyrically, too, Springsteen's songs took a step up the genetic ladder. His conviction that 'You're born, and they bury you' lay at the very heart of his code. Thus all *Darkness*' characters were struggling with their own mortality, ruthlessly waging a secret war against breakdown, clinging to jobs or homes, leading lives of quiet heroism. They were blunt, forthright, broke and screwed-up, luminously 'real' and piercingly American. Springsteen's detailed sense of organization, the structure and texture of the words – their literary architecture – was a creative *tour de force* for a man who said, 'I can't sit for all them hours reading a book.' Here the key role models were naturalistic writers like Chuck Berry, and, in *Cliffs Notes* form, O'Connor and Steinbeck. Certain fans still hold Springsteen's real career to have begun with *Darkness*, the lawsuit a necessary lull between the pagan he was and the missionary he became – the start of a trajectory that led to *Tom Joad*. Still others think he never quite recovered from watching *The Grapes of Wrath* on TV.

At their sorry nadir, Springsteen's civics were an empty roar, his lyrics a few paint-by-numbers stabs at moral instruction. He'd say, for instance, that 'there's a promise getting broken . . . I wanna change that'. Exactly how he meant to do so remained fuzzy. A year or two later, Springsteen would enlighten the public with the news that 'There's no place to take aim. There's nobody to blame . . . It's a little bit [the fault] of this guy, a little bit of that guy.' Yet if the thoughts behind them were satirically duff, the songs were still deftly idealistic: the idea that every life buoyed a whole – society – whose parts were logically related. His comparative slowness in getting off the mark (finding the old man inside the young one) jars strongly with the Springsteen of middle age, the epitome of Tennyson's aspiring human, 'forever seeking something new'. The explanation is simple: Landau.

Springsteen's longest and largest road-trip yet opened in Memorial week 1978 and wound down, eighty cities later, on New Year's Day. In 1973, acting as a sacrificial 'butt-fuck', he'd sworn he'd 'never do another shed – ever'. Five years on, Springsteen was ready to cross this symbolic Rubicon. He played arena-sized halls in twelve cities, and nowhere at all smaller than 2,000 seats. Although some of the best reviews depended on the nostalgic forgiveness of the writer, Springsteen was by any token a famous, highly touted and, above all, 'true' star – he was about roots and community, not merchandising and spin-offs. As Lynn Goldsmith says, 'These days, he'll take a limo, even a helicopter to a show – he's four-square in the music biz – but the Bruce I knew was a simple guy, true to his self, who loved to play,' demonstrating anew the redemptive power of old-time rock and roll. In an era lacking heavyweight musical gods of its own – the Stones, Who and Led Zep all having opted for semi-retirement – Springsteen now constituted a soul of encyclopaedic continuity. As Weinberg puts it, 'Bruce encompassed the history of performance.' The gigs were an oratorio of old and new. There weren't any other icons with an act like his who crossed all or most class lines: the shows drew men, women, mothers clutching kids, and tough, T-shirted barrio types, all of them stamping and yelling, 'Br-*ooose*!' (About the only group absent were blacks – of whom, one wag said, there were more on stage than off it.) Also present and screaming were the teenage girls, many of whom, by encore's end, would have poured over the footlights to maul Springsteen. During 'Spirit', a longtime live set-piece, he'd make his own reciprocal leap into the stalls. There was a neat psychological touch to the fact that he was offering himself to them, as it were, raw and bare, yet at the same time walking away each night unscathed. They loved him. At 2 a.m. on 6 July, local Los Angeles radio broadcast the news that Springsteen would play a one-off date at the Roxy, scene of his west coast coup in 1975. Long lines began forming instantly.

Re-creating Springsteen's intricate-yet-sparely-done riffs almost seemed too much to ask, even from a man of his intoxicating gift. But he normally pulled it off. Unlike those – the name Bowie comes to mind – who rarely doffed their velvet street togs to break a sweat, Springsteen was an all-action hive of euphoric, mesmerising pop and percolating rock; playing notes like bolts of static. He took the set at a clip, chasséing, bouncing the Fender off his thighs, wildly 'up' in parts, yet grafting the scion of blues on to the root stock of a mass riot. It was all close to a 'privileged moment', when traditional star–fan barriers break down. From San Diego to Toronto, the gigs connected on aural, visual and, above all, gut levels. Springsteen delivered. He was rock and roll future, past and present. That jump into the crowd served as a central symbol for a show that, night after night, was a blood-hot, dynamic four-hour commiseration with the fans' lows and celebration of their highs. He was that good. In Seattle, said the *Times*, 'the capacity crowd went crazy over Springsteen's incredible set . . . the whole house was up and participating, not wanting it to end'. In Los Angeles he was carried off at the curtain by the band, 'dead', then bounced back, gladhanding and bawling an hour of juke-box giants. A week later, in Phoenix, CBS's Arnold Levine shot the nine-minute orgy of 'Rosalita': the first Springsteen's UK fans had seen of him since *Born* would be that video of him mugging, singing, pulling a silly walk out of John Cleese's repertoire and being swarmed by girls on *The Old Grey Whistle Test*. The show's MC, Bob Harris, caught a later dithyrambic rave in New Haven: 'Bruce played from 8 p.m. to midnight . . . a great gig. As he ran past me into the dressing room, I asked how long he needed to cool off before the interview. "Let's do it now," was the casual reply. Within thirty seconds of the last encore, he was sitting with me being charming, focused like a laser . . . Two hours later, we amble up to a club, Toad's Place. Springsteen sits down, orders a beer, then waves to the bar-band. The end result is that he sidles onstage with them at 3 a.m. and starts pounding out "Pretty Flamingo" . . . Bruce just had that attitude and edge to him. *That's* a rock and roller.'

Springsteen didn't, though, just sing, play the guitar and dance all night. Most concert-goers like something to share, and in the hours and days after the gigs his various raps did the rounds as much as the music. The homespunnery didn't always work. A witness to a long, rambling harangue in Dallas reports Springsteen's words as having been cut short there by a 'spud to the chops'. But generally the intros were a treat. The ability, for instance, to strafe Freehold with the binding force of a road trip yoked to an ego trip: 'One of you guys wanted a lawyer and another wanted an author . . . Well, tonight youssa both gonna have to settle for rock and roll.' Springsteen could have been excused his moment of revenge when he sang 'Growin' Up' that night in LA. Doug and Adele themselves were front and centre. Six weeks later he returned triumphantly to the venue he'd last played as a 'butt-fuck'. Then, he left in tears. Now he sold out the Garden, three of fully ten New York-area gigs he did down the road. 'I hear you gotta paper strike,' Springsteen chortled, as he ran forward to the lip that first night. 'Well, y'heard the news?' On cue the lights flared and the drums boomed into Elvis' 'Good Rockin' Tonight'. Later in the show Springsteen got to introduce Tex Vinyard. Later still, he turned to his old neighbour and ex-manager, pointed a finger across the city lights to Jersey and said, 'It's a lot further from Freehold to here than you think.'

Springsteen gave the band a long leash. But all the leads ultimately were held in his hand – pacing, staging, lighting, sound, vision. That the subsets looked on him with due awe, as much as warmth, didn't deter some amiable high jinks. On stage the E Streeters pulled up several trees. The skittering, always melodic rhythm, Federici's cheesy, analog keyboards and the punchy sax breaks – all came off as an uncanny, convincingly earthy collage of sixties pop. There were touches of Monkees-like hamming between Springsteen and his two foils, Clemons and Van Zandt. Offstage, too, they weren't above ensemble horseplay. Springsteen spent Independence Day in Hollywood by climbing on the roof of a building with Clemons and Tallent to deface a billboard plugging *Darkness*. At a hissed warning of 'Cops!' he shunted down a fire escape and bolted like one of the switchblade-toting punks of 'Jungleland'. It was an authentic rock-and-roll prank (and, as Springsteen said, 'an artistic improvement').

Much as the frat-pack antics of the band thrilled fans – and stories like that got round – several factors combined to prop Springsteen's benign empire. As well as the music, there was what Richard Williams calls the 'powerful mystique around his prowess' as a live draw. Most A-list stars played for ninety minutes. After three hours, Springsteen would just be hitting his stride. Backstage, he was interested not in snorting junk or full-body rubdowns but in locating a club where nobody hassled him and he could happily belt Manfred Mann hits till dawn. Even when he was forced to relax, he was apt to be out jamming with the Knack, Beaver Brown or Southside Johnny. Springsteen, thus, was the real thing. As *NME* said, 'You look for the catch, the flaw, the giveaway. And you look and you look and you keep looking until you finally concede that there isn't a catch. He's it' (if not quite the free-flowing vessel of spontaneity: the author Marc Eliot notes that 'when Bruce wanted to go shopping to buy jeans, he'd insist that [Darvin] accompany him and stay for sometimes up to eight hours at a clip until he chose just the right pair. The idea he had was to fastidiously capture the perfect "casual" look'). *Rolling Stone* and the rest could plead with fans to consider the mythic, nostalgic side, but most stubbornly made up their minds on the basis of whether they liked the cut of Springsteen's jib. Here, too, he scored highly. 'Everything counts,' he told the *Chicago Tribune*. 'Every person, every individual in the crowd counts – to me. I see it both ways. There's a crowd reaction. But then I also think very, very personally, one to one with the kids.' Coming from anyone else, cynics would have wondered whether Springsteen had managed to get drunk on the two or three beers backstage, and, for tactical reasons, wanted to revel in a display of pro-kid populism. But he really meant it. A friend in Seattle asked if a gig there had been 'almost like having sex'. 'Not "like". It *is* sex,' said Springsteen.

Believers in the unwritten law that pop stars (no less than sports gods and pin-ups) need to fit into a virtual family would have done well to look hard at him that summer. If Jagger was the Flash Harry and Bowie the officially sanctioned ponce, Springsteen carved out a niche as a bug-eyed, door-to-door preacher, testifying and turning heads one at a time. Amid the cheap shots and formulaic din of most gigs, that 'Welcome Back Boss' tour was a new dawn. People talked. Interest focused not just on the shows and songs, but on the crack-up with Appel and long lay-off. Something heroic and high-minded was inferred and Springsteen was given the status of a latter-day saint of rock legend. In particular, his business plan appealed to those for whom dewy sentiment, at worst, did for dry reviewing. To men like Dave Marsh, Springsteen was keeper of the flame, a human repository of the kind of hopes and day-dreams first stirred by Elvis. He was a golden man in an age of lead. About his only rival that year was Graham Parker, an ill-kempt pub rocker and thus somewhat below these pundits' radar.

It wasn't, though, just a grim tribe of prigs and coke-tooters – with no real interest in 'rock and roll future' or anything else alive – who colonized Springsteen. He was deservedly famous at the level of 'real dudes'; with men, women and children, including those teenage girls. Famous – all the gigs, the quotes and quips and the code of which he said, 'I decided a long time ago, I know who I am . . . I try to keep my perspective on the thing.' In contrast to the sycophantic projection on hand elsewhere, most fans admired Springsteen for his apparent coolness to the hype, the shill and the trappings of 'shit'; that and the sucker-punch of the songs. After three years, a new album wasn't bought, it was seized on. Even amid high-profile releases by Dylan and the Stones (not to mention the floodtide of posthumous Elvis), *Darkness* shipped gold, with advance orders of 600,000. It would have taken an anti-PR genius to blow this deep, far-flung fan-base. Springsteen wasn't that.

As well as devotional awe from his male peers, he got full shrift from the women. Springsteen had spoken of being sick of 'kids throwing their panties at me'. A man needs to be on nodding terms with plenty of underwear to enshrine it in policy. Springsteen, it's true, steered clear of the kind of *Satyricon* that turns platinum-selling LPs and manic tours into nightmares of greed and envy, hazed over by dope, drink and rooms groaning with so much luxury they're squalid. He was, however – says one woman – 'like a fox down a hole' in the world of 'uncomplicated fucking'. This particular source remembers Springsteen 'rooting himself silly' across America. His libido was less about two sexes than two personalities, the ones he inhabited for ten years.

Alongside the sometime teetotaller was the priapic stud who craved a constant supply of 'fresh tail' (the woman's words) and other striking combos. Springsteen's seduction technique, always winning – a couple of sodas, a lunge up the skirt – was still of a piece with his mutual scuffles in the fields around Lake Topanemus. If he'd 'done fifty chicks' as a teen, not improbable for an erotic apprenticeship of seven years, the ratio would have doubled as a rock god. Springsteen liked sex. The number of his lovers doesn't detract from his fame as 'real' and refreshingly free of the 'star-zone bullshit' of a Jagger or Bowie. It may even add to it. The girls who tossed lingerie or doffed their shirts, baring their breasts (often with BOSS daubed on them), were just as loyal as a Landau or Marsh. They, too, put down their $7.98 for *Darkness*, proving that Springsteen's audience wasn't just deep, but also broad.

The album was out that June. For the most part, *Darkness* abandoned the clarity and punch of *Born* to concentrate instead on the problems and pressure of late-seventies America. The cliché of the leering, dumbed-down pop archetype was lost forever. Springsteen's lyrics posed a number of unanswered questions on decidedly non-teen topics like the means of production, unemployment and the recession. A strong, if silent sub-plot was his own emotional slump. *Darkness* – the first album he made after fame struck – saw him caught between the extremes of sentimen-tality and fatalism. The result was cutting-edge, angst rock. Pre-hype Springsteen could never have written a cut like, for one, the title track. As a rule, musicians' answered prayers tend to get recycled on to their albums, as gradually they become famous for their deconstruction of fame. (Springsteen's friend Bowie reached this pass in 1973 with *Aladdin Sane*.) *Darkness*, too, was set against record label and media hopes, not to say hysteria: by its success or failure Springsteen would become a doughty, long-term player or one of those evanescent '70s fads like Evel Knievel, 'Bird' Fidrych or clogs.

Bluntly, it was a pivotal, what's-it-all-about LP, as he said, 'where I spent a lot of time focusing . . . What do you do if [it] comes true? Where does that leave you?' Opinion polarized between those who thought Springsteen's conclusions whipped-up and fake, and others who valued his prudent nod to maturity. (As one of the key cho-ruses had it, 'Mister, I ain't a boy, no, I'm a man.') The fingerprints not just of the suit, but of hard lessons in life, were all over *Darkness*' grooves. 'I had a big awakening in the past two, three years,' Springsteen said. 'Much bigger than people would think. Learned a lot of things . . . it's all there on the record.' The overall focus was on blue-collar types scrapping for dignity and (a Springsteen keynote) control in the teeth of the giant forces tyrannizing them. From at least three tracks wafted an echo of *Death of a Salesman*. Unsurprisingly, *Darkness*' tone was, as he said, 'down. It's less romantic . . . On *Born* there was the hope of a free ride. On *Darkness* there ain't no free ride. You wanna ride, you gotta pay!'

Springsteen thus conscientiously if self-consciously reclaimed upmarket pop, carrying out Landau's great advice to 'de-glib'. He simply overdid it. Among the lyrical themes were darkness (real or imagined), fathers, sons, jobs and faded dreams. Cars also returned. Nine out of ten tracks mentioned them, though, this time up, the drivers were apt to be crashing, not fleeing. For the next two albums, and particularly *Nebraska*, escapism was on the way out and confrontation – whether with bosses, spouses or oneself –

triumphant. The rationale behind Springsteen's new vein of realism varied. A sense of duty and, increasingly, fixation on the moral ambiguity at the heart of the Dream wasn't wholly absent. But there was also a strong whiff of self-preservation, an awareness of the need to stay a nose ahead of obsolescence. Many of Springsteen's man-of-the-people effusions were in the service of his own shelf-life. But since artists' motives are nearly always mixed, only purists griped.

Darkness' sound, if not old-fashioned, recalled the best of Springsteen's C&W idols in bringing a brash enthusiasm to the job at hand, and keeping it brief. Long-form epics were out. If *Darkness*' best tracks tended to follow a formula – a muted strum tapering into a full-band, embattled chorus – nobody did natural talent better. Springsteen, having shaken the echo from his voice, could still belt a melody, while Clemons and Federici, in particular, flexed musical brawn. *Darkness* also began the tradition of flinging as much on the studio floor as on vinyl; Charles Cross lists over twenty-five songs that never made it. Springsteen's dogged perfectionism – whether doing untold takes or retooling the cover art – seemingly contradicted the wild, free-form vibe of the gigs. (As he said of a show in San Francisco, 'I kept making mistakes . . . and this guy in front yells, "Hey, it's OK. You can fuck up all you want" . . . I live on that kinda spirit.') *Darkness*, by turns, could be measured or curiously flat; a matt coat where *Born* was all gloss. To the *Chicago Tribune*, 'like its predecessor, it favors bombast over subtlety, but this time the music is almost frighteningly brutal . . . Springsteen brandishes his guitar and voice like blowtorches'. What stuck was the sheer feral snarl of the vocals, bringing with it the verdict: plenty of tension, little release.

Darkness fell with 'Badlands' (named after Terrence Malick's cult film), due warning that it was something other than feel-good pop, and went on from there to get Oedipal. Lyrically, 'Adam Raised A Cain' echoed both Ibsen's *Ghosts* and the James Dean role in *East of Eden*; musically, it stumbled through sonic orbit via a call-and-response chorus and the kind of revved-up guitar channelled, by Fleetwood Mac, into the BBC's 'Grand Prix' theme. Whether flogging a basic I-IV-V harmony or reprising the piano part of 'Born', 'Candy's Room' was elegant filler. In 'Racing In The Street' the debts were to another film (*Two-Lane Blacktop*), old heroes (Martha and the Vandellas) and a new peer (Jackson Browne). The vocal Sherpa on 'Prove It All Night' was Graham Parker. Elsewhere, *Darkness* ranged from the patchy to the potent. The mundanity, the 'sense of terror, waste and sheer loss' of Doug's life came horrifyingly clear on 'Factory'. At one moment lilting and the next coiled and snakelike, the second half, in particular, was music for all seasons. The title cut was classically well made, destined for some kind of after-life on 'Unplugged': not a single dud line, not a chord you could live without. Springsteen conjured a dark fable, in quiet-storm format, where redemption could only be had 'on that hill/with everything I got', a raw, harrowing awareness that we can never escape our fate.

Darkness' methods were those Springsteen, and others, would use to show what the world really was. Romps about Harleys, boardwalks and back-alley rumbles gave way to a dualism of loss and love. 'What it is,' he said, '. . . is the characters' commitment. In the face of all the betrayals, in the face of all the imperfec- tions . . . it's the refusal to let go.' *Darkness* was a state-of-the-race album, an entire shopping list of social ills, bent on dashing hopes of a re-*Born*. (Its singles flopped.) As a marketing ploy it may have been weak, unconvincing and, above all, wilfully confused. As an artistic snapshot of its times, and all time, it worked. *Darkness* was masterly.

5

'I Felt Like I Was The Beatles'

'The quiet backstage was broken by the clatter of boots from down a guarded hallway. Seven men ran out toward me, one after another, in an animated locker room procession . . . Springsteen led the charge. He paused a few feet from me and waited for a flashlight escort to the mikes. His fiery brown eyes were covered with an electric glaze. With his fists clenched and his weight shifting abruptly from side to side, he seemed like a loose power line crackling in the night.'

Like the writer Ken Erickson, most who saw the *Darkness* tour dwelt on Springsteen's manic glee – how he bundled up his whole life and flung it against the stage – marshalling his songs with a near-mechanical edge and yet pouring so much into them that every one became a call to arms. The shows might have been less slick than before, but they still had all the eternal virtues: wit, scorn, stamina, power and compassion; part party, part revival, all buoyed by the heartland vocals. In Seattle, Springsteen played until 1 a.m., then ran back on for four separate encores. The night ended with him dancing atop a twenty-foot speaker stack, yelling and screaming, 'I'm just a prisoner of . . . ROCK AND ROLL!' Five thousand fans wove home coated by snow, sweating. The whole thing ended on New Year's Day at the Richfield Coliseum, Cleveland. At the previous gig Springsteen had shown his wry, rumbustious and ratty sides in the space of a few hours. Before the first note of the first song, he set the mood by playing a tape of the Ronettes' 'Frosty The Snowman'. Once on stage, Springsteen did a thirty-strong set, plus encores, climaxing in 'Good Rockin' Tonight'. By contrast, the finale was him flaying an 'asshole' who tactlessly celebrated by heaving a firework at his feet. During the seven-month saga he'd played, coast to coast, to a million fans. Even the Stones didn't do business like that in 1978. Springsteen was the arch live draw in America. He wouldn't go back abroad. It added to the mystery and lure of his image, an aura compounded by both distance and myth. Fanned by Roger Scott and a few like-minded DJs,* Springsteen buzz regularly did the rounds in Britain. He was said to be 'planning to do' it that fall; testing for films; readying a live album; and dating the vamp Rachel Sweet – none of which ever happened. The gossip was compelling, both for its more or less true gauge of his fame and for the idealized, lyrical haze through which the disciples saw Springsteen's star. It didn't, however, say much about the man.

Everything now went overboard. Even other rock gods watched with mingled awe and envy the hysterically pitched raves in the press. It was a challenge to their own capacity for hero-worship. First, Jagger weighed in with his vivid 'I'd fuck 'im.' Wendy Williams ran with the theme by adding, 'He can lick *my* twat any time.' 'God help Bruce when they decide he's no longer God,' noted Lennon. Bob Geldof, who'd already muddied the waters of their latent rivalry by calling Springsteen 'a rip-off', nonetheless stooped to his own E Street pastiche, 'Rat Trap'. Such beefs as there were were either too tritely positioned or came too late to

---

*Tony Parsons, for one, raved of a New York show, 'Springsteen is the only geezer I'd actually pay money to go and see . . . This ain't just the best gig I've ever seen . . . it's like watching your entire life flashing by and instead of dying, you're dancing.'

halt *Darkness*' smash. No self-respecting scenester was without it. As Graham Parker says, 'If you were dicked off at the Floyds and Zeppelins, Bruce was the one it was okay to like.' (Reciprocally, in an inverted black mass of hype, his friend's gag that 'Graham's the act I'd pay to see' fulfilled the same role for *Parkerilla* as 'rock and roll future' had for *Born*.) Springsteen was becoming the high priest of what Scott termed 'the Bruce cult', and others dubbed Bossmania. Its devotees came in all shapes, sizes and sexes, but more than a few were critics. At core, they had the same relation to Springsteen as he did to his bleak childhood. The operative word was nostalgia.

First, there was Dave Marsh, already at work on an in-house biography.* Meanwhile, names like Robert Hilburn, Dave McGee and Peter Knobler all came round, like stops on the El, above copy on Springsteen. In the *New York Times*, John Rockwell hastened to join the chorus. 'It's not difficult for this writer to say that, as a *performer* (as opposed to a composer, a singer, a guitarist, a musician, a record-maker or whatever) Mr Springsteen is the best he's encountered in rock-and-roll, ever.' The first pulp title, *Thunder Road*, was already out in February 1978. Charles Cross, the Seattle freelance who'd been 'baptized' at the Bottom Line, went on to found the fanzine *Backstreets*. To hacks starved of spiritual nourishment and desperate for beauty, joy and truth, Springsteen was as if heaven-sent, God's rocker, proof that pop hadn't lost its soul. In a trade with a centuries-old tradition of deifying its greats, it was only logical that he become a – or the – consensus star.

Springsteen also knew the flip side of fame. Instead of ambling out of gigs, he learned to sprint through the stage doors of theatres and coliseums, and make his way home through side streets and roped-off alleys. ('Isolation' was his one-word take on life a year or

---

*The age-old snag of 'access', specifically whether Marsh could quote *Born*'s lyrics, had been a rumbling sub-plot in the 1976–77 lawsuit. Springsteen liked Marsh. Appel's view was that the author was 'part of the team that's screwing [me] . . . his book eventually came out, was a huge success and did irreparable damage to my career'.

two later.) He was fully alive to the mania that inevitably dogs American celebrity. The most memorable such lunacy came when a middle-aged woman bumped into Springsteen in New York and switched from fawning on him to frenzy when he wouldn't join her for a drink. 'Cunt! Prick! You should get herpes!' she yelled after him as he walked away. More often, public and press competed to heap honours on him. In the *Rolling Stone* awards alone, Springsteen was Best Male Vocalist, Best Songwriter and Artist of the Year, beating the Who and Billy Joel. *Darkness* was runner-up only to the Stones' *Some Girls*.

By then Springsteen had broken with his lover. There'd been a time when he dreamt of 'the big drop' – even a child – with Goldsmith, but careerism had done for that. The actual rip came on tour when, rummaging through the bag they shared, she dug up a letter and pictures from her successor. Springsteen was already seeing an actress called Joyce Hyser. Here, almond eyes, hair and accent all made for a plausible Jersey Girl, as tirelessly shrill as she was 'on'. Around 1979 there was a rash of partner-swapping in the E Street Band; Springsteen was first to go down. His instant obsession with 'another fire-eater' may have been, as a hand says, 'sad'. It was also very much on the cards. Hyser's attraction, for Springsteen, his mind no longer hemmed in by the gulag of Asbury, was obvious – 'brains *and* boobs', a wit puts it. They lived together in Holmdel for the first part of 1979. By Easter, Springsteen was back in the studio (this time, Manhattan's Power Station), leaving Hyser to her own desires.

Almost all the songs on *Darkness*, not to say his narrative raps, had shown Springsteen's compassion for the bewildered souls of the 1970s. Yet Hyser, along with the musicians, tape-ops and gofers at the Station, learned something about him his fans didn't know. Like most *engagé* rockers, Springsteen had, they felt, more time for humanity than for humans. When not actively working, he rarely or never kept up with the group. A man who met him at home found him 'not easy to warm to . . . kind of skittish and fidgety even around Joyce'. It's true that literally thousands of fans and well-wishers would speak of Springsteen's innate charm and charisma.

They were right to. But if anyone leaned on him as an emotional prop, they made a gaffe. What Hyser and the rest really got wasn't friendship, but friendliness.

'I don't run around too much . . . I kinda keep to myself. You know, if you grow up in a slum, you just want it like that. You don't show, like [any] emotion.' So Springsteen said in 1975; and the complex self-lure had only grown four years later. Lack of an internal hitching-post was clearly a major factor in driving the young Bruce out on his quest for a viable alternative – for light in a shady world – a trek which took him first into song and then words. That slog had begun in 1958. Twenty years on, Springsteen could still tell a bandmate, 'I love crowds from their faces, but there's like a wall between us – I feel so alone, I can hardly keep from yelling out, I'm a guy, just like you.' It was no idle boast. Springsteen's 'loneliness at the top' was very real. He still lived a few miles from where he grew up. There was some cash on hand, two or three longtime allies, and, says one of them, 'shit in the way of friends'. Apart from Hyser, Springsteen's only other adult relationship was with Landau. He met the band's allegiance with affection. By the late seventies he was keeping an edgy truce with his parents (Adele had made an onstage cameo at Madison Square Garden); still strolled down the Asbury boardwalk; and knew scores of people to wave at. Beyond that, Springsteen had what he called a 'dark pit'. He told a colleague he'd dreamed of a mix of 'party and arty' companionship with Goldsmith, but got only the latter. Another four years' graft since *Born* had served to deepen the isolation under the carefully sheer façade. The photographer Joel Bernstein spent a week living with Springsteen in 1979. 'He'd pad around, affable and low-key, kind of mumbling over a bowl of Cheerios or maybe slugging a beer.' There was a band room with a clock, a TV and a few framed food labels on the wall; but, says Bernstein, 'not much of a human touch'.

Work, which over the years had become habit, brought its reward. Springsteen was making money for the first time in his life. Mike Tannen had renegotiated a basic dollar-an-album royalty for his client; *Darkness*, hitting number five, sold over 700,000 straight off. Live fees pushed Springsteen's gross income into seven figures. (He still had just $20,000 in the bank.) Yet the cash wasn't the chief reason he flogged himself on the road. When a man plays 118 consecutive gigs in thirty-seven states – sweating off five pounds a night – it's apt to be because he wants to, not from some grudging duty. What's more, after a week or two off, Springsteen would be trawling Asbury for more. That spring, he guested with the band Beaver Brown; duetted with Robert Gordon; and turned Marc Brickman's wedding into an *ad hoc* rave. Then he went back to the Power Station. Slowly, the picture of a driving and driven workaholic emerges from his stage–studio cycle in the seventies. As always, he felt emotionally more secure with a guitar in his hands. All the tours and myriad retakes were in the service of great music; but they were also a Siegfried Line against the pit. 'I eat loneliness' may have been over the top, but there's no doubt Springsteen worked to keep the rest of life, and the world, at bay. For someone who buffed his lyrics through twenty drafts, his few love letters were sadly underwritten.

Springsteen's evolving character, his wry self-effacement, spiritual apathy ('Puts on a good show, don't he?' he said of the Pope's visit to New York) and warm, bluff pragmatism tended to mask what went on under the skin. To his mates he was, simply, the Boss. Most speak of Springsteen's phenomenal charm, his *savoir-vivre*, his managerial skills, even that unusual thing, his niceness. As Weinberg says, 'With Bruce, what you see is what you get. There isn't some public image out there. I've known him for [twenty-five] years, and he's exactly the same way now.' According to this reading, Springsteen was an artist who took his craft – but not his fame – seriously. 'His price rose, but nothing else,' says Grice. It was never a question of him sitting slack-jawed while minions wheeled in drugs and comics. But, kicking thirty, Springsteen was both man and child, never patronizing his eleven- and twelve-year-old fans, even when talk turned to music. He admitted he 'dug Abba' to one pre-teen neighbour. A man named Kenny Pentifallo recalls Springsteen gleefully letting rip at a local coconut-shy to win a stuffed lion for his son. Another Jerseyan, Brian Pringle, saw his hero loping down the boardwalk one day that summer. He was 'sweet – warm, real and totally tuned in' to Pringle's two young cousins. Yet Springsteen could also hold his own in a roomful of lawyers or cutting deals with CBS. His key view of himself was of a man on the move. It was an important part of Springsteen's self-image that he never wanted to be like Doug, with whom he shared a name but not a sense of mute despair. 'Some guys they just give up living/And start dying little by little, piece by piece/Some guys come home from work and wash up/And go racin' in the street', he'd sung on *Darkness*. That said it.

Springsteen's childhood division of the world into the white of good and black of evil, with nothing between, gradually broke down with maturity's sly compromises. He could – and did – still maul those he felt failed him and his code: Appel; the odd fan-with-firework; and bootleggers. That summer, he was cutting songs like 'Under The Gun', 'Loose Ends' and 'Be True', eked out while others tossed off their own under-the-counter 'shit'. It was too much. In August 1979, Springsteen issued writs in Los Angeles against five defendants – a woman named Andrea Waters and four shops – claiming a total of $1.75 million damages for copyright infringement. A second, parallel action began in November. Springsteen (who'd been known to kick off shows by yelling 'Bootleggers, roll 'em!') eventually dropped, or settled, most of the suits. But they did nothing for his good mood. Earlier in the spring, he'd fallen off his dune bike and, in an eerie replay of 1967, torn a leg. He was laid up for a month. This time round, instead of fighting with Doug, he rowed with Hyser. Springsteen always seemed able to test and break affairs on points of principle. He made melo-drama of his lovers' every lapse, pumping them into grand, operatic treachery. Already, by mid-1979, there were growing signs that Hyser, too, would join Darvin, Goldsmith and the rest. That Springsteen was reviewing his core relationship to the world was heard in a quote, using his stock metaphor, he gave the BBC's *Glory Days*. 'I thought, maybe I was the guy . . . I get to go down the high-way. You're scootin' down there, it's great, you feel good. An' then you realize there's not a lot of other traffic on the road, the cars passin' you have those real dark tinted windows, and you won't see in them too much; and you realize it just adds up to a big, "So?"'

Springsteen, in short, became the latest and not last of a long line of rockers to hit their starting marks, then ask '*Now* what?'

He did, still, enjoy a varied social life to break up the litany of fame. The ripe earthiness of Springsteen's music – 'Dollhouse' had more true drama in the rip than even 'Darkness' – was matched by a sex drive that went his own way, usually to good effect. As well as the critical Valentine's cards, he got plenty of the other sort. It was between keeping home with Hyser and his first wife that Springsteen met Joyce Moore, a Monmouth College senior. A mutual friend called George McDonald recalls how this unmodified, pre-Aids tryst ended, all too literally, in tears.

'Joyce, as it happened, was also seeing a guy, Jim Cobanis. He had a date to meet her on campus. When she didn't show, he took off to the local bar. Sure enough, there was Joyce slumped with the Boss . . . All hell bust loose.' Springsteen duly came out of it with a black eye (small ocular beer next to Moore, who was nearly blinded in an auto wreck straight after the row). A second man, Don Vogler, also remembers 'Bruce charm[ing] a few co-eds out of their jeans around '79 to '80'. In the tight Jersey communities, full of sharp eyes and tongues, gossip – most less sourced than the above – regularly went round. Some of the wilder tales of Springsteen's libido are in the realm of myth, since detailed accounts of sleaze – in one case his having bedded a local teen and her mother – are given without attribution, but Grice's view is that 'he started pumping iron not as a health fad, but because of having the crap kicked out of him by Jim'. Seventeen years on, from the far side of domesticity, Springsteen would tell *The Times*, 'I've had one relationship – several women, but always the same relationship.' His passive-aggressive, anarchic sex life contained few insights until his marriage in 1985. Meantime, Springsteen was kept on the true path of righteousness not by any moral code, but the gym.

He was on hand that June to celebrate Marc Brickman's wedding to the band's travel agent, June Rudley. Springsteen played full-bore versions of 'Thunder Road' and 'Fire' at the reception. More to the point, the service began a slow revolution in his policy on 'the drop'. Introducing the songs 'Two Hearts' or 'Stolen Car', Springsteen often dwelt on long, if mind-numbingly trite synopses of the Brickmans' rabbi. 'When you're alone, without anybody, your dreams and fantasies are all you've got, and when you get married, when you meet someone, that's the first step toward making those dreams and hopes a reality'; all unexceptional. To Springsteen, though, this homily was 'hot poop'. Both on the lyrics and in private, he now came down heavily in favour of wedlock. His main qualifications were that living together was in some cases better; and that he, for one, needed 'space'. He used to say that he didn't make married music. But by late 1979, weddings, divorces and the pram in the hall all featured in the new songs he cut at the Station.

The dual motives with which a man who did some of the deepest public thinking since Dylan 'rooted himself silly' illustrate, more than most Springsteen sagas, not so much the twain as the twin sides of his life. The serial seducer had a respect for monogamy that could bring a wry 'I envy you' to Brickman. One of Springsteen's lovers says that if fans thought he was the nearest one could get to being a saint, 'he was fucking close to being Satan', too. The parts made the whole man. At thirty, he was clearly someone trying to raise his emotional game. Meanwhile, for five years the 'fresh tail' kept coming.

Aside from Hyser, there were literally dozens of women who filled out the time between gigs. As well as the ones who stuffed lingerie or love notes in his pants, there was, says Todd, 'a second kind of chick' whose strongest motive, after lust, was ambition. By mid-1979, 'Born To Run' had been officially adopted as New Jersey's rock anthem; Springsteen himself narrowly avoided being voted the state's 'youth ambassador'. Jimmy Carter quoted him in the White House. Democratic uniformity, plus his own talent, meant his fame was being standardized. The girls who offered sex, even 'love', for a possessive grip on his arm were after – as Kern herself says – power. What made it more intoxicating was that Springsteen responded not slavishly, but with winning cool. ('You doing me till

we're both the same colour?' he asked of one dusky groupie.)
Slowly, like the tide coming in, the one-nighters crept on to affairs
and relationships. For Springsteen, marriage was only the chronological, logical next step.

Five years before, Darvin had used to grin at her lover's nasal
Jersey slang. She may have been, as she said, 'no head doctor', but
she possessed a certain earthy wit. Publicly, Darvin always laughed
along when Springsteen lapsed into his 'demz' and 'doz' argot.
Privately, she bridled.

Even a band member, in those bygone days, furtively nicknamed
him Fog. Springsteen hardly ever seemed to have read a book
except ones on rock. He had scant feeling for words and cheerfully
preferred doggerel to verse. His lyrics had a certain street-smart
charm, but even they stuck squarely to a Jersey mentality.
Springsteen, co-tutored by Landau and Goldsmith (and buffed up
by the lawyers), hit creative maturity over the next three years. For
him, the gap between *Born* and *Darkness* was the Iron Curtain
between twenty-five and twenty-eight. Now, with the new album,
Springsteen meant to plunge into the thirties, dragging a still
mewling genre with him. *The River*, as it became, marked the first
time he and Landau fully staked out their mutual turf. The exact
boundaries weren't fixed, but several thematic claims were there to
be jumped. Springsteen would tell Brickman the latter's wedding
featured 'in about half the tunes' on *The River*; significantly, the
back cover showed a collage of a cardboard cut-out bride and
groom in front of a flag. Into the camp, meantime, came Senator
Bill Bradley, ex-Rhodes Scholar and NBA star, once and future
presidential hope. His arrival at the Power Station was another
milestone down the road to Springsteen's annexation by pols of all
hues, one that reached its apotheosis in, aptly, 1984. But the spec-
tre riding pillion – the 'big mo' – in all the best songs was neither
faction nor family. It was organic. By the time he wrote *The River*,
Springsteen made a distinction between mere invention and creation. He wanted the songs to have fully formed 'plots, fates and
all', like the old films he hoovered up at Holmdel. 'Part of the
thing is that when I write [a track], I write it to be the movie – not

to *make* a movie, to *be* one.' By mid-1979, Springsteen's newly cinematic eye was trained on dozens of lyrics. 'The Ties That Bind',* 'Point Blank' and 'Mary Lou' all emerged as willed, well-turned vignettes. As a writer, Springsteen now had both art and craft. His credo became increasingly utilitarian, striking out at social ills and the spectacle, as he saw it, of a society atomizing into 'shit'; yet still, for the most part, joyous and life-affirming. (Musically , too, the LP covered all bets between Fred Rose and the Raspberries.) 'I think most great songs do [that] – say, "Hey, take this and find your place in the world" . . . It's a pretty wonderful thing for a record to do.'

The River sessions began on 4 April 1979. After a month off convalescing, Springsteen dug in again in mid-May. As usual, there was plenty, even too much material. One of the band recalls 'Bruce coming in most afternoons with a new first draft . . . It was like painting the fucking George Washington Bridge. You get one cut down, and . . . *hel*-lo, another's up.' Digs, for once, weren't a problem. Through choice or need, Springsteen had tended to work in low-slung rooms like 914 or the CBS studio in Manhattan. Even the Record Plant could evoke, and often did, the marquee-jam of a sold-out dive. The Station held no such terrors. Anyone entering the converted church on West 53rd Street was met with soaring, steeply angled ceilings in a neat ecclesiastical touch. The acoustics revealed themselves, to the connoisseurs of such matters, as 'true'. There were no dead spots. Springsteen settled in there for a year.

All the first four albums had taken a handful of chords and flayed them into the most striking music of their day. The trouble was that Springsteen the writer was anti-climactic compared to the wild, atavistic trouper. In some ways the whole point of *Darkness* was its ordinariness. Laudable as that was, a general beef was that the albums were too slow coming, and paled next to the gigs. Critics were divided on whether they were deep or merely 'difficult'; a multiplying version, like Russian dolls, of the same idea, or exercising a wilful negative vibe. ('Factory', for one, was either

---

*Then the album's working title, first heard in November 1978.

suggestively slow-moving or – as *Sounds* said – 'fuckin' boring'.)
Navvying in places named Plant and Station (and, later, Factory)
was neat symbolism. It was also useful shorthand, and there was
real graft to Springsteen's art. Anyone thinking he was just an
ungilded prodigy, cranking out hits-in-waiting live in the studio,
should have seen him, slumped at the desk, minutely deconstructing ten, twenty or thirty mixes of a three-minute song. Peter
Philbin would tell Fred Goodman of listening to seventeen separate takes of one track. 'I'm sitting there thinking, "What is this?"
And then Bruce goes, "Now which one is better?" *Which one is
better?* Flip a coin!' One of the band calls it 'a third playing, a third
listening and a third plain BS-ing'.

Even so, Springsteen kept his commitment to go flat out for
anyone he liked. He was 'just a king' to Chuck Plotkin, a friend of
Landau's co-opted to mix *The River*. Above all, during that long,
ultra-stressed year, there was what one source calls the 'manic
democracy' of his work and another likens to a lift's ability to come
to any level. Springsteen never talked down to musicians. Weinberg
nominates him as 'the most patient guy I've met'. Early on at the
Power Station, Springsteen took his drummer aside and told him
he 'wasn't cutting it'. Interminable, solo sessions with a metronome
finally paid off. But Springsteen's loyalty never wavered. 'That's
what I mean about patience,' says Weinberg. 'He could have got
someone else. But he gave me time to find myself.' It was the same
after hours, when Clemons and Federici were prone to party till
dawn. Springsteen never joined in; but he 'didn't lower the
boom . . . provided you stayed clean and showed up on time'. As a
co-worker, son had much the same traits as father – both Doug and
Bruce, in all their rigidity, were 'hard but fair'.

Bill Bradley, for one, relates it back to the 'smoke-filled room of
a political think-tank . . . It was "Let's do it this way, that way" . . .
Very measured, very nuanced, like something out of a Tammany
Hall bull session.' Joel Bernstein also sat in at the studio. 'The
band all loosened up by vamping history-of-rock hits. Then Bruce
strapped on an acoustic and went through the basic riff. Roy Bittan
scored it. Next the drums and bass, and last the whole group came

in. But everyone was tired and in the end they only hit it twenty times that night.'

What Bernstein heard was the LP's title tune, one of the best songs Springsteen wrote. 'The River' closed the first half of the year-long saga. All in all 'about ninety' tracks would be variously hummed, sung, rehearsed or recorded. The total bill came to $500,000. CBS's Walter Yetnikoff duly 'went bazootie' when he got it. But Springsteen stayed resolutely above sordidly commercial concerns like budgets. 'The release date's just one day,' he said. 'The album's for keeps.' It was funny, and had the added bonus of being true.

The MUSE gala that September had its origins in a bid to 'do something' about nuclear power. It was the irony of the cause that it stood far ahead of public opinion, fighting to order all kinds of plant closures, only to see counter-forces barge in from the right – the pro-job wing. Particularly around Jersey, much of MUSE's logic was lost on the voters. Relatively few, and certainly not the thousands of families working in the field, bought into it. No Nukes began when rock had one of its cyclical bouts of morality, a fit of conscience. Things gathered pace after the near-meltdown that spring at Three Mile Island (less than eighty miles, by chance, from Holmdel). Jackson Browne, fresh from localized blitzes to save the parks, the trees and the whales, duly signed up a drab-if-worthy tribe of west coast rockers of the likes of Crosby, Stills & Nash and the Doobies. But it was Springsteen, attracting mass awe, not just admiration, who was most use to the cause. Browne and the promoter Tom Campbell began lobbying in June. By July, Landau had hammered out the logistics of ticket prices, a mooted live LP and film. Springsteen's panjandrum, armed at all points and logically unstoppable, single-handedly turned the gigs from a post-hippie orgy into a five-night stand where every step and nuance was glossed to the last note. One result was that No Nukes was *the* rock-music event of 1979, if never quite living up to its hype of 'Woodstock 2'. Another was that Springsteen wrote one of his best songs, the alternately obsessive and depressive 'Roulette'.

Amid the anaemic, soft-rock bias of CSN, Browne and James

Taylor, Springsteen stole the last two shows. His set, a weird amalgam of old ('Rosalita') and new ('The River') – if no 'Roulette' – welded traditional, fist-pumping pop with revolutionary sound effects. Powerful but polished, the songs had as much to do with state-of-the-art mixing as with graspable tunes and Springsteen's dread of synthesized clones. The encore, Gary Bonds' 'Quarter To Three', was at once raw, human, android-precise, witty and real. After five minutes' ovation, an MC appeared to urge everyone to go quietly, but there was no problem – most of the 20,000 fans were in a daze. 'It was a Springsteen crowd,' wrote John Rockwell. 'One got the impression the other performers and perhaps even the nuke issue itself were barely being tolerated', something confirmed by the graffiti daubed backstage: BOSS WALKS ON WATER WE SINK. Overnight the last two words were rubbed out by an unknown staffer who still agreed with the main thesis.

More remarkable, as well as more poignant, was the row which boiled over next night between Springsteen and Lynn Goldsmith. It was his thirtieth birthday. Here some disparity exists between his take ('She was doin' something she said she wouldn't') and hers (Goldsmith swore she'd only agreed not to shoot from backstage, not ten rows back). Though few openly said it, a number of Springsteen's court were shocked, as unable to doubt the hot fire of their old friend's rage as they were to explain it. In fact, the whole squabble had its origins in the pre-show summit. Springsteen had done his best to hint that Goldsmith stay away. She stood her ground as he stood his; and the exact definition of 'Don't dick with me' was never settled. What's certain is that Goldsmith, of all people, didn't need 'unauthorized' shots of her ex (she already had him posing in the shower); and that despite, she says, being 'frozen out' by Landau and blacklisted by CBS, she never seriously considered suing. She might have had a pretty good case. As Springsteen dragged her onstage, the floor of the Garden was shaking, fans surging up from their seats and cooing Br-*ooose* from the rafters. It was like a collective orgasm. Joel Bernstein, also taking photos, had 'never heard or seen anything like it . . . the place was literally bouncing on its axis'. Amid the din, something like the noise in a shambles, Springsteen's hissed aside carried a lethal chill:

'We're *done*, babe.'

Most of the music of No Nukes was gravely beautiful. Springsteen apart, its pace was dreamily slow, its mood sublimely sober. Neither of those qualities, however, vouched for the triple album or the film. They bombed. Concerts with a cause are always, or usually, hard to package – as George Harrison had found. In the end, MUSE raised only $300,000, less than half the hoped-for profit. It remains debatable whether it did any lasting good toward a non-nuclear future. But it worked wonders for certain bedraggled, California rockers, thin smiles plastered over their ruined features. With the Doobies, for one, the lasting impression was of fey, reclusive souls, scrupulously ecological, organic, rural, who found themselves co-hosting a binge in New York; an ordeal for which the band were rewarded by seeing sales of *Minute by Minute* treble in the month following the gigs.

For Springsteen, MUSE brought almost royal fame. Until then, isolated with relatively few, if fanatical disciples, he'd used his often impoverished leisure to indulge his gift to the core. After 1979, he broke through to the 'great average'. People who'd never heard of Browne or the Doobies knew full well about the Boss; partly because Landau planted him squarely centre stage; partly because he now added a second brand – Events – to the portfolio, all the while carefully nursing the flagship label. As Dave Marsh wrote, 'MUSE placed Springsteen firmly and permanently in the pantheon of American superstars.' It also nearly landed him in court. Goldsmith, said the *New York Post*, and she denies, wanted to sue for $3 million. The threat passed, but, making every allowance due, there was something odd about Springsteen's pledge 'never [to] put someone in the position of being humiliated'. The intended note of fellow-feeling rang false. A number of fans and fellow stars at MUSE, notably Meat Loaf, used the word 'jerk' to describe him. For Springsteen, of course, the impersonal joys of rock were inextricably twined up with personal concepts of loyalty and trust. These Goldsmith broke. Still, it was a bad scene.

Perhaps the most immediate – and long-term – effect of MUSE's near-pandemic good vibes was, though, neither more deification nor 'shit'. It was artistic. Admitting the whole event had made his album-in-progress seem 'sick', Springsteen ordered the band back into the studio. (Final mixing of the Clash's *London Calling* was duly shunted across town.) The original plan had called for four months' work on *The River*. By late 1979 there were growing signs that, yet again, CBS's due-date was too tight. Sessions finally wrapped in August 1980, when the label curtly took possession from Springsteen, who found it hard, even then, to let go. Over sixteen months, he'd put in 170 days' work, typically from 7 p.m. to 6 a.m.: 1,870 hours. The album, on first release, made him $1.7 million. Having begun in spring 1979 and ended in late summer 1980, Springsteen earned $909 per hour, $24,285 a week, or (for purposes of comparison) $1,262,857 per annum – seventy times more than the average blue-collar worker. It was a lot of cash, though, cumulatively, Springsteen lagged far behind the Rods or Eltons. To his credit, he still lived well within his means. Instead of rock-star staples like drugs or jets, Springsteen only splurged, if then, on a Camaro or Harley. He was a generous boss and, says Grice, 'tabbed' several old friends around Freehold. Springsteen also found ways of subtly probing the reaction to an offer of help. 'Bruce never made you feel bad . . . He had a sense that he was lucky. Always approached things with a kind of let-me-give-something-back attitude. I dug that.'

As well as the healthy ASCAP flow, Springsteen won an array of glittering prizes and, all in all, more gold than Bruce Jenner. In *Rolling Stone*, he'd again pick up Artist of the Year, Best Album, Best Single, Best Vocalist and Best Songwriter awards in 1980. Landau was top producer. In Britain, where his star was at warp strength – even pulsar – Springsteen figured in heavyweight raves by *The Times* and *Guardian*. Roger Scott, and others, kept him in heavy rotation.

Dave Marsh, meanwhile, chose the moment to publish *Born to Run: The Bruce Springsteen Story*. Leaving aside the hagiographical spin, infinite regress and stark contradictions of the book – a marker down the way of both their careers – there was a sub-text at work: or at least a fatty degeneration into hero love. Marsh, of course, had long been 'practically family' (his wife became Landau's key assistant). For an author, especially, that kind of access can cut either way; as can an obsessive eye on statistical niceties. (Marsh also wrote *The Book of Rock Lists*.) At least, though, it had the slant of someone who'd known Springsteen for years. Elsewhere, scissors-and-paste merchants who never met him – as few had – could be heard talking in his voice, and critics who could barely spell his name screwed up their noses at things which had a bad smell for him. He was the star of editorial brainstorms and debates, leaders in trades and front-page reactions in some of the top titles in North America. If Yetnikoff had gone 'bazootie' for his own reasons, so, too, did the media for theirs. It was one of Springsteen's journalistic buffs who coined the term 'high concept', the gist of an album expressed in a couple of emotive words. *The River*, for example, was 'Chuck Berry for the eighties'.

In fact, Springsteen's slavish copyists did him no good. With a few notable exceptions, he was infinitely better than his press. A visitor to the Power Station remembers him 'standing there, towering physically and symbolically over all the hangers-on and toadies', a kind of rock in a 'seething, bubbling swamp of white-suited spivs'. Bill Bradley speaks of the 'quiet command' of Springsteen's presence. In a trade bloated with vulnerable limelight addicts, flitting between ecstatic fame and private clinics, he was a self-possessed, sane, if limited Jerseyan: the one who'd grown but not swelled. To *Melody Maker*, Springsteen came over as a 'courteous enthusiast . . . anti-drugs, a non-drinking, non-smoking rock 'n' roller'. Graham Parker happened to meet him in the Navarro hotel, New York, one night that spring. 'Landau was sitting down in the lobby at 4 a.m., just checking it out . . . we got talking.' As a third party adds, 'Jon said Bruce was wiped out, kaput – doing twelve-hour days at the studio. We BS'd, then Springsteen came up and asked how Graham was. "Knackered," he said. "Just barely making an album." Bruce immediately laughed. "Can I help?"' The result, brokered by Iovine, was two tracks on Parker's *The Up Escalator*. This same

casual gift-giving provided scores of songs, not least Warren
Zevon's 'Jeannie Needs A Shooter'; there were more. Springsteen,
almost always, was the pros' pro. Whether rescuing careers, bailing
out friends or meticulously giving credit to anyone who caught his
ear, he was the one other rockers revered. Among the new fans
Springsteen made in 1980–81 were Clapton, Page and Townshend,
three men who knew all it was possible to know about fame, yet
whose misconceived disdain of lesser mortals like Parker gave way
to unstinting raves for *The River*. Bowie had long deemed this
pedlar of ravishing tunes like 'Growin' Up' worthy of, as he says,
'the gods'. Even Lennon, in the last days of his life, 'dug the Boss'.

The B-side of his undoubted passion was a dogged perfectionism
that, around the twentieth take, could pall. It wasn't a modest ambition: Springsteen flaunted it; and though it was always in the service
of the song, it's not illogical to say he risked it helping his career –
specifically, by a hit single; Lynn Goldsmith reports him as 'seriously pissed' when the Pointer Sisters, not he, scored with 'Fire'.
He was rabidly focused in the studio. Reviewing *The Wild* in *The
Real Paper*, Landau (yet to see 'rock and roll future') had once urged
Springsteen to 'just throw some hot ones on the vinyl'. Six years
later, one of the band on *The River* would warm up the culinary fare
by calling it 'oven-baked, not nuked'. First Springsteen went back
to the Power Station with more songs. CBS ponied up the overrun
costs. Aside from the actual cutting, the sessions eventually lapsed
into all-night polemics on mixing: Springsteen would spend hours
ranged over the board to find the right drone or toot for each
track, while Landau dozed in the corner. There were the usual
agonies over sequencing. Finally, as with *Darkness*, production
bogged down at the artwork stage. 'Shit-shooting and ass-sitting'
was one wag's view of the process. It was all a long way from the
sweetly grainy, take-one tradition of Springsteen's heroes.

From artistic growth, Springsteen moved both forwards and
back to classically American populism. He wasn't overtly political.
Marsh, among others, took the quixotically radical view that rockers were the marching bands of the revolution. Yet Springsteen's
partisanship didn't cut that deep. He'd voted once in his life. To

him, socialism lay in ten million *de facto* covenants between friends, family or either side of the industrial divide. 'It's the whole thing,' he said in 1980. 'It's terrible, it's horrible. Somewhere along the way, the idea, which I think initially was to get some fair transaction going, went out the window. And what came in was: the most you can get. The most you can get and the least you can give.' It wasn't a party-political point, but a sad variation on the Spenglerian one of moral decay. In the late seventies, Springsteen liked to visit his sister Ginny and her husband. Their fun-free lives, held in check by the grip of deep debt, struck him as symbolic of 'the type of things people do that make them heroic . . . small, little things that happen in the kitchen, or between a man and wife, or between them and their kids'. He worked the theme into *The River*. The complex and deadly pressures bearing on society was Springsteen's text, not 'big picture' activism. Haste and superficiality – both of which he tossed in the studio – were the twin evils of 'your and my America'. In a left-leaning industry, he saw his mission as to offer the best music, thought and 'real hope' to the people. He was a community worker.

Springsteen did, in time, proceed to a familiar litany of Republican ills. 'I'm not sure what you think about last night [when Reagan was elected], but I think it's pretty terrifying,' he said in November 1980, the same month he read Joe Klein's biography of Woody Guthrie. For the next four years, Springsteen would identify numerous breakdowns of the notion of government serving the people. He chafed once or twice, in private, at 'the gipper'. In 1984, Reagan himself stooped to the tactical gaffe of basking in Springsteen's fame, winning the well-earned rebuke: 'the President was mentioning my name the other day, and I kinda got to wondering what his favourite album must be'. He neatly backed off from the taint-by-association. Nor, however, did Springsteen jump on the Democratic bandwagon. A year or two later, his music took a conscious tack back towards emotional, not civic, traumas. Springsteen wasn't ideological. Rather, he was romantically wed to certain personal views that weren't necessarily owned by left or right. Again, in his faith in Lincolnian values of graft, family and fair play, he was, if anything, a 'good Tory'.

Meantime, Landau and the rest were busy banning from their man, and thus his thinking, most of those who'd historically been his mortar. Unless you worked with him as a musician or roadie, you didn't get to meet Springsteen, let alone talk to him. He was either in the studio, on a plane, or sealed in a twenty-four hour hermetic pod on the road. Off hours, he'd stay in Boss Acres or holed up at the Navarro; a life, he'd later tell *Rolling Stone*, 'centred too much on [his] music'. Springsteen, in short, no longer experienced 'your and my America' outside a loyal but narrow clique. The result was that his causes, at this stage, were too often theirs. Springsteen may well have done No Nukes as an act of charity, or good citizenship. What's more, one of the organizers, Danny Goldberg, told Marc Eliot, 'Bruce was very concerned there be a political message in the film, which was a happy revelation to me. It hadn't been clear exactly how into the politics of the show he was, but as it turned out, he was extremely so. He didn't want this just to be a concert.' In practice, that meant Springsteen debating whether or not 'Quarter To Three' was due illustration of the gigs' protest; plus editing the Mitch Ryder medley on the LP. In fact, by corralling their friend into pet political playpens, men like Browne may have scared up less radical zeal than would have come untutored. One witness adds that 'pantomime stalked the scene' as Springsteen was first 'agonizingly' talked through the shows' manifesto. Tellingly, he was the only MUSE artist not to sign the no-nuke pledge in the programme.

In later years, of course, the set-piece galas were merely the scaffolding. Springsteen's major focus, outside the proprietary albums and tours, was main-street issues like jobs and family. Norman Mailer, on this point, calls him the 'Everyman rocker'; Bill Bradley, 'a modern Walt Whitman'. At their best, Springsteen's inspired riffs throbbed with the heady rhetoric of Utopianism, quiet and nervous in most cases, yet buoyed by their moral thunder and lightning. The gibe that he 'knew nothing and cared less' beyond a half-dozen cherry-picked fetishes – that he 'thought foreign policy was his LPs' British sales strategy' – was a vile obloquy. He certainly cared. But, *pace* those who'd co-opted him, Springsteen's causes were invariably backed from a stance of personal, gut fealty, not in thrall to any agenda. On most points of principle, he was loyal to his art, as genius is meant to be. Springsteen was always or mostly amenable to those who stirred the generational drama of his youth: provided they got through. He'd already bought and read a copy of Ron Kovic's *Born on the Fourth of July*. Then, by chance, he actually met the author staying at the same Los Angeles motel. From there it was a short step to the Vietnam Veterans of America. This particular band may have touched the nerve of his having 'scammed' the draft. Or it might have spoken to a life – as he admitted – eking away into death, obsession, egoism and trivia. Springsteen, in short, wanted to 'do something'. When the vets gave him a signed helmet and lined up for his autograph, he duly launched a brilliant strategic retreat towards a policy of duty. One result was an August 1981 benefit which raised over $100,000. Springsteen struck a rich, key note in his speech ushering the VVA's Bob Muller onstage. 'It's like when you're walking down a dark street at night, and out of the corner of your eye you see somebody getting hurt in a dark alley. But you keep walking because you think it don't have nothing to do with you . . . Vietnam turned the whole country into that dark street, and unless we walk down those dark alleys and look into the eyes of those men and women, we're never gonna get home.' The parabolic echo rang out. Springsteen wanted to see America live up to the Good Samaritan's ideals.

The newfangled *artiste engagé* was one thing. Many fans, notably the young, female ones, were more interested in Springsteen's burgeoning career as a sex god. And rightly so: for better or worse, it was half his appeal.* For all his artistic upswing since *Born*, Springsteen looked younger than then: too callow ever to grow a beard. At thirty, he was lean, clean-cut, with a cloud of curly, yet trim hair. For a spell in the early eighties he toyed with Dickensian sideburns. Springsteen's bristling hank struck some as a clichéd shorthand of blue-collar *mores*. To others the stubble was part of his compassionate, humane vision of street-level solidarity. Either

---

*As he still says today: 'Get their asses moving and their spirit will follow.'

way, Springsteen hit the new decade with serious – if serio-comic – broadsheet types unable to agree on his facial hair.

It was an instructive debate, proving that for all the talk of Woody Guthrie and Hank Williams, the best way to arouse the hacks was still via the old rock erogenous zones: danceable beats and a randy show. There was a gag in the second MUSE concert where Hyser, dressed gigglesomely as a nurse, dragged Springsteen offstage. The 'macho Boss' *shtick* also met with a full range of gay hamboning. In terms of high camp, Springsteen's live act was alpine. He was known to soul-kiss Clemons and bat his eyes, interminably, at Van Zandt. A number of the fans who joined him to jitter through 'Rosalita' and the rest were, oddly enough, male. He didn't, though, as some thought, use up his erotic life onstage. Nor in the studio. ('I get into the routine of fucking my album,' he said.) In adulthood, Springsteen's ideal mental and sexual level stayed that of a teen voyeur; or, as an ex gnomically says, 'Bruce didn't like champagne. Loved champagne bottles.'

On that final MUSE show, when he hit what he called the 'wall', Springsteen was faced head-on with a dilemma he couldn't sidestep. Was he or wasn't he still a frat-house rocker? Or, more tritely, *had* he been born to run? The answer found Springsteen caught between poles, chewing up hoary pop chestnuts and stirring them into his *sui generis* witches' brew. *The River*, his first LP from the far side of thirty, was also his most schizoid. 'Chuck Berry for the eighties' hardly began to say it. Among the roll-call of merely musical models were Johnny Cash, old gods like Elvis and Dylan, and modern rock on parade: the New York Dolls rang through on at least two tracks. The result was a farrago of R&B, C&W, rockabilly, pop, folk, soul and the kind of manic, black-and-white sixties shout-outs that served as a throughline. Thematically, too, *The River*'s metaphor ran wide, if not always deep: from the Bible, via Mark Twain, Thomas Wolfe and Theodore Dreiser to the sort of *auteurs* who swashed Landau's buckle – Howard Hawks, Frank Capra and John Ford. That his manager's and other hands at once enriched and confused the work was in line with Springsteen's quote to the *LA Times*. 'Rock and roll has always been this joy . . . but it's also about hardness and coldness and being alone . . . I finally got to the place where I realized life had paradoxes, a lot of them, and you've got to live with them.' *The River* was a stream of such forks. The lyrics touched on everything from God to 'little dolly with the blue jeans on'; from his father to Kojak; with all in all, says Fred Goodman, 'more cars than the Indy 500'. Yet Springsteen's verbal perversities still fitted neatly into his pop. It worked.

One of the reasons was that *The River*, if meandering, was part of a full-fledged landscape. It balanced the joyous derangement of *Born* against the black heart of *Darkness*. A 'concept' was the dire word used by *Rolling Stone*; 'triptych' by *The Times*. It was neither of those, but *The River* did, nonetheless, round out a saga begun on 'Thunder Road'. The same Mary who wove across the porch to Roy Orbison was now a jaded, cash-strapped housewife: emblematic of a society facing Depression-era debt at home and cocked snooks abroad. Springsteen himself said of the album, 'It was about trying to get connected back with your relationships. It was the first one where people were married on it.' Most of the characters, like him, were adults, scrabbling for sense in a world where divorce was rampant, kids regularly toted deadlier guns than the police, and a third of all college graduates would go, long-term, on the dole. When you hit your thirties and the Eighties in the same breath, vestigial joy is bound to rub against experience.

Springsteen's legendary capacity to dwell on lowbrow, if not lowlife, pleasures was still a sub-plot. Burt Reynolds, 007 and the Batmobile all got name-checks. There was an old-fashioned, bubblegum single. But the story-line of *The River* was Springsteen's journey from reckless youth into brooding maturity. For years, he'd mostly been about the hips downward; now he was about eyelevel up. If there was a focal, core theme, it was the Springsteenian one of promise corrupted, of compromise:

Out on to an open road you ride until the day
You learn to sleep at night with the price you pay

In grasping the facts of middle age, just as the condition hit,

Springsteen not only mocked his Utopian self. He'd been naïve. In particular, the notion that there was unemployment, and that a bad marriage was as likely as any other kind, struck, for one, Bill Burroughs as 'two givens of not having been born yesterday'. Springsteen, though, had erred in good company. As even Burroughs said, 'most people are complete idiots until thirty, and partial ones thereafter'. What's more, seeking the consolation of human love wasn't the worst response to joining the real world. Most of *The River* was warm, if wry, proving that, to Springsteen, naturalism was akin to romanticism. Or, they differed as man and boy: idealism was the youth of realism and realism the idealist's dotage.

As for the music, Springsteen had been under heavy stress – the label's, and Landau's – to do an 'up' album. Any other rocker would have truckled to please, or drawn the line. Springsteen, while flaying Top 20 formulae, followed them to a T without selling or copping out. The result was a pristine, sixties mix, vocals layered lavishly on top, neatly invocatory keyboards and frog-in-a-storm sax somewhere behind, spliced by the rubbery weave of the rhythm. Though *The River* slipped in and out of type, the sheer bar-by-bar class of the writing was the glue that held together the hazy concept. The proof of it was that 'Roulette' and 'Be True', two potential hits, were left on the studio floor.

What remained was a hopscotch through pop styles. Springsteen's avian pastiches – of the Byrds and Eagles, respectively – opened and closed the album in a frame, but, in between, the music veered from barrel-house rock to sobering *mise en scènes* of death. 'Sherry Darling' and 'Out In The Street' cited and cannibalized, in turn, Graham Parker and Elvis Costello. The lyrical text for 'Two Hearts' was Ecclesiastes (biblically, a cousin of 'The Price You Pay'). Springsteen stretched out in the raunch-by-rote riffs of 'Crush On You' and 'I'm A Rocker'. *The River*'s title track slyly bolted an old Hank Williams chorus to utterly fresh, quicksilver bursts of piano and harp. 'I Fought The Law' and 'Little Queenie' were, similarly, the grid-points for 'You Can Look' and 'Ramrod'. Berry was again the star of the crunch-rock 'Cadillac

Ranch'. On 'Independence Day', Springsteen's acoustic strum and vocal added warmth and body, not to mention an Oedipal blast – all the better for being muttered – at Doug. The rest of *The River*, with one quirk, was an engaging flux of country and blues. 'Hungry Heart', with its four-bar phrase and trebly, latex mix – virtually channelling Frankie Lymon – brazenly harked back to the Wall. Audaciously commercial, singalong pop pitched somewhere between Buddy Holly and the Beach Boys, it was an exclamation without a point: gravy for CBS. It also gave Springsteen his first major hit.

As a document of his, and our, twenties, *The River* was astonishingly bold and equally vague. That was its strength. It was a synoptic LP, Springsteen's high-water mark to date. Everyone from Lennon (playing it non-stop the week he died) down admired the sixties lineages deftly blurred by Springsteen's Guthrie-via-Dylan dirges and ear for a hook. 'Hungry Heart' (heard on the film *Risky Business*) brought him a vast new following. A few made it a point of duty to slag. Julie Burchill, in *NME*, used the word 'bore'. *Time Out*'s Frances Lass asked, 'what *would* he have done if he'd failed his driving test?': as usual, car imagery abounded. Elsewhere, Springsteen's dial-spinning musicology and refusal to quarantine himself from life redoubled the global fame of *Born*. *The River* sold over two million copies. Its tunes obviously helped; as did PR, and the genuinely if unexpectedly romantic causes for which he sometimes did war. Lack of competition also played a part. If, in 1980, you liked amplified, boyish rock and social argument, Springsteen was your man. For all this and the juke-blues eclecticism of the playing, *The River* was a rip.

Live, it soon burst its banks. The tour that bowed in Ann Arbor on 3 October 1980 cared less for musical punctilio than for the entire CV of rock: part Harlem revue, part rival state-of-the-Union address, it crisscrossed America twice and slew most of Scandinavia and Europe; even the most jaded hacks basked in the London shows. Yet, instead of doing it big and glossy and sentimental, Springsteen kept the music stripped-down, taut and cathartic: there were exactly four rehearsals. (Even they took place in a barn in

rural Lititz, Pennsylvania.) Whether droning the minor chords of
'Independence Day' or haring through 'Promised Land', he was a
feral, power-aerobics workout for body and soul. Muscular pressure
from Landau and Barry Bell, Springsteen's booking czar, ensured
that not a single $12.50 seat went unsold. But, this time round, the
PR and hype were mere signposts in a people's crusade. Springsteen
had only to turn up and the house came down. It wasn't just that
anyone buying a ticket could look forward to a four-hour medley of
thirty years' musical fads; but also, says Parker, that 'Bruce *gave* a
shit'. As Bittan told *Rolling Stone*, 'He's older and wiser, but he
never strays from his basic values. He cares as much, *more*, about
the losers than the winners . . . He's so unlike everything you think
a real successful rock star would be.' In Denver, Springsteen happily went out for an evening at a fan's home. Three days later, in
Seattle, he showed up at the Old Timer's Café, paid the $1 cover,
ordered, then mildly asked the bar band, 'Can I play?' Gradually, as
the saturation trek wound through California, Springsteen would
find a way to work these, and similarly demotic yarns, into stage
raps. He had the uneasy task of holding such stories together with
nothing more than insecurity, but Springsteen's vast, startled guf-
faws of pride rang loud and true. Few dramatic 'swishes' compared
for variety.

At the shows' core lay the classic stage relationship between
loved and lovers. It was mutual. The lunatic ravings emanating
from other stages might have done for the brainwashed children of
punk, but to a hard core of America's thirteenth generation, they
were a sign that the time had come to look to their own futures.
First, after suffering all the romper-suit jingles of both new wave
and New Romantics, people flocked to Springsteen for fun. Shows
like his didn't exist just to entertain, but to absorb a minimum of
three hours' repressed frenzy; a coup against the whole orderly,
moneyed, respectable, banal reign of Sting and co. *The River* was a
neoconservative phenomenon, harking back to a simpler, white-
bread era, when guitars ruled, 'pop' was so rendered, and volume
dials were set to eleven. In return, Springsteen gave more than
laughs and a little learning. He gave himself. 'I always keep in my

mind that you only have one chance. Some guy bought his ticket, and there's a promise made between musician and audience . . . It's at the heart of everything.' Some time around 1980–81, Springsteen took over from James Brown as the 'hardest-working man in pop'. Those twenty-eight- and thirty-song sets were a fanfare of the genre's best tunes, new and old, from Guthrie's 'This Land Is Your Land' to Creedence's 'Who'll Stop the Rain?', Elvis to Sonny Curtis, Gary Bonds to the Beatles.

Such was demand, Springsteen could have sold out Madison Square Garden sixteen times. He settled for twice at Thanksgiving and again pre-Christmas. (The New York state attorney later investigated 'several hundred complaints' of ticket touting.) Half clown, half Charismatic, Springsteen opened on 'Born To Run' and ended, thirty-four songs later, in the Mitch Ryder medley. It was staggeringly full. And far-flung: put the whole thing together and you could hear the old Yankee gag to lost tourists, 'You can't get there from here.' His takes of 'Thunder Road' and 'The River', bringing their message to millions as they had to thousands, or one-on-one, would grace his *Video Anthology/1978–88*. Those New York shows were some of the most intimate, if not confessional, nostalgic, *ecstatic* concerts ever, utterly unique; yet, somehow, Springsteen repeated them, night after night, for twelve months on the road. As John Rockwell wrote, 'There are many things that make him the finest performer in rock . . . His themes may arise from the despair of working-class lives. Yet his ultimate message is affirmative, a vision of the promised land . . . and the way he proposes to reach it is through the joyous energy of rock 'n' roll.' He'd been the Boss. Now, *The Times* had it, he was a 'theme-park God'.

The designation was hard won. As Rockwell added, 'Springsteen has integrated his theatrics and lighting into the music better than ever.' In the *Globe*'s words, the 'cool insouciance' was in stark contrast to the 'hawk eye for detail'. That barely did justice to a set that was sound-checked and buffed for hours on end. Marc Brickman – whose spots and strobes would dazzlingly punch up the songs' riffs, fading again when languor called – was a vital, if unseen presence; so, too, Bruce Jackson at the mixing-board and Springsteen's roadie

Mike Batlan. Batlan carried his boss's $185 Fender Esquire every-
where – if he went in a bar, the guitar went with him. Above and
behind these three was a court led by Landau, Marsh, tour manager
George Travis and sundry thick-necked PAs, one of whom says: 'I
protected Bruce from himself . . . You know, he's got a big Italian
heart. He trusts everybody, and he doesn't see when he's being
screwed. And he'd never act on it, anyway. I did.' A man named
Nick would take on the day-to-day running of Springsteen's house.
The Fifth Avenue firm of Parcher, Arisohn & Hayes, still there
today, lent legal clout. The result were shows that not only rede-
fined what rock should look and sound like; their smooth running
gave Springsteen room to unwind. On tour, he still stuck to fried
chicken and burgers. He took commercial flights, rode in rented
cars, and stayed in the same one-star hotels as the band.
Springsteen only went to parties if they did. The back-up wasn't the
main reason he could afford to relax – that came from onstage – but
it helped.

Whether at showcases like New York, or less exotic shacks in the
heartland, Springsteen never let up. From the instant he reeled on
like a tuned-up version of John Wayne, the gigs seemed to go from
zero to sixty in ten seconds. Without the satin jackets or maquillage
of the 'hair farmer' bands (his one nod to glitz was his guitar strap,
studded like a horse brass), he drew his charge from within.
Springsteen was born to perform.* Not that the tour was all testos-
terone-crazed mayhem. Nearly every knees-up was in turn a set-up.
Thus, Springsteen would gently deflate 'Because The Night' with
the brooding 'Stolen Car' – or flog the audience from behind a
copy of *Short History of the United States*. It all worked, partly
because the band were so good, cocked for the cue, still rooted in
the soul-revue pranks of old. Van Zandt was self-styled
Obergruppenführer, the nexus between frontman and back line.
Under his helm, the E Streeters were ten cool hands and a hot rasp
of wind. Springsteen himself played from the gut. Though his

---

*Behind the scenes, he was auditioning for roles in remakes of *Breathless* and
The Wild One, as well as a film version of *The River*.

moves tended to be more brawny than balletic, evoking both the dogged locomotion of track and the soaring majesty of field, the proof was in the tape. He went from 150 to 130 pounds on tour, from a thirty-inch waist to twenty-six.

Much of it was musical mugging. In the course of a show, Springsteen would march, mince, strut, dance on the piano and flay the guitar – Batlan retuning it – all the while playing, singing and leading the crowd in mass shoutalongs. As 20,000 voices took over the intro of 'Hungry Heart', you had a rare glimpse of what it was like to sit in with the E Street Band. Springsteen never overpowered, still less ignored, the fans, even when his mind was elsewhere – dedicating 'Drive All Night' to Hyser, for one, or roughhousing with the boys. The male-bonding rites took two lines. There was Springsteen's cod homo-eroticism, whether necking with Clemons or goosing Van Zandt. On top of that came comic, not to say corny touches like him snapping a crutch or breaking free of a stretcher – revived, as it were, by rock – and goofily preening through 'Fire'. Still, raw pop and storytelling remained Springsteen's twin peaks. For all his hammy charm, he was no actor.

In Philadelphia, the day after Lennon's murder, Springsteen's set seemed to contain so total and powerful a slice of life – its grit, frailty, courage, incalculable and often freakish despair – that it *was* life and not a show. 'If it wasn't for John,' he said from the hushed stage, 'a lot of us would be in some different place tonight. It's a hard world that makes you live with a lot of things that are unlivable. And it's hard to come out here and play tonight, but there's nothing else to do.'

The first half of the tour rounded off on New Year's Eve. Springsteen spent the break at home with Hyser. He and CBS were awarded $2.15 million damages (little of which they saw) against Andrea Waters, the bootlegger trading as Vicky Vinyl. Later that month, Marsh's book became the first rock title to hit the *New York Times* bestseller list. Springsteen then co-produced an LP, *Dedication*, for Gary Bonds. (One track duly furnished his first hit in twenty years; Bonds repaid the favour with a '64 Chevy convertible.) He was back on the road from late January to March. There was no higher office, he felt, than exercising the moral imagination needed to whip the fans into a state of Bonds-era frenzy. It was Springsteen's genius to deliver the goods, night on night, wrapping oldies from rock's lost youth around unsparingly dour hymns and tragicomic ballads. Crooning 'Can't Help Falling In Love' in the same musical breath as 'Jackson Cage' wasn't the act of a man given to many hang-ups.

He broke again on 5 March. A week later, Springsteen rang Landau with a bombshell. He was sick, with a combination of fever, laryngitis and 'near-death' (later diagnosed as flu). After frantic activity on the transatlantic phone, European dates were put back two months. Springsteen spent three days in bed, then strolled incognito around the juke bars of Asbury. He jotted the one word *home* in his diary, and that said it all. This same black book contained the start-date of the tour's final leg, 14 June at the Hollywood Bowl. It was another no-nukes smoker.*

Things went well in Los Angeles, though, for once, the mix mangled Springsteen's vocals and the runaway truck of the twenty-strong band hit a wall. Two months later, across town at the Sports Arena, he hosted the VVA benefit. Of this Bob Muller says bluntly, 'Without Bruce, we wouldn't exist. There wouldn't be any vets' movement.' Within a year, Muller's organization would be protected by an act of Congress. Single-handed, Springsteen had issued a clear call to arms, and hundreds of state and local ex-servicemen's groups joined up. Their first move was to put together a home office and a newsletter; symbolic but important steps down the road of self-respect. It was a major milestone, too, for Springsteen. He took a hard look around that summer in California – with solid, bottom-line results for MUSE, VVA and others – altruism that served not only causes but also his own, unspoken needs. He had several, overlapping worries. For all the theatrical good vibes and public effusions, Springsteen was at

---

*Springsteen played this one-off set with various MUSE vets, rather than the E Streeters.

breaking point with Hyser. His father, meanwhile, had had a stroke. Backstage on a hot tropical night, swabbing himself with a towel, he turned to a British writer and murmured in a rare moment of inner emotion, 'When you lose people, you don't really want to go tooling round – "Ooh, ooh, I gotta crush on you" don't stack up any more.'

Springsteen did, though, open the new Byrne Arena, across the Hudson from Manhattan, that July. His six nights there sold out; he could have done ten more. A Freehold woman, Kathleen Stanley, serves as ironic proof of how far Springsteen had come. 'There were hundreds of people in line all day for tickets. Everyone was yelling, playing radios, or passing out drunk in the heat . . . the fire brigade showed up and hosed us down like animals. It was wild.' Even the Monmouth County Thrift could have seen no odder sight than this: a mini-riot, complete with vomiting and loud oaths, all for the 'dorky' exile who'd once trudged those same streets in his bib overalls. In the event, there were plenty of fireworks, vocal and visual – at one point, Springsteen donned a ten-gallon hat – on the first two nights. ('I never saw *nothing* like it,' he later said. 'I felt like I was the Beatles.') On the third, the pyrotechnics came from an unknown fan in the bleachers. As before, Springsteen's rage shook the crowd cold. It was short-lived. The concerts' normal ebb and flow returned overnight, and an *ad hoc* set at Clemons' new club was a foam-flecked steeplechase. The four hundred local fans were so tightly packed, their hands, once up, couldn't get down.

After thirteen countries and a million seats sold, the tour wound itself up on 14 September 1981. Springsteen celebrated the 'final rites of Bossmania', as he put it, in a spree of Kahuna punch and Dave Clark Five tapes. For many critics, his career spiked with those 139 shows. They were a peak. He'd risen to this international acclaim – second only to Dylan's and considerably more lasting – with an act as smart as it was brute. In just less than a year, he became a rock nova, the one post-sixties star to hold a candle to the likes of the Stones. By chance – there could have been no collusion – the Stones themselves opened their 'Campaign '81' the very week Springsteen folded camp.

Meanwhile, the revamped European tour had woven through West and East Germany, France, Spain and Holland, along with virgin turf like Switzerland and Denmark, that spring. In Paris, Springsteen told *Melody Maker*, 'I haven't changed my way of living . . . The sell-out doesn't occur when you take your first limo ride – it happens in *here*.' He thumped his chest. Springsteen was, though, keen to gauge the distance between the 1975 ride and this one. 'It's nerve-racking . . . I've changed so much since the last time I was here.' Much of the pre-tour blitz would consist of putting blue water between the old Boss and the new. With what one paper called 'balls' and another 'amnesiac loathing', he did only one pre-*Born* song, 'Rosalita'. On 11 May, the British tour – his first UK appearance of any kind in five and a half years – opened in Newcastle.

One of the reasons Springsteen's semi-joyous vision worked (there were 700,000 applications) was that it touched on a country that had gone wrong. Not only was 1981 the summer, oddly, of both the royal wedding and the worst English riots of the century; as in 1975, the chart was top-heavy in aesthetically clapped-out lags with creative nerve centres shot from posing: MOR merchants like Barry Manilow, or a fungus-ego'd mob of Romantics and ex-punks. Here was a figure who could strike a responsive chord in the heart of every true fan, not to mention tap into the fad – where the premium was on image, not academic consistency – for Americana. Finally, in short, London *was* ready for Bruce Springsteen. After Manchester, Edinburgh and Stafford, he hit Brighton – culturally twinned with Asbury and scene of primal Mod punch-ups – on the spring bank holiday. It was raining. Richard Williams (who'd first presciently called him the 'future of rock and roll') met Springsteen on the beach. 'At this stage, Bruce really *was* different. We walked along the front for an hour, and what struck me was that when I asked him something, he seemed to be honestly and clearly answering. He wasn't a slave to his fame or management [Springsteen had yet another Elvis biography in hand] . . . Landau would ask, "Going out, Boss?", and we did. There were no heavies, nothing.' According to a second journalist,

'Pete Townshend was in the same hotel, surrounded by goons. How can you respect someone like that? What a contrast to Bruce.'

Springsteen's six London gigs were touted as a second coming, and actually were. Opening with 'Born' and turbo-charging through a set weighted not only with golden greats but novelties like Jimmy Cliff's 'Trapped',* he may not have been – one critic said – 'rock and roll's future tense, but its past perfected'. He was certainly the luck of a generation. The warmth, wit and human touch of the shows belied even the venue's 'shed' acoustics. In the days ahead, Springsteen's UK fame soared to galactic heights. Slumped in the Wembley dressing room nursing a beer and a copy of U2's *Boy*, he was tired, happy, effusive, a would-be dispenser of truth and sanity to a world maddened by 'shit'. 'Now, *that* was a gig . . . I've always been haunted by the two we did [in London] in '75. I've got absolute total recall of those shows because the first was so bad and I was ready to blow up fuckin' Big Ben.'

When the *son et lumière* faded after the last note, the hard facts of Springsteen's coup remained. He'd made it in the spiritual home of sixties pop. Britain loved him. *The River* spent eighty-eight weeks in the chart. Townshend himself was, he said, 'gobsmacked'. Members of the Stones, Pretenders and ex-Pistols all paid court. Elvis Costello was granted an audience and agreed that 'Bruce's boss', rich for one so wary of praise. Suddenly, Springsteen's reputation as an Asbury cult dissolved under pressure from both without and within. As he said, he 'nuked 'em'. The tour's fallout was immediate and global, money and plaudits pouring in, reviews and interviews at every turn. Now he belonged to the world.

Popular and critical kudos, star-struck sibyls and even the odd stalker – all the coin for which a rocker trades in his name – were around and about him full-time. Many fine judges, like Andy

---

*Springsteen had bought an old Cliff LP in the duty-free zone at Schipol Airport, with the genre-hop result heard in London.

Peebles, call the Wembley gigs Springsteen's best, and some of the nights of their lives. Cynthia Rose swears they 'literally did change' her. What's more, for several years now, Springsteen had been slaying his heroes. This ironic light now had to be cast on Townshend, whose next album ran on guitar-and-glockenspiel riffs and a river theme. Springsteen even had his own famous fans, including a woman named Obie who trotted the globe after him, and others who dabbled in love notes, lingerie and polaroids. In Birmingham, one naked girl splayed herself, Ecstasy-like, atop his rented Rolls. The response generally was wild, *The Times* opining that 'among the pussy cats of American pop, Springsteen roars like a lion'. To *Sounds*, he 'touched universality'. Springsteen came in for a drubbing from certain rock nabobs, and, of course, narked *NME* – by which sign alone, he'd made it.

The British kudos bounced back to the US. Each rave rising on the horizon from *Melody Maker* was swiftly added to the press kit. Since the depth of Springsteen's fame lay in its dispersal, merely collating the stuff was a full-time job. (Landau now had a staff of six.) The fanzines lapped it up; every word. Ironically, about the only person not thrilled by his good fortune was Springsteen himself. An old friend saw how he still 'missed the rhythm of life', always reacting too much – witness the fireworks – or not enough. He said his salvation was in 'loving', but failed to add 'in being loved'; the 'big drop' remained over the hill. Shortly after the tour ended, Springsteen was on hand when Clemons married Tina Sandgren in Hawaii. His friend and foil's wedding can only have underlined the barrenness of a being hazed over by the twin totems of sex and rock and roll. Springsteen had proposed to Hyser. Her refusal was the flag for a harangue about 'cunts' who gazed soulfully, spouted EST and emoted for TV movies. (Hyser did, though, aptly, go on to grace *Spinal Tap*.) Springsteen's mood darkened when his second Obie-styled 'blood bud', Van Zandt – now morphing into Little Steven – announced that he, too, would marry. Before long he left the band. Springsteen responded with a bout of 'shit-shooting and ass-sitting' in a Los Angeles studio. He cut a demo of a new song, 'Mansion On The Hill', and strummed the early chords of a rockabilly 'Vietnam', aka 'Born In The USA'. Then he had dinner at the Beverly Hills Hotel. Financially, at least, Springsteen's dues-paying years were over. When the lease on the Holmdel farm ran out, he rented homes a few miles east, first in Colts Neck and then Rumson. The latter had a large, fenced-in yard, bow windows, a pool and Bonds' gift parked in the drive. Springsteen also bought a house in Hollywood.

Those sessions in LA were a musical brewing and annealing – a shaping, distilling, sharpening and hardening of Springsteen's well-meant fetish for social healing. It found its apogee in his sixth album, *Nebraska*. He was, as he said, 'no statesman'. Nor sage: his few metaphysical asides were satirically dim. ('That's what I [care] about,' Springsteen said in 1980: '. . . going out and meeting people I don't know. Going to France and Germany and Japan and meeting Japanese people and French people and German people, meeting them and seeing what they think, and being able to go over there with a pocketful of ideas or go over there with, like, just something, to be able to take something over. And boom! To do it!') Whether fundraising for MUSE, underwriting the VVA or bailing out Bonds and Ryder, he was, though, a loyal all-weather friend in the face of hard facts and fiscal nuts. When he left the Seattle café that wet night in October 1980, Springsteen met a man, Pat Fosh, hunched over a 'bucket of slop', cold, ragged and – as he says today – 'dragging my ass down Skid Row'. Springsteen not only gave him money. He sat and spoke with Fosh for an hour, 'not patronizing or bible-thumping, just asking me stuff . . . Bruce told me I had a God-given right to life. He actually got me thinking. I owe him that . . . The songs are great, but what he gave me to roll with was even better. Hope. You know, Bruce convinced me I could make it.' (Fosh now manages a software house.)

Springsteen's own freefall continued apace in 1982 – 'rock bottom', he called it. Even under the dire stress of his father's stroke, their mutual sparks still flew on his trips home. In the strangely mixed brew of tyrannical 'shit' on Doug's part and benevolent neglect on Adele's, Springsteen was forced to find strength and order with a series of career-struck women. None lasted. *The River*'s 'Point Blank' had been an angry shot at Goldsmith's defection. There were others. Neatly, of course, he also self-satirized. Part of Springsteen's next album, though, went beyond modesty to masochistic debasement. Hyser, too, now left him. Compounding Springsteen's low spirits was an appeal, launched by the National Organization for Women (NOW), demanding he stop singing of 'little girls' in his lyrics. Rock hacks, like others, gladly wreak extra pain on artists slurred by a list of centrally vetoed *isms*: sex being but one. The flak duly flew. Down the months, Springsteen had to fight to the last ditch to win back this key constituency. He sent in the shock troops. Instead of sitting in Black Rock, CBS spin-doctors spent long nights swanning round Yorkville, reassuring NOW they had nothing to fear from Springsteen, who was 'more right-on', their own expression, each album. It worked.

Springsteen's solitude, the way his 'I'm A Rocker' riffs were more written than lived, had its drawbacks. He enjoyed hanging out in the obvious sense – of playing 45s or staying up all hours with his girl – and the business of making a life outside of sex or music was so tedious and time-consuming he never made much more than a few stabs at it. He was a dab hand at softball, but that was his one and only extracurricular bent. When not in his study writing *Nebraska*, Springsteen was glued to late-night TV. He watched both John Huston's *Wise Blood* and, again, Terrence Malick's *Badlands* that winter. Springsteen rang the latter's author. Those twin tales of breakdown, despair, delinquency, murder and intrinsic banality chimed with a mood he called 'beat'. Springsteen's stark, alienated LP in turn asked the questions: 'What happens when all the things you believe in when you're twenty-five don't work? What happens when things break down? When you're alone – can you live? Can you go on?' Artistically, Springsteen's world-woe would be compressed, summarized and brilliantly vented in *Nebraska*. Personally, it meant he often sat home in Colts Neck, or trudged for hours through the tangled black gum and dripping leaves, then drove to Freehold to stare at his old homes. An analyst would later tell him: 'What you're doing is . . . something went

Born in the USA.

STATE DEPARTMENT OF HEALTH OF NEW JERSEY

BIRTH No. 129—

49-068129

After Doug Springsteen deep-sixed his plan to hitch-hike to the Monterey pop festival, Bruce donned a mortar-board and gown to graduate on 19 June 1967.

BRUCE SPRINGSTEEN

I am a 1967 graduate of Freehold Regional High School. I was quiet and shy and liked to putter with cars.

The 'New Jersey wailer' solo (left) and flanked by Clarence Clemons and Steve Van Zandt (below). From a shaky start, Springsteen glossed his set into a well-rehearsed, blocked routine that was as much Broadway as boardwalk.

The Harvard Square Theatre, where on 9 May 1974 Jon Landau saw 'rock and roll future'.

Those titanic early shows soon became lore. Springsteen's albums may have been on the short side, but at three hours, the gigs never were: epic rave-ups that flouted the laws of nature long before chaos theory had a name.

The Hammersmith Odeon, November 1975. As a slogan, it was five and a half years early.

To some, it was like looking through the pinhole of a scenic souvenir charm and seeing a whole pink-suited Apollo revue – except this was England, and the star was wearing Levi's. And that hat.

With 1978's *Darkness on the Edge of Town* and 118-date tour, a second-wave cult finally turned Springsteen from a novelty into a star.

As Lynn Goldsmith, who took this shot, could bear out, the next two years were often grim, and the street was rarely easy.

Although Springsteen alone had 'the shine', it wasn't as if his career was an effortless feat of unsculpted, free-form self-expression. Among those who helped down the way:

The E Street Band (left to right: Van Zandt, Weinberg, Federici, BS, Clemons, Bittan, Tallent).

Adele Springsteen.

Jon Landau.

The Big Man.

By the time of 1980's *The River* – still the best, one-stop slab of what made Springsteen great – he was both a radio star and a pin-up.

wrong, and you're going back to see if you can fix it, if you can make it right.'

Still searching, Springsteen drove south down I-95 for several days. Along the way, he struck up a rapport with a woman named, for the purposes of the story, Mary. There were other such convivial pit-stops. Yet even in these serial seductions, Springsteen emerged as a closet misogynist – happiest (like Just William in those Richmal Crompton books) when surrounded by members of his gang. Time and again, Marsh's and the others' panegyrics offer words like 'clique', 'club' and even 'clan' to describe the 'blood bud' he became when not shunning the world in toto. Mary herself notes Springsteen's 'lights-out' look (and the fact that, as his shows went from zero to sixty in ten seconds, so something similar happened in bed). Also on the road, he saw shops boarded up and NO WORK TODAY signs tacked to rusty doors. If Springsteen chose the man-bites-underdog view of Reaganomics, there was proof enough for it to feed on in 1981–82. One of his best songs that winter was 'Murder Inc.', a scorching critique, in part, of the red-braced plague on Wall Street. Both the personal and social angst fuelled Springsteen's need for bustle, activity, trial and error, anything to convey a sense of shock and protest. He'd infused *The River* with tolerant cynicism, but by the time of *Nebraska* his scorn had turned sour. An acoustic (later, *Unplugged*) LP had been, for years, the unmistakable maturity milestone for rock's second generation. Springsteen came home alone that New Year, white-faced, shocked and angry at the 'dismal shit-pit' within and without. Now he was ready for an album.

On 3 January 1982 Springsteen settled on to a bedroom chair, turned on a four-track cassette deck and picked up his guitar. In three hours he recorded *Nebraska* and half the songs that became *Born in the USA*. He then stuffed the tape in his pocket, where overnight it narrowly avoided being washed along with his jeans. The demos' lodestar was Hank Williams, Woody Guthrie and the motel-room blues of a Robert Johnson (whom Springsteen hadn't, in fact, yet heard). Also first-drafted were two Bible-based lyrics, 'Lion's Den' and 'Wages Of Sin'. The snarl of 'My Love Won't Let

You Down' was translated, with remarkable bite and fidelity, into a lost soul's guide to sex. These were songs to, and of, their times. Conspicuously absent were any prime cuts for MTV, *Dance Fever* or the rest. (*Nebraska* did furnish Springsteen's first conceptual video – a black-and-white short of fast cuts, disturbing close-ups and frothy symbolism in which he didn't appear.)

After four months of trying and failing to score his home demos, Springsteen had another half-album's worth. Over seven nights at the Station and Hit Factory that May, the band cut 'Glory Days', 'I'm On Fire', 'Downbound Train', 'Working On The Highway', 'This Hard Land', 'I'm Goin' Down', two *Darkness*-era outtakes – 'Darlington County' and 'Frankie' – and, not least, 'Born In The USA'. The last spiralled up from its 'billy' roots into a bone-breaking, six-note rocker. When it was released two years later, few of the song's fans could have known that the celebrated chorus was a dirge, or that the protagonist, Springsteen himself, 'wanted[ed] to strip away that mythic America which was Reagan's image, to find something real . . . He's looking for a home.'

While Springsteen casually wrote new, platinum hits-to-be, the *Nebraska* tape was subjected to every alchemic trick known. Not only were Landau, Van Zandt, Plotkin and a bevy of mixers and mastering men unable to work up the shellac; their slog never cashed in on *Nebraska*'s raw, folkish credentials. Part of the trouble was Springsteen's voice. On the original cassette he'd sung in a low drone that defied amplification. Efforts to recut 'Atlantic City', for one, repeatedly broke down in a crash of steel and drums, the lucid vocal mangled in a garage-group roar. For once, he, the band and the songs weren't a continuum. Nothing worked. Thanks to the low-fi recording, there were problems even pressing *Nebraska* on vinyl. Springsteen drove a dub of the tape to Sterling Sound in New York. He flew one to Precision Lacquer in Los Angeles. Anyone doubting the hair-splitting zeal he brought to even off-the-cuff projects like this should have heard him arguing over v.u.'s and i.p.s.-counts, hour after hour. Finally, *Nebraska* gelled. Springsteen made the intelligent, inevitable choice to release it solo (as he said, 'bare'). The long-suffering Plotkin duly engineered the final cut. Springsteen then took *Nebraska* to Walter Yetnikoff. They met in the CBS boardroom. Yetnikoff flipped on the album, beaming and stroking the vast contours of his chins. His idea of a good song was 'Hungry Heart'. Forty minutes later, he slowly crushed his cigar – and, says a well-placed source, 'sagged like a shot bear' – before groaning, 'We'll do our best.'

In later years, when critics praised *Nebraska* as a classic, they also puffed it as a manifesto; not just expertly done, but a document. In Britain, Roger Scott peddled it as 'two fingers to Maggie'. Across the Atlantic, Greil Marcus's *New West* rave began, '*Nebraska*'s the most complete and probably most convincing statement of resistance and refusal that Ronald Reagan's USA has elicited' and went on from there to get heavy. (By the end of 1981, Reagan's business plan seemed to be backfiring: interest rates were kept at record high levels in order to force down inflation, while at the same time unemployment soared. As the newly homeless moved into the streets and parks of major cities, polls showed that two-thirds of all Americans felt Reagan favoured the rich.) Marcus was stretching it. Springsteen's focus for *Nebraska* wasn't, in fact, political or partisan. It was personal. The winter of 1981–82 was a bad time for him. He had little to do outside his work. Hyser had left. He was alone. Speaking of this era five years later, Springsteen said, 'my relationships always ended poorly. I didn't really know how to connect with a woman.' It was also the winter he first entered therapy, a period when he began experiencing a personal emptiness, 'a floating thing, like I'd gotten lost', he told one reporter. He was drinking. Such was the backdrop to the guitar- and harp-based songs, full of bemused loners and broken souls, that Springsteen cut on his Teac porta-studio.

Still, despite the public's blind misconception, Springsteen sang not to 'say something', but to shout himself hoarse. Forty-eight hours after strumming the gruff elegies of *Nebraska*, he was letting rip at the Stone Pony. So it went, for Springsteen, month after month. The soc-hops and raves poured out, thick and fast, fast and thick, all year. He guested with Clemons, Van Zandt, Beaver

Brown, Cats on a Smooth Surface, Southside Johnny, John Eddie, Sonny Keen, and, not least, Nils Lofgren. There were roughly two home-town gigs – plus the Monmouth County fair – weekly from March to October. Springsteen shamelessly flung demos at the disco and dance markets. He wrote seven of eleven tracks for Bonds' new LP, *On the Line*. He collaborated with Dave Edmunds. He even appeared at the studio with a synthesizer. It's tempting to assume Springsteen recognized his creative volte-faces as easily as he made them. It's slightly harder to believe the stylistic yin–yang wasn't connected to what Motz calls 'Schizo-steenia', the party rocker grappling with his conscience. Jamming with Lofgren, after all, was one thing; writing hits for Donna Summer was an act of surreal eclecticism.

Springsteen's fame evolved along with his music. For seven years, he'd transcended just *playing* rock – he'd lived it. He didn't portray; he defined. Along the road, he'd picked up an image as straight and whole-hearted, if not wholesome. 'Bruce plugged the SE [safe energy] into MUSE,' says one marquee-name friend. It was doubtless this taint that, along with the personal and social welter, led Springsteen to *Nebraska*. He'd matured – he was thirty-two – and as he did so, he began to value direct action. Springsteen's creeping radicalism would duly hit a rubiginous peak in 1995. In the meantime, he was emotionally and artistically in flux. He seemed to appeal to everyone. Springsteen was a great symbolic character precisely because there was something elusive about him: his high-precision ambiguity was like a faulty bulb; the nearer you went to it, the less clear it got.

Thus, just a week after eking out 'Used Cars' and the rest, Springsteen was mugging his way through 'Lucille', lathered like a jogger, ranging over the hills and dales of doo-wop, funk, R&B and Britrock. Notably absent were any torch songs. Most of these gigs said exactly what Appel said, that after years of knowing Springsteen you found, suddenly, you didn't know him. In fact, he was neither troubadour nor cash-harvesting pop star. He was both. Sometimes Springsteen went small, stage-hopping round Asbury; often he went large, playing for 700,000 at a 'Rally For

Disarmament' gala in Central Park. By then, anti-nuclear (and, by extension, anti-Reagan) feeling was at its highest since the 1962 missile crisis.

'All 'board,' the home-boy had sung on *The Wild*, 'Nebraska's our next stop.' The man who got there had changed. Nine years on, all the anger, the pain, the bile and frustration he felt were made flesh in that one state. *Nebraska* was bleak. But Springsteen, to his credit, refused to romanticize the night, or bow to record-label nags. The album was doggedly, proudly sheer, stripped and stark: Springsteen without clothes on. *Nebraska*'s redeeming news – what Roger Scott called the 'flash of gold in the pan' – is that 'folks can make a stand'. They need to. For the most part, Springsteen offered cold hope, raising moral questions about Reaganomics – not to say his own, chronic depression. He'd come, relatively young, to a time when, like a Dylan or Lennon, he'd had to ask himself, 'What am I talking about?': and got no answer. *Nebraska* was his 'difficult' back-to-roots LP, musically and otherwise. 'I always considered it my most personal record,' he said. 'It felt to me, in its tone, the most what my childhood felt like.' Shunning several CBS ideas, all of them half-baked, and with no inner voice, Springsteen followed the old saw and wrote about what he knew. The result was ten unusually and crisply journalistic sketches, miracles of thrift and expression, tableaux, that, if not always *vivant*, were alternately wry, dire and fully human. Springsteen could paint living portraits in a line or two. Even Dylan took more than that. The dour colloquialisms were spot-on, as was the soft-pedalled imagery, where love was found only through death and a rebirth of will.

On his first album, Springsteen had done a slap-happy skit of Van Morrison, specifically *Moondance*. This was his *Astral Weeks*. Above all, Plotkin's finish left *Nebraska* with a welcome lack of Lucite. The vocals were unrecognizable from the Boy George register of 'Hungry Heart'. They set off the saturnine riffs. At last, Springsteen's voice went unpropped; you could *hear* the lyrics. On *Nebraska*, he came over as a word-boffin, with a glossary, wrote the *Source*, 'pure and deep as the second law of thermodynamics'.

Everything was broken down. The odd splash of echo, reverb and Springsteen's falsetto coos – or raw howls – were the sole effects. Even the 'Atlantic City' video, a sop to the CBS flaks, was defiantly monochrome, a hand-held blur of hobos, bus depots and slums on the far side of town.

In *Nebraska*'s title cut, Springsteen took a late-night TV jag and turned it into a full-blown saga. His treatment of Charlie Starkweather, *Badlands*' real-life, homicidal hero, related to Norman Mailer's doomed genre study of Jack Abbott, the killer author. Like Mailer's, Springsteen's compassion could curdle. (His protagonist's flat, disembodied self-rationale – 'there's just a mean-ness in this world' – struck one of Starkweather's ten victims' relatives as 'crap'.) The music, at least, exposed the muck under the myth – a trick Springsteen also pulled off on 'Atlantic City'. 'Mansion On The Hill' and 'Johnny 99' both solidified *Nebraska's* pivotal role between the great older country acts of the fading pres-ent – Chet Atkins, Johnny Cash – and those who'd follow. On 'Highway Patrolman', Springsteen reverted to the brother's-keeper text of 'Adam Raised A Cain'. It was the tarnished jewel in *Nebraska*'s crown. The moody, rich voice set against the spare guitar lent the plot – itself worked into two films by Pam Springsteen's ex, Sean Penn – dramatic clout. Freehold, *circa* 1955, was the landscape of 'Used Cars', hanging together conceptually with 'My Father's House'. Of the last tune, Springsteen said, 'that was bottom . . . I'd hope not to be in that particular place ever again.' So *Nebraska* ended, on a morbidly droll note, ditching us beside the road, poking a dead dog, or waiting for a truant bride, yet still 'find[ing] some reason to believe'.

Not even the oldest rock critic whose memory went back as far as seven or eight years could recall a braver LP than *Nebraska*. A few surly types slated it as 'Born To Crawl', something like one of the Lomaxs' field-project tapes. Springsteen got a graphic lesson in the dilemma of leadership, of pandering to mass hysteria while simultaneously making the fans want 'what they need'. Richard Williams, for one, thought the whole concept 'at best put-on, at worst patronizing'. Yet reviews generally bristled with words like bold, ballsy, visionary, clear and classic. Perversely, for the *ne plus ultra* of Americana, it did better overseas. But, even at home, the terms of trade were in Springsteen's favour. *Nebraska* shipped 600,000 copies, the same as *Darkness*, if not *The River*. It hit number four. Consciously or not, Springsteen ploughed a line between art and sales. He fully deserved his recent promotion from water to earth.

By late 1982, *Nebraska* had been quoted by millions – some of whom bought it – in their mass riot at Reaganomics. The backlash against double-digit unemployment, inflation and interest rates was in full flood. Even Republicans winced at the worst bits. The topper came that October, when the White House announced the purchase of a 4,730-piece set of ivory china for $209,000; on the same day, the Agriculture Secretary blithely declared tomato sauce to be fine as a vegetable for school lunches. Springsteen, among many others, erupted. This was exactly his kind of politics: emotive, tangible and explicitly American. So deeply did he hold to the value of gestures that he gave up ketchup himself for a week, partly because he felt his sacrifice would be a gut demonstration of his horror. Springsteen was good at humanizing hard issues. He was less good at aspirational logic or high-flown rhetoric. 'People have lost the ability to dream,' he said. From the jaded perspective of 1999 the idea that you could 'have it all' struck even Mailer as 'odd – you'd have to be *on* something to think that'. Yet Springsteen's idealism was very real. He was, he said, a 'thinkin' fool' if still 'trickin' it out'. Meanwhile, his *de facto* protest took off in a blaze of patriotism and propaganda, with a large propulsion of fear. Among the *ad hoc* ads for *Nebraska* was one saying, 'This Land Is Yours. Grab It. NOW.' Within twenty-four hours, a quarter of a million fans had laid claim.

Doug and Adele Springsteen were still in California, one house-bound, the other taking the bus every morning to her desk job. Their best days were when Bruce visited. Such moments were prized, and all the more so for their rarity. Much of the time their son was either a past memory to cherish or a future guest to await.

They didn't speak of him in public. Still, Adele, ever the Brooklyn Neapolitan, often told friends she worried. He didn't have a steady job. Far more disturbing was the fact that he didn't have a nice girl, let alone a wife. When Springsteen visited San Mateo that December, he came under a nonstop salvo of maternal concern, complaint and would-be matchmaking. In time, it backfired.* As Springsteen continued to brood over the 'dead flop' of his affairs, marriage became an increasingly touchy subject in his few dates with the flesh Adele brought him. 'Ma,' he snapped finally, 'gimme a break.'

As Christmas came, Springsteen was a killer in one-night stands around New York. Deaf to Adele's reproach, he lived his boast of 'proving it all night' in Rumson and the Navarro and Lyden hotels in Manhattan. Springsteen in those days was nagged by insomnia and – says an ex-partner – often found himself lying in bed with his woman, crying that, at thirty-three, he'd 'blown it'. After one unusually long mutual ruckus, he started strumming the guitar. 'Money, money, money,' he rasped. Then struck a chord. 'Gals, gals, gals.' At this orgasm of creative drama, he suddenly broke down and began sobbing again. 'When's *my* turn?' he asked through the tears. That New Year's Eve, he was best man when the bells tolled for Van Zandt and Maureen Santoro. It was a bitter-sweet scene. Late that night at the Harkness House, Springsteen 'zombied up' at the bride's provocative remark: 'Hey, Bruce. Bet you're next.'

It's sometimes the simplest acts that illuminate the hardest problems. One day that winter, Springsteen drove himself to the Stone Pony to watch, and probably sit in with, Bobby Bandiera. Backstage, he made out a familiar figure dressed in jeans and cowboy boots, her long red hair framing high cheeks and a sharp, almost beautiful, upturned chin.

---

*Adding to Springsteen's dark mood was a bizarre scene late one night in a hotel, when his downstairs neighbour rang up to complain of the noise. By sheer coincidence, it was Goldsmith. His first words to her, still harping on about MUSE, were 'Why'd you do it, Lynnie?'

'We've met,' he said.
'Have we?'
'Sure. I can't remember your name. Mine's Bruce.'
'Patti Scialfa.'

6

Made In The USA

With *Nebraska*, Springsteen had been making 1940s music to compete in the 1980s. Several CBS pashas had variously wheedled and yelled at each other, wanting to know how long 'WY' (Yetnikoff) would take it. The grudging consensus was that, since Springsteen had long crossed into the black, he *was* boss, money- and otherwise. Within reason, he could do what he liked. Fortunately, CBS knew, there was an easy remedy for this sorry state of affairs. The first item up on the post-*Nebraska* agenda would be plastering him on TV.

Arnold Levine, the man who'd shot the riotous 'Rosalita' clip, duly made his pitch for 'Atlantic City'. Here, some artistic difference emerged between label, director and star. Springsteen had no objection to a video – he just didn't want to be in it. Levine's ploy involved panning from the window of a car, changing gears visually from neon glitz to off-boardwalk rot. It was MTV's most complex (and only) jigsaw puzzle yet. But it worked: 'Atlantic City' went into heavy spin over Christmas 1982. People talked. Critics loved it. (In 1993, *Rolling Stone* ran a list of the top hundred such films ever. 'Atlantic City' came in thirty-seventh.) Levine's *cinéma vérité* was followed by a minor epidemic of playfully similar non-plots.

Meantime, studios promptly turned out three big-budget scripts for Springsteen's perusal. A fourth was in the pipeline. Such kudos couldn't have been bought, not least for a man who'd yet to even act for a camera.

In the end, for the usual reasons, the Hollywood projects died in the crib. But the low-key 'Atlantic City' nonetheless led, logically, to the multi-media bonanza of 1984–85. A label staffer named Celia Ryle sat in on a summit at Black Rock, where 'four or five medal-lion men' discussed packaging the next album. At the word 'MTV' a responsive gleam came over Landau, passing immediately into a long, detailed riff on demographics and key targets. Ryle recalls an 'almost porcine' look of greed on the others' faces as they totted up the gross.

Apart from Landau's obvious pleasure, the meeting was no great success. The lure of the cash was offset as far as his client was concerned by the perennial crisis in his sex life. In those days, Springsteen's friends didn't hear of much good news. In fact, there was a lot of grousing. Springsteen's image was, as a female fan rightly put it, 'the guy who had everything'. The reality was a newly middle-aged man who found it hard to function away from the studio or stage. As he later said, he was trading on the 'luxury of extended adolescence'. To the raves he won for the songs and shows was added new respect for his trying – sadly without success – to keep misery quiet. Landau was sympathetic. And versatile: unlike some managers, who concentrated on fixing tours and left private matters alone, he kept a fatherly eye on everything. 'Boss,' he said, 'I'm sorry.' Then he snapped open his briefcase. Over the next hour, Landau laid out the marketing plan. Within eighteen months, Springsteen would pass from stardom into one of the major global brands of the decade.

His depression, meanwhile, gathered pace. 'I thought, "This can't be happening to me. *I'm the guy with the guitar*",' Springsteen told Marsh, almost with understatement. As *Nebraska* limped down the chart, he was in a mood of gloom and dejection bordering on angst. One of the band says that 'Bruce even admitted – "I went through a shitty time. I thought of blowing out my brains."'

Probably he said it, and maybe he thought it, but it wasn't a course in keeping with his credo, his character, or even his Catholicism. Springsteen's grim and deep loneliness was, though, a matter of record. One night in Los Angeles, swigging hard from a bottle, he turned to a record producer and said it aloud: 'Without all this, I'd be a goner.' Even five years later, from the far side of marriage, Springsteen insisted, 'Isolation is the most dangerous thing on earth.'

He began 1983 on the road. This time, though, Springsteen went not by jet, but in his navy Camaro, with a motorbiking friend, Matty DiLea, riding shotgun. It was no tour: the two cruised rather than scuttled down the blue roads and back highways, stubbornly sticking to the worst neon-lit motels and, as Springsteen later said, 'putting about ten points on Cuervo stock'. In late January they hit California. Springsteen now had a full twenty-four-track studio built in the garage of his LA house. Over the next month he cut another Ron Kovic-tinged hymn, 'Shut Out The Light', 'Sugarland' (prefacing the *Tom Joad* LP) and a revamped 'Follow That Dream' – none of them of the rootsy, Mitch Ryder type. He also did a song called 'Car Wash', notable for being written from a woman's point of view, and thus in touch with 'real folks'.* At the time it was thought they and the Power Station tracks might make it into the shops by summer. In the event, *Born in the USA* was nearly a year late. Springsteen gave Landau and the band the impression he needed 'six months off . . . No gigs, no recording, *nada*.' In practice, that evolved into a schedule that made *Greetings*' seem woefully laid-back. As well as covering the social waterfront from Bob Seger to Prince, Springsteen commuted back to Jersey, sat in with Bandiera's band, rehearsed his own material and continued his listless practice of doing a song a day; by July he had eighty. Through all this, he felt 'put-on . . . low . . . Like it was all down to me.'

---

*Unlike the prince of romantic legend, Springsteen didn't, however, feel able to don an old cloak and disappear into the female masses. For scheduling reasons, he turned down production jobs with both Darlene Love and Ronnie Spector.

And it was. If Springsteen gave up, slumped, collapsed, there was no marketing plan left. Landau and the suits who'd rallied to him, the band who'd plighted their troth, all would simply be sacked and cut loose as has-beens, men without a mission, rich, but not the plutocrats they became. In his Rumson house, abject and alone, Springsteen nearly went under. But he held up. Therapy and his own bloody-mindedness won through. As so often, Springsteen began going forward by turning back. He huddled with Van Zandt in a bid to keep his old under-boss, now launching a solo career, in the fold. (When that failed, Springsteen complemented the split with his own distinctively fond 'Bobby Jean'.) He licensed 'It's Hard To Be A Saint In The City' to John Sayles's barband fable, *Baby, It's You* (reminding him, he said, of when 'everything lay ahead'). He even made up with Appel. Springsteen not only recouped his last publishing rights for $425,000; a year later, weeks before they all recharted, he bought out Appel's stake in the first three albums. That, as he duly said, was that. (Later in the eighties there was a full-bore reunion, involving a ritual hug, Springsteen's prize jacket and an offer of a loan. Both men's rage for personal success – their manic ambition – blew over when Springsteen made it, and was at last left alone to reckon with himself. Hence, 'Mike an' me got closure'.)

Over the next twelve months, Springsteen provided the world with an epic example of grace under pressure. His new Rumson home, on the southern bank of the Navesink river and just a mile from the sea, gradually became the scene of continual partying. Friends dropped by to hear rough mixes of the album and stayed for barbeques in the back yard. Shockingly, instead of steaks, Springsteen flung vegetables and fish on the grill. His salad days were starting up. He still played softball most summer afternoons. Now, too, he began running six miles a day. Soon Springsteen would be pumping iron. Whether due to a 'wellness' regime, or being decked by Jim Cobanis, his weightlifting ethic paid off. As early as May 1983, *Rolling Stone* noted, 'Springsteen's muscles have swelled to Popeye size.'

Musically, too, he seemed to be in full revolt against his past.

Polishing Clemons' solo LP and ogling the likes of U2 were staple after-hours fare. But sitting through, let's be brief, Prince – whom Springsteen thought 'one of the best performers I've ever seen in my whole life' – signalled the worst. By mid 1983 he was keeping company with Michael Jackson. Finally, Springsteen heard a club mix of Cyndi Lauper's 'Girls Just Want To Have Fun' and declared it 'incredible'. Hard-core fans used the same word for his next move. In 1984 Springsteen gave up three of his best songs to the dance-floor, and thence to the epic U-turn: 'I was always so protective of my music . . . now I feel that stuff isn't as fragile as I thought.' Like Lauper's girls, he was just 'after a gas'.

The general lightening-up of Springsteen's mood and music was set against personal ennui and the fall-out of E Street's first defection. For seven years the Asbury Jukes had plied the ritual of low-rent gigs, often quaffing their fees in two or three hilarious after-hours. These 'musicians' musicians' had only one wish – to play – and they idolized Van Zandt, who promised them the fulfilment of their dream. By 1982 he'd formed his own like-minded gang, the Disciples of Soul. They toured the US and Europe in 1983. Van Zandt formally exited, though never making for the grindstone, next spring. In fact, he'd been edging out for years. The steady inflation of Springsteen's sound didn't just, a friend says, 'chill Steve's butt'; it made that frost seem like the inevitable outcome of a decade's giantism. As Van Zandt said, 'You can make a very good living – a *very* good living – selling a couple of million records and selling out arenas . . . I didn't think we needed to be any more successful.'

He quit: citing the usual 'musical differences' in public; sacrificed, it was murmured elsewhere, on the altar of Landau's ego. Though few openly said it, insiders knew of a death-struggle for Springsteen's soul. As Appel told Marc Eliot, 'I'm sure [Van Zandt's] departure had to do with Landau, whose goal seemed to be to get rid of anybody who posed a threat, professionally or personally, to his relationship with Bruce.' Whatever the cause, the result was the first mortal crack in a band of what, till then, had been fanatically loyal vassals under Springsteen's sway. He treated them well, but expected them to be true and pure – 'Bruce went ape' when Clemons opened his own club – and wore anything but the one venal sin, disloyalty to the top. Told of Van Zandt's plan, Springsteen had his wits about him enough to throw his spleen into the music. For months in the summer and fall of 1983, he did nothing but sub-*Nebraska* songs, dour evocations of long dark shadows turning black. The logjam was broken by 'Bobby Jean'. Here he famously pumped blood into the tag of a grim life making for great art. The song was Springsteen's half-angry, half-affectionate homage to lost love.

Springsteen was also running a rule over his other major relationship, to rock. He'd discovered some brand-new things since coming off *The River*. It was, he told Marsh, a case of 'Whoa, I've made a big mistake here. I always had the idea that rock and roll will *save* you . . . Well, it won't. Not in and of itself it won't. It's not gonna.' Springsteen's epiphany had the effect of rebooting *Nebraska 2* into *Born in the USA*. He tossed his garage tapes and went back, for the most part, to the gravelly Graham Parker skits last heard on 'Fade Away'. For the new dates, Springsteen's LP boasted one of the perkiest cast of characters since the days of Phil Spector's *Christmas Album*. Clemons let fly with a volley of legato riffs. Weinberg slapped out crafty-bugger cousins of Ringo's beats. Bittan swung. Inevitably, some grouched at the so-called 'cop-out'. Others duly smiled at the idea of hacks getting nostalgic over a lost culture, and argued that Springsteen had no culture to be nostalgic for. Actually, what he had was a counterculture – an identity that was defined by what it wasn't. Other rockers followed their relentless philosophy of drink and drugs. Springsteen, on the other hand, with several rare exceptions, was blushingly normal. In 1983–84 he went back to base, but making it larger. Live, much of the band's soul-train riffing now gave way to arch, enormo-dome flummery. In an odd sign of the times, he reversed his latest ban on T-shirts but not 'scuzzy', unauthorized books. If his career, for a decade, had been a long, persistent search for 'truth', for a year or two it met with an equally dour campaign to flog his wares. It was the sad but sane, logical upshot of losing his religion. Springsteen swapped principle for pragmatism.

When it came to fixing blame for the fall, cynics were spoilt for choice. CBS, Plotkin and sundry mixers and engineers all hacked away at the sound, until, in some places, not a hook or hoot remained of *The Wild*, where once jazz, funk and pop had all shown up for the party. The most culpable, yet brilliant, was Landau. He, above all, knew Springsteen needed a loyal opposition as well as praise. To this day, certain friends are startled on perceiving him grubbing amid studio and backstage rooms. What Landau did best was review. Now, as the moment of relapse loomed, he reverted to type. Late that summer, Landau took the bold step of writing a minute, five-page screed on the nascent *USA*. It worked. Thousands of artists had been blocked before; hundreds, like Springsteen himself, had wrestled with what it meant to be a rock star. But never had one man hit the wall as gloriously as he did. Late that year he was in, aptly, the Hit Factory, turning out take after take, song by song, mix on mix. All that remained now was paring down the hundred cuts to give the album balance. Technical EQ-ing came, in turn, from Bob Clearmountain, a sleight-of-hand guru who'd conjured the Stones' hit *Tattoo You* from studio out-takes. Significantly, his forte was buffing the voice and drums in a jewel-hard mix. Clearmountain took Springsteen's first drafts, picked them up and shook them inside out until they were clean and crisp – if sometimes starchy – as a freshly laundered sheet. The effect was to give a vital boost to the songs' anthemic potential. When Springsteen walked back to the marble and gold lobby of the Lyden, his Manhattan bolt-hole, he knew he had a smash on his hands, perhaps the best rock album of the eighties. After two years of intermittent depression and manic activity, he was Born again.

Nils Lofgren's fame, by contrast, remained frustratingly embryonic. This hyper, journeyman guitarist and affable soul had already grazed Springsteen's life in 1969, when both auditioned for Bill Graham in the same night. Years later, the word 'karma' would be used to describe the two men's meetings, their mutual lurches up the Jersey shore. That was stretching it, but in the mid seventies they'd each tapped the same vein of hit-hungry nostalgia. *NME*'s issue of 15 November 1975 – virtually a Springsteen love-in – presciently asked on the cover, 'Where does Nils Lofgren fit into this?' Distantly, was the answer for eight years. Then Springsteen began putting out feelers. Lofgren, whose own record label had just folded, was at a low ebb. During the course of a night at the Stone Pony, they renewed a mutual love of primal R&B which wasn't – didn't want to be – more than 'fun'. The two then jammed together at a Red Bank club that Christmas. Slowly, the way all such decisions were made, Springsteen sealed it. After a *de facto* audition the next May, Lofgren (beating out Bobby Bandiera) was in. There were various impressive-sounding rehearsals which seemed to show he could play a *lot* of guitar, and Van Zandt, his predecessor, rather less. Without attributing occult powers to him, he gelled.

Springsteen himself spent the holiday compiling his wish-list for the year. At the top were the two words 'Love' and 'reaction'. Below that, '*drums*'. Formal nightly conferences still went on at the Hit Factory. An officer at the 18th Precinct, across the street, remembers 'Bruce and the boys walking in . . . always in shades and black leather, like some kind of crime family.' In fact, in the control room with Springsteen were just Clearmountain, looking gaunt and harried, and Plotkin. Landau would show later. Springsteen listened to various mixes, echoing beats and riffs with snapping fingers. When they were done, he'd sit gloomily in his chair for a moment then give his verdict, a clenched 'yep' or 'nope'. Hours and days dripped by like this, and 1984 rolled around. The proverbial year, and his own, began in a 'Jersey joke-telling' contest at the Pony. Springsteen's Italian gag, about the priest and the dwarf, came third.

When he drove home up Ocean Avenue that night, he was intrigued to see graffiti and call-signs painted in huge white letters: BOSSA and HE WINS – WE WIN. There was a riot of fan activity around his gates. For the first time since *The River*, Springsteen was being doorstepped. He rolled down the window of the Camaro as he went by. After a half-hour of frenzied autographing, he gave his dry chuckle and said something about food. Springsteen drove up the lane to the house. A few minutes later, his minder Jim

McDuffy came back with supplies of pizza and coffee and blankets, in preparation for a siege. It had started to rain, hard.

It was grim in the winter in Jersey, and the dark fell early. Then the courtyard lights came on and Springsteen's blue car passed, idling, shuttling between Rumson, clubland and the studio. Work on his album proceeded at its stock, glacial pace. Springsteen would set out most evenings, stopping for a quick word at the gate. He drove fast, and skilfully, angling over the back roads that went from dirt to tar, then speeding up the Parkway. At the Factory, he'd slump in an anteroom furnished with worn velvet couches and fat chairs, tables piled with books and homeopathic medicines, cassettes, fruit and beer. A soiled rug covered the floor. It was the same dark, male lair Springsteen created at home or away. He loved sitting up all night, listening to mixes, prowling the control booth or cutting in the studio proper. Beyond that, though he didn't show visitors this (and never would), was a safe – as large as a vault – where Springsteen kept his tapes. Ever since a fan casually walked off with demos from *The River*, security arrangements were elaborate.

'I want to get girls into the group,' Springsteen had said. That was in 1974. A decade on, he retrieved his ambition of broadening the band, if not the sound, making for more cloudy poetry about 'real folks'. Here again, Landau pulled a masterstroke. For years, he'd known something was missing. The tours had been orgiastic sell-outs, but market research showed up a hard truth: most women were unwilling to sit through four hours of frat-rock and male bonding, even with Springsteen to moon at. They wanted a proxy; someone to actually root for. There was only one real bet. After their reunion at the Stone Pony, Springsteen had casually dated Patti Scialfa 'and gone out for a burger. We had a nice rapport.' She added vocals to one of the new tracks, though they didn't make the final cut. Then came an audition. At last, in June 1984, he called back. One thing Scialfa noticed right away about Springsteen was that he was a shy talker ('because his music's so loud', Bill Bradley adds). No matter how manic the roar around him, he kept his voice at the same low, muffled drone, except when laughing. Whether or not it was a ruse was moot, but it had a ruselike effect: Scialfa listened hard to every word he said. After thinking it over, she joined exactly three days before a world tour began. 'Ten minutes to showtime, they still didn't know where they were going to put me,' she told *Q*. 'I ended up by Max [Weinberg]. I had a big notebook with my words like cramming for school down at my feet.' Scialfa was also coming down with laryngitis.

Even in those unsettled days, Springsteen was never short of female company. But the friendship – as it still was – with Scialfa was different. Down the months, he'd suddenly display an unusual concern for closed rehearsals, and made several trips to her room to buff, as he told a friend, 'them harmonies'. The noises from these try-outs sullied any objective appreciation of the music. Scialfa was then turning thirty-one. She'd grown up in Long Branch, went to the University of Miami, toured around New York and finally eked out a living guest-singing on the Asbury run. Like Springsteen, she was, if not a barfly, a confirmed club-hopper. Opinions vary as to how talented she was. Scialfa made a neat foil and focal point onstage, little though that had to do with music. But she, too, gelled. Early in the tour, Springsteen playfully called her by her first name, Vivienne. There was a quick flash on Scialfa's face that neared the hue of her hair. Not until that moment had it dawned on her that she, who 'really dug Bruce', might also be in love with him. Scialfa said nothing more, and the scene could easily have been forgotten but for a third party's glance of it. In telling – and retelling – the highlights of the saga, this source is adamant. 'Patti was puce, *absolutely puce*.'

Meantime, Springsteen took to the road again, mingling late-night trips to Rumson and down the back alleys of Freehold with days cruising the Parkway. He'd often stop off at a neon-topped grill. Springsteen always chatted with the waitresses and other diners. At Dock's in Atlantic City, he sat at the counter, bolted meatloaf and spuds washed down with milk, then signed autographs for an hour. Springsteen licked off his white filmy moustache, deeply, engagingly and always, says Grice, a 'kid at heart'. A friend stood by the door, 'watching Bruce do his meet-the-troops bit . . .

we were late for the studio'. Springsteen was delayed, in part by the crowd, in part by the sudden arrival of more fans, who had to be obliged with photos. Scheduled to be in New York at 9 p.m., he didn't swing out of the restaurant till eleven. As he did so, in a final touch of the circus vibe of the night, a woman ran out and squeezed her bare breasts against the Camaro window. Dragged back, she announced herself as 'Sherry Darling' and explained that she was 'Bruce's legal wife'. Meanwhile Springsteen, oblivious to most of these ravings, waved gaily from the speeding car.

There was more to his drives, though, than just nostalgia or the mania of the fans. Springsteen also liked to veer off the highway. His next album would be less cryptically folk than *Nebraska* and more big-canvas American: pop slices of the heartland; low-slung retail strips, convenience stores and hometown streets. Most notable of all, Springsteen managed to animate his landscape's heroes. Populism became his text, as solid and irrefutable as Rushmore. Unlike Dylan, who practically put on social comment with long pants, Springsteen had spent several years, and at least three albums, finding his voice. He compensated for lost time in frequent, direct action. His charity was abundant, whether in taking veterans off welfare or quietly donating cash to food banks. He lived out Whitman's text:

I seize the descending man
O despairer, here is my neck . . .

But Springsteen wanted to rouse America, not coddle it. The songs on *Born in the USA* cut a swath between radicalism and die-hard love for the nation's, and his own, lost innocence. Like Whitman, he was a 'good conservative'. There was nothing anarchic about Springsteen, and his protest even at Reaganomics didn't always cut deep. He wanted to see America live up to its dream. 'With countries, just like with people, it's easy to let the best bits slip away.'

As he drove west on Asbury Avenue, then turned north on the freeway, Springsteen passed rusted-out suburbs pummelled by rain and offering a continual row of clapboard shanties, junkyards and malls. He saw low, shake-sided slums untopped by roofs and dirt pavements where the broke stood and stared. In Eatontown he met men, gaunt and red-eyed, panhandling at the country-club gates. By Red Bank, there were NUKE IRAN slogans daubed on walls now black with moss and smog. Even home in Rumson, faces sheered up at the door and begged for food, as well as relics. This was the America, full of hungry and homeless, where a slow trickle-down of the manna given the top rank left a full third below the poverty line, that fixed itself in Springsteen's album.

'The joys and hopes, the griefs and anxieties of the men and women of this age, especially those who are poor or in any way afflicted, these too are [our] joys and hopes, griefs and anxieties.' Springsteen may have deep-sixed religion around the time he bowed to fleshly gods like Elvis. But he still cleaved to those words from Vatican Two, the most lucid expression of the modern Catholic church. In 1984, mere altruism hardened into a sense of destiny. He had the cookie of wealth yet ate the cake of poverty. Springsteen was perfectly suited in personality, temperament, courage, context and patriotic *mores* to the moulding of a charitable sub-career. He was a loner from the start, long known to embrace family 'shit', the maker's mark of philanthropy. Springsteen was moody, brooding, dour and, for years, intensely uptight in his approach to his music and the challenges and hassles of being a rock star. As the first push gave way to consolidation, he looked round. 'Every person, every individual counts – to me,' he said. Difficult and self-obsessed he was, but always with feeling.

All that year, Springsteen read. He soaked up Flannery O'Connor sagas and William Fox's *Dixiana Moon*. He duly finished *Death of a Salesman* and later bought *Journey to Nowhere*, a book of photos of post-industrial America that would fuel *Tom Joad*. He rediscovered Robert Frank's anthology *The Americans*, and the grainy black-and-white shots of David Kennedy and Eric Meola. Such things, as well as exploring Robert Johnson and Guthrie, dramatically altered the architecture of Springsteen's world. Before *Nebraska* there was a lazy tendency to think of him as a *de facto* liberal. He wasn't; but within three years, he'd taken over from punk the role of lightning rod for those socially, and variously, anti-Reagan. Of all the ironies of Springsteen's thirties, his political conversion was probably the most noteworthy, if only for its exquisite timing. It occurred on a rare upswing. Yet, while Springsteen's own life got better, he experienced it as having worsened. It was a tribute to his fellow-feeling. Because not everyone had won, he wasn't happy in the skin of a winner, fretting over the fallen and lost souls on his own doorstep. Meanwhile, Springsteen bought a three-storey white-porticoed villa, upriver in Rumson, that he wryly called 'the mansion on the hill . . . the kinda place I told myself I'd never live in'.

Rich, clear-eyed, with his newly buffed torso, Springsteen was also catnip to the ladies. He'd long been used to perks such as the notes and photos pinned to an endless flow of bras and panties, along with phone numbers, love odes and keys heaved at his feet. In time, these alms had grown into a gladiatorial sex life. For someone who, generally, had the manners of a governess – he never swore around women – Springsteen's amours would have raised eyebrows on a pirate brig. One night in 1978, after waiting outside her flat for a friend to leave, Springsteen shinned up Goldsmith's fire escape and banged on her window. 'He started yelling at her,' says the friend. 'Bruce began going through her closets and screaming about gifts he'd given her – camera gear, books. He was on such a rant, he even grabbed a copy of *Born to Run* on the table. The record flew out of its sleeve and nearly decapitated me.' Five years on, rotationally dating Scialfa and the flesh he brought home from bars, Springsteen still had an exotically flush libido. In particular, he enjoyed giving high-school girls and college co-eds the thrills of a Cinderella. There were literally dozens of them.

In 1983, Springsteen met a waitress at Clemons' club in Red Bank. Recalled only as Jenny, she was a scenic strawberry-blonde, permed and squeezed into a low-cut top, jeans and heels stacked higher than Abba's. Late that summer she took a job at D'Jais, a bar on 18th and Ocean in Belmar (a dozen blocks, by chance, from Sancious' old home on E Street). Springsteen came in each Wednesday night. Regulars grew used to the sight of the local icon sitting quietly in a corner over a beer, then roaring off with Jenny in the Camaro. He always came back. Springsteen's yen for roots and community led him to join in D'Jais' softball games and summer picnics. 'Nobody hassled him,' says Brian Pringle. 'He was one of us.' Jenny met the fate of all Springsteen's lovers, but his first wife, a noodly model-actress, eerily conformed to type: she, too, was a sinewy ash-blonde, clad in size-two tops and matching skintight jeans cinched round her waist. According to Pringle, the likeness wasn't just striking. 'It was spooky.'

For all the fame, the cash, the maturing music and social conscience, the hard nut remained: for years, he'd been a mental wreck. Sexual frustration had begun to taint both his lyrics and his moods. By late 1982, Springsteen was belting a song called 'On The Prowl', in which the central thesis – 'I'm lookin' for a gal, gal, gal'* – was met with wild whoops from the floor, if no action. Even as Springsteen filled out his life with a steady diet of one-nighters, he remained emotionally starved. A fan named Gina Esposito saw him one night sitting at the Stone Pony. 'I almost felt sorry for him. It was like he had nobody to talk to . . . But maybe he was happy like that.' There were certain other clues. Springsteen's body language was an analyst's dream: hunched, eyes down, hands drawn guardedly over his lap. Another friend, echoing Toni Hentz, thought him still 'kind of dorky', a well-meant man who only really shone with a guitar.

Springsteen himself made the link. 'I don't live that much differently,' he said in 1984. 'I'm still in Jersey and I go down the clubs . . . I still see a lot of the people I always saw.' All that was true, and old cronies who met him (like the protagonist of 'Glory Days') found a kindred soul who'd lope over and blurt a name. 'My man,' he'd say. He'd put his arm round your shoulders. 'How you *doin*'?' Looking up at that face, seething with warmth, even Grice thought that 'Bruce was the same guy.' The change was all in scale. In the sixties, there'd been Freehold; in the eighties, Rumson. Then, he'd been Baby, or Buck; now, Boss. Meanwhile,

---

*He slurred the words, so one might have missed some of their subtlety.

on 25 March 1984, Springsteen first sang the song that archly yet quite aptly foretold his arrival as a brand name, 'I'm Bad, I'm Nationwide.'

Production of *Born in the USA* continued through early 1984, and even then – after two years' fitful work – Landau would have to prise the tape from Springsteen's fist. Many of these revisions could have been done by the original Mandarins, whose name for themselves was the Humans. No one else qualified for the title, so, to them, the rest of the world was somehow unreal and there to be shunned, if not scorned. Springsteen, of course, wasn't slagging anyone. But it would be wrong to think that the idolized keeper of the rock flame and the cranky, reclusive worry-wort were incompatible: the man who spent hours and days holed up in the Factory was as real as the magical nice-guy and clubber. A writer who frequently worked with him diagnoses Springsteen's condition as that of a 'graphomaniac' – a person with a dour perseverance in one and the same basic idea: here, an obsessive shuffling of raw, two- and three-chord songs into something greater than their parts. He had help doing so. Along with Plotkin and Toby Scott, Bob Clearmountain now stood tall. He virtually ran the final sessions. Not least of the feats on Clearmountain's CV was his being a maths whiz. Much of the buttressing that went on that March were similarly number-crunching drills in adding and subtracting fractals from the mix. At times, it was more a lab than a factory, with white-coated men reverently speaking, in trade argot, of clean-ups, damping and DIs while Springsteen mumbled his layman's 'yep' or 'nope'. Mainly the latter: proud, fastidious, above all touchy, he never found it easy to let go. The compromises and frustrations grated. Any attempt to impose a rule-of-thumb schedule caused him apoplexy. But a new CBS deadline loomed. Late that April, *USA* finally went to bed: twelve colloquial-style studies, some stark enough to be speech-song, forty-six minutes' work variously written, rehearsed, played, sanded and spit-shone over five thousand hours. It changed Springsteen's life.

Landau, of course, was ever-present. No fans threw panties or stalked *him* (recently married to ex-*Stone* editor Barbara Downey), but it was he who signed off and made the major decisions – which tracks to include, when to go live. Springsteen was content with the walk-on roles so long as the overall vibe was right. On one occasion he played softball with the band while Landau chaired a key studio summit, partly because he felt his serenity proved 'I trust the guy'. He had good cause to. Nearly five years ago, 'Hungry Heart' had been casually offered to friends, then, at the same brisk clip, retrieved, a process richly illustrative of Landau's role. He did something similar with 'Cover Me'. This dread of charity and non-materialism was a fixed and sincerely held principle, one he pursued with a mastery of wheedling tactics. Both those hits would have grossed Springsteen thousands as covers by, respectively, the Ramones and Donna Summer. Instead, they netted him millions. Time and again, Landau's ritual performances as his kid's Janus were convoluted, ingenious; sometimes even ingenuous. Too often, they were castratingly rude. Almost always, though, they wrought miracles.

One spring Sunday at the Lyden House, Landau – 'unusually forcefully', in Springsteen's words – spoke up. For both artistic and, by luck, commercial reasons, *USA* needed another song: a lead single. Even rock's album of mental pictures can have produced few more potent images than Landau demanding a 'Prince thing' and Springsteen, after raving and kicking over a few chairs, grabbing his acoustic guitar and writing it. For lyrics, he began with the satiric cliché, six words fixed on the blues-rock idiom. 'I get up in the morning': bumped, for truth's sake, to evening. The rest of the song was a snarl of ennui, claustrophobia and world-woe. As to music, it hijacked the thudding disco beat of the likes of Chic (another of Clearmountain's crew); with synths that managed to be both tossed off and fussy. As soon as he heard 'Dancing In The Dark',* CBS's Al Teller knew it 'had the smell of an absolute monster'. Springsteen launched the song at Xanadu's bar on 26 May. That same month it tore up the chart, backed by one of the best

---

*A line from *Born*'s 'Backstreets', as well as the title of a William Powell musical released, oddly enough, the very week Springsteen was born.

outtakes, 'Pink Cadillac', to make neither *Nebraska* nor *USA*. Springsteen's deft one-two punch translated into his self-styled 'commercial début', a number two smash. Ironically, it was kept off the top by Prince.

The rest of that spring and early summer was a tide of waxing enthusiasm, Springsteen for the market, the market for Springsteen. On 1 May CBS opened the shrill, stupeyfing sales blitz that ground down, with one lull, at Easter 1987. There were press kits, cut-ups, sell-ins, fold-outs, posters, banners, trannys, ads and TV clips. Springsteen mimed through his first concert video. He had his rear immortalized by Annie Leibovitz for the *USA* cover. By Memorial Day, he began gearing up to tour behind it. This time round, there were a few, significant changes in line-up. Van Zandt left; Lofgren and Scialfa joined. Since 1977, too, a series of stealthy pogroms had culled most of E Street's original gang. The 'amnesiac loathing' now did for Marc Brickman, the man who'd lit the shows for ten years. After being fired, 'no one would hire me,' he told Goodman, 'because I wasn't with Bruce any more. Rumours circulated – Jon [had] some influence in ruining my reputation.' Springsteen then tried to rearrange the furniture, literally, by having the group swap places onstage. There were several hangar-sized try-outs. When that backfired, balked by a bass-led mutiny, he took to rehearsing in and around Asbury. On 8 June the band brought down the house at the Stony Pony, going on at 2 a.m. and straggling off, tired but happy, at dawn. That same week, *Rolling Stone* officially broke news of the album. According to Arthur Baker, a key slogan was 'Later for the subtlety.'

So far, Springsteen's value had lain in what he was rather than what he said. Until May 1984, by simply being, and mainly sticking to the stuff of albums and no-frills tours, he'd done no wrong. He was the one who stood aloof from the naked lunges and greed of most bands. He eschewed 'shit'. But now Springsteen did something new. He went into mass production. The original plan had been to release *USA* in June, then hit the east coast in July and August. Long before then, there were sly hints that the original itinerary was far too modest. Both the single and album flew off the racks. Ticketrons' phones rang night and day. Landau's and Barry Bell's growing expectation was that this was the bank year of a superstar for whom dollars – and pounds and yen and guilder – would teem down on the tills. It was a manager's dream break, taking an archaic dramatic device, the gig, and twisting it into a sales jihad. Now more than ever, Landau pushed and shoved for his man, made him rich and secure; and generally coped with the nitty-gritty, leaving Springsteen free to work. Money-wise, the latter had been near-subnormally *naïf*, a word that was now too embarrassed to venture outside inverted commas, or without the attached 'faux'. His beliefs had been simple, useful and universal, and helped to undermine the dire farragos – at once postmodern and fossilized – of seventies pop. Springsteen was still a potent, deviant force, but he no longer bucked commercial norms. Along with Michael Jackson, Prince and Madonna, he *was* the mainstream.

Springsteen began his pursuit of gold by pandering to TV and radio gods. On the tour's opening night in St Paul, he sang 'Dancing In The Dark' twice, not in joyous encore, but a crass lip-synch for Brian de Palma's cameras. Springsteen's twitchy, manic and ultimately St Vitus's dance (with the starlet Courteney Cox) struck even Marsh as 'self-conscious . . . his enormous, fluorescent grin simply didn't jibe with the anguish of the vocal'. Springsteen himself thought the shoot 'great'. He was now appealing to seven- and eight-year-old children. MTV aired the clip nonstop. He took a half-step up the genetic ladder for his next move; Springsteen turned 'Dancing', 'Cover Me' and 'Born In The USA' over to Baker to convert into dance-mix – and, thus, race-busting – hits. The results didn't win many new friends. Landau and his client's hopes that the edits would somehow endear him to a younger, black audience were sadly misplaced. The old acolytes carped at the profaning of holy writ. Baker fumed under a volley of hate-mail and critical rants about suborning anthems. 'A fuck-up' was Springsteen's confidential report. 'I blew it.'

Aside from the music, there were some signal changes that summer. Springsteen's diet and gym regime had pumped him to Rocky volume. A bodyguard squired him everywhere. He'd also bought his first Jersey home. A friend who stayed there had the sense of 'a star struggling to care' and fixing, instead, on making a life. 'One of the things on my mind,' Springsteen said, '[is] to maintain connection with the people I grew up with, the sense of community . . . The danger of fame is in forgetting.' Even as the king-making machinery swung to its zenith, he spent his few free afternoons on the public beach. At night he rehearsed – even there, sweating like a welder – then drove to Rumson. Springsteen's new seat was flanked by icons of his past, pickups, Chevys and the '60 Corvette. The house itself was that of a moderately sloppy bachelor, not a wasted, narco-dependent wreck. He sometimes invited a fan in for a beer. Springsteen no longer haunted D'Jais, but was known to drop in on the Jefferson motel in Asbury. He made a friend of George Smith, the sixty-year-old bartender there. They went to dinner together. On other litmus-test issues, Springsteen also pursued an individualistic, rugged road. Of course, he basked in the fiscal high noon. But he did so as his own man – seldom yielding an inch, for example, on personal habits. Springsteen was still hellbent on honouring the factory hands, vets and anyone else staking the minimum $15 ticket price. So he never did drugs, rarely drank and wouldn't let anything 'fuck me up for the kids'. Even as he questioned his work, his musical commitment was total. He cared.

His inner life was a tragedy. In later days, Springsteen often spoke of his romantic flops, adding that he was in the same cage 'for thirty years with a lot of chicks' – one of many variants on the theme – till a therapist charged 'two hundred freakin' bucks an hour' to help him get off the wheel. After Springsteen split with Jenny, there were still seniors, co-eds, grads, actresses and – all of a type – models, as well as the odd backing singer. Most of these trysts were more *corps* than *coeur*; as were the blouse-lifting rites of the groupies. Certain fans continued their habit of doffing their shirts to him. One seventeen-year-old who kept a more or less fixed vigil at Springsteen's gate once threw herself at his feet as he trudged out with pizza. She was naked. Another girl left gifts in his mail-box: polaroids of herself in duly striking combinations with

men, women and farm animals. Somehow, Springsteen kept on a
tight rein and merely smiled. Meanwhile, he wasn't afraid – he
needed – to subject himself to raking truths. In public, Springsteen
sang:

At night I wake up with the sheets
soaking wet and a freight train running
through the middle of my head

– while, in private, he weighed the 'pros and cons of emigrating,
suicide, becoming a monk, and the other usual crap. In the end, I
figured I might as well marry.'

The dismissal of the 'usual crap' was Springsteen's masterwork.
On 4 June 1984, *USA* was released worldwide. Five months later,
Springsteen had a hit album and a hit tour; and he fell in love. Her
name was Julianne Phillips. He'd first seen her, in fact, acting in a
.38 Special video and in two TV romps, *Summer Fantasy* and *His
Mistress*. They met, backstage in Los Angeles, through the
inevitable Barry Bell. Overnight, the couple fell through a trapdoor
and found a surprising thing: the thirty-five-year-old Jerseyan and
the Oregon prom queen and Elite model, ten years his junior, were
mutually centred round their loneliness. They worked. To see them
arm-in-arm only a week later was to be left in no doubt that both
were on the path of self-discovery. Springsteen, he announced, was
'figurin' shit out'.

That meant a (thunder and) lightning romance, with sex,
lunches, dinners, TV, movies, gyms, tanning salons, aerobics,
roses, lingerie, limos, pools and meeting-the-family all neatly
condensed by Springsteen as 'gettin' real'. Especially the sex.
Phillips' startling beauty (her scripts somehow always called for
her to don a bikini) palpably altered the Asbury crazy-gang tone
of the tour. In October, Springsteen had told Kurt Loder, 'I'm just
not really looking to get married . . . I've made a commitment to
my job right now, and that's it.' Two months on, he'd changed
tack. 'It's not a question of wanting to do less. It's just more a
question of wanting to round out your life.' Between times, they'd

bonded in health clubs – his in Jersey, hers in Beverly Hills – and in the grey backstage rooms of hockey stadia. At least one musician resented the intrusion of a lover into the inner shrine, glowering at Phillips whenever she showed. From this Springsteen drew what his friend calls the 'drop-dead conclusion' that 'Juli deserves' – he looked at the band – '*all* your love.' Scialfa's conclusions she kept to herself.

By then, *Born in the USA* was six months into a two-year boom. Previewing the album, *Rolling Stone* had said 'it's . . . not a heavy, message-oriented LP. It's simply a lot of fun.' They meant it as a compliment.

Time has a curious way with music. Albums last. The best ones, of course, are those that duly pass the ten-, twenty- or thirty-year rules: LPs that chug on from one era to the next. To do that, there isn't much point being 'simply a lot of fun' – you need to *say* something, as well as keep the music on the move. Springsteen did so on *USA*, a rock tapestry of first-person, working-class lives. On one level a howl tuned to the damaged psyche of the Vietnam vet, it was actually a kind of mass-market version of Allen Ginsberg's *America*, with touches of Guthrie, Dylan and Phil Ochs vying with the usual suspects, Elvis and James Brown. Springsteen aimed for breadth on *USA*, so much so that it was swiped by both Reagan and, for sheer numbers, stadia full of unfathomably squealing twelve-year-olds. The whole was given a blue-collar rinse. Above all, it had the virtue of being topical, not least on Springsteen.

For years, even by the standards of his confessional age, he'd stuck close to the facts in his work. You could trace Springsteen's life by listening to the albums in order: the bleak youth and love of pop; the need to reconcile dreams with harsh truths; the abyss under the wit. For years, too, a sure sign of Springsteen's mood had been his poses on the LP covers. For sheer *joie de vivre*, it was hard to beat *Born to Run*. The dazed stare of both *Darkness* and *The River* neatly meshed with the passion and rebuke of the songs. On *Nebraska*, he'd gone for a snap of a two-lane blacktop as stark as a brick wall. All four shots spoke of Springsteen's sense of the narrow frontier between success and rout: the same one that forms the national character. Now he wrapped himself in the imagery of the Stars and Stripes.* Springsteen's wasn't the first LP to filch the American flag, or Americana; Chuck Berry, Hendrix, Sly Stone and Grand Funk Railroad had all done it. Fourteen years before, the MC5 had belted *Back In The USA*, a cult classic produced, oddly enough, by Landau. But none of those sages had ever stooped to musing about the sheer span of their country, whether from Whitman's pastoralism to urban junk, Thoreau to Twain, Emerson to Elvis. Springsteen did. Better still, his album had a weary, endearing, personal charm, as though he'd wandered into the studio one night – instead of over two years – and knocked out his thoughts on the state of friendship and love. Its second half, in particular, was autobiographical. 'As I get older I write about me, and what I see happening around me,' Springsteen said. 'So that's *USA*.'

The album was a failure: at least a failed stab at writing *de profundis*. 'I wasn't satisfied with it,' he added. 'I didn't think I made all the connections.' One external qualm about *USA* was its hack vocabulary, with fire joining girls and cars as stock images. Richard Williams calls it a 'scam . . . between them, Bruce and Landau took themes that had worked in the past and blew them up into cartoons'. Thus the old cast of *Greetings* and *The Wild* made their comeback knock-kneed and laughing: just more Top 20 vaudevillians. Unlike Jackson's or Madonna's, though, Springsteen's LP had a curiously poetic ability to pinpoint the language and bluff facts of America. Its flop was one of nerve, not vision. Four years later, Springsteen told *Rolling Stone* he preferred his new album to *USA*, which he shrugged off as 'a rock record'. No crime there: but, instead of being down and dirty and breaking like the wind, it just piled on every possible beat, groove, synth and riff possible, adding weight rather than meat. At worst, *USA* was the aural mirror-image of how Springsteen looked: matey but muscle-bound. As Paul Sexton says, 'it all veered between a cliché and a caricature', with the obvious goal of 'finally living up to his billing'. Springsteen

---

*Also opting for the patriotic look was Springsteen's wardrobe of red cap, white vest and blue jeans. For added symbolic value, he wore a cowboy belt.

agreed. 'I've had a large cult audience from when I started . . . Then I hit *Born in the USA* – and suddenly a lot of people who weren't interested in my music before and haven't been interested since bought that record.'

USA was both big and heavy, yet with flashes as fresh and slick as a new dab of paint. One of the album's strengths was the way it used the history and form of rock as a trampoline, lurching woozily around from hoarse arias to ballads. The anthems, of course, were set in a different plain. Most cuts, though, arrived on vinyl sounding spare and stark, all the better for being given the lean treatment rather than the Spector glitz. Between them, Springsteen, Landau and Plotkin came up with a smoke-and-mirrors gem (half from the *Nebraska* archives), an album that betrayed the folkie sentiment if not the gamut-running glee of *Prodigal Son* days. At its best, it was neat and nippy and recalled some ancient, but never-forgotten, plot-lines – there were touches of *Liberty Valance* and *The Postman Always Rings Twice*. Like a Swiss army knife, *USA* provided different tools for different needs: there are times when headbanging mayhem comes in handy, and others when nostalgia does the trick. It was the evocation of these various moods – a slab of what it was like to be thirty-four, rising thirty-five, in 1984 – that gave *USA* its bite. Like anything good, it went both forwards and back: among those who leapt on the juggernaut were half the Brill Building's singer-songwriters, the novelist Bobbie Ann Mason, two presidential hopes and PR firms unnumbered. Springsteen turned down $12 million to license *USA*'s title tune to Chrysler.

Plato called songs 'spells for souls for the creation of concord'; at best, Springsteen's slogans were balm to a republic polarized by debt. (At worst, Landau's hype concealed a grisly truth – 'Born' was boring.) Hollow and clunky in spots, the uplifting swell of raves about joy-rides and glory days ultimately won through, fuelled by plucky riffs and synth-pop hooks. The band's two 1974 intake all but turned the record inside out. Notably Weinberg. The original *Village Voice* ad hiring him had said 'No Jr. Ginger Bakers'. Ten years on, the template had duly shifted to John Bonham. Landau had spent much of the decade between nagging Weinberg to simplify for the studio; *USA*, and particularly the title track, was their mutual coup. It was left only for Clearmountain to punch up the drums, stiff-armed and meaty when not sounding like Led Zep's entire rhythm section. Clemons was conversely muted. The result was a foot-pumping, chipper, if hoary classic. Springsteen, of course, possessed a prodigious rock memory – some of *USA*'s licks could be carbon-dated. All in all, it drew on pop's richest mineral deposits, with trace elements of blues and rockabilly, and a lode of C&W, roving giddily from party noise to dirges. The mix's relentless modernism didn't obtrude many trendy lyrics, full of babies, sha-la-la's, little girls, misters and '50s nonsense syllables like 'knock-a'. Springsteen's dry, friendly voice soared like a stunt pilot.

The lead-off track, another morality tale which took wing from Kovic's book and a script also called *Born in the USA*, and which millions read as a war-cry, had an identity crisis as deep as Springsteen's. It was a saga of cold hope and failed American dreams, what Landau had called 'a dead song', one of the fillers on the original *Nebraska* demo. From there, Springsteen shook it off, slowed it down and pumped it up in a take-two jam, Weinberg's 'greatest single experience I've ever had recording'. The syncopation made the song jump up and down the block. Weinberg whammed out a backbeat that 'USA' used as a launch-pad to all-time Golden Great transcendence; it and 'My Hometown' reigned supreme as the album's bookends. Inevitably, some seized on the motto, not the message. Springsteen's allegory was milked by everyone from 'real dudes' to the White House. While wisely failing to 'explain' the lyric, others did so for him. Crowds at the Los Angeles Olympics flogged the chorus as a *de facto* national chant; Safeway, sundry beer, burger and pizza chains and scores of bootleg ads – not to say a Chrysler knock-off – all got in on the protest. At its most visible level, plastered over hoardings and chalked on walls, its theft was rife, a riot of swagger and jingoism, and near instant. Triumphalism was the donkey on which Springsteen would pin the tail of the song's perversion. 'It's not ambiguous,' he said. 'It had an enormous amount of pride, pride in being American. But they missed the shame in it.'

'Cover Me' was the typically minor-key, yet spicy follow-up, an example of the not-that-well-concealed art of paradox which says bouncy beat, but listen to the *words*. Elsewhere Springsteen goosed his material with in-jokes (the 'Batman' theme dogging 'Working On The Highway') and the familiar nods. 'Downbound Train' started out like a Keith Richards riff and swerved, via Elvis and Hank Williams, into one of those great country, busted-heart lines, 'Now I work down at the carwash/where all it ever does is rain.' 'I'm On Fire' retooled Springsteen's Pointer Sisters gift, though with a darker vibe. Fragility had gone from his voice, replaced by a virile adult's sense of sex and – at a stretch – menace. The intro, treated by most fans as a bit of randy foreplay, was also loaded with a mix of threat and promise worthy of a paedophile.

'Bobby Jean''s tune mined its cheesy, Memphis-cum-Detroit roots (echoing both the Supremes and Love Affair), with new life breathed in by the plot, a *buon viaggio* to Van Zandt. Sentimental yet sharp, it worked. There were no mixed messages to burn on 'I'm Goin' Down', a throwback to the days when Springsteen was seventeen and ogling his lifelong totems, 'pussy 'n' pickups'. 'Glory Days' similarly evoked the pear-shaped emotional vista of the Castiles. The requisitely ethereal model for 'Dancing In The Dark' was 'Every Breath You Take'. Musically, it was potentially lethal only to diabetics; lyrically, 'Dancing' wove a darker spell than the sugary disco paean. It was an end-of-the-rope song, sharing *Nebraska*'s dire, three-word gist: no way out. Freehold, and specifically Doug, had, of course, long become a narrative *idée fixe*, the throughline of *Darkness* and half *The River*. But where he'd once tapped into a child's revenge trip – Springsteen's own Inner Brat – most of the later songs tracked down the equally strong sense of doe-eyed wonder. Aptly, *USA*'s closer was the treacly 'My Hometown', a moving and affecting elegy in a discount-Dylan strum. Springsteen had told friends he wasn't ready to marry, but only a man weighing his options could render uncertainty, hope and longing with the parting lines 'I'm 35, we got a boy of our own now/Last night I sat him up, behind the wheel/And said son, take a good look around . . . This is your hometown.'

Predictably, there was a fuss about *USA*'s sales; or sell-out. To some, Springsteen seemed to be making an almost heroic bid to kowtow to an entire industry's gods. For them, it was all over for 'rock and roll future' the moment he hired Arthur Baker. Springsteen could never have gone global, others sniffed, without the well-timed CD and video booms. They all missed the point. No one shifts twenty million copies (and seven hit singles) by luck, or even marketing. *USA* remains one of the top ten rock albums of all time. Reviews, and royalties, still tick over today. Its façade of being macho and even bovine grew with its fame. That, too, was a mark of having made it. There was something almost mythical about the story of its rise to the level of a catchphrase. And something inevitable: *USA* was Springsteen in his pomp. But it was more, and in its tireless glorification of what, at first, seemed trite and small-town, the album duly laid full-time siege to posterity. It spent 126 weeks on the chart.

The red, white and blue Terror, or holy war, that made Springsteen part of the ether began on 7 May 1984. An 'awareness' campaign choreographed by CBS pumped, successively, 'Dancing', *USA* and a tour. The label sent 350 field kits to its sales force and PRs. Reps huddled with key distributors. Listening parties for buyers and DJs were held in twenty cities. By 18 May, a well-oiled machine was delivering posters, banners, logos, replicas of *USA*'s cover and over-all gush to record stores. TV ads and word-of-mouth attracted huge numbers to the album's launch. The charts measure success or failure by first-week sales. On 7 June, three days after release, Springsteen had a platinum smash.

He didn't appear to weep over the loss of what he'd called 'that gas . . . [of] not going on for eight billion people . . . and getting fat'. Springsteen may not even have been conscious he was in the pres-ence of his 'privileged day'; he was interested, mainly, in having a good time, sex, and, of course, drilling the band. Dry-runs contin-ued in and around Asbury through mid-June. Landau and George Travis, meanwhile, drew to the tour an entourage of mixers, min-ders, truckers, tweenies, goons, roadies and riggers, not charming so much as overloading them with a sense of duty. ('Bruce is going to change people's lives; your job is to help him do it' is one memory of the pep talks.) Most of all, they were creating on an epic scale, sweeping past *The River* and aiming at a larger vision of what rock could be. Everything now went to undreamt-of levels of profit. 'Tour 84' opened at the Civic Center, St Paul, on 29 June. It vectored west and south before breaking at Christmas, whistlestopped the Orient, blitzed Europe, recrossed the Atlantic, jagged between Washington and Chicago, barnstormed Jersey, and tore to a finish in California. In terms of sheer numbers, it *was* a crusade; with, once again, at its centre, a man unable to connect with life, yet unable to let it pass by without trying. For Springsteen, it was a haunting and haunted saga of projecting a front. He was, in fact, chronically down for at least the first four months.

Fans weren't watching him any more. They were adoring a god simulating himself against a vast diorama. Springsteen's success doing so was beyond doubt, as was his failure to recoup the spontaneity and edge of old. The questions raised by the tour's balance-sheet are, first, whether the price paid for going 'nationwide' was too high and, second, whether the same end could have been got for less. The answers lie largely in the mind of whoever asks; but Springsteen's professionalism, skill, good intent and talent for bending with the wind all stood out. So, too, did the band, self-styled knights of the Grail, always solid and intermittently thrilling in their pursuit of rock-and-roll ideals. The shows survived even outdoors. Springsteen animated the sets with a judicious number of *Nebraska*-era blues, jeremiads that set up the emotional gear-shift of the belters. The vocals and backing on 'Thunder Road' were a feat of musical action, as well as of the frame they were set in; the lights were gouged into blinding spots of red and white, shocked into insignia by cross-beams of blue, flaring on the 'I'm pulling outta here to win' punch-line. Recognizing that such moments are sacred, Springsteen stuck to note-by-note replays of the classics. There was one glitch. The slow, hypnotic weave of 'Racing In The Street' gave way to a moment that took the breath away – and not by being transported on wings of song. The aesthetic jolt of 'Cover

Me' struck one critic as like 'a turd in the Tate Gallery'. Springsteen privately agreed with this bleak assessment. He began doing the song in Baker's self-consciously 'wacky' way.

Elsewhere, the shows flowed on a wave of upfront rhythm, full of attack and drama, chintzy organ and Bittan's synth fugues. As on record, the thrumming density of the drums injected volume and velocity; you could *feel* the beat. It was a fat noise. The gigs were both ferally loud and fully audible, the intonation perfectly true – an amalgam of Led Zep, choral clarity and pain-threshold blare. Springsteen mostly sang as though shouting the words from a passing car. Yet the actual set, despite its scale, was far from being a stylistic free-for-all. Both lights, and the giant flag backdrop, were ravishing, the staging vivid and lean on boss's orders.

Sometime in those fifteen months' road work, he ceased being a star and became a symbol. That Springsteen wasn't just a rocker, and had the politician's need to convert, he'd already shown in a quote on tour. 'If I leave the stage feeling, "Well, if I played just one more song, maybe somebody out there would be won over" . . . If I feel I could've done more, it's hard for me to sleep that night.' Live, he gave everything, every time. The critic Lawrence Grossberg would coin the phrase 'inauthentic authenticity' to describe icons like Springsteen – their moral centre *was* their image. In that sense, it was, truly, 'an act'. On stage, Springsteen wooed his fans with his witty platform manner, his flat-out charm, the '*Howdy, Detroit*'s coming fast and furious. No one else could hold a candle to his striking affirmation of pop. Further testing his power to consist of the inconsistent, Springsteen managed to conceal from his audiences all the hurt and 'shit' caused by the last decade of neglect. The rich, fulfilled man they saw still saw himself as an emotional wreck. There were really, of course, two Springsteens: the randy rocker and the man who went off on solo drives through Freehold, where he'd sit gazing at his past. Musically, too, the party raver co-existed with the crooner. He did the fast tunes in a kind of fit of hormonal frenzy. On the slower songs, the brawny, pensive Springsteen suggested an introverted ox. Some nights, Joel Bernstein says, it was 'like he was plugged into a piano-roll . . . the shows were so formulaic, if I missed a particular pose, I knew I'd get it again next time'. To others, this sameness wasn't necessarily a flaw. For them, Springsteen was the best retail rocker since the salad days of Jagger.

Frequently reeking of embrocation, swathed in gauze, Springsteen jogged on stage like an athlete to the track. Bernstein's shots of him, hale and headbanded, hit almost iconographic heights in the eighties. 'How ya goin'?' he'd yell, or 'Missed ya,' before cuing in 'Born In The USA'. The song was given full anthemic treatment. Springsteen's right fist shook aloft, and few in the 20,000 crowd emphasized lyricism at the expense of drama. He kept it up, with one break, for four hours: laughing, hamming – playing the Fender as though trying to rope a steer – and even lecturing, moving in the opposite direction to the expected dramatic snap. By tour's end, Springsteen was spicing the mood with a stump speech on foreign policy. He kept it personal. 'I wanna do this next song for all the young people out there . . . When you grew up in the six-ties, you grew up with Vietnam every night on TV . . . I'd like to do this for you, 'cause if you're seventeen or eighteen out there, next time, they're gonna be lookin' at you . . . Because in 1985, blind faith in *anything* – your leaders – will get you killed . . . 'Cause what I'm talkin' about is . . .' and, *boom*, the lights and drums pounded into 'War'. Everywhere he went, he'd tell his fans about growing up, school, church, the draft, about Doug and Adele, and then he'd pick a girl from the front row (seats there were scalped for hundreds of dollars) and jive with her. He danced himself dizzy.

'Born In The USA' was a good title for a tour. Depending on how you took it, it was a patriotic hug-in, a leaden plod (with crowds duly decked out in tricolours), or a cool threat to the smug, Morning-in-America tub-thumping of both presidential hopes. At its dismal nadir, there was a ghastly misappropriation of Springsteen as a rock-and-roll Rambo. With his bandanna and pumped-up pecs, he certainly looked it. What's more, whatever rabble-rousing he tried on the fans – 'Ain't it *great* to live here?' – came right back over the net. It was a gag, but somehow it bypassed the crudely xeno-phobic, and seemed, rather, both wistful and wry. Springsteen never meant for audiences to cosy up to the self-satisfied dross of Stallone's film. At core, he was more sad than angry, or even proud. 'We live in times that are pretty shattered . . . It's tough to think there's a generation of kids out there whose memory of their home is going to be a welfare motel. Too many of us [are] living in what amounts to being refugees [in our] own land.'

Down the weeks and months of globe-trotting, Springsteen never acted like a spoilt child of fortune. He played each and every of the 170 shows as though his life, and the crowds', hung on it. The tour had its own highs. Springsteen mingled, and sometimes duetted with old friends like Van Zandt, Southside Johnny and Mitch Ryder. (The last remembers 'talking body-building with Bruce as much as music'.) He sold out a ten-night stand at the Byrne Arena in Jersey. Fans pressed close to the stage there swore they could read the lips of the girl he brought up to dance. 'I love you so much,' she said, and judging from the female yelps in the 20,000 crowd, she spoke for all. It was dramatic, and unique, to hear whole stadia singing along *a cappella*: not choruses or songs, but entire, four-hour sets. The Who's John Entwistle, no stranger to mass hysteria, joined in for an encore. 'It was like playing to a jet engine, with those chicks. I've never before, or since, heard a sound like it . . . Bruce himself was a bit New York, but a gent . . . I remember him asking if I'd stay on for the rest of the tour. It could have been straight or it could have been a wind-up. He wasn't laughing when he said it.' Even the *Nebraska* monologues (fleshed out with drums, synths and chime effects) got them whooping along.

The next weeks saw a sub-industry of major print and TV tributes, one of those cyclical fits of goodwill towards a given artist. (Those with long memories made the link back to 1975). The luvvaganza made even *The Real Paper* hype sound like *Hansard*. It brought Springsteen to a wider audience than *Born* ever had, and complemented the CBS sales and marketing drive. There were some surprising converts. Via Weinberg and his wife, the Tory columnist George Will came to a show in Maryland, dressed down for the night in grey flannels and jacket, with a puckish bow-tie. He made a strange bedfellow, as well as a right-wing darling out of

Springsteen. 'An evening with Bruce tends to wash over into the A.M., the concerts lasting four hours,' Will wrote. 'Of course, [everyone] is making enough money to ease the pain. But they're not charging as much as they could, and the customers are happy . . . If all Americans made their products with as much energy and confidence as Springsteen and his merry band, there would be no need for Congress to be thinking about protectionism. No "domestic content" legislation is needed in the music industry. The British and other invasions have been met and matched.' Will added that he didn't have 'a clue about Springsteen's politics'.

With that column, a new image was born, one that booted Springsteen to all-American symbol status. He was certainly 'real' but he could also be flip, and, in a particularly arch way, he could often be both at once; he was the perfect rock star for both ironists and those who like their heroes straight. The nation now got behind him. On 12 September, the *CBS Evening News* ran a long profile. The *Tonight Show* star, the wag known as Johnny, now did 'Kingsteen' sketches. David Letterman duly brought up the rear. The legend was working well, and his offstage shyness and flag-waving gigs gave Springsteen a charismatic hue; a 'pop enigma' in *The Times*'s phrase. *Entertainment Tonight* buffed the CV anew. *People* weighed in with its own join-the-dots chronology. MTV's 'The Boss' contest traded witlessly on the myth. That tidy salvo put Springsteen under extra strain, and he responded by closing down. His tart views on fame were a sign that he'd entered the phase where he'd had enough. 'It's the old story of getting elected to a club you may not want to be a member of. But you are, anyway. You're just another trivia question on *Jeopardy*.'

Springsteen turned thirty-five in a rare drunken coma at a Buffalo club. Guests noticed his intensity, something apparent in the way he partied: an obsessive toping, a desire to 'get wrecked', the need to render himself insensible, a yen for Cuervo. When Springsteen drank, he quaffed. The tour's first leg wound up that week. By mid-October, he was in Tacoma, scene of a *Rolling Stone* feature, as well as the local rave: 'Everything about the man and his music is honest and straightforward, and even those who don't care for his spare arrangements and working-class lyrics acknowledge he's an unusually generous and sweeping performer . . . in all, he and his band played nearly forty songs.' Springsteen's sweep didn't, however, extend to 'Rosalita', deep-sixed for the first time in eleven years.

Elsewhere, a few critics knocked the tour as a coup not of musical enterprise, but of size and revenue, the scale more extravagant than anything Springsteen had done before, as if grandeur and overkill had replaced the last atom of spontaneity. In the sense they were slogan-ranting rallies, the gigs put some in mind of, aptly, *1984*. Men like Richard Williams weren't actually disloyal to Springsteen, but committed thought crimes. Those *vox pop* singalongs in Detroit, Pittsburgh and Oakland raised the risk of his knack for charm amounting to hypnosis. Generally, though, reviews were all Springsteen and Landau could have hoped for. The shows appealed to purists and tourists alike. On both vinyl and stage, *USA* left nothing to chance: the title track won the blue-collar vote, for instance, while 'Dancing' could be relied on to raise interest in smoochy disco-lovers. From the song's first bar, Springsteen would be fixed on the women, in love with his grin and the way he ground his hips; his hair, under the band, would start coming down, along with the sweat, into his deep brown eyes, until the girls would look at each other, and, after suffering all the bland doodlings of the New Romantics (who were neither) – and the dread Jacksons' tour – start to yell. That fan plucked out of the stalls was a proxy for 10,000 others.

By general reckoning, Springsteen had a striking hit-rate backstage, too. It usually began with something like:

'Omigod, omigod, omigod. Bruce!'

'True, o doll.'

'I love you'

– and went on from there, via a rubber chicken and limp salad buffet, to the hotel. Broadly, according to one woman, 'he'd get somebody who had good legs and knockers and charm the pants off her for twelve hours. Next afternoon, he'd go, she'd stay.' Springsteen's partners tended to be big-haired, amenable and chosen for their 'boobs, not brains'. They were pickled in hero lust and some thought he, mutually, needed love. He was, in fact, lonely.

During this next tsunami of fame, he spent much of his time alone with Landau. Though his promos policy remained in doubt, still swinging to the hard-sell and back, Springsteen's views on money were decided if complex. Always taking a stand against commercialism, he was an almost equally fervid non-hippie, once saying of bootlegs, 'Nobody likes the feeling that they wrote a song and in some way [it's] bein' stolen from them.' It was no fluke that Springsteen enjoyed an unprecedented 95–5 split with concert promoters in 1984–85. Even the Stones settled for ninety.

Whatever the theory of Landau's corrosive tactics, the fact was that, in 460 days of Bossmania, five million fans paid $110 million for seats alone. Merchandise raked in another $60 million, with Springsteen netting nearly $2 a copy for *USA*. When all the numbers were totted up, the eleven-country trek grossed a cool quarter of a billion dollars. While in Los Angeles, Springsteen was visited on equal terms by any glitterati in town. He appears to have been distinctly unimpressed by them, but did his best to be civil. Hence the snaps of him with Liz Taylor or Princess Stephanie. But Springsteen's main entanglement was on the campaign trail. As he crossed the plains on the tour bus, the small towns' signs and clapped-out neon wheeled and fell away to reveal America's main visual drama, his own name, alongside 'Reagan' and 'Mondale', in lights. Over the years, he'd been studiedly apolitical, or bi-partisan, voting exactly once in his life. Temperamentally, at least, as a nostalgist and free-thinker, Springsteen veered close to both main parties. There was, therefore, scope for what could be called either horse-trading or exploitation.

This is the place to recap a lifetime's fear – almost a phobia – of joining things, including causes. Late in his forties, Springsteen would bend knee to some of the star-system pieties of men like Sting. In a bid to buoy up his sense of involvement, a belief in 'dudes', he became, to some, like the 'holy fool' in *Boris Godunov*, alluding to awful truths; to others, a heart-warming faker. He certainly drifted leftward. By the nineties, Springsteen clung to a view

of life rigidly divided into rich parasites and jolly peasants, identified as Chicanos by names like Louis and Miguel and *de facto* heirs
of Tom Joad. This Manichean take on human nature came to him
late. While much of his populism would be made into rock's Magna
Carta by hip bletherers, they studiously missed his conservatism.
His manifesto was, like Jefferson's, 'life, liberty and the pursuit of
happiness'. Springsteen was in a direct line from the republican
work-and-play ethic of the Founding Fathers. He was interested in
pushing goals, not agendas. Between doing the rounds of club and
college gigs in 1972, Springsteen had made his sole trip to the
ballot box – to listlessly poll 'for George McGovern, I think'. Three
years later, Ray Coleman had asked him if he were 'politically
minded' or 'studied world events'. No, said Springsteen.

True enough, he was shaken by Ronald Reagan's election in
1980. Many were. Springsteen still seemed happy with the music-
does-the-talking apathy for which nature made him. A full term of
recession and Cold War-mongering later, he was stressing, 'I'm
just a singer; I don't get involved in that stuff,' when asked about his
party affiliation. Two weeks before that fall's election, Springsteen
added, 'I'm not registered to one side or another . . . I don't think
along those lines.' His detachment went both to and fro; as late as
1996, he told *The Times*, 'I don't sit down and think I've got a message or I've got something I gotta say about the state of the Union.'
Among his latter-day list of pet hates were Ollie North, George
Bush and Bob Dole; Springsteen liked Jerry Brown, Jesse Jackson
and Bill Clinton. Even then, it was his habit to apply the morality
yardstick to those in power, not ideological dogma. He was, he
said, 'nobody's poster boy'.

Purloining *Born in the USA* was, therefore, Reagan's epic *faux
pas*, an exquisite folly. The President's exact words, at a campaign
stop in Hammonton, a farm community near Atlantic City, ran:
'America's future rests in a thousand dreams inside your hearts; it
rests in the message of hope in songs so many young Americans
admire – New Jersey's own Bruce Springsteen. And helping you
make those dreams come true is what this job of mine is all about.'
It was 19 September 1984, the first time a Commander-in-Chief

had ever mobilized a rock star as a character witness. Reagan's press office couldn't immediately say what Springsteen song might be his favourite.

While Landau schemed and Marsh seethed from his crouch in the bus, Springsteen sat tight. One source reports him as 'mildly embarrassed for the Gipper, not foam-flecked. I think Bruce was secretly amused.' Three nights later – after news releases and position papers had been unrolled for him like reels of silk before an emir – he made his blunt, simple retort on stage in Pittsburgh. 'The President was mentioning my name the other day, and I kinda got to wondering what his favourite album must be. I don't think it was *Nebraska*. I don't think he's been listening to this one.' Springsteen cued in 'Johnny 99'. That lyrical cocked snook was a godsend to the rival campaign. Yet it, too, bungled its chance. 'Bruce may have been born to run, but he wasn't born yesterday,' quipped Walter Mondale, then claimed to have been 'endorsed' by Springsteen. It wasn't so; and the interval of four more days and countless 'wonks' and 'bull sessions' produced a second, public snub. The cumulative farce of that week left Springsteen more sorry than angry. 'They basically tried to co-opt every image that was American,' he'd say in 1995. 'Including me.'

These false gods having slurred his good name, all he could do was head down the lonely trail, hoping that by playing enough gigs and hawking enough albums he could put his own word over. It was both old-fashioned, and happened to be something Springsteen did uniquely well. He loved performing. The shows' video director, Arthur Rosato, says 'logically enough, Bruce got more remote as the gigs and entourage got bigger. He was still a genuinely good guy. If you could fault him at all, it was on grounds of self-confidence. "Everything I've done, I owe to Jon," I remember him saying. It was loyal, but it was weird. He short-changed himself.' This fact deeply moved those who saw him backstage. Whether sitting in his father's lap (a replay of 'My Hometown') or eagerly asking 'What'll I say' to Reagan, he could seem the tour's junior intern, not its boss. There was something engagingly coy about Springsteen. A visitor to one of the June rehearsals in Clemons' club remembers it ending with 'the band all scattering into two different restaurants – the sushi bar and the diner – and Bruce sheepishly tucking into the pork chops . . . He was nearer-my-coronary-to-thee, but all the happier for it.' Later still, he was worried that 'they told me not to eat in them places. They'll be pissed.'

There were no Bacchic orgies or Dionysian rites at Springsteen shows. The only visible lark backstage was ping-pong. By now, even Clemons was interested not in groupies but in finding a quiet corner to meditate. Springsteen himself retreated to a private den before and after playing. As well as vocal warm-ups – often with his backing singer – there were rumours that he pursued his set policy of active bachelorhood. According to the same friend, 'When Bruce was tired, he screwed himself awake again.' Thanks to a stream of 'dolls', the old rock pro duly became the randy beachboy once more – or, at any rate, lapsed back into the normal state of a pop god. None of these lax couplings troubled the average fan. But they were the talk of the forty road crew, some of whom now obscurely called Springsteen 'Toss'.

His other, well-earned fame was for charity. The perception of men in Springsteen's songs shows an eye for weakness, not strength. *Nebraska*, in particular, reveals a near-neurotic fellow-feeling. The broad parallel between the kind of liberalism worn by Reagan pre-1952 and by Springsteen post-1982 is compelling. Both men stumped for civil rights and dues. Both were convinced they stood for the working man rather than any special interest. Both gradually became converts to a more radicalized agenda as they got older. Cynics said Springsteen was now also moved by a pre- or post-political need to put clear water between himself and the President. As Marc Eliot notes, 'His staff set out at once to find places for Bruce to make public appearances, statements, and donations designed to clarify his position as anti-Reagan, anti-Republican, anticonservative, antidupe.' An *NME* bard would ask – though the blue pencil cut it – a question rife that year, if 'de Boz, frankly, gives a fuck. Yes or no?'

Whatever his motive, Springsteen began to donate money,

goods and services. He did so quickly and efficiently. Charities and food banks down the way would be visited by Landau's assistant (and Marsh's wife), Barbara Carr. She listened to the various beefs, took notes and generally paved the way for Springsteen's warrant. Those passing muster would be invited to set up tables in the arenas' lobbies. 'This is your hometown,' Springsteen then told the crowd, making his own matching pitch for the soup kitchen, union or cause *du jour*. What's more, when the gig was done he gave the local hands tips on how to fund-raise. Springsteen told them to involve the whole community, not just rock stars like himself. This sounded a good idea: a man who explained, at last, how his guilt pangs had driven him to 'give something back' from the millions earned. Some nights, Springsteen would divvy up as much as $10,000 a show.

It was more than do-goodery. Springsteen wanted to 'boost folks' belief in stuff', or, at least, make them think. After a gig at Giants Stadium, he'd scarcely signed his last photo when he hit on another way to put his house rule on life. He added it in a PS: 'Be your hero. Be your own Boss. BS.'

Springsteen backed clinics and strike funds; he sang for Africa and anti-apartheid; and gave cash to aid agencies. It was a new world he loomed over, unique in place, peculiar in time. Mid-1980s America, with its phobia about health, its dread of age, its need for instant satisfaction of every whim – its greed-is-good *mores* – was crying out for such leads. Alongside the clear-sighted vision, there may well have been a streak of careerism. Springsteen's public-spirited image didn't exactly harm sales. His meet-and-greet surgeries were full service: they included spin-doctoring. Less publicly, less predictably, he still funded pet causes, many vet- and union-related, long after the last note of the last song. That he did so incognito, without fuss, shows the angst he felt in both being responsible for getting rich, as well as wanting to disown his kind. Springsteen gave a fuck.

More than once, he said he needed to be there for 'the dead dreamers . . . the lonely'. That took a rare talent for dreaming and loneliness. Despite, or because of, 'rooting himself silly' – his lover's words – Springsteen had no resources but music, the gym, tequila jags and sex. And so the groupies kept coming, until Los Angeles. Joel Bernstein (who Springsteen called 'the most mysterious guy in showbiz') remembers the very night Phillips shuffled up, backstage, with Barry Bell. A second photographer snapped the scene. 'You could hear the gulp.' Springsteen stood staring at her from bulging brown eyes out of his aura of black fuzz. He'd always said he fell for the same woman. The likeness between Phillips and, say, Karen Darvin was there: each had ski-bunny looks, fine, high cheekbones and a dizzy smile. They were also akin mentally. Both were career girls. Neither particularly liked rock and roll. Phillips' own tastes (for the MOR soul of a Lionel Richie) soon surfaced. One notably tart scene ended with Springsteen's prize LPs strewn across the floor, along with the couple's dinner. He ruefully claimed she wasn't 'buzzed' by Elvis, or even the Beatles. Phillips did, though, amply fulfil Springsteen's long-time 'doll' criteria. For someone who found women unreadable – 'them sub-texts', he'd say – scenery was what counted. That first night at the Sports Arena, Springsteen told a friend, 'I knew.'

Phillips was then twenty-four. She'd grown up in the lacy, prim suburbs of Portland, Oregon. Her spiritual home was the flashier, more topical one of swimsuit modelling and B-films. She was dating the actor Peter Barton. Yet by Thanksgiving 1984, a month after they met, she and Springsteen were keeping house. The clip was brisk and rested, at least in part, on Phillips' organizing ability, corralling him in the days and hours between gigs. A member of the crew heard 'her hauling off at Bruce about being late . . . and him just mumbling, real meek . . . Pussy-whipped. That's when I knew they were doing it.' They were together in Rumson for Christmas. In February they visited Phillips' parents, vacationing in Palm Springs; Springsteen arrived wearing a suit and tie. According to a family friend, Betty Fulop, 'everyone [was] delighted . . . Bruce was very quiet and subdued, didn't smoke or drink.' The first most of the world saw of Phillips was when, late that month, she and Springsteen sat together at the Grammys. While, oddly, Richie, not he, won Album of the Year, 'he was consoled,' *People* noted drily, 'by

Juli's company'. In fact, to a Shrine Auditorium staffer, Tom Modi, it seemed 'they were all over each other. His right hand and her left one were going at it.'

Taking the Grammys as the proper start of Springsteen's trajectory – he won for best male vocal – he'd be in global orbit for two years. There were gongs and medals in Britain and France. He was a popular sweep at the *Rolling Stone* music awards. *Born in the USA*, with its Old Glory motif and 'simply fun' tunes, was a coup of songwriting, packaging and market engineering. It was also proof of Springsteen's consistently good, if lucky, timing. As technology would have it, *USA* was the first-ever CD made in America, and one of the first anywhere. The passage of a year or two would see hundreds of thousands trade up from the original vinyl, every sale tending to more Bossmania, as well as more cash in Springsteen's bank account. It wasn't, strictly speaking, an LP at all. *USA* was what the labels like to call a multi-media event: a hard kernel of music wrapped in hype. As well as Springsteen's voice, the PR, too, was pitch-perfect.

Landau, in particular, roved over the bottom line with an actuary's eye. In time, he duly booted his client's art into an industry. Part of Springsteen's CBS deal was a healthy cut of the licensing. There were literally scores of *USA* spin-offs, everything from T-shirts and cups to customized lunch-pails and framed posters; if you could wear it or use it, Springsteen and the band were on it. Meanwhile, the 'back end' – TV specials, videos and foreign rights – would add even more to the pie. As Federici told *Backstreets*, 'We started out as a group, and turned into a super, giant corporate money-making machine.' Springsteen himself spoke of 'a blitz'. Jack Rovner, his CBS manager, as quoted by Marsh, used another fell b-word: according to him, the campaign was 'designed to give rock radio stations and stores an equal chance to climb on the bandwagon'.

A few fine judges were awestruck at Springsteen's sales, which they seemed to regard as pop's answer to McDonald's or Coke. To others, it was the cool profiteering that took the breath away. Even by playing 'sheds', he seemed to deny everything he'd taken years

As 1984 came round, fans weren't watching him so much as adoring a god play-acting himself against a vast diorama.

Bossmania.

That same year, Springsteen's 'red-headed woman' (third from right) joined his boys-only band – one of the steps on their downfall, and his own saving.

Meanwhile, he married the model-actress Julianne Phillips.

Duets – Springsteen with:

Patti Scialfa.

Sting.

Mick Jagger.

Springsteen's second wedding, in 1991, was a lesser world event than his first. There was no publicity strip-tease or press helicopters buzzing the reception. It did, however, set up a successful and lasting marriage.

Most of Springsteen's comeback gigs in 1992–93 were solid, if uninspired. On good nights, at least, he redeemed what the new band couldn't cut. Now in his forties, he still had the moves.

Legend.

The 'sawdust Steinbeck' who
toured the world, doing some
of his best and most human
work, from 1995–97.

1998's Amnesty International reunion. From left to right:
Tracy Chapman, BS, Peter Gabriel, Youssou N'Dour.

Springsteen, looking like one of his own lawyers, leaves the High Court in London. 'I came to defend my right to my music,' he said. 'It's a big part of what you are . . . what you come up with when you're sitting alone with your guitar late at night is one of the most personal things in your life.'

to build up. Then again, mass-marketing was in the game plan all along. There comes a point when all Rock Superstars want to cash in on the long years of scuffling and apprenticeship by a crass fling at the 'great average'. Bowie reached this point in 1983 with *Let's Dance*. It's hardly surprising they'd want to mop up, particularly those who'd long paid their dues, but some were better at it than others. There was no other period than that from *Rumours* to, say, *Nevermind* (partly cut in the same room) when the industry seemed so dwarfed by economic change, or so totally ruled by PR. Positioning was all. Springsteen 'knew just how to seduce the camera', says a well-known photographer. 'When to frown, when to smirk, when to give his little giggle . . . Anyone who thinks Bruce shrank back, waiting for Landau to call, has a very warped view of Bruce. And, in the case of those goods and chattels . . . he dug them.' Other pop *ingénus*, of course, had done the same or worse. Springsteen's old role-model Dylan springs immediately to mind. Even the Grateful Dead, in the end, went for the pay-off. These commercial pales are often, even compulsively crossed by everyone in rock; few can wear their hippiedom as a halo. Most felt Springsteen's bonanza to be well earned and overdue, as for an elderly and respected actor winning a tardy Oscar. 'I felt proud of him,' says Todd. Springsteen wasn't mercenary; he was mercantile.

Along with recording, touring and flogging logoed goods, Springsteen soon bent to the fourth sales god, videos. 'MTV provides all the physical information that's a big part of rock and roll,' he said, sounding like an ad for the station. 'My attitude is that it reaches a lot of people and I'm interested.' He was, of course, one of pop's great hams. Early in the art–commerce *anschluss*, Landau had met with Brian de Palma. 'You know,' he said, 'Bruce can't really act.' It took some time before the director realized it was a reassurance, not a warning. Over the next twelve months, Springsteen did live or semi-live clips of 'Dancing', 'Born In The USA', 'Glory Days', 'My Hometown' and 'War'. They were perfectly good, even though the tension, the sense of waste and loss, and even the joy of the songs were all reduced to corny lip-synching and a series of colour-supplement shots. Along with John

Sayles, Springsteen managed a bit of business in 'I'm On Fire', though it, too, failed to catch light. It was unfair, and wrong, for one critic to say 'the only flair Bruce has is in his nose'. But the nonstop airplay and heavy rotation perhaps flattered these rheumy, if well-meant shorts. By and large, the films worked less on raw talent or production values and more on the sheer greed of TV in general, and MTV in particular, for product. Here, again, Springsteen's timing was perfect.

Still, in making his killing, Springsteen wasn't flaunting luck or cant, but survival. The rock landscape was littered with artists dumped by labels for marketplace reasons. As an overpowering talent, and twelve-year vet, Springsteen viewed *USA* as a chance to put his long experience, ceaseless globe-trotting and ear for a hook to good use as a pension plan. He wasn't alone in doing so. The tag team of Landau and Teller kept the album and back-end ticking over for years. Beneath them was a sub-court of flaks, PRs, shock-absorbers, ciphers and grunts. The actual merchandising came under the wing of Winterland Productions. Bootleggers and fringe entrepreneurs in T-shirts and such – virtually a cottage industry – were pitted against the entertainment lawyer Paul Schindler. By 1984, Springsteen tended to collect attorneys as he'd once done cars. A sidelight on his gilt-edged name came that winter when Peter Bogdanovich needed four songs for his film *Mask*. 'No problem,' said Schindler. He quoted $160,000. Universal Pictures balked, and used Bob Seger's music instead. In a final twist, director then sued studio for 'loss of the commercial value of [Springsteen's] name', which he put at $10 million.

Early in the new year, the tour swung south, one-nighting in Louisville and Columbia, skirting the Carolinas, before hitting the Carrier Dome in Syracuse, New York. The 40,000 crowd there was the largest of Springsteen's career. His album had sold six million copies. CBS were releasing its third single. Now, in the same week, Springsteen made two different, but twinned decisions. The moral of the first – to do summer shows at the 70,000- and 80,000-seat sheds – was that not even he could be a cultural icon with a strategy to tread water; 'Bruce now [went] big', as *NME* had it. And he sang on 'We Are The World', America's response to Geldof's *ad hoc* group Band Aid. Much to Springsteen's credit, it wasn't a case of peons ferrying him in limos while he casually skimmed a few salient horror stories on Ethiopia. He flew to LA by commercial jet, rented a Corvette at the other end and drove himself to the studio. An industry figure called Ken Kragen happened to be at the door. 'I was looking to see if there were any hang-ups out there, and in came Bruce . . . by himself. He walked across the street away from the crowd and said, "What do you want me to do?"' Later in the session, where he duetted with Stevie Wonder, Springsteen reeled off facts about famine, 'like Audrey Hepburn', says a colleague on 'World'. That one song would raise $50 million. Seven months later, Springsteen also donated his time to Van Zandt's anti-apartheid anthem, 'Sun City'.

He spent the early spring plotting the summer. Friends say Springsteen got more 'creative' in staging – which he did, if you think of stagecraft as something external to music, laid on with a trowel – but he also worked at his own fame. As well as meeting with Landau and the rest, he hung, ominously, with Jagger and Bowie, sat for interviews, and shot a video. In March, the band flew to Honolulu for two days, did a CBS gig, then regrouped in Australia. 'He seemed pretty loose,' says Joel Bernstein. Soon enough, Phillips would be a sunny fixture on tour.

Onstage, generally, things went well. Springsteen and especially the band, that miraculous tool for making a little go far, were rightly touted as more 'real' than a Prince or Madonna. As *Rolling Stone* said, 'Bruce seems a regular guy . . . the resonant vision [shows] a gift for popular expression . . . His concern for his characters, and by extension their millions of counterparts in his audience, seems genuine.' It was; Springsteen convincingly filled the jeans and work shirt. His very garb seemed like a natural show of his charm. More to the point, Springsteen was the goods. He stood for a tradition of theatrical, camp rock which harked back to James Brown, rather than the faux-boffins hunched over their synth programmes. At its best, it was a tight, taut package which brilliantly counterpointed the bouncy, upbeat tunes with a wry social conscience. Springsteen wasn't the first to see the potential of linking the worlds of Elvis and Dylan; but he did it best.

Offstage, it was a different story. Springsteen was being sucked into the decadent mania of American celebrity. His tour was marked by almost a full-page map in the Jersey weekly, captioned 'The Boss' and listing his various haunts. It was like a miniature of Springsteen's life, reducing his space by hyping him as a 'draw', Jersey's finest, while flogging him as a 'homeboy' who'd made it. His own path duly veered between those two poles: the hard-line, rigid need to keep his life private and yet the equally rigid one to perform. Springsteen was becoming a street-level, not just a critical star. On one hand, that meant fans hanging out of windows cooing 'Br-ooose', whenever he walked by. At its darker nadir, Springsteen's fame drew the cranks and fringe nuts who attend American 'names'. As well as the autograph hounds, there were the stalkers and dumpster dippers: human scavengers who stole his trash. He'd always been chary, even remote, with friends – now he was being hit on by total strangers, some of whom, he griped, 'you'd think took a shit with me'. It was enough to make him paranoid, and it did.

Springsteen was poignantly alive to the old one of being alone in a crowd. His simple neglect, along with the cumulative leads of men like Brickman, Clemons and Van Zandt (whom Springsteen told, 'I'm next up'), would forge a U-turn on marriage. 'I don't rule it out,' he'd tell *USA Today*. 'If it's the right moment, the right relationship, the right person, maybe you'll change the way you do [things] . . . I'm kind of married to the job. I love women. I love kids. I've been with my sister and her kids and see where certain feelings they have match the intensity that I get onstage. It's a different type of experience, and not something I want to miss.' If the Springsteen legend draws strength from its similarity to the Christian one of self-denial and redemption, it also had a more modern root. He was a social analyst in the classic fifties style, plagued by a nagging regret for something he realized he'd 'blown' and wanted back. That thing being family.

Springsteen's first marriage was proof of the problem, not its solution. He fell for the wrong woman. It wasn't, in fact, so odd a choice – he and Phillips followed in a line from Joel and Brinkley, Richards and Hansen, and preceded the likes of Bowie and Iman as pop star–model mergers – but it was bad enough. Even Marsh was left asking, 'What the hell did [they] have in common?' Phillips, after all, had led what *People* called a 'charmed life'. One college friend in Long Beach recalls her 'reading her rights', as she put it: the right to party, to shop, and tool around in her father's MG. All of these spoilt-child staples were fed during her leafy, Lake Oswego youth – about as far as one could get, state-wise and otherwise, from the woolly, end-of-the-line world of Asbury. Phillips was, however, a mini-name herself. What's more, she'd been a drop-dead, $2,000-a-day model. She wasn't the first amenable woman to call on Springsteen backstage, but she was the most exotic. It was typical of his cripplingly low self-worth that he could say, 'Juli's the star, not me' and mean it.

Phillips, in fact, was almost an ideal mate for Springsteen, who liked his females to be ornate and emotionally uncomplex. She scored highly as the first, 'a perfect-10' in the Elite agency's slang, a 'fox' in the band's and '22-carat doll' to Springsteen. Phillips' looks, in particular, turned Scialfa's eyes the same hue as her Irish roots. According to one *USA* source, 'All in all, Bruce'd had more models than Ford. Then there was Patti, who'd already fallen for him . . . go figure. Fists never flew. Sparks did.' Marrying Phillips wasn't, though, just wishful thinking; Springsteen was also expressing his core American conviction that he had a right to the 'pursuit of happiness', and it's doubtful whether many men would have differed in principle. She was stunning.

The man Phillips was dating that spring could have traded his Levi's and cracked boots for the cutaway and stovepipe hat of a Victorian grandee. *USA* might have been a mildly subversive take on the place, but in saying 'it may only sell to me and my Ma', Springsteen didn't necessarily want it to happen. In the event, of course, it made him a populist hero; more a quasar than a star; a vivid staple in the world's imagination. For eighteen months, he rode the *zeitgeist*. Springsteen became a, or the, leading light of the 'rockocracy', public nova number one. He was a global, cash-flush phenomenon, and he spawned an industry. So profitable was he that he became like the medieval Church, whose vast estates fed cloisters full of devotees, burnishing myths and diligently drafting metaphysical tracts. Many of these were journalists' books rehashing other journalists. Shelf-space-wise, the Springsteen business boomed in 1985. His 'own private Dow Jones' – his phrase – spiked that summer.

With his kryptonite hit and *de facto* coronation by the White House, Springsteen brought not only unparalleled fame but also a sense of *noblesse oblige* to the job: he believed it was payback time. Hence the lavish gifts to strike funds and hunger programmes. At another level, too, Springsteen moved people's lives. Entire families banked on him. Fans wrote and said, 'Bruce, I'll do whatever you tell me.' It suited even his enemies to collude in this mythopoeia. Whole sermons were preached on whether or not Springsteen's text – and what he seemed to say on the Union – was a Good or Bad thing for the man in the pew. Questions were asked in Congress. To be fair, no one fretted at this giantism more than Springsteen; and the speed with which he later junked it is the surest proof that, at heart, he didn't buy it. In the meantime, he dwarfed the overstuffed and undernourished rock landscape with a pop-political wallop that couldn't be denied and wasn't ever copied, let alone equalled – not by the bloodless Bowie, not by the cartoon cut-up of Madonna, whose Minnie Mouse voice mewled beside Springsteen's. His only rival, in fact, in the rock-authenticity stakes was Tina Turner. Her *Private Dancer* was the retro counterpoint to *USA*.

More than some of the press underwent a change with time. Despite the flood of books, mainly hagiographical, Springsteen had been largely absent from the tabloids between *Born* and *USA* – mostly, no doubt, because his head was usually higher than his feet, rendering him bad 'copy'. But print acreage was only the most trite form of kudos in 1984–85. His pecs-and-plaid look would star in Joe Davola's rocumentary, as well as a slew of videos and a *Whistle*

Test special. David Hepworth's own BBC profile was still in the works when Springsteen won the ultimate TV accolade, a *20/20* slab called 'The Conscience of Rock and Roll'. So great had the curio trade become that several broadcast media descended on 'shabby but magical' (CBS) Asbury, looking for clues. The locusts – as they were known locally – retrod the myth, as well as the Springsteen cult, while his inner life, and tanked relationships, remained off-limits to most Bossmaniacs and known only in part and guarded detail to cronies. Generally, the grubs lowered his personal and musical message to a level that became the norm, not the exception. Springsteen's apotheosis in film and folklore did him no good.

Abroad followed suit. In London, Roger Scott's evangelical work paid off in a long interview on Capital Radio. Several rungs down the evolutionary ladder, Springsteen's boot-and-braces image was taken up by the National Front, twisting Old Glory into a Union Jack. He became the ring-pull of the lager louts' canned sadism. A number of *USA*'s lyrics went through ingenious makeovers into football chants. No less an abortion took place in Moscow, where Springsteen was ruthlessly hyped as anti-*yanqui*. That, too, was a warped picture of him.

Everything was so bent, in fact, that, by 1985, he was claimed by both wings. Springsteen was either the very best or the very worst of America. He didn't make for any lukewarm feelings. To the Industrial Workers of the World – the Wobblies – he was the 'thinking-man's Boss'. The rockers Morrissey and Peter Buck, conversely, would pan his 'Philistine' and 'Yahoo' yens, respectively. Among other musicians, Keith Richards, Roger Waters and the Band's Levon Helm grouched at the 'consensus star' aspect of it. To most, though, he was a kind of male version of the Statue of Liberty. The usual suspects of Bowie, Elton and Clapton all salaamed. Rod Stewart, he informed the world, 'really dug' him. In 1986, Rhino released *Cover Me*, an anthology of acts who'd worked Springsteen's turf, from the Hollies to Johnny Cash. It was a tidy hit.

Springsteen's fame, and the backwash of crazed fans, had its downside. At the very centre of several protective rings round him were Landau, Teller, Bell and the double-act of Carr and Marsh. But the most powerful man on tour, bar one, was Bob Wein. Springsteen's minder, and thus the bulwark between him and the world, was a dour fixture backstage, in planes, and the lobbies of hotels – literally everywhere it wasn't vital his boss be alone. Under Wein came Jim McDuffy, the ADC. A Special Forces vet named Terry Magovern rounded out the clan, one that made Elvis's look like the Algonquin set. At a technical level, Springsteen swore by his roadie Mike Batlan, his trainer Phil Dunphy and the monomark Nick, who kept his houses in order. On the road he fraternized with George Travis and Art Rosato. It was an impressive train. As the tour criss-crossed America, all the entrepreneurial, clerical and brute skills of the suite, magnified by sheer numbers of money and fans, were focused on the lone figure in the spotlight. It changed him. Sadly and not surprisingly, Springsteen slowly lost touch with 'dudes', and, inevitably, himself. The entourage began to 'do shit' – like hosting his parents – for him. Eventually there were sixty in tow. 'Short of a travelling palmist or a trained bear,' says a hand, 'Bruce had 'em all.' Except, of course, a wife.*

Similarly, Springsteen's act seemed to cut to the heart of an identity crisis. To some, he was still a Dylan-*manqué*; to others, Stallone with a backbeat. Offstage, too, he was an artful dodger of the pigeonhole. Brian Pringle remembers him playing softball in the park – 'a nice guy who seemed like you or me'. A drifter named Jim Eddy says Springsteen crouched down next to him in a Belmar alley. 'He told me that, basically, he'd been down and out, and it wasn't like I was in it alone . . . Stuff like that. Then Bruce gave me a hundred bucks.' Yet, other times, the studied blankness, and the minder, kept Springsteen at one too many removes. The history of the tour was the story of his acquisition and mistrust of fame. As an artist, he warned, 'you don't rake in the dough without some sacrifice on *Billboard*'s altar'. A rich man, but an honest one. 'Like Santa

---

*It was doubtless this need that led *Good Housekeeping* to name him one of its '50 most eligible bachelors'.

Claus at the North Pole,' he once called himself. And: 'you get in a situation where the myth of success is so powerful [it] overwhelms the story you may think you're telling'. Friends, fans and members of the Springsteen mafia, together with most of the lovers, agree that he was a mixed bag: cool, yes (the band never heard from him off-duty), but wry, well-meant and almost lewdly warm with a crowd. He eked out Bossmania with a grin and a shrug, awaiting the day – he guessed 1987 – when context would again meet character. If nothing else, he wore his doubts like a campaign medal.

In March 1985, Springsteen, band and crew met in Hawaii. As well as rehearsing, writing, and poring over gates with Landau and Teller, he played godfather at Clemons' son's christening. At one stage, Springsteen asked how it felt 'having a kid . . . y'know, the whole vibe'. Clemons replied, 'like nothing else. Even rock and roll.' His candour on this point was, he felt, the 'curtain-raiser' to what came, as Springsteen heartily believed in family. To their mutual surprise the former 'guys' guys' had found common ground on women and children. 'When he was holding the kid,' Clemons told *Rolling Stone*, smiling, 'I looked into his eyes and thought, "Well, he's gone."'

On the 19th, they hit Sydney to placards railing at 'RIP OFFS' and 'POOFTAHS', apparently in reference to the odd soul-kissing. Throughout Australia, Springsteen never quite dodged flak (lest the world doubt) about his being rich, famous and American. There was a ruckus at the airport involving Wein and a tabloid hack, who somehow mutually fell over and earned a splash in the *Sun*. 'What gives?' Springsteen could only ask after yet another to-do, this one over ticket sales. Sadly for him, he was in a country which makes a fetish of pricking myths. Eleven years earlier, Rupert Murdoch's best had staged a similar pantomime round another Jerseyan, Frank Sinatra. This time up, the travelling press corps soon restored normal service. Still, the local media went down fighting, their drawn salaries in their hands. 'BOSSY!' was only the most obvious rant. 'The [Sydney] papers fanned the flames' was Marsh's understatement.

Springsteen stayed at the Sebel Town House, worked out at City

Gym, swam at Bondi Beach, walked round Nielsen Park, drank Foster's in a Paddington bar, looked over the Gap, and had dinner with the widowed mother of his sound engineer, Bruce Jackson, who'd emigrated from Sydney to New York. Fans waiting outside the hotel were rewarded by frequent sightings and Springsteen's game policy on photos and autographs. 'Please don't bother any of the guests,' he told teenage girls as he signed multiple *USA* covers. He also made donations to two hospitals and the Vietnam Veterans Association of Australia. Short of scoring a century against England, it was hard to see what more he could have done for the place; the hassles over ticket touting and punch-ups outside the Entertainment Centre weren't his fault. 'I'm here to *rock* it,' he said.

There, too, he scored. The shows in Sydney, Brisbane and Melbourne weren't Springsteen's best; nor did they dent his popularity, the basis of which was captured in the *Herald* lead, 'the Saviour of Rock and Roll'. Joel Bernstein remembers them as 'fabulous, if sort of pat . . . It was a formula.' Art Rosato, who shot every night on video, would then sit with Springsteen in the cutting room. 'Bruce was glad to see even the kids at the back of the joints jumping up and down to the beat. Around then, he kind of extended the "hot spot" from 10,000 to 40,000 – you can see it on film.' That rare feat, and a storming duet with Neil Young, were précised by the *Sun*'s superb phrase, 'Bruce came, saw and conquered'. He was now famous in three continents.

He soon cracked a fourth. The eight Japanese gigs' features were the routine ones of Asian rock: early starts, curfews, polite crowds and dim smiles. The reaction to Springsteen's 'Adam and Eve' rap in 'Pink Cadillac', in particular, was like one of those *Life* photos of a cinema audience wearing 3-D specs – people literally goggled. But when he cut the guff, he likewise tore down walls. The small but wild crowd at Kyoto (where fans waved US and Japanese flags sewn together) thought they'd seen it all by the interval; Springsteen had already given one of those two-hour, more-dash-than-cash epics of Asbury days. He then ran back on to flail the likes of 'Rosalita'. As he left, grinning and yelling *Aishitematsu!* ('I love you!'), the shrieks, howls and cherry bombs burst. The strong hint was that, as far as Japan went, the feeling was mutual. That night, Phillips flew in. They took in the Hiroshima memorial, before leaving for a week's shopping and surfing in Maui.

On 3 May (thirteen years to the day after the first demos), Springsteen proposed. Word went out on the 6th, Phillips' birthday. The lapsed St Lima Catholic agreed to – in most views, wanted – a church wedding. Plans were delayed first by Springsteen's dread of *Globe* stringers with Sonys skydiving down, rolling even as they were arrested. Next, Phillips' parents, Bill and Ann, aired equally sound fears of New York. The answer to both sides was to marry in Oregon. Phillips' mother knew just the spot, Our Lady of the Lake, a 1950s church set on a manicured lot trimmed with fir and azaleas, where she played the organ every Sunday.

The next week was a Niagara of leaks and counter-leaks. As caterers and florists got into gear, somehow the news – the biggest in Portland since VJ Day – wound its way south and east. MTV began a 'Bruce buzz' spot on the 8th. On the 9th Bill and Ann well-meaningly told an old friend, who happened to be a DJ. Overnight, charter jets of paparazzi swooped into Oregon. The Phillips' home was besieged like the Camp on Blood Island, as reporters mingled, swarmed and occasionally brawled with police. Local station KKRZ set up a 'Springsteen hotline' to give fans 'up-to-the-minute facts', or, failing that, anything to hand. Even the local freesheet, normally a grim file of petty crime and store coupons, went full-colour and acquired a certain half-shod drama babbling about the 'royal wedding'. Robert Hilburn called it one of pop's 'hottest bits of gossip since the "Paul is dead" rumour in the sixties'. In Asbury, the *Park Press* noted, 'You can almost hear the sound of hearts breaking all along the shore.'

Springsteen showed in Lake Oswego on the 9th. The service was set for the 15th – put forward, when he saw the mob, to the first legal instant, 12.01 a.m. on Monday 13 May. Springsteen spent the weekend trawling the local night life in towns like Sublimity and Boring. When their after-hours brew proved insufficiently heady, he settled for a pizza. Nobody bothered – or even recognized – him when he walked in for it. There was no pre-nuptial, nor formal rehearsal. Springsteen did, though, meet with Phillips, the priest and others for what he termed a 'sound-check'. At the run-through next day, he went down the parquet aisle (an upmarket copy of the boardwalk) and stood at the altar of Botticino marble with its carvings of *rossa verona*. Early summer sun sifted through the bowed Rose window. Clemons, Duffy and Magovern watched from among the fonts. Father Paul Peri – an interim pastor who left the diocese a week later – read the text. He stopped the ritual at the vows and studied the couple through his pince-nez. 'You get the rest,' he said. There was a laugh. Afterwards they stood outside, in the landscaped yard, beside the rug-brick chapel with its oak trim. It was a bright, warm night. The pines and firs threw up a shadow against the bronze lamps. With the harvest moon, it seemed that the trees, the bushes, the cut brush and all the grass had been varnished with ice. It was light enough to read by. You could smell the cottonwood blossom. Springsteen looked up over the Gothic transept to the fletch with its gold cross. 'Man,' he said quietly. 'Good times.' Then they drove to the Phillips' house, two blocks away. Doug and Adele were there waiting for them.

The actual event was a composite circus–carnival. At midnight on Sunday, all the lights went off in the Phillips' home. The press and paparazzi duly folded camp for the day. Thirty minutes later, in scenes reminiscent of *Mission: Impossible*, a van with smoked windows pulled up to the rear of the house. A dozen black-clad figures ducked in and were driven, in pitch dark, to the car park of the local school. There they met with a second party, ferried in, also incognito, from a Portland hotel. Both groups then stole, under police escort, into the church. There, too, all the lights were off. A few stone arches were strung with Easter candles. It was silent. There were fifty-three guests. Also invited, though outside, were the Oregon state troopers, who blocked all four doors. In the end, there was no problem – most of the media had skulked off for the night.

At quarter to one, the lights and the pipe organ welled up. Springsteen came down the aisle sporting an electric-blue suit and open-neck white shirt. He was joined at the rail by his three best men, Landau, Clemons and Van Zandt (the last in his 'formal' check bandanna). Phillips herself wore an off-white lace dress, white boots and a waist-length veil. It was a minimalist Catholic service. There was no mass. The ceremony faltered over the rings – the ushers were on the wrong side – but otherwise went off well. Father Peri never tried to inject artificial colour, spurious drama or untoward speed into the night. At 1 a.m., the Springsteens were married. They and their guests then walked down to the bare-walled and tiled parish hall. One of Phillips' friends squeezed off shots from a hidden camera. Bride and groom cut a three-tier cake and drank Krug from silver goblets. There was a minor scene outside on 'A' Avenue – a lone fan had to be evicted – and, in the week's mounting lunacy, the service was taken as a success. But it amounted to little more than a lull in the nonstop frenzy which in turn fed on the same low view of human nature it had allowed itself to entertain. As Springsteen said, 'The real crazy thing was the wedding. I'd planned well, and we managed to outwit the press. And suddenly, what do I see on the roof? A seven- or eight-year-old boy with his Instamatic. The son of a bitch! Anyway, it didn't make any difference since one of our guests sold his photos.'

The reception, too, was like a parrot house under water, a superior freak show loomed over by the *National Enquirer*, Suzy from the *Daily News* and low-flying Hueys. The 'quiet gig' Springsteen planned wasn't best held in the chi-chi aquarium of a glass-walled home in Tualatin, west of Lake Oswego. There were more paparazzi on roofs, others who sat and squatted (like a Marx Brothers skit) in the caterers' hampers. At the party itself, long-haired rockers in rented tuxes mingled with the Phillips' country-club set, 'clocking', says one, the 'airhead' mall-rats and aspirant debs who swarmed the bride. Some of the culture-lag that did for the marriage was there that evening in the Willamette Valley. The whole day was animated by constant media hassles, making it both farcical and poetic. Doug, for one, seemed shaken and angry at the helicopters buzzing – at illegally low level – virtually outside the door. Adele shed a tear. Springsteen's own emotions ran the gamut. From jail, to freedom, and then back to jail again – all in forty-eight hours. 'I remember the night that I got married. I was standing at the altar by myself, and I was waiting for my wife, and I can remember thinking, "Man, I have everything. I got it all."' And, two days later: 'I don't believe or comprehend the world that I live in.'

Meanwhile, the Portland FM stations, MTV and, overnight, the press from Berkeley to Boston all danced a lurid, coast-to-coast conga. The *New York Times* managed to splash the story on 14 May. Most of the tabloids went into war-is-declared mode to break the news, which wasn't much, in banner capitals. Upper-case puns on the word 'Boss' were the norm for Los Angeles. In Chicago, the *Sun-Times* ran an entire leader on the scoop. Op-ed pages bristled with the mixture of congratulation and gossip so vital to sales that, in Jersey, it was moved to the front page. As the *Park Press* had said, it was a dark day for waitresses, models and co-eds all down the shore. It was blackest of all for Scialfa. While Springsteen married, she did a tape of solo songs, 'contained, down tunes' and big Dusty Springfield ballads. She began shopping it round. Few singers were ever so bent on pitching their ground entirely on their own love life. It was an album of blues Scialfa hawked that winter. There were no takers.

7

Brilliant Disguise

The honeymoon was brief. Springsteen was back making the 'Glory Days' video on 24 May; rehearsing; then flying to Europe, where he at last relaxed the quota on indoor, smaller-than-life gigs. He agonized, and took flak, over his decision to megatour. Even the band had their doubts. It was like presenting an unwanted love child to a set of fusty grandparents. They were uptight, but now it was there they'd come to terms with the thing, even learn to love it. Only a few churlish souls reminded Springsteen of his long-standing ban on stately homes and soccer stadia. The six weeks that followed were his devastating trump. As David Sinclair says, 'Sure, he lost his virginity. Why not? With a repertoire and personality that strong, who wouldn't go for the bucks . . . It made the whole thing universal.'

Springsteen landed in Dublin on 31 May. For him, the tour was a world within a world. He and Phillips spent the day in a roped-off suite at the Gresham hotel. At dusk, he took a helicopter out to test the first gig, Slane Castle, a natural bowl carved between hills and the banks of the River Boyne. All the band later spoke of the sight. The stage had been built in the lee of the crenellated pile, a single grey road leading across a high plateau, then up and down through orchard-bushed fields, around a slope of forest to the top of a rise where they could look down and see the crowd, the numbing queues and, backstage, the red shirts that darted like a shoal of tropical fish. Less visible, though all too plain on the ground, were the fights. Officially, the capacity was set at 65,000. Thanks to gate-crashing and forgery, there were probably twice that many *in situ*. Half were drunk. The two-lane road leading through the village up to the cow pasture where the gig was looked like Dunkirk. All round, Slane was embellished with tents, trailers, fires, bin-liners, mud, Portaloos and kebab shacks. In the castle itself, eight hundred guests of Lord 'Hank' Mountcharles drank champagne and ate polenta. Several teenage girls jammed up against the wall screaming at anything alive, or, when that failed, Ron Wood. Clapton, Townshend and Bono were on hand. For some compelling reason, Elvis Costello came as a rabbi. And that was only the sound-check.

What happened on the evening of 1 June is history. Springsteen ran on, dressed in jeans and a polo shirt, at 5 p.m. In a bid to rehumanize, Diamond Vision screens, flanking the stage, beamed the prancing-ant stars to those in the far reaches. They were the lucky ones. Up front, a combination of heat and drink made for a sewer. It was bad enough for Springsteen to appeal for calm. After that, he complained to the band that 'it's like fuckin' Fellini down there'. He needn't have worried. The twenty-seven-song set was so strong it could sustain even the normal 'pissing and puking' – the Garda's words – of a festival crowd. The sight and sound of 130,000 Irish bawling 'Born In The USA' was the tour's most surreal one, no small prize. Block harmonies also ruled on 'Badlands' and 'Atlantic City'. The riff and rabble-rousing chorus of 'The Promised Land' was duly seized on by the site's head-bangers. By 'Glory Days' and 'Thunder Road', a quarter of a million hands slapped in chiselled unison. In 'Dancing' he pulled Scialfa out to boogie. A hard nut, Springsteen. While he shook a leg with the woman who loved him, his bride of three weeks worked backstage among the ambulance crews. The set ended in a salvo of 'Born To Run', 'Twist And Shout' and 'Do You Love Me?'. Musically, it was a triumph. Personally, it shook Springsteen to the quick. He'd faced his largest, and wildest, mob on opening night.

Springsteen, of course, was a big star, perhaps *the* big star. On tour, he came over not only as warm and witty, but as a man who had something to say. The donations and pledges won not just headlines but the kudos of most right-thinking hacks, as seen by *Melody Maker*'s 'he stands for Good against Evil'. All that counted heavily in Springsteen's favour, but he now toured like Phil Collins. It was that bad.

Springsteen had risen purely on talent. But he was kept on top by a sales and marketing corps that Richard Williams, who saw the plan, describes as 'military'. By Slane, the new model army of reps and rat-tailed PRs was on the warpath. As in 1975, though on a bigger canvas, hype was all. The whole of the cow pasture and the fort beyond was crawling with security cordons, stretch limos, chalet girls, Sherpas, ecstatic VIPs, press briefings, photo-ops and all the prefabricated glitz that goes with an Event. The posters read simply BRUCE IS BACK. A month later, at Wembley, CBS outdid itself. The hospitality pit was screened from the rest of the gig by a slab that took the form of a giant, mock Cadillac; the right pass entitled the glitterati to step through the doors into a toytown Asbury. Normally sane rock critics went 'mental' (as this one did) over the Ferris wheel, the shelves piled with Bud and the crisp tang of 'Bruceburgers – 100% beef' frying backstage. To the *Guardian*, it was 'America redux'. Other 'qualities' followed in kind. Meanwhile, the red-tops perfected a new vulgarity by daubing their pages with busty shots of Phillips (34-22-34). Both up- and down-market left the shows floored by Springsteen. The *Mirror* man said that he 'got a sense of professionalism and nous, not of Napoleonic shit'. Many of the plaudits, in fact, were chiefly negative. They made the distinction between Springsteen and what he wasn't: addled, vacuous, with spliff in paw, gnarled and greedy. Still, the gravy train rolled on.

It was a tour, as the *Mirror* said, when the word 'work' acquired a new tinge. Attitudes about stagecraft, about value-for-money, about the respect due fans, even those projectile-puking up front, changed radically. To compensate for the altered acoustics of the gigs, Springsteen doubled the size of his sound system. He made a personal gesture to scale by wearing loud shirts. More to the point, the songs were as strong as pig-iron, or at least as Springsteen's musculature. The band all got their moments in a set which sounded, at best, as if the Who were casually guesting with James Brown and the ghost of Woody Guthrie. Lofgren worked. Scialfa, too, though there was surely poignancy to be seen in her eyeing Springsteen's back, taking her cues from his every breath. The E Streeters alone were virtually always better value than most head-liners. Nothing spoke up for Springsteen himself like sales: a million fans applied for tickets in Britain, many of them, oddly, middle-aged women. Demographics like his would have sunk other artists' careers, but being drooled over by housewives only seemed to symbolize his all-round, family image. Springsteen was unstop-pable after that. As well as the titanic coup of *USA*, all six old LPs recharted. More even than Prince or Madonna, he was *the* approved star of 1985, partly on form, partly by, unlike them, quot-ing and living Emerson's success mantra, 'To know even one life has breathed/easier because you lived.' Landau was quite right to be proud of him.

Springsteen gave freely while in Britain. He made gifts to Oxfam, Chiswick Rescue (for battered women) and the Durham Miners' Wives. This last deeply hit home with the group's leader, Anne Fiddick, still agonizing from the coal strike. 'We met an incredible guy. He'd followed events on TV and in the press and he wanted to know how we managed to live and organize the move-ment from within the communities so that it spread nationally . . . He told us about his father.' Less moved was the MP for Newcastle Central, Piers Merchant. As he says today: 'Springsteen didn't seem to be aware that many miners were bitterly opposed to the action, [which] was harming rather than helping their future . . . He played into the hands of the romantics . . . I felt him ill-informed and, though he was a welcome guest, it was unwise of him to get into a local controversy.' In twenty years, Springsteen had gone from a 'dorky' Jerseyan into a man posing convincingly as Arthur Scargill, with his name bandied in the House; a high-court judge even probed his merchandising. A long way for a single life. Springsteen gave the Durham group £16,000, thus earning further raves from Marsh, who ranted at Merchant: 'This version of George Will had in the past been supported by the fascist-style British National Movement.' It was the very idea of a Tory talking about Springsteen that shocked his diarist out of his studied fraternal cool. Did it never occur to him to blame the 'endorsement' on the BNP, or to air Merchant's decidedly non-fascist views on issues from Aids to Amnesty? Again, Springsteen was ill served by his clerks.

From Newcastle, Springsteen flew to London, then (in a jet specially diced into two suites), Göteborg. For three weeks, he duly wove a loop through Scandinavia and Europe. In that first Swedish show, played in midnight sun, he made the encore into a public Valentine for Phillips. 'D'you love me?' he bawled – the crowd confirmed it – before turning to the wings. 'They're rootin' for us, darling,' Springsteen chortled, then counted in the riff. In Milan (where he could have sold the stadium five times over), a US marine stood surreally at attention, holding the flag, for the full four-hour gig. Springsteen brought down the house in Munich and Paris. In both, many of the lyrics were actually inaudible, and more were left incomprehensible. Still, Springsteen's genius was to build on the universal values of shoutalong songs that contained both fact and fantasy. He was everything and was everything at the same time: an '*oproerling punker*' to Dutch TV; '*un chat cool*' for *Le Monde*. In the course of the summer, most sub-editors' imaginations would be left stranded with nothing but a well-thumbed copy of the press pack, and a thesaurus, for company. By the time he hit Wembley, he was officially Boss again.

There were signs that the cult had reached Shinto level. Every afternoon Springsteen worked out in his hotel gym, then casually took in Bond Street, the CBS office, or lunch at Santini's. By now, the press had transformed into bipeds in the grip of collective frenzy. The pack soon learned that it could feed on Bossmania by yielding to it in certain practical, if novel ways. One well-known tabloid bribed a chambermaid for a pair of Phillips' panties. Exactly what it meant to do with them remained a tad fuzzy, but cash changed hands. The grubs won their greatest victory in running down sundry pre-nuptial 'glamour' shots; but even these bikini-clad pouts only deepened the vacuum for more flesh. Sometime in that first week of July, Phillips had an identity haemorrhage. She'd later tell friends that was the stage she'd gone, like Alice, 'through the looking-glass', slumping, eventually, into the role of celebrity-without-portfolio. It was a rude baptism. Springsteen himself, shielded by Landau and the other flaks, not least a local handler named Sharon Wheeler, moved through London, he later said, 'like Prince Charles'.

Those Wembley shows were high-tension, scenic orgies. The stadium was rigidly split, like the *Titanic*, into three classes. In steerage, those who paid £14.50 absorbed, as a matter of course, a dose of violence which few other pleasure-seekers would have stood. A mix of oafish stewards, brawls, burger bars and queues held sway until 6 p.m. By then, the crowd's 'Br-ooos'ing was much like the growl in a slaughterhouse, a sort of low baying in 70,000 chests. Four hours on, as the last notes, windswept, echoed among the cans and soggy programmes, they went home happy. Travelling soft class, meanwhile, were the 2,000 backstage VIPs clutching their ersatz US passports and Cristal, everyone from Bowie and Sting to the Australian cricket team. Paul Jones, the man who'd caught Springsteen's ear with 'Pretty Flamingo', was there with the writer Steve Turner. Despite the surface gloss, most of them, too, were in a state of cramp, herded into a pen well away from the action. Many never made it out of their shanty to watch the show. They missed a classic. Onstage, Springsteen was a dour, pent-up and angry spirit, reeking of Swarfega, who unleashed a shattering new bolt, 'Seeds', and elsewhere snarled over the bat-on-bin drums and rinky organ. Yet there was enough of a spark in him, enough of the bluffness and good will, to make people care. 'You genuinely wanted the best for him,' says Jones. Even leather-clad, Springsteen had a homey, period charm, a panto greaser, more Fonz than Brando. His gigs had always suggested jolting, three-chord progressions in old trucks, and still rarely wove from within a tyre-tread of the asphalt. At best, no one since the Beach Boys had given London such a slab of American pie. People saw the practice and perspiration involved, but knew they'd witnessed a set created by something more. At worst, the famed Springsteen nuances barely survived, and the only contrast was between the puffed-up, shamelessly demotic chants and the slower tunes trundled out towards the interval. For any Rip Van Winkle who'd lost the plot around the time of *Greetings*, the three London rallies would have seemed like a recipe for a nightmarish gig. As stadium rock, they were perfect.

Springsteen now had a command of any form. He could play in the largest 'shed' as well as the smallest dive. The band was superb, and Clemons was especially winning in his old role as the feed. The moment, in 'Thunder Road', where he caught his boss in his arms was marvellous. Ten years ago, Springsteen's appeal had been against 'plastic soul' and the fag-end of glam. In 1985, he was a heartfelt refuge for those bored – as millions were – by New Romantics twiddling their Korg knobs. His security phalanx bespoke not just a star but a saint of pop culture. Personally, nothing now so moved Springsteen as the idea of himself as a loner: as far as possible, he kept to his own on tour. 'You only ever saw him with his wife,' says Julia Collins, a CBS PR girl. 'Though there was a time at Leeds when I remember him murmuring to Patti.' It was more than that. At least one of the crew at Roundhay guessed what only intimates fully realized; 'they'd already fallen'. The jolt for this verdict was a scene where 'Patti ate some candy, then said her hands were sticky and would he lick them off, [whereupon] she stuck two fingers down Bruce's gob.' Private oats belied public tact. Springsteen's no-press policy showed the classic tug between myth and man. Onstage, he was in control of his world. Offstage, he was uptight and paranoid. His chief husbandly advice to Phillips was 'Watch it. They're everywhere.' Straight after the last encore of the last show at Leeds, he flew back to Jersey. Springsteen declined to grace the decade's major gala, Live Aid, six days later. After years of buoying up charities, he temporarily had no more use for them. 'You've got our stage [at Wembley],' Landau told Bob Geldof. 'The set's on us . . . that's it.' Both manager and ward still invariably dealt with conflict by withdrawing the gift of their labour.

In a week over a year, Springsteen had played to three million fans. *USA* was still in the Top 10. 'Glory Days' was the summer's designated hit, on both radio and video. It couldn't get any bigger, yet it did. The final US stadium gigs would duly make it the highest-paid tour ever. In what seemed an instant, and was only twelve months, Springsteen had left the likes of Prince standing. He was the last true rock star. There weren't enough like him, which is why Geldof felt his loss so much.

Unlike previous tours, Springsteen didn't waste much energy on sound-checks or drills. He did, though, tune up at Clemons' club in Red Bank on 1 August. When he left, in the small hours, a teenage boy asked him for a lift. 'Hop in,' said Springsteen, and they took off in the Corvette. That one fan sat in for the mass of critics, who increasingly viewed 'the boss' in his own terms. Springsteen was doing what every major icon eventually does – beginning to drive the way in which people saw him. Slagging him now was either crass, boorish or downright unpatriotic. Few tried.

These were the scenes that attended the last, gate-busting leg of Bossmania: in Chicago, whole families moved their homes on to the street, sleeping under the Loop for nights on end, all on the mere buzz of tickets. Illinois Bell went into crisis mode to handle phone bookings. In Washington, calls by fans to Ticketron tied up lines to the White House. Springsteen's name was plastered over the *Wall Street Journal* and his takes and yields debated like those of a blue-chip stock, which he was. In New York, the local agency sold 240,000 seats in a day, more than for King Tut. Springsteen's Jersey shows did better than any other pop event of the eighties, grossing $7 million over six nights. Even Sinatra and Dean Martin got in on the act, cracking Boss gags. The man who'd gone to Europe in late May was a rock star. The one returning six weeks later was a test case of whether America was mad or sane. On this last point, Springsteen himself had his doubts.

'When I was young I felt excluded from the community and I wanted to gather people round me . . . I thought that by being a musician I'd succeed. But the opposite happened: the community gathered round me, or rather round my music, and me, I'm excluded.' In practice, that meant that people, like Dino, related to him as Boss rather than, as he'd hoped, as Bruce. The twenty-eight shows that summer gave further scope to the clan. There was serious frenzy. Everywhere Springsteen played, he came under a storm of notes, gifts, bras, teddy bears and, in Jersey, a whole wooden leg. His hotels were swarmed, his cars rushed. As well as Liz Taylor and Sean Connery, fellow Jerseyans Jack Nicholson and Meryl Streep, sundry mayors, senators and governors all paid court. The Springsteen voice entered the national consciousness as a fixture, until it was turned up so loud it began to warp.

On 5 August, opening day, *USA Today* ran a front-page splash by Springsteen's friend and perennial next-President, Bill Bradley. Neither Reagan nor even Piers Merchant raised hackles like this pat, well-meant eulogy. Marsh was to fume at Bradley's 'wooden prose . . . parochialism . . . egregiously false . . . distortion', such that even Springsteen might have been struck by the irony of it: a noted author and two-term senator unable to agree on his meaning. (As Bradley disarmingly says, 'it summed up how I felt about Bruce. I'm no pop guy. What's the beef?') On stage that night, Springsteen took a break to address the dome. 'I'm reading a history book,' he said, 'and thinking a lot about where this country's been and where we're going. And where we're going is pretty scary.' He urged them to visit a Veterans Affairs hospital, 'and then you'll see what stakes we're playing for in 1985, born in the USA'. Even that eminently sane (if fat) hope caused a row. He may have been the one not to do product ads, but Springsteen's name still got tossed about like a frisbee by most groups.

The tour's last lap was the closest Springsteen came to making *USA* convey, rather than hint at, his tough, sometimes bitter musical soul. 'Seeds', for one, showed he was about more than bouncy riffs and full-throttle choruses. Storylines like 'This Land Is Your Land' and the other calls for renewal wed a frisky beat to the kind of moral seminar rarely heard in factory-sized sheds. Instead of being 'brill' (*NME*), the Giants Stadium gigs were brill but with a sort of push–pull cry of rage. On 'Johnny 99', the guitar was touched into a long, deep note under Springsteen's dry baritone and rasps of harp; something like a death-sigh. That one ballad proved, for all time, that he'd earned his fame the hard way, through songs with melodies and linear plots, not by sleek chore-ography or snappy threads. The shows sold out everywhere, every time; as *Time* said, 'the fulfillment of one of pop's dearest ideals . . . sensationally good music that's also great rock 'n' roll'. It wasn't just that millions heard Springsteen. He heard them, too, and, amid the belters, those folk-tinged odes about the doomed and disenfran-chised lent the gigs a sense of familiarity far beyond glib populism. They were vast shows, but they were also feverishly communal, ones of mutual substance. They were intimate.

The final week, in Los Angeles, contained a nugget. After 'The River', a red spot picked out Lofgren, strumming a riff within a chord of his 1970 'Beggars Day'; Springsteen bobbed up, peered into the faux-Grecian bowl, tugged at his jerkin, then did his rap about Vietnam, blazing into a brassy, bottom-heavy 'War', all Led Zep whamming and blues guitar. The all-too-real, if soapy, message was vividly brought by the music. Federici's cinema-pit organ spun into a frantic plot device. While Springsteen's head had obviously been turned by the same funky Detroit sources that fired the original, there were several subtleties under the rocks-and-dirt vocal and manic gyrations (the last, in part, so he could read the lyrics taped to his wrist).* As the song ended in a squall of reverb, the band revved into 'Working On The Highway' and sprinted to the half with 'Thunder Road'. In the second set, 'Cover Me', 'Dancing' and 'Hungry Heart' roared out in a salvo. The white lights flared, Springsteen grinned, and on came his manager. Landau's guitar cameo on 'Travelin' Band' confirmed the wisdom of his career path. It also brought the house down. 'It's too late to stop now,' Springsteen yelled. And there, with him slumped on his knees, it all ended.

The real Springsteen was, at heart, an ordinary man who hap-pened to have the gift of seeming both a best friend and an effigy.

---

*'War' was later released on vinyl and video.

He loved his wife, baseball and burgers. He could be cheerfully crude after the second beer. But he also felt an obligation to play – to give something back, beyond the coy, call-and-response japes of the megabands – to take his wry, danceable rags to the biggest feasible audience. He did so. The tour swept from the Baltic to the Sea of Japan, from numbing cold to 110° heat. Onstage in Dallas, Springsteen was swarmed by a plague of crickets, and choked by diesel fumes in Miami. In Britain, there was no problem with smoke. The problem was with mirrors. Dozens of Wembley fans got in on the sweat-and-testosterone act by bouncing back the sun as it sank below the stadium rim. Even then, Springsteen kept smiling. Those shots of him pacing, laughing and goofing on the piano (all caught on Rosato's video of 'Born To Run') were the tour's abiding scenes. He gave generously, not least to food banks – $35,000 in Dallas alone – but *USA* was always more circus than bread. Around the time of Giants Stadium, *Rolling Stone* sent a reporter to gauge ground-zero reaction. Phrases like 'He's just like everybody else . . . Acts real . . . Ain't stuck up . . . Humanitarian . . . Doesn't come out with earrings and make-up . . . Bruce is America' went round like a Mexican wave. According to this reading, most of them adored him not for being 'bossy' but for the exact opposite reason: his normality. At bottom, the shows were an unforgettable celebration of American potential. Springsteen succeeded because he lived as a man, not a mere pop god. Above all, he made a connection, vitally, between manner and matter.

Less successful – in fact, parodically inept – were bids to make Springsteen 'mean' something more than raw energy and a concern for the fallen. His lyrics were filched by everyone from politicians (Reagan through the Mayor of Freehold) to overheated rock hacks like the one on *NME*. 'In Los Angeles,' she wrote, 'the American Psychological Association meets and are asked what they see when they look at the country in 1985 . . . A lot of Americans simply deny and will not face some very severe problems, they say . . . One spokesman adds that "particularly disturbing elements" include the search to find scapegoats for the farm debt crisis, unemployment and [our] low profile abroad. He says the nation as a whole is experiencing a "significant failure to grasp the subtleties of human motivation"'; though no worse, surely, than *NME*'s failure to grasp the subtleties of reviewing a pop show. (It was the moral humility one most admired.) Springsteen's tour threw up its share of such nabobs. The result was the emergence of huge caravanserais where 'think' pieces were doled out like gruel in a soup kitchen. Most of the alleged insights and the dozen books served no purpose but the careers of those who touted them. As usual, Springsteen was better than his copyists. Sure enough, his heretical refusal to write just about cars and sex (though they were there) did him proud. Springsteen's laments on blue-collar life bucked a formula. The ones about unemployment, in particular, struck a nerve. Yet amid the shrinks' phoney arcana shone 'real dudes', like the well-named Amy Human, who cut to the bottom line of Springsteen's lure: 'I think he's good-looking – and he's got a cute ass, and everyone knows it. He's the most patriotic guy around . . . I feel that.'

Bluntly, the Bossmaniacs' response had been akin to mass sex. But soggy attachment was only the most obvious form of tribute. Fans also paid good money for their homage. By October 1985, Springsteen's fortune was estimated to be more than $50 million. *Born in the USA* provided him with an annuity. 'My Hometown' would follow 'I'm Goin' Down' as the album's seventh hit. As he left the closing-night party and drove the short haul to his Hollywood home, Springsteen said, 'I'm happy . . . the bubble is in the middle of me.' In the days ahead, he saw, and underwrote, a Workers Project play called *Lady Beth*; took out ads protesting 3M's decision to shut their Freehold plant; spent a week fishing in Mexico; revisited Rumson; and generally began life with Phillips. As the well-earned credit and cheques rolled in, there was only one cloud on the scene. Immediately after the Sunset Marquis bash, two of Springsteen's roadies – including Mike Batlan, the man credited with taping *Nebraska* – quit, as they said, 'in disgust'. Their lawsuit against him would rumble on, with occasional jabs in the press, for the next six years.

Professionally, Springsteen, backed by Landau, would walk crab-like to the wings for much of the late '80s. 'The plan was that he'd start to scale down,' says an ex-colleague. 'We took the view, "If it ain't broke, don't fix it." Bruce took the view, "I'm the boss, I'll do what I have to do." He never much liked being an icon.' The idea of Springsteen's next few moves was to shatter the iconography as surely as a rock lobbed through a stained-glass window. He talked about wanting to 'reintroduce' himself as a writer. The whole *USA* fit was 'insanity . . . a distortion'. All the band, especially Clemons, would be marginalized over the next four years, at which point they were fired.

Springsteen's final bow to Bossmania came that November, when Landau sent him a tape of four live tracks, 'Born In The USA', 'Seeds', 'The River' and 'War'. It was another simple but shrewd ploy from a man pregnant with them. Springsteen's long-time distrust of a concert album began to wilt, and by Christmas he was debating whether it would be a one- or two-LP set. 'A gasser' was Landau's considered verdict of the sales potential. For Springsteen, the marketing plan worried him far less than the usual flap over sequencing and production. A pivotal moment came when, for the first time in ten years, he listened to 'Thunder Road' recorded at the Roxy. 'That kinda opened the thing up to take in the time span,' Springsteen told Marsh. 'If we're gonna use that and "War", what's the matter with all the stuff in between?' For a full decade's worth of material, obviously, the original plan was far too timid. *Bruce Springsteen & The E Street Band Live/1975–85* would come in a box set in three formats: three cassettes, three CDs or five LPs. CBS spent $3 million plugging it, which helped rake in $30 million in orders. For a man planning to throttle back, Springsteen still followed eighties voodoo practice of doing every-thing bigger. The accretion of detail was, in its own way, fair enough; but somewhere a single, five-alarm album waved wildly to be let out.

Personally, too, he wanted to wind up, to settle down. Here some gap exists between Springsteen's words and action. Everyone had acknowledged the genius of most of his albums, notably *Born to Run* and *The River*. What wasn't as well known was the way he worked. Springsteen wrote almost nonstop from adolescence onward. He scrawled lyrics or chord charts in the backs of cars, on planes, even sitting at dinner with Phillips. It nagged her to see that drive, that 'bug', she said, that took him daily to the studio – any studio, anywhere, locked studies, attics, anything. The cycle that emerged was vicious: Springsteen would do or say something work-wise that hurt Phillips; her hurt would put her out; her moodiness drove him to work. He spent much of the first half of 1986, along with Landau and Plotkin, whittling down 200 hours' tapes to 216 minutes' music. The project was musicians' manna, and jam to the fans. It did nothing for Springsteen's marriage.

A culture war loomed. Essentially, it was between Springsteen's old-shoe habits – some said chauvinism – and Phillips' go-go career. 'I want to be thought of as an actor,' she said. That fell manifesto was, writ large, a key policy clash. Notwithstanding Freehold (and the fact that 'Hungry Heart' was the blithest song ever about abandonment), Springsteen had a rigid code on chil-dren. He wanted them. Other than the *Sun*'s scoop, based on quotes from a barman who served Springsteen, that the couple fought 'because she wouldn't give him a baby', there were several clues down the way. Clemons always spoke of the way his boss 'looked sappy' at his godson. Half Springsteen's onstage babes-in-the-woods skits were pure *Jackanory*. Old friends and colleagues duly remarked how much he 'dug kids'. In the 'Glory Days' video, he'd acted a construction worker with a wife (played by Phillips) and two sons; he was making a film, but it was a real-life yen if ever there was one. Although the marriage had its other stresses, it foundered on a simple, core truth. Springsteen had been stuck on a romanticized view of himself as a loner. By his mid thirties, his manager, best friends, bandmates and both sisters were all family-bound. Such things found a way of subverting his 'married to the job' mode. Phillips' own career, meantime, took off precisely on account of her newly honed CV, a crocheted tapestry of modest talent, fame and ambition. A mutual friend remembers a day in Rumson when she lit off with a suitcase, while, at the kitchen table, 'Bruce shifted his gaze', unable, apparently, to cope.

It wasn't one-sided. Springsteen may have been the Boss of

Bosses, but, like most of us, was just an entry-level adult. Anyone putting him on a perch missed the humanizing neuroses cushioned by cash and fed by a passion for brooding on life. What was 'wrong' with him? For one thing, the hard lessons learned back in the house on South Street still cut deep. Self-reliance was in and about him as much as the twelve-bar tunes he wrote casually (though polished endlessly) every day. Springsteen hinted at this when, speaking of *Tunnel of Love*, he told *Rolling Stone*, 'I wanted to make a record about what I felt, about really letting another person in . . . That's a frightening thing . . . It's difficult, because there's a part of you that wants the stability and the home thing, and there's a part of you that isn't so sure . . . I mean, there's days when you're real close and days when you're real far away.' This ambivalence was a moral variant of Phillips' rule on motherhood. She insisted on contraception. He wore a condom over his heart. Springsteen knew it, and when the blow fell a spokeswoman quite aptly told the press, 'My sense is that he's very upset a lot of the coverage has been negative toward Juli'. Speaking of that era to *Q*, he went on, 'I'd gotten very good at my job, [and] for some reason thought I was capable of a lot of other things, like relationships . . . When you get older, you start to realize there are all these other things that you're really bad at, that you've been failing miserably at for a long time.' A dawn feeling ran through this *mea culpa*; Springsteen's divorce would be the dying fall of a lost soul. Better days, as he sang, lay at *Tunnel's* end.

Phillips, for her part, emerged as a stock type: imaginative, fiery, with a creeping embrace of touch-therapy slang. ('I'm taking a dip in the lake of me', she once told her spouse.) The moans from some of Springsteen's fans weren't that he'd got married, but that he'd plumped for a California Girl. By California, they meant someone who managed to convey enigmatic depths, in whom there was, perhaps, less than met the eye. On screen, Phillips tended to smoulder with all the allure of damp mulch. For her, though, these few scenery-chewing cameos put a rarefied gloss on the perennial job-v.-family debate. Like Springsteen himself, she found working easier than living. Phillips was a sane but narrow soul with no use for the pram in the hall. She was as much a product of her age and time as he was. It's a plausible and adequate theory on the rip that Phillips wanted to live, or in the existential sense 'make it'; that Springsteen had done so; that both did their best; and they should probably never have married.

The world, of course, had gone mad for him. Just as with other fits – the name Madonna comes to mind – a backlash was due. To his credit, Springsteen began it himself, anticipating the so-called 'Boss burnout' as he came off the road, did only a handful of gigs, and gave no interviews. As he later put it, 'I really enjoyed the success of *USA*, but by the end of that whole thing, I just kind of felt "Bruced" out. I was like, "Whoa, enough of that." You end up creating a sort of idol, and eventually it oppresses you.' This icon fatigue showed a cool and distinctly sly self-reproach. Springsteen knew he didn't need to boost his aphoristic name for rock, but for stability and 'them one-on-ones'. Hence his decision to sit out 1986 with just his wife – and, increasingly, Landau and Plotkin – as company. He never, or rarely, called the band. A sure sign that he'd shrunk from his own fame was the spate of soundalikes suddenly staking a claim to his turf. Of these, the Jerseyan John Eddie was only the latest martyr to the 'new Bruce' cross. Old lags like Bob Seger and John Mellencamp were also tarted up to fill the void. In this cod-Bossmania, Springsteen himself occupied an honoured, if odd niche. Essentially, he was semi-retired as a pop god. As a human being, he was taking a 101 course. 'Sometimes you do your best,' he told *Q*, 'and you pull out people's insanity or you pull out parts of your own. It's not completely predictable, and when you lock into it on a very big level, it's a big wave that you ride and you try and stay on and think, What was that about? What did I accomplish? Where did I fail? I thought about all that stuff.'

For a year, then, Springsteen was famous for what he didn't do. He turned down Chrysler, said no to Hollywood, kept stum on Chernobyl, vetoed Earls Court, passed on Amnesty's 'Conspiracy of Hope' tour and failed to vote. He didn't become a father.

Nor did Springsteen get any less astral. Seger, Mellencamp and the rest all had their fans. As well-manicured rebels, they were no worse, and usually better, than a Sting or Bono. You sometimes met people who said, 'Bob rocks' or 'Johnny kicks ass'; you never heard anyone say, 'Those guys speak for people like me'. That was precisely what, for years now, they'd said about Springsteen. So much acreage was devoted to his alleged political nous that not enough was left for his real gift – spotting people's hopes and fears and expressing them. It's this which caused Bob Muller to say, 'Without Bruce, there'd be no Vietnam veterans movement', or battered wives or miners or No Nukes to feel he was rooting for them, or Salary Men in Kyoto as well as the home team in Jersey to give him a hero's welcome, or women from Slane to Seattle, even into his forties, to tell you how cute he was. A year off wasn't going to change that.

Springsteen may have been a husband and would-be father, and a shrill critic of market forces as embodied by Reagan or Thatcher; a lover of the underdog and the dispossessed. He might, as was quietly claimed, have had the attention span of a gnat, and that same insect's knowledge of higher civics – a whim of iron. But in the end he was a working rocker (exactly twenty years on the job), and even off-duty he went at it nonstop. First, he edited and mixed the live LP. It was nothing for him to listen to thirty separate takes of a song. Nor was packaging ignored; according to Joel Bernstein, a total of ten thousand photos were sifted for the sixty-two-page booklet. Above all, Springsteen, in the words of a close friend, was a 'one-thing-at-a-time guy'. He spent months playing and replaying tapes, ironing out lumps, adding overdubs – a process Plotkin calls 'like going down in a sub'. Alongside the chronic fidgeting, solid work was done. By summer the new baby was in Bob Clearmountain's incubator.

Almost no one remembers provincial gigs, and even the galas are soon forgotten. But Springsteen did a number of these – haunted and richly telling – that year. In January he took to the Stone Pony to fund-raise for the Local 8-760 union picketing the 3M company. Then, that fall, with the live LP done, Springsteen guested at Chuck Berry's sixtieth-birthday fêtes and a benefit for autistic children, a cranky and oddly inspired set that yielded a video of 'Fire'. Between times, he took part in a seminar around the play *Lady*

Beth and settled two debts of honour, reconciling with Appel and writing 'Light of Day' for Paul Schrader. Springsteen also managed a side trip to Paris, where Phillips was living *en attique*, co-starring in a Nathalie Delon film called – friends couldn't help quoting – *Sweet Lies*.

When he returned, a godlike hero sprang before the public, as word and rumour of Springsteen's altruism, charity and anti-Republican bile, tricked out as homilies – not to say his new album – did the rounds. His PR sabbatical ended. Like an Elvis or Sinatra, he was a pervasive cultural fixture: someone people related to, who was, in fact, lonely and unknown. Wein's strong arm was just the brute expression of Springsteen's own Zen-like affinity for solitude. As he sat in Rumson that autumn, refusing to talk, the media filled the gap with gossip and blazoned scandals. The story of his marital crack came out. Other press hordes burst into Asbury, to gauge the local react. The *Guardian* ran a feature on the town, comparing it to Bognor, while in the tabloids it was 'randy', 'bawdy' and full of 'beauts' with bikinis or 'bare boobs'. Another wing of the cottage industry worked flat-out servicing the needs of Springsteen's fans. Titles like *Backstreets*, *Badlands*, *Candy's Room*, *The Fever*, *Jackson Cage* and *Rendezvous* all fed the maw. A 'Bruce Line' in Los Angeles did a roaring trade supplying the pop equivalent of phone sex. As for the books: they weren't much, but as models of the pathology of stargazing, they stood alone. Springsteen deserved more.

The 'burn-out' was all internal. Springsteen felt it, along with a number of rock-biz types. They tended to be the ones who made it a point of honour to vent. Some of the original legmen rightly felt they'd lost him to the masses. Springsteen, for his part, had trouble distinguishing between attacks on Bossmania and attacks on himself; 'they kick a guy when he's up'. Geldof, for one, chose his post-Live Aid slump to spout on pop, circling from the general ('It's all be-bop-a-lu-la') to the specific ('kids actually look to Bruce for gravitas'). This brought a curt transatlantic call. Geldof's friend Van Morrison joined the Celt consensus. 'For years people have been saying to me – you know, nudge, nudge – have you heard this guy Springsteen? I just ignored it. Then, four or five months ago, I was in Amsterdam and a friend of mine put on a video. Springsteen came on and that was the first time I ever saw him, and he's definitely ripped me off. No question.' The implied sneer of another pop idol's dig – 'the sun god' – sums up a view some had of him. One of the colourful quirks of the Year of *USA* was its effect on long-running rivalries, feuds and, at worst, raw envy. To blame him for winning fans was like blaming a spider for catching flies. The true culprits were the home-grown acts, with their camp Jerseyana, who simply did it worse than Springsteen did.

There was something in him, deep and loud on the first albums, that responded to the romantic. There's no doubt that, within the vast province of the word, Springsteen 'loved' Phillips: she was pretty, rich, spoiled, a slim, tooth-white girl who could have stepped out of a Scott Fitzgerald novel. Wanting a romantic match, though, and feeling romantic towards the person you're married to aren't the same thing; and to be left dogging her through Europe was a study in what Phillips calls 'gaga masochism'. Of course, there was a cautionary strain in him. He stayed his hand. There was no murmur of divorce in 1986. But that Springsteen feared the worst was clear from an interview he gave *Q*. 'I felt at the end of *Born in the USA* that I'd said all I wanted to say about [certain] things . . . My battles were elsewhere.' It was a dark year, and a dire form of suffering. Phillips' rages were sudden, mad and allegedly violent. Springsteen's moods tended to roil slowly, like an oncoming weather front. When the storm broke, he'd do what he'd always done: get in the car and drive for hours up the Parkway, or down Colts Neck Road to Freehold. Increasingly, he took to dropping in on his old clubs – unannounced and often, it was noted, alone.

Bossmania flared again on 11 September, when the live album was officially confirmed. The gears of the marketing machine promptly dropped into fourth. CBS had to pull other new LPs from the presses, to try and keep pace with preorders for Springsteen. By early November, an eight-song sampler, 'War' to the fore, was in spin. A full-colour 'marketing overview' for *Live* jostled with print and TV ads. Queues began forming outside record shops. 'We're selling them as fast as we can get 'em out of the box,' Don Bergentry of Sam Goody's store said. So they did: another retailer was reminded of 'when Elvis croaked'. Springsteen product, said Record World, was 'flying out the door'. It became the ultimate Christmas gift – a beefed-up version of the sort of treats the Beatles used to dole out for the holiday. Ironically, yet again, the one man not cheered by his festive smash was Springsteen himself. On 10 November, the day *Live* was released, he flew back from another summit in Paris. After eighteen months, he was already mired in a dying and joyless union. It was 'black, black, black', says a friend, recalling the era. Yet it was good luck to have come home, where so many people led lonely and frustrated lives, and to have fallen straight into another woman's arms. Springsteen's change of address for Scialfa, from 'doll' to 'darling' came that winter. It wasn't, at this stage, a clear-cut affair, more an understanding. Technically, Springsteen's marriage went on.

Although he lived with Phillips on and off for the next eighteen months, it was a sham. Springsteen became increasingly fickle in observing the niceties of home life, simply turning away. As things got worse, he had a succession of nights out in bars and road-houses, hazed over by beer and whatever shapely flesh caught his eye. Or he might reel on stage for a jam. As often, Springsteen just sat there, a lost soul of the Dashiell Hammett school, grizzled, gaunt and dark-eyed, scrawling inky notes on a napkin. When people approached, he was civil. Springsteen had the true knack of talking to fans on their own terms, chuckling, and in the words of one woman, 'making *you* feel the star'. More usually, he was off-limits to both friends and the stock rites of celebrity. Although Springsteen, *Sounds* said, was 'bossa again', his table was never crowded. He seemed too remote, too lost, even for those who knew him. A few, used to the turbo act, failed to so much as recognize the lone figure in the corner – Springsteen's gloom blanketed his looks. As he metaphorically, though quite factually, said: 'Fame, on its best day, is kind of like a friendly wave from a stranger by the side of the road. And when it's not so good, it's like a long walk home all alone, with nobody in when you get there.'

Live was mixed, and ready to be boxed, by 5 October. Springsteen flew to San Francisco, spent the day with his parents, then closed out the children's benefit with 'Hungry Heart'. That same month, he gave each of the band the new album with the words, 'Here . . . when you have kids, and they want to know what you did for ten years, play 'em this.' ('That's when I knew we'd be fired,' says one musician.) The LP itself was a fact of life for the rest of 1986. Springsteen was with Phillips over Christmas, alone again in the new year. He won a hatful of gongs early in 1987 – everything from Best Album to Sexiest Male Artist – then went back to work. Most of the fresh tracks were done in his home studio (over the garage) in Jersey, spare, mid-tempo blues with a human focus. 'The only thing I ain't got honey/I ain't got you', he sang ominously in the first cut. If there's such a thing as a designer padded cell, it may have been the drab room where Springsteen faced the mike each day, trying to come to grips with marriage.

Amid the downsizing, Bossmania's forty-song testament, *Live/1975–85*, imposed tribal magic and collective lunacy on buyers and sellers alike. At Tower Records in Manhattan, the manager, who'd already placed 'our biggest initial order for as far back as I can remember', told *Time*, 'it's going to be the hugest LP of the year, maybe the next five years. I want a big truck to pull up in front of the store at 9 a.m. on November 10, with a cash register in back. For the first few hours we'll just sell 'em right off the truck.' It was an authentic mob orgy. For those unwilling to stake the list price, $20–30, street vendors sold knockoffs, pirating *Live* the very day it was launched. Around Times Square, the familiar terrain of sex clubs and crack bars blanched at the riot of fans, back-alley hucksters and police, all jostling together in splatter-art vein. It was like Brueghel retouched by Jackson Pollock, with dabs of Arthur Daley. Normal protocol was suspended as New York suffered a municipal breakdown. They'd seen nothing like it since the Moptops. About the only person not mining drama from *Live*'s oddly flat, if panoramic landscape was Springsteen himself. That same morning, he flew in from Paris, stopped off at Landau's office, lunched at McDonald's and stood in the line for *'Crocodile' Dundee*. No one recognized him.

It was a perfectly good album. As a souvenir, *Live* vividly recapped at least one half of the decade's sound and vision. The problem wasn't the songs, which were majestic, but the choices. The latter-day, dome gigs exerted a bigger pull than the club dates, as did the gilded swag of *USA* over *Greetings* and *The Wild*. It was the old story, common to every anthology: they're like a sports round-up or a porn film – all action and no context. A series of climaxes soon turns dreary. It was a pity Springsteen didn't seize his chance to level the hoary rites of the 'live' format, perhaps by some of the scores of shelved tracks or at least the Detroit oldies (none of which made the cut). There were, true, two songs he'd written and given away, as well as a smattering of covers, from Guthrie to Eddie Floyd. With them, *Live* was more than another relic, if less than epic. It stood in the same relation to its raw material as *Match of the Day* does to real football. The game's bitty, full of delay and defence and odd spasms, yet with a ragged cumulative rush – and then the highlights shriek: watch this nonstop, one-act frenzy. That's what *Live/1975–85* was: end-to-end heat that somehow missed the gig's sense of loss and tension and release.

As well as the warmed-over fare and singalongs like 'Hungry Heart', the album flowed on three *Darkness*-era tracks. 'Paradise By The "C"' harked back to the sweat-and-sawdust vibe of the Upstage; 'Fire' was Springsteen imitating Elvis as he might have imitated Springsteen; and there was a taut version – surely definitive – of 'Because The Night'. Most of *USA* was there, as well as generous slabs of *Born* and *The River*. Springsteen showed what *Nebraska* could have been if he hadn't been feeling suicidal; though if he hadn't been suicidal, it wouldn't have been done. The guttural voice worked on all but the production numbers, where the crowd took over. 'This Land Is Your Land' unwound with a snap that overcame the sickly-sweet fable of the lyric. Closing the set, Tom Waits' 'Jersey Girl' duly brought the greasers from 'Sandy' full circle, cruising Ocean Avenue on a Saturday night. Springsteen's – and here, Landau's – sense of pace was perfect.

A war broke out over the album's sales. *Live* shifted three million copies in a month (making Springsteen $7 million off the bat), fifteen times more than Dylan's *Biograph*, but 800,000 less than CBS hoped. Hence the slurs that it 'tanked'. It never entirely recovered. Over Easter 1987, *Live* went into freefall. By then, most retailers' gloats had turned into groans. 'It went up like a rocket, and came down about as fast' was Tower Records' bleak verdict. The label worked out a deal to extend shops' credit, and thus delay returns (conveniently keeping millions in red ink off the books at a time when CBS itself was on the block). Even in this crass transaction, Springsteen's knights errant gleaned a backlash, by both a fickle public and a false press. For them, it was an act of faith that he, and they, battled against dark forces – not just questioning non-fans' motives, but, as one says, 'wishing bad *juju*' on them – giving them the sense of being trailblazers and gutsy outsiders. In fact, Springsteen was one of the most revered artists on earth. *Live* simply ran out of steam. As usual, the paranoiacs missed the point. The album, by most standards, was a roaring success. It also closed out a chapter for Springsteen and the band. As an ex-colleague says, 'I, for one, knew we were fucked. That box should really have been a coffin.' Springsteen himself hinted as much. 'We all sat there listening to it and sensed that it was the end of something . . . next time would be different.'

It was. In PR and accountancy terms, Springsteen's star was still rising early in 1987. For the third straight time, he was *Rolling Stone*'s Artist of the Year (as well as propping the Worst Dressed list). There were glittering prizes in London. He was toasted by the Paris *Académie*. It was Springsteen who inducted Roy Orbison – now both a hero and a fan – into the Rock and Roll Hall of Fame. Paul Schrader's film *Light of Day* opened to affable reviews. *Live* spent eleven weeks in the Top 10. 'Fire' did warm trade in America, as did 'Born To Run' in Britain. On the surface, everything seemed to be normal. Springsteen was a, perhaps the, man of his time. It was apt, then, that as the eighties wound up, so did he. This downturn was largely his own doing. In the post-*Live* months Springsteen went through a schizoid backlash to his fame, and later saw the whole 'Rambo shit' as a kind of out-of-body experience in which he'd never truly functioned. 'It's the Boss with all the fans,' he said. 'Not me.' *USA Today*'s Bruce-v.-Elvis readers' poll was only the latest sad distortion of 'rock and roll future'. Springsteen made his gaffes, but he was never going to sit toad-cheeked on a bathroom throne. Both 'Shut Out The Light' and, more poignantly, 'Bye Bye Johnny' were wry musings on the Elvis, or Bunker Syndrome. As Bruce Jackson, who worked for both men, says, 'Bruce learnt from the King's mistakes. He wouldn't be wooed by the good life . . . Bruce's tuned in to his friends and the band. [Presley] did three tours in a row without talking to them.' That kind of isolation, which he saw as 'pathological . . . nutso', would be a key note of Springsteen's life and work for the next decade.

What some took as a U-turn was a sane and logical tack to a more human orbit. In Marsh's spot-on prose, 'A negative mood began to swell for the first time since *Born to Run* . . . With program directors talking about "Bruce burn-out", there were no further attempts to generate a hit from *Live*. With no airplay, sales died out.' That still ignored how much Springsteen chose his turf. As he said that year, 'I don't believe the essence of the rock 'n' roll idea was to exalt the cult of personality. That's a sidetrack, a dead-end street . . . I feel like to do my job right, when I walk out onstage I've got to feel like it's the most important thing in the world. Also I got to feel like, well, it's only rock 'n' roll.' Springsteen's very awareness of his faces suggested which would prevail. The DIY sessions in Rumson – where, if a car drove by and honked, a retake was in order – were a self-reaction to 'USA''s 'sick' perversion into a national roar. For fifteen years, Springsteen had only felt truly alive when he was playing. Now he wanted to feel that way less and less. 'I like being on stage when I'm there,' he said. 'When I'm not, I don't.' There didn't seem to be much of a future in recycling 'Dancing' into his forties. Nor was a check of the past that rosy. His marriage was dead, the author of *Greetings* had become an excuse for beer-swilling aggro, and many of the old fans quit. The fallout from John Hammond's death that summer hit Springsteen with a virulence few could have guessed. For instance, a CBS staffer saw him 'sobbing on his way out of the room where there'd been a wake'. Springsteen's sad hunch was that it 'was the end of an era, both for us and him'.

It wasn't a great year. In quick succession that fall, Springsteen sang at both Hammond's and Harry Chapin's memorials, as well as a mass for a Freehold friend. He joined a New York benefit for street children. Other groups and galas were rewarded with either money or a song. Some time in 1987, Springsteen became more a figure than he was a musician. Even the acolytes knew that his fame lay as much in what he stood for – the rites of empathy – as what he did. 'Mother Theresa in plaid' was one only half-glib tag. Springsteen evolved from being rock unbound to the patron saint of the unhappy. Items in *The Times* and *Guardian* and a TV special merely added ballast. The profiles' interest was clearly historical, as Springsteen was the man who'd bridged the gap from Dylan to Princess Diana in all his human intensity. The word 'holy' was used about the covenant between him and his fans.

That was pushing it. Springsteen's well-meant court weren't always fraught with humour, with the result that they missed his own. For example, he roared at Cheech Marin's *Born in East LA*, a movie spinning off a video and song spoofing 'USA'. Springsteen also later licensed his single for a skit by 2 Live Crew. Amid the funerals and crack-ups, he still stage-hopped around Asbury and bars like McLoone's in Sea Bright. He clearly tried to control his fame, as much as vice-versa. One night that November, several teenagers knocked on Springsteen's door. The result was a rock-and-roll party he threw at their school hop, bawling Chuck Berry hits and, in one version, 'hanging there till midnight, gargling punch and being the life and soul of the gig'. Springsteen's old fan Doc also saw him around the same time. 'Bruce was sitting in his car at a red, bopping up and down, with Jackie Wilson blasting off the radio. I remember him with his T-shirt and crew-cut, real neat, kind of smiling and clicking his finger at me. Whatever it meant, he came over as a regular guy. I mean, in the same room'; if cocked for the door. When the light changed, Springsteen duly 'took off like a drag racer'.

Wherever he was going, it likely wasn't home to a cooked meal.

'I've got only one job, and it's called Bruce,' Phillips said, but in fact she was so busy – not to mention his schedule – that they rarely met. Springsteen's *Tunnel* vision, the songs he did that spring, were, as David Fricke says, 'very . . . political, only now explor[ing] the politics of the mattress and the heart'. This conception of sex-struck lyrics was by no means as flip as on *Born to Run*; nor was it just Springsteen's idea. As well as the root material of his marriage, there was the fact that Bono, among several others, had dared him to write 'something from the gut'. He duly did. Tracks like 'One Step Up', 'The Honeymooners' and 'Lucky Man' were more than a noisy whimper of self-pity; they were as deep a recce as anything in the arts of the human condition. It was in those long nights in Rumson – usually alone, or with one colleague at a time – that Springsteen hit on the dirty secret of life, the gulf between myth and reality. 'It's easy for two people to lose each other in/this tunnel of love' he sang on the title tune. 'I'm fucked,' he told a sidekick. Temperamentally, Springsteen was a more orthodox soul than the emotional junk-bond dealers around him. To them, the views he held, the things he said about fealty (like many an autodidact, he toyed with words) sounded like a put-on; so, they said, big deal – get a mistress. Springsteen's response unfolded with a portly deliberation. 'Maybe a change . . . is . . . gonna come.'

Her name was Patti, and she set her cap at him. By then, Springsteen was in dire shape. His songs were larded with break-up verses, pinched and laryngitic, and he carried on much the same off duty, holding imaginary raps (more like seances) with Woody Guthrie. There was still something deep in him that pined for roots and domesticity, and a life away from the planks; not to say sheer fun. That was her. Where he always planned his moves and weighed options, she did things on the fly: a Lucille Ball type who auditioned wearing dyed leopardskin pants and a klieg-lamp smile. Springsteen was dazzled. The two enjoyed some convivial outings in 1987. In 1988 speculation turned into media McCarthyism (pairs of their used Rome Excelsior sheets were bid on like a stock auction), not untypically missing the point. Springsteen wanted – almost a morbid need – a sense of security. She gave it to him. No greater analysis is needed than that. In the year ahead, all three parties would be put to trial-by-tabloid, though Scialfa alone wasn't guilty.

Springsteen was onstage, that autumn, again bending knee to Roy Orbison. This 'black and white night', shot at Hollywood's Coconut Grove, featured an A-list cast of bravura cameos. The rich filigrees of Orbison's voice were the star. Springsteen added elegant filler. His solo on 'Oh, Pretty Woman' brought off the trick of being both light-hearted and moving. He drifted amiably through the other hits. Despite being artistically edgy, Springsteen stayed true to his creative canons, namely a continuous probe of rock's joys and leaden depths; once you accepted the lows, even they had a kind of integrity. In *Rolling Stone*'s words: '"It was fun," said Springsteen afterward, his arms draped round Orbison's neck. "Lotta fun, playing guitar . . . and just *being* there with this guy." Then the Boss headed out the door, still humming "Dream Baby".'

From time to time Springsteen couldn't sleep for fear. As well as his marriage, there was his money. He was among the millions hit in the crash of 1987. Coincidentally or not, he began calling the band a month later, at Christmas. They heard what others, like *Billboard*, announced in January. 'The Boss is going back on the road . . . The Tunnel of Love Express tour will stop in at least 22 cities, according to a label rep. She says Springsteen will be performing with the E Street Band and not as a solo act, as rumored.' This last point, in fact, had been the subject of several summits, during which the Boss took mortal form: plagued by worries about his wife, full of doubt on his niche for 'history 'n' all', and still haunted by the fear that fans might, suddenly and terminally, go south. Above all, Springsteen still wanted love and reputation, respect from the whole world. His end was clear, but he was rethinking the means. *USA*-style pomp was out – one of its by-products, he said, was 'you'll be trivialized and you'll be embarrassed . . . I guarantee it' – but he wasn't ready to peel back the layers of head-banging rock for good. In the end, the loudest voice in Springsteen's ear may have been his accountant's.

The tour was shaped by two upsets, one consisting of peerless gloom at his marriage, and the other, less sharply defined, pertaining to the blows of that winter, including burials, memorials and Black Monday. *Tunnel of Love* itself (out the same week as the crash) outdid *USA* as the iconic cry of a middle-aged male, whose recent trials – those requiems, that lonely vigil in Rumson, with Ollie North on TV – all called forth a sense of being wise, or cynical in the ways of America; of kicking forty. This was maturity in bafflement. Bluntly, Springsteen had learnt there was no answer to the devotion–betrayal cycle. Not even his titanic success could remoralize a man as down with his wife as he was alone. Springsteen's own verdict on the LP cut to the bone: 'That sense of dread, man – it's everywhere. It's here, it's there. It's on the street . . . it's in the bedroom.'

The lyrical gist of the album shed light on the murk of *Nebraska* (often tantalizing in what it skipped), as well as *The River*'s 'Stolen Car', though this time the demons were inside, not out. Most of the best music, oddly, was pure pop. *Tunnel* was a sunny place for shady characters; depth came with a series of steadily more dark and twisted sub-plots. There were several new wrinkles. According to Andrew Greeley, 'Prayer, heaven and God are invoked [in *Tunnel*] as though they're an ordinary part of the singer's vocabulary.' A second writer managed to find glints of 'masturbation, deception, disgrace, infidelity, fear, rage and self-loathing' in the pan. *Stop Press* wrote it up as a 'Kinsey Report for the eighties'. In this reading, the very title was a tacit metaphor for a vagina. In fact, *Tunnel* in all but name was a concept album. If there was a key theme, it lay in the song 'Brilliant Disguise', or, as Bono has it, the 'hypocrisy of Bruce's heart'. The therapeutic style allowed him, for once, to share some of his hopes and dreads; the cadences (here, wry and low-key) spoke not of being born or running, but of winding down, journey's end, nowhere to go. Springsteen failed to hint that, by some happy chance, wedded life had introduced him to an earthly bliss. *Tunnel*'s 'ride' allegory was crudely, yet well put – juddering up sheer gradients or swooping down, turning blind corners along an inky, waterlogged rail towards a light (that of the oncoming train) at the end of the line. What singled it all out was Springsteen's bewildering balance: on the one hand, a native, quixotic faith that dreams are there to grab, like roses; on the other, an alien cynicism that the bloom, once picked, will prick. For him, and us, that ironic nudge spoke volumes. A gifted salesman of his own traumas, Springsteen got at least one foot in the doors of perception. As Bob Harris says, 'your air of doom struck a chord', with fan and star alike. Cutting *USA* to human size was both inevitable and intelligent – Springsteen walking before they made him run; the genius lay in making his mid-life crisis universal, and not just in the beholder's eye.

Musically, *Tunnel* spoke in a kind of fluent but modestly spare code. The songs' terseness, along with the slick arrangements, was smoothly convincing. Many of *Tunnel*'s genre larks were sweet soul, or the sort of ballads-with-beat best left to Orbison. As usual, the nature imagery came from listening to country and folk. The album boasted reggae, blues and even waltz time-signatures. Springsteen opened it playfully *a cappella*. It was hard to identify much trace of rock.

Equally memorable was the shorthand playing, at once supple and potent. In both 'Tougher Than The Rest' and 'Spare Parts' well-crafted riffs underpinned the lyrics, though it was the title track where mood and technique fully chimed. Ten bars of cod-disco then a reverb-heavy beat and swelling guitar were more than a pretext to pain: 'Tunnel', updating 'Wild Billy's Circus Story', struck sparks. Where a song like 'Born' was barking street-theatre, this was lean, focused and stately. The chorus was one of Springsteen's best – sunny and dark, at the end of his vocal tether. 'Brilliant Disguise' and 'One Step Up' both had the feel of confession, with rumbling drums preserving the mood. 'Walk Like A Man' was pure autobiography. Springsteen's Oedipal rage had never been in such magnificently naff context; it was this mixture of self-absorption and rapt interest in the sensual side of things, particularly female things, that made *Tunnel* so odd, yet so good. Elsewhere, there were lifts from Bo Diddley, Del Shannon's 'Runaway' and 'Highway 61'. 'Ain't Got You' flaunted the overall vibe of George Michael. 'Cautious Man' managed to filch a gothic sub-plot from Charles Laughton's *The Night of the Hunter*. Here, though, Springsteen made the words 'love' and 'fear', tattooed on opposite hands, into a sign of his own commitment phobia. More than anything, it was a supreme self-rebuke.

Tunnel, for all its scaled-down values, wasn't released in a vacuum. There were no fewer than five videos, mainly directed by Meiert Avis, along with promo CDs, T-shirts and the like. CBS sold 30,000 engraved bolo ties, of the sort Springsteen wore on the cover, more than they'd once shifted of *Greetings from Asbury Park*. Full-page ads were taken in both the dailies and trades. It was the third wave of a complex relationship with the PR mill of which neither it nor Springsteen ever tired, despite occasional barbs to the contrary. For *Rolling Stone*, where a 'Boss' orgasm was an annual event, not even a stylistic U-turn could keep him off the Best Dressed and Sexiest Male Artist rolls.

On a cyclical note, *Tunnel* continued Springsteen's '80s habit of following one radio-rock album by one home-made one. It was a moot point whether it was objectively 'good', or whether – like a Dylan – his name, and the loyalty he kindled, shifted the idea of an LP to fit his words, themes and shaky tunes. Early notices slated *Tunnel* as 'thin', anaemic and downbeat, rather than fully fledged, sombre fare from the home front. Some of the hacks had to be educated up to it. By 1988, *Newsweek* would spot it as a 'great record – an affirmation that rock 'n' roll can grow up', while for *Time*, ultimately, it was 'the best album Springsteen has made'. Ten years on, *Q* would include it in its readers' poll of all-time greats, a list lacking either *Born*. Commercially, as well as artistically, Springsteen himself wasn't vying with his past. As Landau says, 'Growth from record to record isn't part of the plan . . . When we put out *Tunnel* we certainly didn't think it was going to be as popular as *USA*. We're not in the business of taking X and forcing it into being Y.' From this unlikely strategem, a smash was born. Aside from the videos, the album's launch had none of *Live*'s hoopla. CBS initially shipped two million copies. But by May 1988, *Tunnel* had sold twice that and went on to go quintuple platinum; even this misfit of rock careerism hit number one.

For fans who wanted to know what the fuss was about in

Springsteen's marriage, *Tunnel* held the clue. 'To me,' he understated, 'the record had a certain doubt to it.' There were several key lyrics. The lines 'You've got to learn to live with what you/can't rise above', 'Now you play the loving woman . . . I'll play the faithful man' and 'Given each other some hard lessons lately' – not to add 'Ain't Got You' – were a direct take on Springsteen's life. He set up fatherhood as a clearly recognizable ideal of 'Walk Like A Man' and 'Valentine's Day'. Nobody could say 'Well I've tried so hard baby/But I just can't see/What a woman like you/Is doing with me' didn't come from the heart, or that 'All That Heaven Will Allow' (the title of a film in which a blue-blooded woman falls for her gardener) wasn't a choice echo. As a further twist, Springsteen chose to bump and grind on video with Scialfa, whose fey vocal could be heard on 'One Step Up' (whose own short featured Springsteen alone, in a bar, pondering his wedding ring). As for the album cover: he looked like a man off to a funeral. Finally, for sheer curtness, there was Springsteen's two-word acknowledgement in the notes. 'Thanks Juli.'

If *Born* had been Springsteen's greatest up album, then *Tunnel* was his greatest down one – exquisite pain translated as exquisite music. With it, he moved from Symbol Rocker into the realm of the true artist. At worst, it was superior pop. At best, it was disturbingly symmetrical, yet still unforced, lean in surface drama but deeply moving. *Tunnel* was Springsteen's masterpiece.

A new tour was an Event, if not a universally welcome one. Early in 1988, the extended group began six weeks' rehearsal. Agency and label teased the press into its normal, where Springsteen went, priapic state. The very scale of the reporting was tumescent. First, said *Rolling Stone*, 'Bruce will likely play small venues' – amended, a month later, to sheds – before Landau announced the inevitable 'summer stadium gigs', all flogged with a self-regard that would have glazed Narcissus' eye. Springsteen himself took various shakedown cruises, from cutting 'I Ain't Got No Home' and 'Vigilante Man' for *A Vision Shared*, the Smithsonian's Guthrie and Leadbelly tribute, to inducting Dylan into the Hall of Fame. He tuned up for the tour proper most nights, between ten and six, in Rumson. At times the sheer density of rockerati – with the band, crew and handlers wedged in a dank practice den – had all the makings of an art-world version of Bombay. Claustrophobia had been a strand in Springsteen's life for years (there'd been nothing state-of-the-soundstage even in 1984), but this was strikingly shack-like. Cabined and confined all winter, the E Streeters gelled.

About the only one not transported by the hype was Springsteen. His aptitude for self-doubt returned even before the first note of the first night. It was, in fact, to have been a solo tour. When that was nixed, vetoed by an unholy mix of marketing and management sorts, he rebelled by dumping, he said, 'all the cornerstones of my set', specifically twenty-one-gun salutes like 'Backstreets' and 'Thunder Road'. Next, in a symbolic but literal break with the past, he moved the band members' places. In the chess game that followed, Bittan swapped with Federici, Lofgren with Tallent, and Weinberg sat downstage. Horns were added. But the real departure was Scialfa. Previously secure in the wings, now she stood front and centre, often sharing a mike with Springsteen and whanging a lusty guitar. A perfectly plausible theory, as Joel Bernstein says, is that 'Bruce was nervous . . . He knew it was time to downsize, but didn't know how to do it.' Scialfa, in this reading, was a kind of Sherpa. For all the manic strumming, the instrument she played best was Springsteen himself, guiding him safely through a dire year. 'She saved me' was no more than he meant.

The Tunnel of Love Express gave a lurch and started on 25 February 1988. Without, the scene at the Centrum in Worcester, Massachusetts, jerked nostalgic memories: tickets had sold out in two hours and touts were asking $500 a pair. Within, Springsteen himself sauntered on holding a stub from an ersatz carnival-barker's booth. 'Ready for a date?' he beamed. Both his formal garb (black pants, dress shirt and gold braid) and opening prank (tossing roses into the pit) were early hints that this was something other than sweaty frat-pop. Whereas Springsteen's *USA*-era motto had been 'I'm just a prisoner of . . . rock 'n' roll', now he told the house: 'I'm a fool for lurve.' Sure enough, the evening took on a treacly mood with a set of ballads, blunt, inoffensive fare – ditties like 'All That Heaven' – which at least warmed the hall, even if failing to sift *Tunnel*'s less smoochy grandeur. The band all flailed away. Springsteen, on the other hand, seemed caught at a moment when something snapped inside him, like a pain pill or laughing-gas; an actor forever about to send in the clowns, but facially numb. His smile looked rictal. 'Seeds' booted the tone into something darker. After a rap about wife-beating, the first set ended with 'War' and 'USA'. If Springsteen the swab, with T-shirt and bulging forearms had pared down, he still weighed in. 'How ya doin'?' was imbued with almost Homeric depth. He closed the half part singing, part prating, dancing on the ivories, and dousing himself with cups of water. 'Should I get the cardiac the first night?' he yelled. And that was just the break.

From there Springsteen went for the jocular. 'You Can Look' featured a near divorce-actionable snog with Scialfa. Springsteen swooped through 'She's The One'; blazed out 'I'm On Fire'; and débuted 'Part Man, Part Monkey', a rare reggae jape. Retooling 'Born To Run' as a fond yet rueful blues was a logical, sane bet. As he said, the man who wrote it had 'croaked'. Other songs betrayed his old-time country and folk sources. There was enough left of the permanent teen, though, for 'Rosalita'. Springsteen topped that with Ryder's 'Devil With The Blue Dress' medley. The jewelled imagery and boiler-room blast relit Bics still flickering from 'Hungry Heart'. Then he was off.

There are words which circulate round a gig, and at Worcester one was 'older'. Yet to most fans – some of whom had seen him twenty, thirty or, in one case, 147 times – the articulate, grown-up songs more than atoned for the relative lack of romps. Not that roots were ignored. As always, the multiple encores proved that Springsteen had the capacity not only to move the crowd, but jolt them. Three years on, he'd returned to earth's orbit wiser and sadder. He still knew how to deliver hoary rock goods, but nowadays his effect lay in more than a calibrated blend of pure ham and volume. *Tunnel* was his finest hour. Live, too, its focus was forensic yet deeply emotional, never pat, warm and vivid lyrics juxtaposed with ravishingly sad tunes about people guilty of lying or cheating, of doubt, lust and 'shit'. They rang a bell. Phillips herself was backstage for the first dozen shows, after which there was nothing left of her marriage but its dirt.

That acoustic 'Born To Run' – collated on Springsteen's *Video Anthology/1978–88* – stood for a tour that, though wry and evocative, never raised the roof as the last had. Despite the Detroit rave-up, many of the oldies were gone. Springsteen no longer moisturized his audience with 'Growin' Up' or 'Ramrod' or 'Jungleland'. Fans got a smattering of belters, but the tenor of the three-hour set stuck more to the emotional centre. Springsteen had grown nearer the old Jerseyan who'd once moved his parents; *Time* was just the first, but not last, to call 'the Boss and the Chairman [Sinatra] . . . America's two greatest singers'. As the local press wrote of the Atlanta gig, 'It was a changed man who worked in black suit and bolo tie . . . What better example of it than a skit Springsteen acted out early in the night with Clemons: they meet at a prop park bench, and Clarence shows off kiddy pictures . . . "There's a little Big Man running round out there," Bruce said with a laugh.' Not that the show was all maturity on parade. Springsteen still turned the air blue with his newly partisan rants ('Don't vote for that fuckin' Bush!' he advised one crowd) and plodded through his Freehold raps, desperately seeking a point. To his credit, though, he rose above the duff retreads of other metastars. The grown man in the skinny tie knew that most fans needed nothing more to finish the job than a quick rendition of a few basic moves. He made them, while hinting how brittle and sad, how much harder to please, was his own life. There was pathos in his bandying of baby snaps. Backstage, too, all was surface calm, tables heaving with fruit, tea and scented candles, though, again, he cut a figure down, if not out, ruing his wife's rush to read for *Fletch Lives*. Springsteen met *Rolling Stone* 'clad in black slacks, black dress shirt, black leather blazer and silver-tipped black cowboy boots, a gold wedding [hoop] and single diamond stud in his left lobe'. As the tour progressed, he lost the gold band and added more earrings.

Meantime, the nightly theatre of the bizarre spun heads on both sides of the footlights. It wasn't unknown for certain fans to walk out during, say, 'Brilliant Disguise'. One man in Atlanta was true to form. The song was just welling up when he flashed the international sign for 'gangway'. Then he deftly manoeuvred out alongside a group huddled in the car park, who also happened to be taking a smoke. 'She for real?', 'Where's his head at?' and 'Come back, Big Man' were among the soundbites. It was the way Scialfa rose above it, like Yoko, that most admired. Clemons' own view could only be guessed. Not only, with a few rare exceptions, was he shunted downstage. He hadn't played a single note on two of Springsteen's last three albums.

'A more important Catholic event than the visit of the Pope' was pushing it, especially since Springsteen's cultists weren't, by and large, still living through him. Nowadays, you could even mildly pan their god without their revenging his insulted name. He'd gone some way to gently doing so himself. Quite deliberately, the 1988 tour never scaled the bombast ladder of 1984. Though still heavy with flaks and fixers (and the hardest of all Springsteen's hammers, Landau), the entourage had been pruned. Now he had a crew of just thirty. Onstage, too, there was a matching dip. Previously, because the gigs had been as much about graft as native talent, they'd tended to bring out the latent cheerleader, much like the audiences in *Rocky*; now, the fans were rooting for the lofty moral of a *Field of Dreams*. Instead of pumping up his repertoire, Springsteen had stripped it to the bone, then added mock-orchestral relish. You couldn't hear a clearer revelation of mood music. The jump-cuts between pop, soul and quasi-classical were a rung up from even *The River*. For Springsteen himself, all the props – the splintered Fender, the studded guitar strap – were in place, but there was no mistaking that he'd run out of adolescent puff. 'The past is a funny thing,' he told the dome in Atlanta. 'It's something that seems to bind us together, and something that can drag you down and hold you back as you get stuck in them old dreams . . . It can break your heart.' He was speaking generally, but it was a telling self-rebuke.

The tour had its individual highs. In Landover, Springsteen declined an interview with Fawn Hall, Ollie North's ill-famed

secretary, with the words: 'I don't like you. I don't like your boss. I
don't like what you did. Thanks.'* A month later, in Palo Alto, he
dedicated 'Walk Like A Man' to Doug – then sang it straight to
him. Next night, he waltzed onstage with Adele. His old friend
Randy Brecker ran into him at Madison Square Garden –
Springsteen was 'pally'. Peter Gabriel got much the same reaction
when he pitched an Amnesty tour slated for the fall. And *any* night's
climax or leaden nadir, to taste, was the steamy floor-show with
Scialfa. Those bumps, grinds and rutting hips, practically feign-
ing the act, served as the gig's central metaphor. It was the
apotheosis of pulp. '[The couple] weren't just acting,' notes Marsh,
helpfully. True devotion was measured by Springsteen's willingness to shock.

After the tour's opening salvo, Phillips, unable, allegedly, to cope,
flew back to Oregon. 'I'm dead,' Springsteen told a crony backstage, and there were other reports – not denied – of him ringing
his wife in tears. (His friend, by contrast, once heard him end a call
by snapping 'Whatever' and banging down the receiver.) By early
May, Phillips learnt what insiders had known for months. The
same week Springsteen was making nice to his father, he split from
his wife. He and Scialfa became rock's most obvious, if furtive
onstage–offstage duo.

'I'd like to get my hands on her,' Springsteen laughed, stepping
through the door to the parking lot, where his band milled around
a red E-type. It didn't seem possible that he'd be so rash. Wizened
roadies stared bug-eyed as he wet his lips. He seemed almost to
drool. The handlers realized Springsteen was in the grip of a full-
blown obsession. But all they could do was watch. It took another
second for him to run his hand up and down the flank of his love-
object, the car.

Scialfa was then thirty-four. She had a willowy charm, a cinched
waist, stork legs, and, more pertinently, both feet planted firmly on
the ground. Unlike Phillips, it wasn't a case of poles attracting.
Scialfa had never been a hostage to the frantic moods of the time.

---

*Springsteen endorsed Jesse Jackson for president.

Her world wasn't Hollywood, but the Irish–Italian ghettoes of Long Branch and Asbury. She was a Jersey Girl. It's debatable whether her choppy guitar and vocal added much to the music, but she did wonders for Springsteen. For once the satiric 'luvvy' ambitions of most groups were amply fulfilled. By that Memorial Day, the pair were also an item, at least within the rigidly controlled pod of the tour. Later that month, Wapping duly splashed its scoop that 'Bruce and Juli have separated because she wouldn't give him a baby'. By early June, the *Enquirer*, the *Globe* and *People* were on side. On the 15th, the first photos ran. PICTURES THAT WILL COST THE BOSS £75M yelled the caption, and from there the tabloids' fits of morality flowered, oddly, into a circulation war. The *Sun* blazed all year.

Springsteen's European tour – pointedly, dome-based – opened in Turin on 11 June. He jammed with the Marleys in Paris; graced the 'SOS Racism' gig; survived Britt Ekland, who, for some vital reason, crashed him in Stockholm; and charmed fans by busking 'The River' while out strolling in Rome. A month later, Springsteen did the same thing in Copenhagen. He wove through both Berlins, Amsterdam and Madrid, along with England. Between times, notices were warm. The *Tribune* praised his shows' 'shrewd feel for the beat of the age'. British hacks still, by and large, touted Springsteen's gift for writing high drama of ordinary folk in ordinary, everyday rhymes, as well as the new depth of the gigs. They were more than mere bellowthons. Even in the love songs, Springsteen duly put some vinegar in to go with the honey. Most shows were a blend of sweet science and basic blacksmith, with a creeping trend towards acoustic, if not solo strum. 'It got me thinking that maybe the band should have ended after *USA*,' says Tallent. 'The *Tunnel* tour wasn't the real thing. The magic was gone.' Yet at Villa Park, the first UK date, the *Guardian* found Springsteen 'still a mesmeric performer with remarkable stamina. He's in no danger of becoming an embarrassment as he still shares his changing experiences and problems with his audience . . . [It was] an exercise in mixing rock euphoria with a very brave and personal line in emotional striptease.'

By then, there was a mass UK yearning: a blood lust. The media exploded. Scant, skint hints of royal crackups gave way, in turn, to lurid non-interviews with Springsteen, Phillips and Scialfa, alongside a '*Sun* World Exclusive' on the roadies' suit. In spite of his own qualms, Shinto awe had grown steadily from 1984 to 1988, at the instigation of the clubs and zines. There was also the fact that most fans were spiritually starved. They'd seen their early ideals and illusions and hopes one by one worn down by the corrosive influence of events and fads – by the slow ruin of the go-go years, by smut and royal sleaze, by the grim spectacle of currency-shadowing, inflation and the poll tax, and finally by their recent diet of Madonna and Jacko. In short, Britain was 'ready' again for Springsteen. The well-honed machinery (now run, along with the rest of CBS Records, by Sony) fired up. A contemporary god re-emerged as from the ether, along with his cult. Its effects were counterproductive. Eulogies of 'the Boss', 'guv', even 'the godfather', stirring reminders of the fans' good luck to be paying members of the clan – all bids to elevate Springsteen to the status of a capo – merely fuelled the frenzy. Throughout June and July, private trips would become unexpectedly public when press and photographers dogged him on the street. If it's possible to convey menace at the Dorchester Hotel, the paparazzi managed it. The concentric spheres of life – the inner worlds of home and family, the public ones of fame and 'shit' – now clashed. All parties took a dunk in the tabloid trough. Springsteen was stalked. Scialfa was slagged as a Jezebel. To their credit the affair was real, even if slighter than they let on, and both took care to hedge it until summer. Then merry hell broke loose.

'It was tough,' Springsteen later said of his marriage. 'I didn't really know how to be a husband. She was terrific . . . I just didn't know how to do it.' In practice, that meant, a month shy of three years into the 'lifetime warranty' he'd promised Phillips (while waving away a pre-nuptial), it was over. Long-lens snaps of him and Scialfa, the latter in her thong, merely added pathos. At that stage, Phillips' lawyer made the official announcement. In a news release, Springsteen then apologized to his wife. He denied that children, or their lack, were a factor. The general hunch in the press was that it was the one issue that had done for them more than anything else. Better, or innermost, reasons aren't available to an author, some of them not even to the parties themselves. 'It was tough' is a suggestive key phrase.

Both Springsteen and Scialfa came to a certain amount of grief in 1988–89. She had another setback with her solo career, and took fire from the *Sun*. For at least a year, he was an emotional cripple. Friends, family and therapists worked on him in shifts, and even then things would go wrong: callers to Rumson found a self-lacerating 'fuck', who still kept Phillips' photo in his den. Mutually, he and Scialfa weathered a storm of abuse in the time-honoured roles of the Shit and the Slut. Their neighbour Kathleen Stanley happened to see the pair at a bar in Long Branch that winter. 'Patti looked like utter hell.' 'It was a tough time but a great time,' Scialfa says. 'Wonderful and very painful.' Phillips herself filed on 30 August 1988. Negotiations weren't onerous, since Springsteen instructed his lawyers to be fair, and a settlement was reached by Christmas. Under the terms of the divorce of 30 March 1989, he paid Phillips $20 million. In virtually all of the several versions of the deal, it was assumed to carry a gagging order preventing her from writing about him. She never has.

Springsteen's world tour wound up on 3 August. A month later he was back live in London, heading a six-week trek for Amnesty International, covering 40,000 air miles in eighteen countries. He'd agreed to the slog as a result of subtle press-agentry by Gabriel, Frank Barsalona and Amnesty's Jack Healey. (The presence of Springsteen's old blood brother, Davy Sancious, may have helped.) 'Human Rights Now!', as it became, was announced on stage in Stockholm. Less well known were the various ructions that threatened to wreck it. Like a stagnant pond, motionless to the naked eye, the tour, though portraying itself as a mere charity, was inwardly teeming with furious, invisible strife. CBS's Walter Yetnikoff, convinced Amnesty was biased against Israel, tried to veto it. When that failed, a coolness descended between label, management and star for two years, at which point Yetnikoff quit. Meanwhile, in a hysterical month of logistics and plotting, Bill Graham, too, blew a fuse. Finally, there was brutal jockeying over the acts' pecking order, which ran: Youssou N'Dour, Tracy Chapman, Gabriel, Sting, all garnish for a one-hour bite of Springsteen. Opening night was 2 September, at Wembley.

'Relevance in rock' – can that message have fallen with a direr thud than words like 'fusion' or 'concept' had in the 1970s? That autumn's ride marked a new high-point for the idea that pop stars can care. Human Rights Now! split critics down party lines. To men like the MP John Carlisle, it was proof of a sad trend yoking festivals to political crises or national angst. Others, like Marsh, thought it a fitting way to 'celebrate the twenty-fifth anniversary of the International Declaration of Human Rights, a document ratified by most of the world's nations, but enforced in its entirety by none'. Springsteen himself had little to say on the ethical aspects of the tour. He did, though, cover Dylan's 1964 'Chimes of Freedom' as part of a four-song EP to plug it. Even this touched off a row. CBS took flak for trimming the CD version of both Springsteen's spoken intro and most of the graphics. In the end, the record paid Amnesty $206,000 in royalties, the biggest single donation ever made to the group. The way Springsteen skinned his best tunes, like 'Born To Run', to the bone, made *Chimes* a study of clenched despair and joyous release. As usual, the music spoke for the man.

One by-product of the trek was a lasting bond with his co-stars, notably Sting. Both clearly enjoyed pricking the loftier extremes of each other's fame. The conception that the self-styled 'greaser' and 'Geordie yobbo' could educate large audiences on civil rights, and that the host governments involved were simply mass roadies, the state 'grunts' who stamped visas or booked gigs, might seem eccentric; but it made sense to them. The two became fast friends. Before camping through 'The River', Springsteen would describe his partner as 'my best pal, a man of bizarre sexual perversity'. Sting, in turn, once slunk up on him onstage wielding a Hoover. On the tour's final night he appeared, in semi-comic tribute, togged up in jeans and a bandanna. The second of October, Sting's birthday, found the pair in the jetset's favourite Aegean sandpit, a beach bar in Athens. For most of the fall, they exchanged amorous triviality for songs, like 'Chimes', that rallied to the cause. Here, the reverse went. A woman named Rose Macnab, part of the night's revue, has fond memories of two very different souls to the public misanthropes. Specifically, they 'loved watching girls shake their cakes'. (She duly reprised Sting's gig with the vacuum.) As a man, the one thing Springsteen didn't lack was drive. As a pop *deus ex machina*, he wasn't so sure. 'My band's happier than they've been in years, but one of the reasons I wanted to do this was to work with others . . . I wanted to get in with a bunch of people who had an idea and subsume my identity into that idea, into that collective, and try to come out with something more meaningful and bigger and better than I could on my own.' This one-of-the-guys effusion would, paradoxically, do for the E Streeters.

Springsteen saw in his own birthday with just a few friends and 20,000 fans at the Oakland Coliseum. He was serenaded by Joan Baez. In the case of Scialfa, art continued to ape life. They smooched through 'Tunnel Of Love' and 'Brilliant Disguise', duets that had long turned both parties into media roadkill; the operative words were 'torrid', 'randy' and 'blue'. That was a lot of text, not to mention the actual tunes, to cram into four or five minutes. Then he bloked out again with Sting. Next the tour barnstormed the sub-continent, blitzed virgin turf like Zimbabwe and yomped through Europe. One day Springsteen found himself eating breakfast in Paris, lunch in Budapest and dinner in Turin. Everything ground down, chaotically enough, in Buenos Aires. A planned global radio feed broke up, and was padded by ads for Reebok, whose sales executives took almost as many bows as the actual stars. It all stood for a crusade that, though well meant, was neither an activist's nor an accountant's dream. For the first time in ten years, there were unsold seats for a Springsteen gig in America. An HBO special about it bombed. More to the point, it felt then, and was later proved, an era's end. For all Springsteen's commitment, the tour was also escapism, ducking domestic truths, fudging the need for change and riveting his focus obsessively on externals. That exotically bold bid to free convicts was actually about a man clutching at the bars of his own ego.

Nowadays, Springsteen was no rock-and-roller. He knew too many actual rockers to confuse the issue. The doomed lovers of *Tunnel* were far removed from the cartoon cut-outs of *Born to Run*, the whimsically ordained instruments of an oversized teen. Straight after coming off the road, he said, 'I had a bad time . . . I'd made a lot of plans, but when we got home, I just kind of spun off for a while. I just got lost. That lasted about a year.' Among Springsteen's roll-call of worries were the divorce, its fallout and the overtime-pay suit. The creative itch also bulked large. He already knew it was time to make for new musical waters. The press had fanned perennial band-breakup rumours for years. But studying the CVs of men like Sting and Gabriel, both of whom had lit out to explore their own careers, now swung it. 'I'm not gonna keep going like a monkey on a stick,' Springsteen said backstage in Buenos Aires. '*Something*'s gotta give.' It was 15 October 1988, a month short of the E Streeters' sixteenth anniversary. From the first, their genius had worked in close connection with his experience. And now the whole thing had come full turn. Springsteen's lush, word-bath phase had been well aired on the first three albums. The darker artist had torn himself from solitude in 1978–82. *USA* was a vivid aberration. On *Tunnel*, Springsteen hit home with songs whose humanism quailed at the bedroom door. Truly it seemed that, after their thirteenth tour, the band were played out as a gang. 'We knew, and he knew we knew,' says one ex. 'All of us needed to get off the jet.' For now, they'd taken wing for the last time.

8

Jersey Girl

For years, in fact until he remarried, Springsteen used to brood over his wife. Often he'd gaze at her photo, while strumming some luminously old blues; if it happened to be night, the frame would be specially floodlit. As well as the picture, he was confronting the fact that, from Ed Sullivan on, he'd barely existed outside of rock. Testimony to his solitary ways spanned forty years, and much of it was Springsteen's own. His earliest memory was of being alone and lost in a field. Now, wry self-appraisal gradually gave way to one-on-one feeling. 'I'm just taking baby-steps . . . closer to a certain kind of fullness I always felt like I was missing. I enjoyed my work, but I felt like I couldn't function without it. I always had a hard time.' Thanks in part to Scialfa, Springsteen's three-year silence wasn't presumptive darkness. He embraced the light, literally, rising at dawn and recanting his life-long love of night and storms and Atlantic fog. When he emerged in 1992, he was sporting a tan.

At the time he divorced, Springsteen wasn't sure if he was a New Jersey, New York or Hollywood native. He played at being all three, saw them as virtually interchangeable, and liked to flit, rehearsing the stuff of countless rites-of-passage mid-life crises.

Early in 1989 he seemed to have hit on California. As well as work-ing on Scialfa's oft-mooted LP, he was demystifying his own glum studio routine, casually laying down demos of what became *Human Touch*. (Among the first cuts was one called 'Trouble In Paradise'.) So lax was it that several of the hired guns weren't told whether it was his, or his lover's, LP they were working on. This wasn't a man smarting with the daily hurt of being a pop god. Springsteen also graced various Sin City spas, including Mickey Rourke's club Rubber. The eternal sunshine, must-have friends and laid-back *mores* seemed to suit him. Especially the last. Springsteen even slipped, once or twice, into the PR jacuzzi, dealing with *ad hoc* TV interviews. One pert local anchor asked if he were having fun in Los Angeles. At that point Springsteen pursed his lips, promising to be 'straight up' in his answer, which turned out to be 'yep'. But the roasting wasn't over. 'How cool is it to be you?' Springsteen told the woman it was pretty cool, signed a CD, then took off into Beverly Hills.

In the weeks around his divorce, Springsteen drugged himself with trivia, recording and stage-hopping on both coasts. On 18 January he was at New York's Waldorf-Astoria for the fourth Rock and Roll Hall of Fame. Pete Townshend inducted the Rolling Stones. Jagger quoted Cocteau while Richards studied his nails. The lights flared, the audience stirred, Springsteen played a solo 'Crying' for the late Roy Orbison, and all shed a tear. Both 'Mad Dog' Lopez and the Castiles' George Theiss were on hand. A pick-up band then tripped through a medley of '60s hits. Springsteen sat down next to Scialfa. Photographers swarmed them before, during and after dinner. This was served under the Waldorf's dusty chan-deliers, and beside a shrine. The hotel had made a sort of pall of guitars, and beneath it a wreath of roses. Springsteen stood at this edifice on the way out. Guests pressed close to the door claimed they saw his lips move in tribute to his old hero. Springsteen bowed his head. Then, again, he was gone.

The facially immobile, emotionally moving presence was Springsteen's forte. In common with other stage icons, he'd been nagged with film scripts over the years, everything from *On the*

Waterfront down. There were rumours that Robert Stigwood offered him £10 million to play Che, opposite Meryl Streep, in *Evita*. Casting an all-Jersey lead – later, so memorably done by Madonna – would have appealed to Hollywood realism (and followed in a long line from Brando in *Mutiny on the Bounty*), though in the end it broke down. Other offers followed. One studio head duly sent him a bowl, huge enough to hold Bob Evans's ego, full of drugs; the fate of a white, photogenic Name living in Babylon. For the next three years, Springsteen drew producers like skin does ticks. As a rule they tended to be maverick types who made Appel seem shy by comparison, and, just to prove it, they called him either 'Boss' or 'Brucie'. Springsteen's tragedy was that, for now, he could neither remake the world nor ignore its creation of him. He put up with the toytown tsars beating a path to his door. No business resulted.

He did, though, release his *Video Anthology/1978–88* early that spring. The title was skewed: fully fourteen of the eighteen clips were post-1984. In that context, it was good to revisit the hoary 'Rosalita' and the other live footage, less soupy and freewheeling than the conceptual kind. The latter offered rich pickings for fans – particularly the end-suite of *Tunnel* shorts – but inlaid in the gauzy fabrics of MTV-friendly 'art'. Such posing cut across the very grain of what Springsteen stood for. But he also knew to mix winning personal charm with glossy technique. There was a moment when his eyes acted out 'I'm On Fire' which was moving and profoundly soulful. The spot where Springsteen dragged 'Born To Run' back from the archive was superb. In terms of a full-fledged retrospect, *Anthology* chiefly toasted the near past, rather than ancient history. For old times' sake, there could have been less *Nebraska* and more of an Asbury zing. As a rocumentary, it was an ironic log of Springsteen's woes, hurtling dizzily between farce and tragedy. As a stopgap, it worked fine.

So it went, and for the rest of 1989 he was back in the role of a *jongleur*. Springsteen seemed to be in permanent cameo mode: joining Weinberg's and Lofgren's bands; duetting with Bobby Bandiera; and punching up gigs by Neil Young and Jackson Browne. As a rule, these sets tended to be everything the *Tunnel* tour wasn't: raw, feral, one-dimensional. And fun. It didn't take a genius to see, for this writer did so, that Springsteen was treading water. The home studio was still open, but a musician who did business with him notes that 'Bruce didn't write many songs, was kind of lazy about mixing, and sometimes didn't show for days . . . A few of us once found ourselves holding a band meeting in a dive uptown, because we'd heard he happened to be there.' On that occasion, at least, Springsteen was 'a beaut'. He stood a round of drinks. But, says the friend, he was 'spacy' on work plans. 'You had to be kind of tough with Bruce to get anywhere.'

Little seemed to reassure him that his forties weren't to be merely a long postlude to fame. The few tracks he eked out in 1989 were, he said, 'the best stuff I've done'. The explanation of that rave was more mental than musical. Bluntly, Springsteen was bored. His struggle against anti-climax led him to blurt out, 'What *now*?' as, yet again, he hit writer's block. The shrewder of the guns sagely guessed it was 'part of a Big Picture'. Springsteen formally divorced that March. Meantime, the two roadies, Mike Batlan and Doug Sutphin, had their first day in court. A judge threw out their claim of $6 million punitive damages. Still pending was one for hefty back-overtime pay. Unsaid but not unknown to Jon Landau Management – who reportedly spent $2 million in a bid to quash the case – was a sub-plot that cut to the bone of Springsteen's populist image. As Batlan said: 'We're suing him for massive violations of labor laws which resulted in our being cheated out of hundreds of thousands of dollars . . . the trial has the potential to expose what may be the largest fraud in the history of rock 'n' roll . . . to expose Bruce Springsteen as a world-class hypocrite.' That was a perversion. But the mere fact of the slur was there.

Be it the trial of the century or 'a drama right out of Abbott and Costello', Marsh panned the techs as two 'comic-opera supplicants' who'd each been paid off with bonuses of $100,000. Many agreed with him: but the growing digs at Springsteen's divorce prompted uneasy reminders of other dodgy areas of the recent past which had nothing to do with pop – such as those shots in Rome. Being caught *in flagrante* was more Tinseltown than Jersey. It jibed with the homeboy image. For years, Springsteen's job, as he'd seen it, was really akin to a mailman's. Here was a song or a gig, and there was someone who wanted to hear it, and he obligingly wove between the two. But once the lawsuit hit, he lost his I-am-a-vessel chastity for the redtop kudos of dirt. At its murky nadir, a scandal sheet skewered him as 'crap'. Not everyone held a brief for the roadies, but everyone began to talk about them. (Batlan, for his part, still gave away nothing of what he thought of Landau and Springsteen – 'a story of money, power and greed', they found out later.) One tactic in their legal locker was to seize Springsteen's tax records. It didn't happen, but *Rolling Stone* and the rest reported each move and counter-move for the better part of three years. Elsewhere, the mere words 'Bruce' and 'disgruntled exes' justified their restless niche in the tabloids. In staccato terms, the stories became versions of BOSSY, full of sleaze, superlatives and triple exclamation marks. For more than a decade, Springsteen's headlines had dazzled. Now, they blinded.

It was, as his friend says, part of a big picture. After the Amnesty tour, Springsteen's wrap was quickly torn away. Thanks to Landau's primer, he'd already come by the intellectual curiosity and background, including a fixation on Johns Ford and Steinbeck, that worked against the risk of his viewing rock, or even the larger body of pop culture, as a closed system. He wasn't ever likely to spoof himself like some Jagger clone. During his three years off, Springsteen underwent a 'spiritual crisis' – a stock event in the life of a matinée star – and broke decisively with his band. He even talked about quitting altogether. For more than a year, he didn't speak to Walter Yetnikoff or the other shills at CBS. Besides Scialfa, Springsteen's only other daily friendships were with Landau, and men like Sting and Paul Simon. They talked ecology together.

Emotionally speaking, Springsteen was now as familiar with the pratfall as with the Icarian high. On one level, the hacks' barbs were entirely valid – not to say mild. His cuckolding Phillips had wrong-footed those who like their idols along the lines of a Cliff. Nothing wicked there. Most of us are prey to Goethe's 'two souls in one's breast'. But that's a tad more high-minded than having two women in one's bed. In some quarters, if only the Ken Starr school of ethics, Springsteen's adultery had rightly tainted his fame. Both he and Scialfa took their lumps in the weeks ahead. Graham Parker remembers meeting the couple at the China Café in Los Angeles. They sat there, with child-like shyness, while 'the press hassled them all night'. Amy Frechett notes how Springsteen's lover was widely slagged as 'Patti Ono' or 'Parking-lot Patti'. She'd 'do anything to get her man'.

Springsteen's own recent record was chequered. He was guilty of some epic errors of judgement. But he was also remembered for the achievements of those years – achievements that were largely unique: conscientiously slogging the globe; doing good by stealth; tub-thumping; and all to the backing-track that was a staple of upmarket pop and dour conviction. That would be for starters. Also in the plus column was Springsteen's candour, his resilience, an oratorical style that fused polemic and popular nous, unflagging zip and devotion to the job. To offset such things against infidelity wasn't just 'crap'.

Springsteen's marriage ended that March, a year after it imploded. He signed off on it, as on so many things, at Landau's office. The actual divorce captivated Wapping for a day or two, till the gossip shoal reverted to the royals. In terms of cash, Springsteen's $20 million vied on equal terms with earlier payouts by Clint Eastwood and Steven Spielberg. (The lump sum, plus $3,000 a week, padded the fee from Phillips' latest B-romp, strung out with a bikini-thin plot, Blake Edwards' *Skin Deep*.) He was always civil about her to friends, and on turf well beyond that when it came to the press. She was 'one of the best people' he'd ever met. Still, a number of fans, notably the female ones, voted with their own purses. Springsteen's sales were that rare rock oddity, high but no longer astronomic, while, with the passage of time, his first LPs seemed to get better still.

Backlash met with burnout. During summer of 1989 Springsteen was sick for weeks with recurrent flu and respiratory problems, though the news was kept quiet. Aside from its physical toll, the bug seems to have caused certain mood swings, all too clear to the hired guns. He was prone to bouts of 'black and blue', 'shit-struck' and increasingly cagey of the band. A colleague recalls a scene when he was in Rumson that mid-July. They were dining out with several hands and roadies, one of whom was oddly silent. Peeved by that, Springsteen asked, in his parody of De Niro parodying him: 'You talkin' to me? Huh?' The man went red. A waiter thought he was going to have a fit and gave him a glass of water. All parties seemed mutually unimpressed when Springsteen then started 'laughing nuttily. It was like a mad joke . . . Everybody else kept stum.' It was no gag: typical of a character, if not a career, in freefall. As Springsteen said of the era, 'I was kind of wandering and lost . . . The best thing I did was I got into therapy. I crashed into myself and saw a lot of myself as I really was . . . I questioned everything I'd ever done.' After trying, and failing, to write new songs, Springsteen already knew the worst. He was blocked. The riffs sounded like warmed-up *Tunnel* and the words failed to do much even at the level of the phrase; as rhymes, they fell like a lump-hammer. They clanged. The plot-lines, such as they were, creaked with woodenly doled-out wisdom. From this, Springsteen would reach the Damascene verdict, 'Two of the best days of my life were the day I picked up the guitar and the day I learnt how to put it down.' Thirty years after first finding Elvis, and twenty-five from the Kent, he was focused on the next forward jolt.

Not yet, though. Art Rosato remembers filming Springsteen 'doing some "thank you" spiel for an award. He looked bad. Then, after a minute or two, he strapped on a guitar and started strumming. Immediately he was Boss again.' In fact, if any disillusioned fan had a kind of Geiger counter with which to detect Springsteen motion – as against action – the machine would have been in a state of permanent frenzy that summer. He jammed in both LA and New York. He sat in with Ringo Starr. As usual, he carpet-bombed the shore bars. Stocked in winter by shuffling bums and a few lags, by June Asbury was a day-glo haven of lycra-clad surfers, beer, slot machines and sewage: not to mention the black-leather stringers who cruised the boardwalk in search of data on Springsteen. Often tourists from London stood outside the Pony, gazing up at the peeling white walls. 'Is this where Bruce plays?' a woman shouted at him one day with a Nikon in hand. In fact, he was there on and off all year; he helped bail the club out of its perennial cash crisis. Springsteen was also asked to record at the Garden State Arts Center – *Born*'s 'opera out on the Turnpike' – but blew it off, shrewdly guessing it would be 'a zoo'. Other such requests tended to be met by a form letter from Landau. Springsteen did, though, cut 'Viva Las Vegas' and 'Remember When The Music' for a Nordoff-Robbins and a Harry Chapin tribute LP, respectively. 'Putting down the guitar', it seemed, was a form of sloth by which he meant to keep busy.

He hit forty that fall, lathered like Arkle, sweaty and drunk, on stage at McLoone's in Sea Bright. Springsteen was joined by half the old band, though the bizarre evolution of his backing singers – including his manager and uncle Warren – gently dashed hopes of a reunion. Halfway through the show, Springsteen told the crowd, 'I may be old, but damn, I'm still handsome!' Everyone, in a source's words, was 'cheerfully wrecked'; and few of the shackful of fans could have guessed they were seeing the last *de facto* E Street gig (bar two cameos) for a decade. After dancing with Adele, Springsteen was driven the short hop home with Scialfa. Next afternoon he was on his silver and blue Harley, heading west.

What he thought about as he rode down I-70, or got up to in the unbuttoned privacy of Hyatts and Super 8s, isn't known. What is known is that he told a casual friend, Woody Lock, at work in a mill in St Louis: 'You know, you can always get off the wheel . . . it really *is* your land.' Three days later, a few Hell's Angels were a spellbound witness to Springsteen's relish for Guthrie's and Steinbeck's America. Patrons of a desert inn in Prescott, Arizona, were greeted by a stubbly but grinning figure asking where 'greaser chicks' might be found. What followed was a novelty even for Matt's Saloon: the house band plunking down covers of 'Glory Days' and 'I'm On Fire' while the songs' author bawled the chorus. (Tangible proof that it really happened came a few weeks later, when the club's owner, 'Bubbles' Pechanec, was struck by cancer. The eventual medical bill of

$100,000 was too much. Pechanec went to see her hospital admin-
istrator to explain, and in the faint hope that some instalment plan
could be worked out. No problem, the man said: the fees had already
been paid in full. He added that her benefactor was anonymous.
But Pechanec, by dint of detective work, tracked him down. It was
Springsteen.) Other stories filtered back, that fall, of his affinity for
his fans, especially the young and game ones. 'That road trip *was* a
trip,' says a Dallas woman who knows. But by November he was
back in Jersey. The lead in *USA Today* over the holidays made sense
of much of Springsteen's last-gasp biker antics. For him, one side of
life really did kick-start at forty. Scialfa was pregnant.

Springsteen's reincarnation didn't spare nostalgists, but it was the
band who suffered most. The result was the breakup of the gang
after seventeen years. Psychological characteristics, therapy and
age all chimed to make Springsteen think, then do, the deed.
Looming fatherhood was pressed into service to add logic to the
split; yet the greying rock market was dotted with working parents,
and, in the case of the Stones, grampses. Springsteen himself
offered simple reasons and seemed proud to do so. His real needs
were threefold. The first was to step off not just the jet, but the
merry-go-round. After two decades' touring, he wanted – there
were hints in 1984–85 – to mend his road-rat ways. Springsteen saw
his second priority as, paradoxically, not only to fire the group, but
to help them. Musically, some of the soc-hop formula had become
formulaic. Personally, the in-fighting had made for a number of old
scores: instead of a choir of angels, it had become the raft of
Medusa, survivors still clinging to the cold hopes Springsteen himself had tossed, like junk from a speeding car. The logical
conclusion of this was a move from having cronies to having chums.
That applied not just to the band but, of course, closer to home.
The third and ultimate stage of Springsteen's plan was, thus, to save
several key relationships.

The upshot was that he rang each of the group to tell them they
should 'feel free to take other offers'.

Initially, the band reaction ran the gamut. It ranged from death-
in-life daze to resignation. Tallent, for one, had already moved to

Nashville, where he was busy as a producer. Having publicly said 'the magic was gone', he was stoic. 'Rumors of ill will', he added, were false. Lofgren was less guarded. 'Right now Bruce's just a little . . . he's searching,' he said. 'He's allowed to be confused.' For fans who'd snapped up copies of *Cry Tough*, there were compensations. Lofgren, too, had his own solo career. Aptly, in the showband tradition of the group, it was the professor – the 'pivotal guy' – who was most studied. Bittan only ever allowed to being on sabbatical. Within a year, he and Springsteen were collaborating on a song called 'Roll Of The Dice' and, ultimately, an album and tour. For these three, at least, the plan worked. Springsteen, as he now said, 'wasn't the guy writing the check every month . . . Suddenly, I was just Bruce, and some of the friendships started coming up a bit.'

Weinberg, of course, was the E Streeter who hardly ever got to come up a bit. But his inner front man was there, waiting to get out. In the years ahead he cut an album of his own, *Scene of the Crime*, published a book, graduated, lectured and became better known in the 1990s – as musical director of *Late Night With Conan O'Brien* – than in the eighties. He took Springsteen's call hard. Weinberg told *Backstreets* he was angry 'being left a legacy I was fired, because I'd never been fired from anything . . . That hurt personally . . . I think there were more sensitive ways of handling it.' Yet soon enough, he, too, was on side. Asked about the chances of a reunion, Weinberg, famously shrewd with a buck, added, 'I suppose there is that chance . . . I'd do it in a second, and I'd do it for free.'*

Meantime, Federici, the original under-boss, told Marsh: 'I got a call . . . Bruce said the band is breaking up. It never occurred to me that I was so involved in the band. Bruce called me at home, and I broke out in tears.' The interesting thing about the above is that Federici was talking of 1970. As with Steel Mill, so with E Street. Then and now, he had a wry streak that remained in thrall to a broad ego and a deep fear of the chop. Three years later, Federici auctioned off his Jersey estate and went west, wanting, he said, to 'write for movies'. According to his friend and ex-booker Jim

---

*The eventual negotiations, in spring 1999, proved harder.

Mahlmann, 'By '93, Danny was in bad shape. He had a tough time coping . . . The last I heard, he lit off in a Carmen Gia for Hollywood.'

Clemons exploded. He took Springsteen's call while on tour of Japan. 'Bruce made me go from being very shocked, to being angry, to happy, all in about ten seconds . . . I've been constantly in a shadow. I wasn't playing what I wanted to hear. My diminishing role in his music had me crazy. He was getting away from that sound, from the sax.' Elsewhere, Clemons compared it to 'like being married to someone for eighteen years, and they say "I want a divorce" when you think everything's fine'. The self-pity of his gripe, which smacked so strongly of his few lyrics, was quickly forgiven. It was a bad time: Clemons also split from his wife; his third solo album, *Night With Mr C*, stiffed, and there were no plans for a fourth. This personal and professional double-whammy sent him into a tailspin of hack work and odd TV roles; as he put it in *Mojo*, 'financially [it's] a strain reorganizing yourself . . . It's a great learning experience, but it's difficult.' When Springsteen showed up to jam with his old foil, trashing 'Glory Days' and 'Cadillac Ranch', that Christmas, Clemons was in a state of near shock. It was, as he says, 'a tough, tough year . . . everything I loved, my whole being, my reason for living, my family and my great music, I lost 'em [all]'. Clemons' own greatness wasn't least in his recovery. His later comments on Springsteen suggested epic restraint, while not ruling out the possibility of affection. They talked 'every now and then', cameos that buoyed the friendship through a third decade.

In one published account, Springsteen gave each musician 'a $2 million bonus, a handshake and his walking papers'. Friends failed to see how he could have shaken down the line; but it was nothing to fret about. After their various bouts of denial and rage, all the E Streeters came to a state of wary respect for their fate. It duly rallied. In time, they became central figures of something like a musical salon, mingling with breathy critics who held back no rave. For the hacks, it was a moment of high privilege; for the band, no more than their long experience, tireless globe-trotting and undoubted skill deserved. All, with varying degrees of success, still plied their trade. None either ruled in, or out, a reunion. Most never stopped hoping. The deep parallel grooves scorched by their feet as they ran to Springsteen's eventual call served as proof of their true feelings. When they got back together, the pack blinked, laughed, and then fell in like wolves.

A few privileged insiders had watched the group, stealthily rife with feuds, and rightly guessed that the motive behind Springsteen's axe was neither crass, nor creative, but personal. He needed a break. To them, the split was a shock, not a surprise. Outside the élite, the story made a bonanza for the trades and tabloids. Both the *Post* and *News* led with the shorthand BOSS SACKS BAND. The broadsheets found the elusive occult angle. According to them, firing the group was a logical, symbolic move, as if by doing so in the decade's last days, he'd in some way kissed off an era. (This kind of cyclical theory was first heard, twenty years before, at Altamont.) In fact, the E Streeters had been on tacit notice since *Nebraska*. The moment Springsteen decided to release it solo was the moment he traded his childlike gaze for a gang's worst nightmare, maturity. Divorce, a new mate and fatherhood were just the latest tokens of a personality in flux since 1982. Laying off the hands was a ritual cleansing of the body politic, a self-inflicted purge. It was a surgical excision. The cut worked precisely because it went deep, and Springsteen gave time to heal. The next full phone-round would come five years later.

Long before then, Springsteen's myth was all but bled dry. His 'Leavin' Train' and 'Seven Angels' both wrung the residual zip from an ostensibly jaded rocker. A song like 'Trouble In Paradise', on the other hand, was perhaps too cleverly titled for its own good. Disbanding and moving to a $14 million seat in Beverly Hills – normal careerism for most pop Baals – left the more credulous fans slack-jawed with horror. Not since the dim days of *Pin-Ups* or *Goat's Head Soup* had the words 'cop' and 'out' been in such proximity. 'What's The Deal?' was the headline in *The Times*. Yet he'd held out longer, and was better, than most peers. What set Springsteen apart from the Jaggers or Bowies wasn't just that he kept faith in the age-old props of rock – great yarns and raise-the-roof gigs – but that he treated them with a seriousness rare since the sixties. His sound on stage was matched by his vision off it. Springsteen was coming to terms with various forms of mid-life crisis. He was both more honest and bloody-minded about them than some knew. A loner at heart, he learnt, with Scialfa's help, to gild the real Bruce behind the fictive Boss. Springsteen didn't just want to make it easier for people – 'kids on the street', he said – to get to know him. He wanted to make it easier to live a street-level life. As one local friend has it, 'he got real'. Nowadays, when *Rolling Stone* probed for his 'toughest thing', Springsteen's three-word reply was 'Engagement, engagement, engagement.' He was speaking of fatherhood, but it cut to the core of his own rebirth at forty.

Ironically, just at the time some of the fans gave up, he most rated the praise ritually heaped on him for years. During those years he'd distinguished himself in some areas, and notably less in others. By the new decade, if Springsteen was a family man, he was also a Renaissance Man. It showed in the way both legends of the past and idols-in-waiting became grist for his open-handedness. In short order, Springsteen partnered Little Richard and John Fogerty; bawled 'Long Tall Sally' at the Hall of Fame; gave work to Davy Sancious, last used in 1974 and latterly a member of Gabriel's band; and offered career tips to Terence Trent D'Arby, who says Springsteen 'kind of played a big-brother support role' and generally helped him through a second album. Restless altruism met with a strange innocence about the world around him, the shark-infested waters of rock. Springsteen was 'one hundred per cent cool' to one would-be business partner. 'Bruce always cut people like me slack', if not a deal. He was generous, too, in licensing his wares. Springsteen gave permission for 2 Live Crew to rap up 'Born In The USA', and thus make a point about censorship. He held off on a bootlegging suit. Celebrity groupie Pamela Des Barres notes appreciatively that Springsteen didn't charge her for quoting the lyrics of 'Dancing In The Dark'.* On 12 February

---

*Springsteen's vigilant (some would add an 'e' to that) office is also widely admired as one of the easiest, or most bluntly clear, to deal with.

1990 he joined Sting's 'priciest garage-band ever' to raise, overnight, $900,000 for the Xingú Indians of Brazil. He gave tens of thousands of his own to friends around Freehold. It wasn't just charity: he was a shrewd patron of musical and civic causes, the rare rocker on good terms with, say, both Bill Bradley and James Brown. He was a role model to men everywhere struggling with family and commitment. 'Guys on the lam' were his forte. Ex-chauvinists had in him one of their own.

There were at least two Springsteens. The first was from the books: the saintly icon of pop lore who neither drank nor smoked, saving himself for the gigs as if his very soul hung on them (as, in a way, it had). *This* was the Boss. After the band went south, Springsteen also migrated, having got to a place 'where I said I gotta stop writing this story. It don't work.' *That* was Bruce. By and large, he acted, and looked, the way people hoped – jeaned, booted, with his hair grown and occasionally tied in a pony tail. There was a touch of Shane MacGowan. As to shaving, he didn't flog it. When he spoke, it was in a dry, chuckly rasp. Springsteen could quote Flannery O'Connor by the yard, and did. He began his day with the *LA Times*. After two decades off, for most of which he was news himself, he kept up with the world again. Springsteen was a 'one nation' Democrat: in broad terms, a conservative. Core American values were fine by him. He liked old films and musicals. The 1920s balladeer Dock Boggs was his idea of a 'hip singer'. His own new songs were larded with relationship lyrics like 'Sad Eyes' and 'Over The Rise'. Between times, Springsteen went to therapy (though never church) and began a family. This was the man who, around his forty-first birthday, 'learnt how to put the guitar down'.

As a work in progress, Springsteen was both heroic and coy. Philanthropy was just one of the areas where a debate raged between two clearly warring sub-personalities: the 'real' dude plugging inclusivity in the face of market evils; and the rich one flogging self-help and a competitive view of man. The former usually, though not always, won through. Broadly, Springsteen saw life as consisting of two basic forces. 'Dead' ones were defined as twisted, socially malformed types who found solace for their demons in voting Republican. 'Live' ones meant those who sought change in the form of a better, if not always larger, slice of the pie. Recognizing that the terms were arbitrary, Springsteen preferred them to 'haves' and 'have-nots'. (A 'have', for instance, could also be live.) Along with a steady drift leftward – first hinted at, with feral volume, in 'Don't vote for that fuckin' Bush!' – Springsteen's own welfare policy was lavish. And catholic: 'saving the rainforest' wouldn't have been on his wish-list of causes a year or two earlier. As well as pet projects like *Lady Beth*, he ploughed in cash to the pro-labour film *American Dream*; virtually kept the VVA afloat; and anonymously gave $25,000 for the singer Mary Wells' medical bills. He quietly donated to a hospital and two schools in Los Angeles.

Springsteen idolized the Dream; he *was* the dreamers' idol.

It was this co-dependence – so heady for the cult – that led him to save what space was left. Springsteen now stepped out of the glare of the public spotlight, first switched on with such voltage in 1975. Parts of it he'd enjoyed, or at least gracefully endured. He wasn't, for instance, averse to praise, so long as it was him who got it and not his alter ego. He certainly wasn't averse to money. But he'd 'slit [his] fuckin' throat' before yielding to the nostalgic yearning for a 'place where you replay the ritual . . . people coming to my shows expecting to hear stuff I wrote twenty years ago', his whole life a melodrama warped by their projected fantasies. The fans' dream became, in that respect, Springsteen's nightmare. Hence his sacking his band; his 'pulling outta here to win'. His tactical exit. Nowadays, of course, Springsteen also kept an organization, offices, lawyers and the like between him and the 'guys on the lam'. Terry Magovern, for one, bulked as a kind of Cerberus. Nothing got by him and his power lay precisely in saying no. He and the other flaks were given their head. But all the heads ultimately bowed to Landau – leaving Springsteen free, he said, to 'boogie'. He responded by jiving under the bar of good taste. It's fair to say that, by 1990, among a vocal minority, he wasn't just not liked, he was disliked. People were hurt. At bottom, Springsteen stood accused of cant, concealing the worst pop-god airs under a papery wrap of virtue. That balcony romp, the firings and the lawsuit all revealed things about him his fans didn't care to know, or hope to hear. Yet, in truth, nothing quite spun heads like Springsteen's move to the Hills.

He duly traded up there, from his Hollywood home, in April. The house in the tony Tower Drive colony lay on a palm-lined, winding valley road, rearing up behind the Beverly Hills Hotel. LA's storied pink palace in turn gave way to a zone of tall mock-Tudors, Spanish villas and neo-plantation manses of gothic dark brick. Valentino's old lair, as well as those where Sharon Tate and George Reeves, respectively, were murdered and killed himself, were near-neighbours; a gory undercoat to all the luxury. The estate sat on two lots, hidden behind a fence topped by a thick row of bushes. Two-hundred-foot-high eucalyptus trees formed a natural wall. The four-and-a-half-acre spread was something of a museum, too, since apart from the paintings, murals and Native American rugs, the grounds were strewn with art. (There was no pool.) The sheer quiet of the place was what struck one caller. This particular friend, a poet, calls Springsteen's pile a 'breath of the tomb'. It was here, up a canyon drive, that he and Scialfa spent their year of role reversal. While she dabbled at her solo album, he watched TV or cruised the mall.*

He splashed out from time to time – on the paintings, cars, his home studio. For a while, Springsteen wasn't above shopping on Rodeo Drive. But his trademark anti-style survived. He went to one black-tie dinner dressed in comfy Levi's and left in a visibly grubby Ford. For him, fighting for 'my own slant' didn't mean kowtowing to the locals. Springsteen's slant did, though, include a fierce loyalty to Scialfa. Nineteen eighty-nine's sleepovers had become 1990's merger. He owed her the real start of his recovery. 'Patti had a very sure eye for all my bullshit. She recognized it . . . it was [her] patience and understanding that got me through.'

Springsteen also took untold grief. Even commuting (he kept the

---

*Springsteen's mail and business was now handled from an office downhill from Tower, at 10345 Olympic Boulevard.

Rumson home) was seen as the worst kind of move by longtime fans. For them, the very term 'west coast' fulfilled a dread. Aside from the hot tubs and EST, there were those in California – the gag went – who greeted the news of a Workers' Revolutionary Party by asking 'When?' Hearts sank, too, at the mere association with the likes of Linda Ronstadt. The maniacs feared for their Boss. In some ways, Springsteen gave due cause. 'I feel that the night you look into your audience and don't see yourself,' he'd said, 'and the night the audience looks at you and don't see themselves, that's when it's over.' His classic 'relevance' criteria had rightly won raves. Now, vocalization was apt to be in the form of the boos and catcalls of the mob. In time, Springsteen sprayed *mea culpae* around, like the one in '57 Channels (And Nothin' On)':

I bought a bourgeois house in the Hollywood Hills
With a trunkload of hundred thousand dollar bills

– yet, in truth, he was home free. 'Goin' Cali', as he put it, was a sane, logical bet. It was part of his convalescence. 'I've always felt a lot lighter [there],' Springsteen said, 'like I was carrying less.' It did 'relax me'. It didn't recycle him. Nor was it full-time. True believers wouldn't have begrudged him his break, as enshrined in one apt bootleg title, *Warrior's Rest*. There was also the fact that, by bunking in his early forties, Springsteen was carrying out the same game plan as Doug, and thus still fulfilling the plot-line of 'Adam'. Nowadays, the two men got on 'great' together.

LP rumours, meanwhile, perked up in response to daily sightings at A&M studios. As well as Sancious and his successor, Bittan, the usual suspects – Landau, Plotkin, Scott – were all seen at the old Chaplin soundstage on Sunset Strip. Always or usually a savvy career mover, Springsteen himself was back doing what he did best. Windbaggery, of course, had long been ditched for colloquial scraps tossed in the general direction of the tune. Themes of love and fatherhood did war with one-beat-fits-all pop; 'Cali' and the rest all mined the same basic, bass-heavy riff. Even so, the *Human Touch* sessions cooked up a storm of breathtakingly safe, emotionally daring work. Springsteen's voice and the born-again lyrics each served the songs. But the more he shot for the new, the more diehards pined for the old. It was about now, late one night at A&M, that Springsteen complained of 'that fuck with the Fender'. He meant himself.

Came late July, the week of Scialfa's birthday. At five on a Wednesday morning, in Cedars Sinai hospital, she gave birth to a son – a perfectly normal baby in a normal delivery. With that, gifts for the child began to flood into Olympic Boulevard from all parts, literally an embarrassment of riches. Sting, for one, sent a copy of *Under Milk Wood*. Within a few hours, press and public were clamouring for news. Springsteen's management eked out Dr Rabin's announcement with the name – Evan James – though not nearly enough data on weight (7lb 9oz) and eye colour (blue) for the maw of their client groups. Meanwhile, all the cross-currents buffeting Landau's boss – everything from joy to terror – came together in one emotional twister funnelling down on Springsteen's work. (Hence, among others, the song 'Living Proof'.) 'The night my boy was born,' he said, 'I probably got as close to the feeling of pure, sort of unconditional love and with all the walls down. All of a sudden, what was happening was so immense that it stopped all the fear for a while.' It was 25 July 1990. That same night, Springsteen met, as planned, with various Columbia and Sony suits and handed them prints of a photo he'd taken of his son.

With fatherhood, Springsteen lined up on something new. Instead of the anonymous, fuzzy love of the youth club, he entered the bear-pit of intimacy. It was a long way from the 'undifferentiated faces' he'd played off down the years. For two decades, that high was what he had for a life. Then, 'I made my music everything.' Now, surrogate family gave way to a flesh-and-bone one. Springsteen said himself that work had ceased to be job one. In fact, he put it third. Newfound roots might have made him, as he had it, 'the most knocked-out guy alive', but after hearing of his nineties agenda, fans could have made a strong run at silver. As for

Springsteen's top priority: a therapist had told him he needed to get away from the 'ego validators and nuts' of old. He made a mantra of it, then a compression: E,v,a,n. Evan.

During those twenty years, Springsteen had played literally for life, a good example of something alien outside the arts, that a star can be plastered on a million walls, yet be quite alone. Springsteen's estrangement crossed over the footlights. 'I avoided closeness,' he said. 'I had many ways of doing that particular dance, and I thought they were pretty sophisticated. Maybe they weren't. I was just doing what came naturally. And then when I hit the stage, it was just the opposite. I'd thrown myself forward, but it was OK because it was brief . . . That's why they call 'em one-night stands.' (The same thing applied, of course, socially, a cheerfully lax ethos recalled in 1991's 'Loose Change'.) Off duty, Springsteen, always wary of interviews, had been about as chatty as a lawyered-up skell. He never did TV, said no to Hollywood, and turned away millions in endorsements. What's more, he was equally stingy, emotionally speaking, with friends. That all changed in 1990–91. Nowadays, even Landau was slapped, kissed and hugged in his python-like grip. Laughter rang through the pink-walled home as Springsteen downed his morning coffee and waffles on the sultry days that winter. For him, everything flowed from fatherhood. He not only talked it; he lived it. Springsteen could wade in and change nappies, fix formula or sing the baby to sleep. He loved to take snaps. Sometimes on Sundays he'd drive the whole gang to the zoo. He also contributed his son's favourite 'Chicken Hips and Lizard Lips' to the 1991 LP *For Our Children*. 'Bruce,' as a relative says, 'didn't just spend cash on Evan that first year. He spent twelve months.' Springsteen was a 'model pop'.

As such, he had to ply between the poles of sloth or semi-retirement, and the dire one of moistening the fans. Both options, mostly the former, gave rise to grouches in the press. In the usual absence of fact, gossip dotted the wastes. Speculation, at worst sleaze, was all. It would have been unthinkable, in 1985, for a 'Boss v. Labour' row to have loomed in, say, *Q*. It did now. Batlan fulminated that Christmas in the letter pages: 'Mr Springsteen has reportedly spent nearly $2 million in an unsuccessful effort to quash this case. His attorneys have failed to have more than a few of the 35 counts dismissed. We, on the other hand, have been successful in obtaining a precedent-setting ruling (vehemently contested by the Blue Collar Hero) that says "roadies" are entitled to the same protection accorded all other workers . . . Unconscionable contract . . . World-class hypocrite'; and so on, over two columns. It didn't change many minds. Even so, it was hard to miss, or to duck the questions now shouted over mastheads. WHAT'S UP, BRUCE? was the least of it.

In fact, that was the best of the story. It took another nine months to play out. The roadies' case crept on until September 1991, at which point – as usual when big money and egos hang in the balance – it was fixed out of court. By then, Springsteen had countersued after Batlan admitted taking tapes and four of his boss's notebooks – full of unreleased songs – and selling the latter for $28,000. No cash sums were given: but as the judge had already rejected much of the plaintiffs' overtime beef and was 'inclined to largely grant the remaining dismissal relief' – and Springsteen's lawyers emerged smiling – most rang it up to him. Both news bulletins and the broadsheets duly stumbled on more 'Boss' puns. The tabloids tended to be jokey. Intentionally, that was.

The trades, meanwhile, talked up a storm of post-natal frenzy. Springsteen was back recording. As well as the odes to Scialfa and Evan, 'Real World' was what it sounded like: a genre study of a man coping. 'Ain't no church bells ringing,' Springsteen sang. 'Ain't no flags unfurled.' Grapevine rumours orbited of a tour. Various bands were mooted. Most Springsteen profiles, professionally, at least, were still consecratory. In an era of screwed-up nihilism and recycled hits by Phil Collins, people needed him. Looking at the album charts between *Bad* and *Nevermind*, Hamlet was always missing.

But nothing revved up the media quite like a live gig. Concerts were both the locus and focus of Springsteen's musical life, and, no matter how good the albums, they were ninety per cent of his fame. For much of the last two years, he'd been in no shape, mood- or otherwise, to play. He saw fit, for example, to pass on a special

Nelson Mandela show, to say nothing of the various one-offs and galas beating a line from Live Aid. He was certainly no Iggy-style suburban zombie, but beer, 'kamikaze' vodkas and, allegedly, the odd Valium increasingly filled out the dead time between tours. The all-night A&M sessions, and others at Soundworks West, still went on – Landau saw to that – and Springsteen got through his mornings, with massive aid from Folgers. But it had been nine months since he last stepped on stage. Hence the drama of his two sets, on 16 and 17 November 1990, at the Shrine Auditorium, Los Angeles.

They were benefits. Springsteen, alongside his friends Jackson Browne and Bonnie Raitt, played for the Christic Institute, a left-of-the-dial Washington think tank alleging, for one, a 'vast military conspiracy' underlying US foreign policy. By and large the words 'pressure group' enjoy more prestige in America than in Britain; so that merely talking about, for instance, 'Pentagon-sponsored terror' can itself become a story. This paranoic clone of Heisenberg's law, still rumbling about Iran-Contra, was much touted in the days before the gigs. In one afternoon alone, the Institute took 217 calls. It raised $500,000. That was nothing compared to the demand for Springsteen.

The first and then only night's six thousand seats went in forty minutes. A second show was added and it, too, sold out. On the Friday, Springsteen – whose 'radicalized' politics now became proverbial – loped on, unannounced, heavy but healthy-looking, and bowed with a classic flash of street wit. 'If you're moved to clap along, don't – it'll fuck me up.' He tuned an acoustic guitar. What followed was a smart, funny and moving exploration of the redemptive, if fickle power of love. 'Brilliant Disguise', 'Reason To Believe' and 'Real World' all variously tapped the vein. *Nebraska*'s 'My Father's House' was honed to a chilling edge. That middle-aged Oedipal wreck alone was worth, at a rough guess, ten times the price of a scalped seat. Springsteen's own domesticity came to play on 'Red Headed Woman', in which cunnilingual leers about 'tasting' a mate could only have had one root. (Scialfa was backstage with the baby.) 'Tenth Avenue' was a model of pianistic decorum.

Springsteen forgot the words of 'Thunder Road'. He did a single encore. All this shouldn't have added up to a coup, but that came from the favourite pop–folk devices: warmth, rhythm, civic smarts (never reducing the raps to polemic) and, all in all, a cheerful patchwork satire of celebrity. When a fan yelled, 'We love ya, Bruce,' he shot back, 'You don't really *know* me.' Browne and Raitt returned for the finale, but, as ever, Springsteen was a hard act to follow. They were competent musicians. *He* expressed the pain and beauty of humanity. It was such a winning performance that even the 'message' flowed; Springsteen's sunlit black moods pitched the songs.

He then spent six months in California.

The grapevine blossomed there like night-budding dementia praecox, and those in thrall to it – with its loud E Street buzz – proved a point. Springsteen had moved on. They hadn't. For the rest of that winter, he toyed with his album; cut a track called, oddly, 'My Lover Man'; sang with the Impressions at the Hall of Fame; and on Lofgren's LP *Silver Lining*. It wasn't much to show for half a year, the same time he'd once taken to raze the world. There were no more fund-raisers, no gigs. No galas. It became his obsession to save his 'road-rat' side from its own stupid obstinacy, a theme that ran consistently through his public and private quotes from *Tunnel* to *Human Touch*. Even so, 'retirement' was a bit too highbrow a concept for the fanzines to justify blank columns. Springsteen was busy enough. He'd just, as it were, changed gears. For the first time ever, he had a day-job.

Springsteen's world was essentially a rural, or at least suburban one, and his life was spent in the car. He and Scialfa liked to take Highway 10, downhill to the desert, where the runners, joggers, skaters, bikers and – briefly – freaks gave way to the asphalt; with only cacti or the occasional skull as milestones. Further east lay the Joshua Tree monument. They hiked through the woods, the sky a pale, mineral blue, dry winter air with a slight tang, the contribution of industrial smog to the beauty of the Mojave evening, thinning trees shedding their clumps of pine. Nannies watched the baby. Such was Springsteen's almost parodically normal life until May 1991. As well as his climbing and camping, he still saw a therapist. Springsteen's few public quips were wrapped in the Jungian assumptions of 'wellness', on which he harped throughout his forties. Coincidentally or not, he didn't write many songs. He did plan a wedding.

USA Today first led on 30 May:

Bruce Springsteen cut a song last year called Red Headed Woman. Now, reportedly, he's marrying her.

Patti Scialfa, the flame-haired backup singer, tambourine player and lone female from the now-defunct E Street Band, will marry the Boss on June 9 in Los Angeles, according to [sources], quoting those 'close to the bride-to-be'.

Actually the date was the 8th, when bride and groom were, respectively, thirty-seven and forty-one (five years older than most papers said). If the facts were fragile, the story was sturdy, and found its way into the yards of newsprint. Unmentioned, but obvious to those on the ground, was that Scialfa was ten weeks pregnant. On 5 June, the couple drove to the County-City office in Santa Monica. They handed in their forms to the clerk. He paused only to sift the fee, and the two names in the black boxes.

'Cool?' said Springsteen.

'Everything certainly, er, seems to be,' said the man.

'Excuse my shitty Jersey manners. I'm Bruce, this is Patti.'

'Aha.'

Nothing all week was more redolent of Springsteen's 'I'm OK' mode. By 1991, his legendary retreat was two, going on three years old. Delusive comic rumours had come to match those about a Salinger or Pynchon. Instead, the man standing at the desk at 1725 Main Street was striking for his charm, his James Stewart-like grin, the resounding echo of his silent 'shucks'. It's true he had what all great stars have – the illusion of ease – but there was more: he was cool strictly in his own vernacular. Springsteen not only chatted to other customers. For that hour, most of them thought that nothing else in the world mattered to him. By one estimate, he shook a hundred hands and signed fifty autographs, and he quite visibly loved it.

Springsteen and Scialfa filed their licence on the 6th. On the 7th, Tower was a place of constant ferment. Tough and decisive, the bride drew up a list almost as well plotted as one of Landau's tours: caterers, florists and friends, waiters in braid, butlers and maids all swarmed in the grounds. At dusk on the 8th, a Saturday, Van Zandt, Federici and Bittan struck up a folk tune under a silk marquee. The ninety guests (including Browne, Raitt and John Fogerty) sat in antique chairs on the lawn. A Huey, hired by the groom, buzzed overhead. After the tragicomic antics in Oregon, Springsteen enforced a strict no-fly zone, publicly asking the press to 'give me a pass'. He had a pretty good case.

On a nod from Van Zandt, just like old times, the band wound up. A heavy watered-silk sky, still bright over the tawny gold vacancy of the Hills, turned red. On the dais the vicar, Phil Zwerling, moved about among his props. As bulbs came on in the trees, Springsteen and Scialfa, in black and white, exchanged vows. They each wore a silver ring. The lights flared, Adele cheered and the Huey, making a throaty whirr, did a fly-over. Springsteen wept. With the time difference, it was nineteen years to the day since he'd first done his CBS deal. Then, he'd talked of rock as 'freedom'; it had become a straitjacket. Now, he inked his marriage certificate. According to one guest, 'Bruce was *beaming*. He was to high spirits what Wisconsin is to cheese.' The most intense and rapid growth of Springsteen's life, saturation-point in overcoming all 'shit', took place that year.

Later in the nineties, it was often said that Springsteen's songs were trademarked by elaborately gushy peals that rang with a kind of faith that could only be called gospel. This budget 'Hallelujah Chorus' traced to the love of his wife and son. The wedding itself was Unitarian. Speaking of the day to *Rolling Stone*, Springsteen combined, in rare inner harmony, the qualities of a seeker and a cynic. 'I'm now a believer in all the rituals and things. I think they're really valuable . . . For a long time, I didn't put a lot of stock in those things, but I've come to feel that they're important. Like, I miss going to church. I'd like to, but I don't know where to go.' He'd never again follow Adele's sabbath lead, but Springsteen groped his way back to 'something like old-time religion', one of the nominally faithful who found other things to do on Sunday morning. Specifically, his anti-Catholicism softened. He didn't, however, 'buy into all the dogmatic aspects', more the secular lure of 'people coming together . . . just to say hi once a week'. One of his guests appropriately gave him a Bible, but it might equally have been the works of Albert Goldman – or Steinbeck.

Courtesy of Springsteen's PR, Shore Fire Media, the news broke on the 9th. It was a lesser world event than in 1985. There was no publicity strip-tease of the kind that had turned Lake Oswego into Oz. It made the 'people' columns for days; Springsteen and Scialfa honeymooned for a week, then drove home, unmolested. Brewing in even his fans' consciousness was a realization that he'd changed, not least in looks. (One paper saluted the 'spruce Bruce'.) Still, he was entitled to say, as he did when asked what had become of rock, 'I made some.' If he'd moved on, the times had too.

Implicit in Springsteen's cultural epiphany was a strong but silent confession. He missed work. In Grice's words, 'he couldn't any more give up writing than Tina could give up fishnets'. Within a few weeks of his wedding, Springsteen was back at A&M. Tunes poured out of him. In most accounts of the sessions, the creative recluse was his old self again: a medium for verses, choruses, couplets, rhymes and titles, actual and imaginative yarns, all elaborated and deepened, 'a journey,' he said, 'toward some sort of connection with both people at large and then a person,' welling up from within. Now Springsteen was ready to go public.

In those interim days, almost all his press was of a tart, not to say bitchy nature. It didn't go unnoticed, for instance, that Springsteen's sole hit in 1991 graced an under-twelves' LP, *For Our Children*. Some of his harangues on life and love could border on evangelical. His 'people coming together' line, with its folksy tone and Main Street fervour, was a miniature of his text. At best, he helped to frame a message for a simple constituency not so much divided as vivisected by debt and war. At worst, he preached. As *Mojo* says, 'hardcore fans were alienated as he seemed to follow the gospel according to Sting, only appearing at $1,000 parties and the like'. A few of Springsteen's foes went to fanatical lengths of their own for the vital sneer. Others sat back, letting the ironies surface. That September, he settled (reportedly for $350,000) with the two roadies. The case, though largely in camera, was widely given in evidence against him. The shorthand verdict was that Springsteen was a phoney. Batlan's rant, above all, dealt his ex-friend's image a blow. Yet the idea of Springsteen as the boss – in every sense – wasn't inconsistent with his sweat-soaked, good-rockin' fame. Even at their worst, docking pay and the like, his 'crimes' were minor. Most fans rightly judged it was all to Springsteen's good that he was also, in part, bad. Amid the black and white, there were humanizing tones of grey. As Charles Thompson once said of William Jennings Bryan, 'he didn't merely resemble the average man, he *was* him'; though, like Bryan, Springsteen still cut an inspirational dash. Star that he was, he led by dazzling others. He commanded, rather than demanded respect. Over the years, he built a strong and loyal crew that adhered to the work ethic he embodied; it brought forward a long-running group of honest, able and lifelong blood-brothers. As Springsteen says: 'I think if you asked the majority of people who'd worked with me how they felt . . . they'd say they'd been treated really well.' One ex-hand, who prefers anonymity, duly calls it 'more like a family than a firm'. Springsteen himself made the point. What's more, he said it with a ring of pride as he learned what it was to raise Evan. That New Year's Eve, Scialfa gave birth to a girl, Jessica Rae.

Whether at Thrill Hill (the home studio) or downtown, Springsteen had periodically thrown a 'hot one on the vinyl' for four years. Some of the new material had débuted for the Christic Institute. As well as 'Real World', there was a bass-fat, rockabilly '57 Channels', and forays into blues and soul. 'Better Days' was self-explanatory. The weirdly alluring, two-chord wonder 'Happy' nearly lived up to the title. As a rule, the songs were a generally good-natured if choppy amalgam of '90s pop, sleepy-time lullabies and ballads. Now, *Human Touch* was in the can. But because Springsteen 'didn't feel I'd gotten to everything I wanted', he started over. It was just the sort of whimsical lark, or kink, that jerked fond memories of, for four, *Born*, *Darkness*, *The River* and *USA*. Meanwhile, on one of his weekly swoops to Tower Records, Springsteen bought Dylan's *The Bootleg Series*. One track, 'Series Of Dreams', caught his ear. He went back to A&M, cutting 'Living Proof' and 'The Big Muddy', gazing through the oriel up the Strip, 'winging it' from two to six every afternoon. (Nowadays, Springsteen did his best work in daylight.) With Bittan, a few friends and up to four producers, he had, instead of a gang, a society to whom he chatted across the board. Then Springsteen made the short hop back to Tower. He was always home by seven for dinner.

The inexhaustible urge towards self-expression made it a safe bet that Springsteen would keep selling his wares. The dicier question was if people would buy them. From the off, all his albums had fallen into two camps: those for everyone and those just for fans. *Tunnel*, for one, belonged to the Boss-Only Club, though it also became a calling card for his more melodic, mature house-style. He took a risk, having wrapped one album in two years, writing and recording a second in eight weeks. Releasing them on the same day, side by side, knocked some out and hit others in the pocket. Creatively, Springsteen's reverse 'less is more' ploy more or less worked. There were some good enough songs. Even so, the sales department's hopes were dashed by this frankly unsolicited blitz. *Human Touch* and *Lucky Town* rose and then fell in the chart. *Entertainment Weekly* even put Springsteen on its cover with the tag: WHAT EVER HAPPENED TO BRUCE?

WHAT'S THE DEAL?, meanwhile, was the lead at *The Times*. The tone was hurt, not as caustic as that in the tabloids – not the *Sun*'s tone – but still a stretch from the raves once routinely vented in the dailies, to say nothing of the fanzines. In the case of *Backstreets*, Charles Cross spoke of a sixty-six per cent drop in sales from the mid-'80s. Clearly, people were nostalgic for the old ways, for the sense of community. So was Springsteen, but he also made clear that he wanted nothing less than to 'pretend [I'm] fifteen or sixteen or twenty . . . That just doesn't interest me.' As he told *Rolling Stone*, 'I'm a lifetime musician.' In the years to come, two of Springsteen's models would again be Jagger and Bowie. He related to them as figures of belonging, of continuity and even, it seemed, of permanence. But not, crucially, as figures of fun.

Starting from the Amnesty tour, LP rumours had made roughly annual bows for three years. Old fans were used to such delays. Some even savoured the wait. Of a process that invariably moved at glacier pace, Springsteen himself had his doubts. As he put it, 'During the long intervals . . . as I was spending more and more time in the studio, when I met [someone] on the street I was often asked, "What are you guys doing in there?" I regularly pondered that myself.' Even so, this one had been epic. More than four years had passed since *Tunnel of Love*. During the time he ground away at A&M – in 'continental-drift mode' – the outside world had been remade. Margaret Thatcher was gone. Reagan had taken well-earned retirement. His successor first waged, then won the Gulf War. Berlin, and to some extent Moscow were free cities. But it wasn't, of course, just the global furniture that had been moved around. There was no more quaintly arch polarization of then-and-now than the way Springsteen looked: pink, scrubbed, with a gem cluster Ringo would have killed for, if anything suited up, not down, for work. His self-confidence as a husband, as a father of two, appeared to be almost as great in public as at home. For Springsteen, the time-out had been a mental and emotional education. But it was also a way across the bridge. He was a man on the move, reborn since 1987, let alone '84, and the music proved it. That oddly tired-sounding twin set nonetheless served as a good introduction to Springsteen's latest, and best role: himself.

The *LA Times* broke the news on 21 January 1992. 'Though neither Bruce Springsteen's publicist nor label would comment, a source said today that he would release two albums simultaneously in the near future.' In short order: the official word came down on the 23rd; 'I'm excited about being done and looking forward to getting out on the road,' Springsteen confirmed; various FM stations began playing 'Soul Driver', then, when the lawyers chafed, the two official singles. These took the form of a cassette trailer for the

CDs. Meanwhile, *Billboard* reported that Columbia was rationing stocks, the idea being that 'shortages cause demand and fuss, cut down on the amount of returns, and avoid the embarrassment of having piles of unsold [vinyl] lying around': the sweet, lilting refrain of yet another sales stunt. A video for 'Human Touch'* aired on 9 March. Landau's weakness for total management was again apparent. The PR and ad machines fired up, even if on the novel basis of under- not over-priming the market. Still, in the last analysis, after every drop of hype had been wrung, the albums hung not on stumbling full circle on to some higher supply-and-demand equation, but on the hopes and dreams Springsteen could stir in the hearts of the audience. Here, too, he scored highly.

As on Groundhog Day, you could tell winter was over when Springsteen broke cover for the year. Over a month, he played clubs in New Orleans and Manhattan; showed at various dinners, galas and openings; and generally engaged in the kind of rites-of-spring renaissance that meant a tour. Along with Bittan, he auditioned and booked a band. A source says the idea was to hire musicians who were relatively unknown but seasoned 'road guys'. In practice, that meant the guitarist Shane Fontayne, a thuddingly dire rhythm section (Tommy Sims and ex-B-52s drummer Zac Alford), and a Ziegfeld folly of conga players, tambourine men and scenic 'doll' singers. With Scialfa, there were a dozen people on stage. It wasn't difficult to spot daylight between the old group and the new, as seen in rehearsal. (For one, nothing quite made up for Clemons' sax.) Run-throughs began that Easter, in Los Angeles.

Springsteen was there on 30 April. It was the very day that the acquittal of four policemen in the Rodney King case triggered America's worst outbreak of civil disorder since the likes of Newark had been razed in the sixties. Springsteen was forced to cut short a rehearsal and drive home to Tower. A curfew covered the entire city. From the bay windows in Beverly Hills he could see the glow of smouldering rubble. A black military Huey kept a holding pattern over his house, and the few others on Benedict Canyon. 'This

---

*A hand-double, not Springsteen, seen stroking the flank of a nude woman.

was one of those things waiting to happen,' said John Mack, president of the Urban League, airing a widely held view of the riot. 'Out of frustration and anger you have people resorting to this kind of behavior, and then it feeds on itself.' Despite the disruption of his own plans, Springsteen soon joined the consensus. 'You can go five blocks and you'll see burned-out buildings,' he told *Q*. 'That was the day when all the invisible walls that get put up – LA is actually a very segregated city – all started falling . . . You can feel them starting to melt away. The inner cities are reaching a critical mass. People have been abandoned, thrown away, tossed out.' Even as he spoke, seven- and eight-year-old kids were throwing rocks and swigging blasts of Octane Booster – a gas additive and makeshift drug – outside his gates. Finally the police and National Guard waded in, collared the ringleaders, and shovelled them off; the rest followed. Springsteen drove down to investigate in his Corvette, 'beat and dejected', he said: 'People were really scared.' The tour doctor gave him another shot and a stronger sleeping pill.

That May, Springsteen's group made a brisk, searing and engagingly sloppy début on *Saturday Night Live*. (It was also his first time ever on TV.) In June, he did a live radio hook-up. Club-hops followed. Ticketron machines began turning over for the formal dates. Other high-profile testaments to Landau's and Shore Fire's smooth press-agentry focused less on headlines, and instead let the word sneakily seep through their client's few interviews. Springsteen did covers for *Q* and *Rolling Stone*. Interest turned into excitement. Excitement turned into frenzy. He sold out eleven nights at Meadowlands in less than three hours. Even so, Springsteen never wavered from his insistence that the shows were essentially a kind of cultural kibbutz, with 'people going away feeling more connected to each other and connected in their own lives and to the whole world around them,' and not just gigs.

The tour's two host albums, *Human Touch* and *Lucky Town*, duly came that Easter. For fans, having ninety-nine minutes' new work, twenty-four songs, was like Thanksgiving, Christmas and Independence Day all at once. As the titles intentionally suggested, they weren't *cris de coeur*. Nor, alas, high points. At best, they transported Springsteen's new life on to CD, using the formula of crisp, trebly tunes to hook CHR (Top 20) radio, while not failing to skim larger social issues. At worst, they were minor genre: the sort of stuff he could churn out left-handed. Significantly, there were no drastic detours from E Street. *River*-era rock kept peeping through Springsteen's varnish as a Mature Artist. Any creative tacks were mere diversions, not U-turns. For years, part of Springsteen's appeal was that he'd run counter to the pop *zeitgeist*; most notably when *USA* poleaxed the chart. Nineteen ninety-two's double-header, by contrast, was AOR's beat of choice. There were some great moments, but, all in all, both LPs suffered from frugal melodies and ploddingly obvious, nineties production, the desperately 'contemporary' blips merely sounding pasted on to the stock riffs. The bad songs were fairly well played: the good songs were fairly badly played. None of the hands projected adequately as a soloist, again begging the question on what musical, as against mental, grounds Clemons and the rest were fired. *Touch* and *Town* would keep fans waiting for the answer. The only recognizably classic feature of most tracks was the voice.

There were, however, several new twists. The happily hitched Springsteen revamped the set girls-and-guitars mythology; he paved his street with gold. The albums' relentless celebration didn't stand too many low-life lyrics, full of champagne, casinos, caviar, breasts and Hollywood. Above all, Springsteen demonstrated that the twin drives of a long life at the top intermittently shot through with self-doubt, depression and even despair, were firstly an ego and, secondly, a sense of humour. Both were gloriously at work on 'Local Hero'. Leaving aside his stardom – a pretty large aside – there were two major themes just over the songs' horizon: partnership and fatherhood. Between them they played cleverly on the fragility of some of the tunes. The overall moral was, as Springsteen said, 'engagement'. For years, he'd tended to escape marches, like 'Born' or 'Thunder Road'. They were great road anthems masquerading as art. With *Human Touch* and *Lucky Town*, Springsteen turned himself in. He abandoned flight for the novel joys of hearth and home. Bachelor perks were tossed for distinctly non-macho,

vulnerable airs like 'Real Man', ten years and twenty IQ points
removed from, say, 'Ramrod'. This was music to happily keep you
company while you did the school-run in your Volvo. No longer
just an edgy pasticheur of pop styles, Springsteen moved from the
ice caves to inhabit the sunny domes of married life. Sadly, alien-
ation had also been the first source of his genius. The shy
resolution and lush tone of *Lucky Town*, in particular, struck some as
a kind of wedding gift to Scialfa. It was a new sort of style, if not
sound, consequent on the pram in the hall. With it, Springsteen
walked out of the dark shadows of his own poetic gift.

After the E Streeters folded, an army of Bossmaniacs had first
gone into shock, then spent the next three years wondering what
kind of music Springsteen would make in his forties. *Human Touch*'s
answer didn't keep them long: the title track was light at the end of
the *Tunnel*. From there the electronically adrenalized ditties gave
way to the solid-rocking 'Gloria's Eyes', where Springsteen cannibalized the Divinyls. 'Roll Of The Dice' quite literally had Bittan's
dabs all over it. With few actual pitches and no little repetition, the
chorus nonetheless delivered the hook. Whether an E Street
throwback, or a ploy to try and log a few air-miles for *Touch*'s hitherto scanty rave-up quota, it worked. Elsewhere, there were cribs of
Paul Simon, ZZ Top and soul merchants like Sam Moore (who
actually sang on three tracks). Half the fast tunes threatened to
warp into 'Philadelphia Freedom'. The best of the slow ones, 'I
Wish I Were Blind', was a refined cross between Dylan and A. E.
Housman. 'Real Man' came dangerously close to Rod Stewart turf.
The closing lullaby, 'Pony Boy', was clearly a health risk to the
sucrose-averse, though it worked for Springsteen's son. There was
something sweetly endearing about the crass infantilism; and
laboured. Crooning it might have made perfect sense to Evan, but
here it came over as gilded and sticky. 'Puke' was the dim view of
the *Source*.

Accompanied just by a drummer, and fortified by a choir of
Scialfa's friends, *Lucky Town* was a softer – some thought better –
bet. With the exception of 'The Big Muddy' and 'Souls Of The
Departed', it was doggedly sentimental. The aesthetic aim was

warm and fuzzy. Thematically, it dwelt on Springsteen's good luck, and neatly pricked both his myth –

Well I took a piss at fortune's sweet kiss
It's like eatin' caviar and dirt
It's a sad funny ending to find yourself pretending
A rich man in a poor man's shirt

and upholstered routine –

Now a life of leisure and a pirate's treasure
Don't make much for tragedy

– as well as scattering a few clues about his well-bedded home life. For all the cod-Dylan phrasing, the words came over loud and clear, the intonation firm: Springsteen rose gloriously to 'Living Proof'. 'My Beautiful Reward' didn't seem to have been sung at all. Springsteen sighed his way through it. For these and other reasons, not least the camp cover, *Lucky Town* had a fey charm. It was certainly worth doing. Springsteen effectively rendered the separate sanctuaries of old and new – 'These are better days' – and lit the gap between them. Whether it rated a whole album is debatable.

It was a while since a release so rift the wise men of the press. Some (including *Rolling Stone*) whooped, others groaned. *Q* called Springsteen 'unembarrassable', so helping explain, or define, his whole fame. He was always 'in the moment'. On this reading, with *Touch* and *Town*, he'd joined the Olympus of men like Bowie, quick-change artists who found the general in the specific. This hitting on universal themes was much praised in, chiefly, *Lucky Town*. For *The Times*, 'there could be no more eloquent rebuttal of the charge that he's in some way drifted loose of his moorings'. Others carped that Springsteen's idea of household reality, and thus his art, came down to the coffee table. As the broad issues waned, and *Touch* degraded further into a Valentine, this might be the most illuminating angle from which to see it.

Both were makeweight albums: not up, not down, but loudly,

philosophically banal. They were Springsteen's first to sound pedestrian, a sorry slump from *Tunnel*. Jon Pareles, writing in the *New York Times*, noted that 'he's starting to seem like a man wrapped up in private preoccupations, running in circles'. The two most frequently heard barbs were that, taken as a whole, the end-product was too cloying and – a problem so simple as to sound quaint – too long. Most agreed that, buried within the two, a great single LP waved wildly to get out. This verdict was an index of the profundity with which Springsteen's best work moved lives.

Human Touch and *Lucky Town* hit the chart at, respectively, numbers two and three. Both ignited sales expectations, but ultimately fizzled. Within six weeks, they were on the way down, then out. The implicit message from the casual, *USA*-era fan was *Today*'s rhetorical one, 'Bruce doesn't give a toss anymore. Why should we?' It's true that Springsteen had moved on. Viewed impartially, the albums seemed at first like the kind of soft-focus MOR best left to Elton. 'Pony Boy' made Pareles's point to an almost embarrassing degree. Some of the odes to family life were, frankly, grim precisely for being hideously accurate. 'Bruce doesn't give a toss anymore' was, coldly put, a slur, but summed up how people felt. There was no denying that, by 1992, Springsteen looked on rock as a job. It was what he did. It wasn't what he was. He even managed to joke about it in his radio hook-up in LA. 'In the crystal ball, I see romance, I see adventure, I see financial reward, I see those albums, man, I see 'em going back up the charts. I see 'em rising past that old Def Leppard, past "Weird Al" Yankovic, even . . . Wait a minute. We're slipping. We're slipping down them charts. We're going down, down, out of sight, into the darkness.' It was wry, and had the added bonus of being true. Elsewhere, too, Springsteen adopted his friend Sting's postmodern motto, 'You've gotta laugh.' Even releasing the two LPs on the same day – in the earth-shaking mould of Guns n' Roses – was a kind of anarchic prank. Overall, he presented a man with a new, much-needed flair for mugging up on life. His self-composure even extended to knocking himself as 'Springbeam'. It wasn't possible to dislike someone in that kind of mood. Springsteen, for the first time in his career, was better than his music.

Under the cosh from longtime fans for behavioural gaffes and going Hollywood, Springsteen lost marks as a Messiah, though not his sure touch as a father, son and soul-mate. Chiefly the last. He and Scialfa had been together four years. Both rejoiced in family life. Bliss was a day out, heading east, in a car big enough to fit the four of them, the nanny and two dogs. Or Springsteen might spend the whole afternoon trying to find the right ingredients to fix dinner, in which pancakes, hash or chilli tended to rule. He was a dab hand at bedtime yarns. Springsteen's story-telling bent, which had hushed domes, worked equally well in the nursery. He could play-act, or read Dr Seuss by heart. Ever the doting parent, Springsteen put aside what he called 'the dread' when in the company of Evan or Jessie. Likewise, he drew closer to his own past. Springsteen still visited Jersey. He threw a lavish birthday party for Ginny, his forty-year-old sister. This production on behalf of his sibling was, in its way, more of a hit than the two he'd done with Landau and Plotkin. Springsteen's other sister, Pam, became his in-house photographer. Relations with his parents also steadily thawed. Adele was a regular caller at Tower. To Doug, surely, was due the 'shit' with which Springsteen was racked in his twenties and thirties and about which, in a dramatic slice out of *East of Eden*, he once raved to his father: 'I'm fucked!' and 'You'll pay!'; a fear of physical contact with virtually anyone apart from lovers, a 'clenched' way with friends, and, of course, 'moods'. That was then. Now, sixty-seven and forty-two respectively, father and son got on well. In part the *glasnost* stemmed from the two babies. 'He was never a big verbalizer,' Springsteen said, 'and I kind of talked to him through my songs. Not the best way to do that . . . But I know he heard them. And then, before Evan was born, we ended up talking about a lot of things I wasn't sure we'd ever actually address. It was one of the nicest gifts of my life.' Of all the dour qualities that could be claimed for Doug, and were claimed by his son, he himself was a sunny presence in Beverly Hills. The extended family 'did crap', every kind of hobby and game, together. Over the Easter holiday, they even mocked up a four-colour paper: Springsteen was sports editor.

Some freelance breaks also came his way, providing public proof that, as a man, Springsteen's type wasn't set. That 'crystal ball' spiel would have been beyond him a few years earlier. By 1992, Springsteen took his career less grimly than others, notably fanzines, did on his behalf. The passion for work, intense as it was, no longer buried his other passions. Springsteen loved his family. As for friendships, they came more easily. His appearance, late at night, at Cheers or the Pony, both still plying their trade, was more or less given whenever he was in Rumson. He could joke about life, as when he told a cousin, 'I may be boss, but, at 2 a.m., them diapers all smell the same.' But Springsteen took it seriously, too, and, with a mixture of gloom and pride, never let up on his crusades. The anti-hunger drive went on. This was in part a compensation for, as he sang, having 'Been paid a king's ransom/for doin' what comes naturally', and partly nature. Springsteen was genuinely 'liberal'; in other words, carbon-based. A deeply ingrained sense of justice led him to give both time and money when he might have been expected merely to sign a cheque. No one could match him in the art of popularizing his causes. He still rode a stable of hobby-horses. By and large, they tended to be practical, not political; adding extra cover where the missing skin ought to be. They were human. Across the country, dozens of kitchens and food banks survived because he'd taken the trouble to save them. In church halls and shelters from Portland to Maine, people who never bought a CD had cause to know, and thank, the name Springsteen. That was fame.

Stories of his niceness were legion, and undoubtedly true. Allan Clarke – the first to cover 'Born To Run' – met Springsteen after a show in 1992. 'Bruce not only remembered me. He was all over me. Basically, he was just the same, still crazy, yet down-to-earth after all these years.' Success may not have turned Springsteen into an intellectual giant, but it had taught him there was more to it than working like a pit-pony. Nowadays, he took time for dozens of charities, family and friends. He met Graham Parker, for one, that summer in New York. 'Bruce lurked around behind the amps at a gig. He was great . . . supportive, warm and real. A nice bloke. If there was a Mount Rushmore of modern Yank heroes, he'd be the rock they'd carve it on.' Even Kurt Cobain, not one to over-praise, called Springsteen 'cool'. Jim Mahlmann's bottom-line verdict: 'Bruce was sweet.' Still, Springsteen's milquetoast image wasn't exactly the core of his inner life. Hard-nosed, professional men also found him cool, and not just because, as Motz says, he was 'second in interest only to Niagara' among American natural wonders. As various managers, agents, bootleggers and roadies had learned, you didn't, notes one of them, 'fuck the boss'. No one got to be so famous, so long, by chance. Yet from the first, in 1974–75, he'd been that rare star with character as well as charm. If Springsteen owned anything he was proud of, it was his reputation as 'real'. He'd earned it.

Springsteen's latest trek, sixty-eight dates on two continents, bowed in Stockholm on 15 June. He played a blinder. Staging and acoustics were both immaculate, sight-lines in exquisite taste. No fewer than twenty-seven songs were belted over three hours. It wasn't the show as Bossmaniacs dreamt of it, but it was a fair set. The crowd went home happy. There was no hassle with 'pissing and puking'. In 1992, the problem was pacing. On any given night, he veered between satori and self-parody, sometimes in the space of two consecutive tunes. For once Springsteen weighted the night not with golden greats, but modern, evanescent pop. Specifically, it was dense with cuts from *Human Touch* and *Lucky Town*. With a 7/20 split between old and new, certain critics would find their minds wandering, to be closely followed by their feet. Richard Williams walked out in London. Robert Sandall caught a mood when he wrote of Springsteen's Bercy gig in Paris: 'After hours of one-paced, wham-bam rocking, it was plain [it] wasn't going anywhere special, that it represented only a muscle-bound facsimile of the strong, simple virtues that make – or made – him great, and that though it had the brute power necessary to move dedicated fans to the usual feats of fist- and lighter-waving, the concert was dangerously short on musical finesse.' Springsteen's five nights at Wembley Arena sold out. There was a generous tonic of wit and sex. Scialfa smooched with him through 'Brilliant Disguise'. He strung together 'Hungry Heart', 'Thunder Road' and 'Born' in the usual salvo, which, thanks to the backing singers, also had the lushness of a gospel turn. Even so, the key to enjoying it lay in the steely coils of nostalgia. There were few, or no, shocks. Later in the year, as self-confidence struck, Springsteen recovered his old sense of *sprezzatura* – the Zerillis' art of making the hard look easy – notably in the pre-song raps. By tour's end, in Pittsburgh, he'd shifted a gear. For now, he trundled down the great proverbial highway. Even 'USA''s familiar contours came and went without upping the voltage, amongst either the audience or the band. It was just as everyone knew it would be, and that was enough. They were content.

Others, of course, thought of a Springsteen solo tour – or without the E Streeters – as a contradiction in terms. For them, the new band was never going to compare. Clemons' absence, in particular, was sorely felt. Nowadays, Springsteen was flanked by Sims and the poly-phonic Crystal Taliefero, both shuffling in and out of time with the riff, crotch-poking and generally pulling poses. As for Fontayne: this cross between Marc Bolan and Slash, hiding behind a rancid ring of black hair, meant to 'extend the vocabulary' of the guitar, his playing of which was both frenzied, yet sadly flat. Springsteen's near-rabid defence of the band, something, to be fair, he made nightly, couldn't curb the misgivings: how could he have traded musical partners like E Street for ones like that? There were other riddles. In Paris, those jammed close to the stage swore they saw a full, working mainframe computer. For the first time, Springsteen used an autocue. Some of the old sweat was deodorized by a spray of such sterile, '90s hoaxes; the beat whirred out with the precision of a tinny musical box. Weinberg himself sat in for a gig at Meadowlands. When he walked on, he grinned. Once he settled on the stool, he gaped. If being fired was Weinberg's biggest jolt of his career, then this qualified as runner-up. 'The only thing you could hear in the monitor,' he told writer Patrick Humphries, 'was the drums. There was no vocal, no piano, nothing of the rest of the band. Then I saw a click track playing, and I thought that was unusual. There's no way that you can do it, in my estimation . . .

there's no way you can do that show while concentrating on keeping it perfect.' As a quote, it caught neatly the stilted, smoothed-down drift of the music.

Most shows were solid, if uninspired. But they were well drilled. Springsteen's ability to forge foot-stamping rock from merely serviceable melodies remained, twenty years on, something of a feat. As to the stage act: the middle-aged women in the front rows were the ideal audience for the raps, which were family-bound just like them. Between numbers, he'd talk about his two 'nice little kids' and fears for their future, while pre-*USA* hits tended to get called 'history'. Springsteen had changed, too. Whereas previous tours had been all about 'letting [his] hair down', he'd had it cut for this one. According to one wag, he now joined the 'select group who suffer from Samson syndrome – once shorn, their muse goes, too'. Springsteen's traditional dowdyism was part-traded for dandyism. His Romany fad, hung with chains, clanking beads and earrings, lacked only Van Zandt's toque to formalize the look. He liked silver jewellery – including his wedding band – and often appeared in a suit or sports coat. Springsteen's biker boots survived. He wasn't sold down the *soigné* river, but the clothes symbolized a set, rehearsed and blocked, where every step and nuance (if not running order) was buffed down to the last note. The air of random charm once surrounding his gigs gave way to one of steely professionalism. Effortlessly special 'presence' became, when Springsteen rapped about family, self-conscious feyness. The music still 'worked'. Even the newer material uncoiled around enough *Tunnel*-type riffs to quell doubts. There was no mistaking the songs' author. But Springsteen himself was clearly undergoing one of his 10,000-mile identity changes. He no longer lived for the fans' love, particularly when he could get the real thing backstage. Some nights he even tossed the final encore for Scialfa's sake. His family followed him everywhere on tour.

'You've got to look into some of those people's faces,' Springsteen told *Rolling Stone*. 'They don't take it lightly, so you have no right to, either. It's something that I've never done and never will. I'll quit before I do.' That was 1978. Now, fourteen years on, he seemed to be pleasing himself, not the hardcore. 'Bruce doesn't give a toss anymore' was well wide of the mark. Even so, some of the fires had clearly been damped down. Much of the stock mood was tender and even tame; 'cute', in one paper's phrase. Casual fans, not to say Maniacs, could be shocked by the air of AOR politesse. The effect of firing the E Streeters was much like doing Shakespeare in modern garb, promptly turning it from art into panto, pursuing its middle-aged quarry through a skein of nostalgia and – witness the click track – trendy ruses. Technically proficient, the new group were sadly lacking in subtlety. Where Lofgren's guitar had been as tanned and leathery as an old football, Fontayne's was safe as milk. The playing was so bland that it became the gigs' most obvious feature, making the great, older tunes seem like nothing more than a bid to draw fire from the pasty textures. For someone with eleven people on stage with him, Springsteen had little to show for it.

On good nights, at least, he redeemed what the hapless band couldn't cut. By the time Springsteen hit his home state in July, the set had been upended. There were fully twenty 'history' lessons. He restored 'Born To Run' to full warp speed. Those Meadowlands gigs were the pop equivalent, and near contemporary, of Independence Day parades: with picnics, frisbees and whole families jigging in the aisles, they finally rose above the mystique of ex-greatness. It was the prodigal's return. That eleven-night stand was Springsteen's best of 1992, and among his best ever. He played on for the rest of the year. On 22 September there was an electric, thus point-defeating 'Unplugged'. A month later, Springsteen raised eyebrows, and hackles, by crossing a picket-line in Tacoma.* In Atlanta, he brought the house down at the Omni Arena (where officials had just banned Guns n' Roses and Metallica). Springsteen let rip in Lexington. He trooped between Chicago and Detroit. In Pittsburgh he mixed barbed comic observation with ballads and

---

*Springsteen told the crowd there he hoped the issue – a strike by city clerical workers – would be resolved soon, but he had a commitment to play, 'and that's just what I'm gonna do.'

bursts of overdriven rock. Those last shows had the same sense of natural zip as the best of 1978 or '80. Albeit late, Springsteen was back on peak form. For those who weren't too cynical to bother being disillusioned, the whole tour brought the verdict: flawed rule, fascinating exceptions. He was home for Christmas.

As well as Weinberg, Van Zandt, Federici and Tallent all did cameos for their ex-boss. (The last would tell Robert Santelli, 'it wasn't a whole lot of fun'.) Even those walk-on jams threw ironic light on Springsteen's band. Pre-tour, nothing had been fixed, in that area, for years. In 1990, his 'Viva Las Vegas' group had been west coast session hands, some of whom, like Jeff Porcaro, made the cut on *Human Touch*. Later that year, he'd done the Christic gig on his own. *Lucky Town*, too, was mainly solo. Using Plotkin as a head-hunter, Springsteen then began hiring full-time in March 1992. Those B-52s and Lone Justice fugitives duly auditioned for their roles in a Greek tragedy. They were doomed. Filling monster shoes was beyond them. Springsteen loyally chafed at suggestions that, specifically, Alford and Sims weren't up to it. 'I just disagree,' he told the *Tribune*. And it was true: as a funk-inflected duo, with plenty of drop-kicking on the beat, they were good enough. All the band, in fact, could lay down a blistering blues edge. Sadly, the E Streeters did it better. *Their* playing had at once borne the weight of dense, knotty arrangements and exulted in a kind of weightlessness. It was a heady legacy; a hard, or hopeless, act to follow. Fontayne and the rest shouldn't have had to try. If Springsteen really meant, as he said, to 'push it out . . . see how it [felt] to play different ways', he could have hired a trio like Dylan's; or gone acoustic. As it was, the sprawling stylistic hybrid, with its overegged guitar, its haggard rhythm and, above all, its hammy posing could only ever be a joke.

The tour was deliberately positioned as a comeback, but after a huge opening fanfare, it stood at the gate like a horse that wouldn't run. In some European halls, there were empty seats for the first time in seventeen years. Once Springsteen hit Italy (always a spiritual, and, for that matter, maternal home for him), he began to rejig the set. In the end, no fewer than fifty-five different songs were tried during the year. Some of the blue-lit classics, like 'Rosalita', returned. By mid-August, the *LA Times* was profiling Springsteen with the words, 'He has two new albums, neither a hit, but his concerts are still hot, because fans want to hear his oldies.' That kind of fame was far from what he wanted. 'Bruce kicked several chairs,' notes a third party, during a fall crisis meeting with Landau; but later saw reason. Bowing to commercial pressure, if simultaneously it raised cheers and receipts, he duly looted the archive. In a world given up to the likes of Nirvana, Springsteen proved he could still hack it. It was a close-run thing, but in the end the tour took its cue from the quick play of his moods and the early music. His repertoire made other rock gods' seem, like an old Soviet baker's, sadly understocked. Nothing compared to his back catalogue.* Even with that band, he, and it, were talismanic. The last leg, in particular, would enjoy a retrospective sheen, like a snapshot capturing more than it set out to. True believers discovered them as some of his best gigs ever. He soared brilliantly over the lumbering power-chords. Above all, as the tour's parameters shifted under his feet, Springsteen responded with proof that artistic innovation, growth and popularity weren't mutually exclusive. He may have been off the job for a while, but he was still, after all, boss.

Springsteen's eighteenth tour, in the end, won some of the richest prizes, if not best reviews, of his career. It wasn't the money train of 1984–85. But, by the time he signed off at the Civic Arena, Pittsburgh, he'd grossed $30 million in ticket sales alone, quite aside from the bonanza in high-end spin-offs. His 'Plugged' show was released on CD and video. It, too, swelled the royalty flow: highpoints included the yodelled 'Red Headed Woman', 'Atlantic City' (prodded by Bittan into something like 'Centerfold'), and the ensemble 'Light of Day'; Springsteen himself hit the sweet spot on 'Lucky Town'. The low point was his doing the gig loud and switched-on in the first place. Privately, there were mutterings

---

*Financially, too, Springsteen took his past to the bank, netting $4–5 million annually from the hits.

around MTV at his flouting the show's format, though only public tact: 'When you have an opportunity to do a Springsteen concert, electric, acoustic or banging on a trash can, you do it.' After the quiet shock of the tour, it was an adequate souvenir.

Offstage, Springsteen was almost a caricature of the contented family man. 'Warm, always warm,' says Judy Kern. Away from the kids, he could still freeze. A friend recalls that he 'wore shades around the house, sat like a furled umbrella, and left most of the small talk to Patti'. But he was cordial, charming and genuinely kind, and he seemed to like people; even bores who pinned him to bar-room walls. Another colleague saw Springsteen unwinding after a video shoot in New Orleans, 'chugging Heinekens and just doing *anything* people asked'. If his crowd-pleasing still spoke of his insecurity – of his coldness buffed, as he wished to have it, up to jollity – he was 'real', too. After his Pittsburgh show, Springsteen took the time to look up an old friend. As record chiefs plucked at his arm, he spent an hour huddled with the Houserockers' Joe Grushecky, a man who, like Ryder or Bonds, had a cult following but no real mainstream success. A few months later, he found himself writing songs with Springsteen in Beverly Hills. After staying several days in Benedict Canyon, Grushecky emerged with a promise of studio dates and 'even gigs' together. It duly happened, and *American Babylon* was only the latest proof that, to most, Springsteen was a loyal ally and no bad co-worker. Like his hero Woody Guthrie, he'd discovered the great healing force of optimism as a moral imperative, getting out of bed each day 'wanting to move someone, or something, on'. Professionally, he may have ebbed. Personally, Springsteen was at the rip-tide of his power; 'a *very* benign despot', in one family view.

Pressed, meanwhile, on his own political choices, Springsteen allowed that 'what Jerry Brown is saying is true . . . And I liked Jesse Jackson when he ran last time . . . But I don't know if people are really organized, and I don't think there's a figure out there who's been able to embody the things eating away at the soul of the nation. I mean, the system has really broken down. We've abandoned a gigantic part of the population – just left them for dead.' It seemed to sum up all the anger, the pain, the bile and frustration Springsteen still saw in the big picture. His ability to be the beer-quaffing barfly and America's soul was true to the master vision of all his best work. In what seemed a flash, and had only been twenty months, it was responsible for both *Nebraska* and *USA*. No wonder Springsteen felt the political void as an inner loss. It drove him 'nuts', he said, that none of the presidential hopes could pick up the ugly vibes. In desperation, he voted for Clinton.

9

The New Timer

Early love of the Motorola and the jolt of his first guitar – 'one of the most beautiful sights I'd ever seen in my life' – frame the backdrop to Springsteen's eternal-teen fixation. Although the next thirty years may have made for some minor shifts of mood, his involvement in and reflections on those seminal noises were the major part of the game-plan. This background made him rightly wary of all or most 'fakes' (hype and PR-types), as well as star-system pieties. Rather, Springsteen devoted himself to music that, if not hoary, recalled the best of the '60s bands in bringing a brash snap to the job at hand, and keeping it real. There was also the fact that he aimed high in the lyrics – concept masking the melodies – and carried the polar burdens of rhythm and blues. He had other lofty tendencies: few such icons not only gave, as he did, but then kept up with the beneficiaries. To Springsteen, 'booting something back' was vital not only for maximum self-fulfilment, but also for minimizing the pain which therefore reduced the lure of rock's joyous peal. He wanted everyone to be as happy as he was.

Meantime, Springsteen bent knee to those old gods and shrines of the past. Two of his first jobs in 1993 were inducting Creedence to the Hall of Fame and officially christening the new Stone Pony.

Springsteen jammed all night with Southside Johnny and Jon Bon Jovi. He stage-hopped on both coasts. The central concept to his career was, after all these years, celebration.

Later that spring, he played an *ad hoc* gig at the Count Basie Theatre, raising funds for a food bank. It was one of dozens of fêtes, galas, roasts and tamashas he now did with the official dates. Charities around both his homes, east and west, knew Springsteen was a solid bet for a 'touch'. When you got him on the phone – provided you could – his voice was typically hushed, seemingly slow, as if he were testing something: your view of *him*. One caller once said that it would be like 'hosting God' to have him play at the man's club. This was the signal for one of those sudden, self-deprecatory fits that constitute the basic pattern of Springsteen's life. 'You shittin' me?' he laughed. 'More like the devil.' Springsteen not only did the gig; he sat around until dawn, charming a small crowd with tales from the road: sex; violence; certain promoters with shot-guns; climbing out of hotel windows; the tour bus; cars; chaos. The old days. 'Bruce was just classic,' says the man, who remembers a 'warm-blooded guy who liked telling blue jokes and stories on himself'. These yarns on the rough and tumble of humanity were, so to speak, Springsteen unplugged. It was a side seen by a relatively few, privileged souls. For mass consumption, the MTV set (originally shown in November 1992) was out that March.

Springsteen was back on tour by Easter. He did a month of arena gigs, starting in Glasgow, then the dome and stadium run around Europe. Though still preoccupied with flogging *Touch* and *Town*, he found time for several covers and a goodly minimum oldies count. Reviews, too, were warmer than in 1992. Among other flaws, those shows had offered no 'human touch' whatever, but only the dire fact of crowds falling into a state of coma over which of the nearly identical sidekicks was worst. It was Scialfa who first caught on. She suggested that Springsteen toss some of the turgid heavy blues and forge another set with more 'lurve' on parade. What they hit on was the most direct and sane solution. Catalogue favourites returned. Scialfa herself emerged for more smoochy duets. Amid the gropes and knee-tremblers, Springsteen's raps were so bed-struck that his first line in London was '*Fuck*.' (His last was an invitation to 'get naked'.) He welcomed several old friends on stage. This second, and final trek reflected a tighter and, all in all, better-run ship. Landau and Barbara Carr went everywhere with Springsteen, with Magovern and a small but fanatically loyal crew again doing everything it wasn't vital he do himself. In the *Post*'s quip, 'Bruce progressed like the Sun King.' One way to see the whole tour, in fact, was to treat it as a travelling court, with occasional viewings for the public to gape and buy goods. At the centre of several inner sanctums, Springsteen was a benign, remote (if not regal) presence. He gave some of his best performances.*

Long before the time Springsteen flew home in June, it had become an article of faith that he was infinitely above and beyond sordid commercialism. Any hint to the contrary was morally bankrupt. The most striking example of the kind of emotional claim laid was the *Globe* lead that ran, BLUE COLLAR HERO. It's true, of course, that Springsteen had said no to Chrysler and the rest. He did neither ads nor endorsements. A club that took space in the local paper 'thanking' him for visiting never saw him again. To an almost unique degree, Springsteen was free of obligation to anyone, and meant to stay so. He was, nonetheless, one of the best-managed men in rock. As well as Landau and his army – and, beneath them, sub-strata like Premier – various attorneys, accountants and brokers all tended a fortune calculated at $90 million. By 1993, the main 'board walk' in Springsteen's routine was the one he took weekly to the office. Those were the kind of corporate facts of life rarely reported. Instead, it was argued *ad nauseam* that he remained simply and wonderfully 'himself'. In artistic terms, certainly, Springsteen did. But if that meant he was still a free spirit, able to go and do as he would in the world, it was flatly untrue. A whole apparatus – Shore Fire and the like – ran interference between him and the public. In granting access to some and aggressively snubbing others, their jobs became hi-tech variations of Magovern's bouncer

---

*Among them was an impromptu karaoke gig he did – unrecognized – at the Stanhope Arms pub in west London.

role. As one ex-friend says, 'Bruce, to this day, never knew what went on in his name. People were chewed out by the flunkies.' A current colleague calls meeting him 'more like an audience'. Springsteen, in that respect, far from possessing his fame, was possessed by it. He led a well-padded existence.

Still, even front-office bullying never tainted the name. Springsteen's personal fame lay in his being 'real'; he was a Jersey boy who happened to have, deeply concealed in him, a flair for matching rhyming couplets with riffs. Those early years left a permanent mark, and gave him a living insight into the dispossessed. Professionally, too, Springsteen's best work carefully measured the gap between the Dream and reality. It was more than slumming, more than the human touch. That sense of community and shared experience was the inspiration and connecting theme of his every move. Closely and personally linked with his audience, Springsteen professed a belief that 'family' should be the guiding star of art and of life. It was that which made him the champion of the lost and which echoed his lifelong charitable concern with the needy.

Another way of looking at him, of course, was to say that music was his means to cover nakedness. The spotlight of the songs was ostensibly thrown on to the person of men like Doug, whose story was told alternately as a hymn and a rant. But it was the interplay of narrative voices which made Springsteen an *auteur*, and allowed him to gild his themes. His characters' fates and his own were fused. What he was really writing about on *Darkness* and the rest was himself. It was a neat bit of transference, letting Springsteen hit his marks without stooping to the first-person singular. Even on the life-slices like 'Nebraska', there was metaphor to his madness. Formal ingenuity and projecting his lot on to others: these, he said, were 'bound up in who I am'.

Who was he? Kicking forty-four, Springsteen still buttressed most of the 'Mt Rushmore' clichés. In many ways typical of his era, he was attracted by the 'realism' of a Williams, overdid, like Guthrie, the importance of 'truth' in art, and notably shared Kerouac's sense of irony and dry wit. The last's touch of physical satire was handed down in Springsteen's poet-hipster beard. Now flecked with grey, it made an aesthetic link to the Beats, as did the totemic plaid and wraparound shades. Springsteen's taste for jangly pop, black cars and herbally scented rooms all swung back to the Me Decade. As to the seventies: *Born*'s commercialism was a direct result of poverty, leaving Springsteen alive to the financial aspect of rock, which eventually landed him in Beverly Hills. The eighties duly charted the rise of both the careerist and the social worker. By 1993, Springsteen's process of self-realization had reached a wary pass. He neither believed in revolution nor shared Clinton's manic hope. His politics were rooted in the idea that individuals could contribute, even bring about change. (As he had.) Springsteen's egalitarianism wasn't strictly socialist, more the self-reliant gospel of men like Twain and Whitman. Closer to home, he enjoyed the reformist edge of both the New York and Los Angeles *Times*. Springsteen often sat over a copy in The Brothers or Spago, his favourite haunts on, respectively, east and west coasts.

Musically, too, Springsteen was a mix. For all his rocks-roots classes and the folklorism that seemed to stun most hacks, he was capable of living in the moment; half the tracks on *Human Touch* unfolded in slang, often the fire-and-ice war between love's illusion and fact. Meanwhile, his own tastes were evolving. As Springsteen told James Henke, 'I like Sir Mix-a-Lot. I like Queen Latifah; I like her a lot. I also like Social Distortion. I think *Somewhere Between Heaven and Hell* is a great record ... "Born To Lose" is great stuff.' Ominously, he even went to Mariah Carey's wedding. He also loyally plugged his wife's much-delayed LP, *Rumble Doll*, out that spring.* The couple spent the second half of the year, largely alone, in California. Their son Sam was born on 5 January 1994.

Springsteen also did two charity events, his only US shows that year. The first, at Meadowlands, was to prop three hunger-related programmes. Worthy yet thrilling, it was exactly the kind of period

---

*Scialfa's label, for its part, wouldn't release the cut 'Lucky Girl' as a single, because of the title's similarity to 'Lucky Town'. The second choice, 'As Long As I (Can Be With You)' was, alas, the voice of compromise.

rave for which he'd once lived. For starters, Springsteen vaulted on
to the amps. The set itself couldn't have been more old-fashioned
had it been MC'd by Jimmy Savile, clanking and saying 'Groovy'.
In the encore, he then flung himself into the pit – still flaying the
Esquire – emerging safe but without his boots. When the crowd
saw it, hundreds of pairs of shoes came sailing on stage. It was an
oddly funny, yet moving moment. ('People *cared*,' says Amy
Frechett.) The actual gig was both tough and touching,
Springsteen bringing off the feat of staying astride it through its
nonstop mood swings. Cameos by Clemons and others were
merely dutiful extras; unlike them, Springsteen had the charismatic
gloss to transcend the formula, leaving fans – some of whom were
there for the fifth, tenth or fiftieth time – convinced they were
watching something passionate, precise, emotionally taut and,
above all, unique. When Springsteen went off, bellowing '*Yeah!*', it
was an authentic cry of triumph.

The second show, at Madison Square Garden, raised $1.5 mil-
lion for the Kristen Ann Carr Fund, in memory of Springsteen's
co-manager's daughter. It, too, was a noble, plausible night. Again,
Springsteen managed to tread the line between party rock, folk
revivalism and honouring the cause. Amid the guest spots, Terence
Trent D'Arby was booed when he ran on for the second or third
set. Springsteen, in turn, was livid. Haranguing the crowd about
'showing respect' was a sad note on which to end twelve months'
solid and, lately, successful touring. On record, arguably, he'd
stopped laying golden eggs after *Tunnel* in favour of more conventional deposits. On stage, Springsteen was that rare, or unique
rocker who could roar like a train and yet whisper in your ear,
often in the same song. Live, he was capable of a power and range
that the albums sadly lacked.

Both set-pieces, in fact, were only the formal end of
Springsteen's charity. By 1993, it ran in close tandem with religion. Orthodox Catholicism may have been 'fucked-up', as he said,
but there were enclaves where holy writ held even in Beverly Hills.
Increasingly, those board meetings were forums for streams of consciousness whereby the Springsteen life was seen as a trek from the

'animal plane' toward God. (Conviction on the part of the lawyers tended to be in the form of 'You're giving 'em too much, Boss.') It was the mature man who, through trial and error, had come to believe 'faith is essential and so is doubt. You're not going to go anywhere with just one, you need 'em both.' Balance. Parity. A full exercise of all the faculties. Living awareness of oneself in relation to others. Those were the ends he groped for, and which led him to brief the suits, 'Send ten grand' or 'Twenty'; there were scores of patronages. He'd always been lavish. Ritualistic fund-raising onstage went back two decades. But Springsteen's last five years had seen the triumph of what he called his 'unbossy' skills. This one-on-one détente with the world reflected a policy U-turn. Pawky raps and anonymous gifts gave way to direct action. Springsteen sponsored clinics, stocked food banks, funded hostels. The obvious virtue of this work often left it unscrutinized, though the worst that could be said is that it was carpet-, not precision-bombing. No major cause was apparently safe from his wallet. It was logical, in time, that he'd take up cudgels for minorities and affirmative action. Springsteen spoke out on quotas, migrants, immigrants, blacks, Hispanics, women. He discovered Aids.

Later that fall, Springsteen took a call from Jonathan Demme, director of, among others, *Silence of the Lambs* and Van Zandt's 'Sun City'. His *Philadelphia* was currently in the cutting room. Demme's opening line was stark. 'I made this movie, and I want it to play the malls.' In a bid to salt the plot-line – gay lawyer dies – for mid-America, he first rang Neil Young, then Springsteen. 'Bruce was so disarming and confident,' says Demme. 'His thing was, "Well, I'm interested, so I'd like to come up with a song for you. If you give me some time, I'll see, but I can't promise."' Springsteen himself would recall adding, 'I'm not very good at [scores] . . . I don't think I can work that way.' In fact, it was the first time, in twenty-five years, he'd ever written specifically for film.

Springsteen recorded the demo at Thrill Hill. The homemade tape – exactly the same version heard today on FM – came in the mail. 'My wife and I sat down and listened to it and we were literally weeping by the end,' Demme said. 'It wasn't the call to action, anthem rock, blazing guitar, out-on-the-highway kind of thing. It was this extraordinarily [personal] song. We laid it in and it was exquisite.' Loud, but only loud enough, 'Streets of Philadelphia' was a suitably spare, sombre jump for the film: soundtrack raised to high art. In December, Springsteen shot a video (also by Demme), wandering around the city, singing what one paper calls the 'saddest track cut this decade'. And among the best: the perfect model for the anti-pop song, in all its compelling, hermetic intimacy, was also Springsteen's return to type. Insofar as he'd always been about sub-tlety and suggestive strength, not just volume, it was a stunning comeback.

The world rushed to heap honours on him. In January 1994, 'Philadelphia' won a Golden Globe. Grammys followed. There was a hatful of foreign gongs. Springsteen's performance of it at a Los Angeles gala (raising $5 million) saw the First Lady leap from her seat. It hit in the US, Europe and Britain, where it outsold 'Born To Run'. Finally, that 21 March, it won an Academy Award. A mere four decades after 'That's All Right', the 'Best Song' Oscar went to a rocker for the first time. Springsteen, watched by his wife and mother, was on hand. Unlike most of the well-scripted winners that night, there was no blast of mad glee, or stock pieties, in tow. He not only stood centre stage, in his tux, and crooned 'Philadelphia'. His acceptance speech was classic Springsteen. It was wordy. It was corny. But it was also that rare thing, immensely honest. One passage brought even the most jaded stars to their feet:

You do your best work and you hope that it pulls out the best in your audience and some piece of it spills over into the real world and into people's everyday lives and it takes the edge off of your fear and allows us to recognize each other through our veil of differences. I always thought that was one of the things popular art was supposed to be about, along with the mer-chandising and all the other stuff.

Aptly, 'Philadelphia' didn't just make Springsteen money (much of which he donated to charity). It also signalled his arrival, as a compound star, into the elite. Around then, when experts were saying Aids might last a thousand years, Springsteen made himself a pop figurehead for a broad base of support and action groups. He laced his few interviews with raves for *Philadelphia*, how 'the country is waiting for something that's going to address these questions of tolerance and how people are going to live'. Ten years after being blithely co-opted by Reagan, he finally put down a marker. Like the film it led, 'Philadelphia' rang enough changes to keep formulae fresh while taking up a charged, supposedly taboo theme – and, with none of the tackier flourishes, made a stand. Artist, and art, were now fully *engagé*; in one gaudy quip, 'beating like a million hearts'. It was this breakthrough – Springsteen, while still in a world that worked through ego and self-help, flogging an ethic that looked on their results as 'shit' – that kept 'him . . . and his aspirations morally pure', his driving force now 'care, not ambition'. From 1994 on, both man and music were busy as 'deliberate, responsible campaigners', not mere chart stars. They were 'real'.

Or were they? Nowhere in the lyrics did Springsteen actually mention Aids, HIV or death. If anything, the Catholic imagery hinted he was, yet again, exorcizing inner demons. Various autobiographical nods loomed at every turn. Being Springsteen, of course, he covered a huge swath. All bases were touched. One could find in the same 'Philadelphia' lines about being 'unrecognizable to myself' and, opting for victim status, a friend's 'faithless kiss'. The range of possible causes and effects was endless. Calling him 'Di with a backbeat' was harsh, but caught a view of the song, with its non-specific root, some had. At the very least, it universalized suffering. Springsteen invited – almost a morbid need – the broadest identification. 'I tried to . . . make it more general,' he said. 'It could be about a lot of things . . . the spiritual, how your soul feels, how everybody's felt, hopefully, like [*Philadelphia*'s] characters . . . I wanted it to be read different ways.'

For all the studied ambiguity, Springsteen, and the hit, were lionized. Both now became a mascot for the great and good. Hugs from the ilk of Liz Taylor testified to yet another endlessly repeated parable on 'growin' up'. He'd already known, for years, the sensuous pull of an audience who trusted and wanted him. But 'Philadelphia' fostered the image of a Name, by endearing him to those, like Taylor, who'd never go near a gig. There was little, or nothing of the egoist in Springsteen. He had radical views on being famous. Even so, all in all, he still felt the 'big F' was due. After the mixed reception of *Touch* and *Town*, he enjoyed his cultural and critical rebirth. Springsteen cut something of a public dash in the Hollywood social whirl – dining at Spago, horse-riding with movie moguls, squiring Demme and Tom Hanks – before, late in the year, he exiled himself, retreated to Jersey and went back to music, if not rock and roll.

Springsteen saw in 1994 at the Hall of Fame duetting, with Axl Rose, on 'Come Together'. This surreal gig ended in mutual fists shaken aloft and the assurance, on Rose's part, 'Boss rules!' Yet the sartorially down-at-heel dude, himself whooping and inserting gags in a show already running long, was only part of the picture. Springsteen's 'good-rockin'' persona was crafted by a pop tycoon who was, in real life, confident, well-dressed, shrewd and vigilant. That January he went to the High Court for an injunction against *Prodigal Son*, a two-CD anthology of demos and out-takes. First, if of secondary importance, Springsteen's writ spoke of 'artistic merit'. But his suit also included the fact that he was in no mood to waive royalties. No one blamed him for that. The whole truth of how Dare International bought the songs – many of which featured in Springsteen's 1998 case against Masquerade Music – never came to light. The name Jim Cretecos was mentioned (he denied it). Quite probably, Springsteen was right to sue. Even so, the papers suggested not a principled stand, but an emotional response to being, as he said, 'fucked'. From the Appel war through to the moment he changed his tune on bootleggers, Springsteen rarely shrank from the law. He cast his net wide, not only for record labels, but also pirate T-shirt and souvenir touts. His dependence on Paul Schindler almost matched that on Landau. Springsteen knew his rights.

All in all, he enjoyed the company of 'suits' who, in turn, plastered his signed photos over their office walls. In 1973, when gigging in New York, Springsteen once spent a night with a group of co-eds, poets and free-form artists, discussing what were called 'social raps'. There he met Kate Rous (then a stripper, now a rock writer), who recalls him saying, '"Kill all the fuckin' shysters" with that throaty laugh . . . As far as Bruce went, they came just between priests and the Boston Strangler.' Not that Rous ever thought of Springsteen as particularly right-on. Rather, she got the feeling that it was a point of pride for him to go it alone: that he fought his own wars; and did so without the props and prosthetics, the dreary crew of attorneys and money men. 'Ain't no way I'm going Wall Street,' Springsteen said. This jibes somewhat with the corporate empire of twenty years later.

Sometimes the cash gave ample scope for his agreeably laid-back streak. Springsteen, for instance, liked to spend whole days and nights – literally twenty-four hours at a trot – watching TV. Old Westerns, fights and baseball (chiefly the Yankees) were his idea of home entertainment. Springsteen was frantic, and furious, at the teams' killing of the 1994 World Series; he made that death seem like the dire outcome of decades of self-destructive behaviour.* Raw greed always jolted him. Springsteen was also, quite physically, shaken by the Northridge earthquake. He won high marks for donating cash and supplies to the injured. The phrase 'local hero' took on new meaning whenever he visited a food bank or anonymously funded a shelter. With his wheezy laugh, his sports-page chat, his airy jokes about wives and kids, there was none of the *patrón* to Springsteen's patronage. It was impossible, around LA, anyway, not to like him. Such was his all-round charity, he even enquired about adopting – at least fostering – O. J. Simpson's two youngest children. Fatherhood, Springsteen said, made him realize there was a 'window onto the grace in this world'. Later in the year, his bran-wholesome image took a minor hit when he subscribed to a copy of Madonna's *Sex*: ironic, perhaps, but far

---

*He then offered himself as a 'human sounding-board' for both sides, volunteering to 'talk sense' to players and owners alike. Springsteen's services as a strike negotiator having been declined, the row dragged on until 1995.

from a bad sign. There was a humanity in the saint of Beverly Hills that set him apart from mere smuggery, and which was all to Springsteen's good.

Specifically:

In March 1994, Springsteen and a friend – the former humming a 'stray tune in his head' – drove to a soup kitchen. The address, in east Los Angeles, couldn't have been worse. Both men worked all morning serving up. After lunch, the friend left on an errand. He returned in time to see Springsteen loping towards him in his vest, having given away the shirt off his back. Later that same night, he cut the song.

In June, Ian Copeland met Springsteen at Gladstone's 4 Fish, a grill in Pacific Palisades. He wasn't only friendly. Springsteen invited other diners into his booth, posed for photos and signed a stream of menus, napkins and bills. The old, plethoric groping of female fans gave way to brotherly hugs and kisses. Springsteen told Copeland he was 'going nuts' alone in the studio. He missed people. In most rockers' cases, of course, such effusions lay in a sad need for love. Springsteen's own self-exertion was noble: to 'cheer folks up'.

Finally, in November, Springsteen visited Patti Smith after her husband died. The reunion took place at the home of Jimmy Iovine, the man who'd brokered 'Because The Night'. According to Lenny Kaye, 'Bruce took Patti's young kid Jackson out for a bike ride, and was generally cool.' Again, whereas most pop gods manage to carry off their act with charm, to outsiders, if not their own clique, Springsteen was exactly the same with friends. 'Bruce really gave a shit,' says Kaye. He was 'just sweet'; and flatly contradicted the conventional wisdom of a star utterly in thrall to PR. Springsteen cared.

His relations in one key area weren't, though, improving.

'The band showed him loyalty because he initially showed us loyalty,' Tallent once told Charles Cross. And, in truth, the 1970s had been a feat of man-management as well as musicianship. In the studio, Springsteen moved swiftly and surely to make the group do more than most thought they could. On the road, he'd been player-coach, never just 'boss'. He was, for example, clearly down on Weinberg during *The River*. But, though blunt, Springsteen didn't lose his cool or fire him on the spot. Instead, he gave simple technical orders and left. Weinberg pulled himself and his beat together. He and the band soon found themselves filling the stage with such zeal – mugging, playing, riffing – that all pop history seemed to crowd on it. But, since 1989, most of the hands had struggled with obsolescence. Bittan continued his session work. Clemons eked out an album called *Peacemaker*. Weinberg himself was on TV. In 1992, an ensemble E Street revue – without Springsteen – raised $250,000 for World Hunger Year, and then regrouped at the Clinton inaugural. It was better than nothing, but less than the dreamt-of reunion. Some of the musicians still lobbied Springsteen. One, in particular, gave several reviews of *Touch* and *Town*, highly selective and yet broadly based, the unifying theme being the word 'shit'. A second old friend left a message at Olympic Boulevard. The six-word gist ran: 'Give us our fucking jobs back.' Most fan mail, that not caught by Landau, said the same thing.

Meanwhile, Springsteen had hit a wall with his work-in-progress. He ground away all summer and autumn. Sessions lapsed into parties, or abstraction, or both. By Thanksgiving he'd cut a total of four tracks. Springsteen's hegira to the craggy fastness of Benedict Canyon helped forge a new kind of exile – he was no longer a working rocker; he was now a house husband, 'house' being the Mansion on the Hill. He spent weeks there, unwilling or unable even to strum the guitar. One musician remembers calling Springsteen to talk money and getting a 'Scud missile strike back . . . The operative word was *pissed*.' Late that same night, earning his own fee at a stroke, his manager rang and read off a list of songs. It was for a hits collection. After that there was a pause, ended by Landau adding, 'We may need some new stuff.'

'With the band?' said Springsteen.

'With the band.'

The prospect didn't swing his mood. Springsteen was badly blocked that winter, not just in writing but recording. Even when the riffs came, they were largely banal, artily intricate and vapid – synths taking the role of Clemons' sax – in a way that spoke volumes for Springsteen's tritely good taste. They were first drafts begging for full band makeovers. He'd moved on, of course, from mere martial music. As Springsteen said, he 'wouldn't know how to write a "Jungleland" ' in 1994. There was truth in his claim to be doing 'grown-up shit' on *Lucky Town*. Even so, the familiar Springsteen tones hardly survived any more as distinguishing licks, and the only contrast was between the loud, shamelessly gospel-tinged carols and the blues wheeled out with their sub-*Nebraska* lyrics. Men like Bittan and Federici could have goosed such tunes in their sleep. As it was, the hands' playing failed to intersect with the musical drama, leaving only a run of bland, note-by-note renderings, most of them generic. Tracks like 'Secret Garden' merely straddled the line where the functional met the facile. Without the E Streeters they were more about craft than art. Springsteen followed the '90s rule-book without breathing any new life into what were, at core, ditties.

Had he chosen to plead extenuating facts, he could have found them in the schedule he kept of bit parts and cameos. Despite, or because of, his own block, Springsteen took on a spate of side jobs. Early that winter, he cut 'Gypsy Woman' for a Curtis Mayfield tribute LP. He stumped for 'Philadelphia' and, in the same downbeat vein, won a commission for the title tune of *Dead Man Walking*. His rock-noir 'Missing' would similarly grace *The Crossing Guard*. Of the guest spots, the high was an impromptu 'Wreck On The Highway' for a crowd of fifty at McCabe's guitar shop in Santa Monica. Springsteen kept his promise to Joe Grushecky. And, that October, he and Neil Young strolled onstage at Roseland to bash out 'Highway 61' with Dylan. In these warm-hearted gigs, Springsteen found the cheerfully raw edge sadly lacking in the studio. He also gave his time and money to keeping the Stone Pony open.

Springsteen was so keen to turn up good new (or old) American rockers – a trouper like Grushecky was among his prize finds – that he characteristically over-hyped and did his level best to 'break' them. When a friend made his annual visit to Rumson, he was eager to interest Springsteen in Band A, another of those rootsy turns with a chaotic, lurching stage show. But Springsteen was already sworn to Band B. His own protégés turned out to be distinctly vaudevillian, with Wild West overtones courtesy of banjo and upright piano. How to top that? By bringing on their sponsor for an encore. It was an odd one: Springsteen thrashing away on guitar as the fiddle and trumpet wove drunkenly over the beat. The friend calls it 'Bruce's *Pygmalion* . . . he wanted to drill these clowns into something closer to an E Street Band'. It never happened; but Springsteen performed his altruistic gigs with the glee of a man not only slumming, but revelling in the fraternal, collegiate vibe. 'An ability to laugh at himself, to take razzing on board . . . *that* was new.' In the friend's view, Springsteen's discoveries on these amateur nights weren't just musical. They were personal. Beneath it all lay strong will and ambition, for others as well as him, though now warmly ordered towards the 'whole man'. Talent-spotting was only one sure sign Springsteen had grown.

Reciprocally, 'cover me' became his motto for other acts. As well as the one-offs, a two-CD feast of Springsteen cuts, by the likes of Lofgren, Bowie and John Harding, *One Step Up/Two Steps Back*, hit in 1997, alongside various songbooks and anthologies. At least three tribute bands did the rounds. Most of these trimmed and telescoped the best tracks without adding much; even in the old days, when Johnny Cash tricked up 'Highway Patrolman' with some raw vocals, he didn't master it musically. Rereadings of old glories were, even so, only one stopgap. As the bootlegs, EPs and compilations all proved, Springsteen's creative silence hit fans hard. In Don DeLillo's phrase, he became 'a local symptom of the Almighty's reluctance to appear'. For those who followed him as a cult, hoovering up every scrap or reported sighting, not even 'Philadelphia' filled the void. This need to connect made for a bull market in Springsteen posters, photos, promos and other spurious 'rarities'. With the auctions and swap-meets, it was easy to forget how long it was since he'd last done a decent album.

Most critics made hay of Springsteen's roots and Jersey persona, but his real code owed more to Catholicism – with, he said, its 'riff of blood 'n' guilt' – and the confessional, for which he substituted his lyrics. He once spoke of having a 'broad church' of Maniacs. Those various conventions, not to say the gigs, met, first and foremost, the fans' need for consolation. Certain shows took on the aura of a spiritual circus. They were the perfect modern embodiment of old-time American idealism – friendly, naïve, provincial. And fun: Springsteen basked in his 'Mesopotamia' raps. Still, narrative pranks masked real devotion. Among the hard core, some of Springsteen's goods traded as relics; 'actual beads of [his] sweat' bid on in one job-lot like slivers of the True Cross. It's not fanciful to say that, to some, he became a kind of composite god-guru, the ex-band his apostles. Springsteen himself, of course, laughed it off. Yet the man who moved a billion viewers at the Oscars was still far gone in mythology.

At the very least, he was a flawed, well-meant soul who'd risen to heroism. If some of the devotees were 'precious' (and the back-end merchandising dodgy), Springsteen's romanticism and rough edge were the real thing. As an ex-lover says, 'You can't fake that stuff on people . . . Bruce was complex, multi-layered, his own guy' – what's called in fiction a *rounded* character; with a strength, a vulnerability, and, above all, a vision you could relate to.

Thus, one starry night in December, Springsteen and his party drove down the canyon road to watch a film in an Anaheim hotel. It was a private screening to raise cash for Tibetan exiles. After the show Springsteen stepped out on to the balcony overlooking the Santa Anas, and began to speak to the eighty guests squatting on the floor and steps around him. Straight in front sat an old monk in a wheelchair who looked up at Springsteen with the rapt air of one enjoying a privileged moment. As he stood in the gloom, framed by a dim reflected glow from the suite, lightning flashing over the mountains, the scene seemed almost parodically unreal – like a gothic stage set. But it was no act. Springsteen spoke softly of his hope for the refugees and predicted the coming of a 'full *perestroika*', broad-based and holy, which would begin in Asia and sweep the world. His final words were met with an awed hush. Then, snapping the mood, Springsteen made a crack, laughed, and circulated through the room. It seemed, to some, as if he were startled by his own eloquence. His parting line to his host was 'I suck at this.' Yet the night raised half a million dollars, and even the most gnarled of the A-list crowd spoke of Springsteen's speech for weeks to come. Given the room to orchestrate his passions, he *was* boss; and the Beautiful People learnt what fans had known for years – Springsteen had a way with audiences that wasn't mystical, exactly, just deeply real. He still cared.

His day job wasn't, however, winning through. Some of Springsteen's songs that winter were a wash; others, merely under-saxed. Both sorts laid a deceptively warm surface over a core of wistful longing. 'Back In Your Arms' was a case in point. There was a lovelorn lyric and a general air of conservatory precision, but nothing like a catchy, still less crunchy tune. Even the full-tilt voice somehow managed to sound tidy. It was hard to fault Springsteen's writing, or the hands' playing of it. Yet something was missing. Most of these sessions were metronomically dull. There were few dramatic or vocal twists, and the tracks unfolded with a grim inevitability. Above all, there was no sense of jeopardy. Any band improvisations were ruthlessly edited, while the old interplay between ivory and brass, at once frisky and locked on to jumbo-sized plunging chord sequences, was nowhere to be heard. Everything, though slick, was oddly flat.

Over that Christmas, various E Streeters still sued for work. Mainly civil, a few of the notes and faxes to Olympic – only Bittan had the home number – left Springsteen aghast; of the many calls, some were 'seriously pissed' or near mad, according to one musician. Now Landau emerged from the night. What he'd hoped for had materialized: Springsteen had established himself as a family entertainer. With 'Philadelphia', he was outselling even Elton. Again, the scores he wrote were scores he settled: proof, Springsteen said, that he was a 'career pro', there for the long haul. That didn't preclude him setting a sluggish pace. Along with his brainwave of an oldies set, Landau now had the idea of reviving the band. It combined savvy retailing with a gesture, and, in a happy sub-plot, might even kick-start the main album. Springsteen agreed immediately.

To intensify the drama he operated in three areas at once. Springsteen settled the *Prodigal Son* suit out of court. He told Columbia to expect not an album of new material, but a hits medley. Finally, he began phoning the band. Just as five years before, each got a personal call. It was a sensational appeal, whether to ego, pride or friendship, and all seven – Bittan, Clemons, Federici, Lofgren, Tallent, Weinberg and Van Zandt – rallied round. Scialfa, too, was on hand.

The reunion was a moment of real crisis for Springsteen, blocked as he was, whose 'career pro' pledges were matched, in private, by ones about quitting. On the outside, one or two scribes had dusted down their 'What Happened?' leads. Insiders, meanwhile, feared the worst. Among them, the rumour was that he'd never do another rock album. Indeed, he couldn't. Desperate, the theory went, Springsteen had been looking to Hollywood for work when, as a fakir with a snake, Landau pulled his stroke. For public consumption, the E Streeters were touted as 'blood brothers', though cynics referred to the high-priced Pooh-Bahs as trophies, part of a shameless second-act fling on the nostalgia run. There was truth on both sides. Springsteen loved the band and, for now, needed them too. They, in turn, never stopped lobbying. The tension had become impossible, and management did the sane thing. 'I don't think Jon can visualize defeat,' notes an old friend. 'He didn't do anything out-and-out sleazy,' he says, pausing before adding, 'though he'd have made a great Jerry Maguire. Deals are his gig.'

The calls to the band went out on 5 January 1995.* On the 9th they were in the Factory. Revisiting the scene of 'Dancing' and the rest was apt, aiming, as Springsteen did, at a week of being hosed down by the hit-spreader. It was the E Streeters' first session since those days eleven years ago; Lofgren's first full one ever. One by one, that Monday morning, they pulled up at the door in their cabs, RVs or, in one case, the bus. There was Federici, just that tad more caved-in round the edges, Weinberg in glasses and Van

---

*In the event, Springsteen did the ring-round amid hosting his son's first birthday party, the din of which could be heard down the line.

Zandt with bandanna. Clemons arrived wearing black leather and shades against the winter sky. (He showed he had better sense in clothes, alas, than in his reading of the band, which he admits thinking would then 'go on'.) Though, as a group, they'd grazed only on the lower slopes of luvvydom, there was a lot of hugging. Even Landau joined in. Springsteen himself was effusive. 'You just get lonely, you miss people,' he told *Mojo*. 'We had good relations, all the guys. I mean, everybody drives each other nuts and all the normal things, but . . . we had a history. I realized that they represented trust and loyalty, friendship, community. The power of companionship. That they were a bridge between my work and my audience.' Dressed in jeans and a torn vest, he was as laid-back as a man being eyed by his wife, staff and Ernie Fritz's film crew can be. Recording started at noon.

Upstairs, past the framed gold discs, in the hangar-sized 'live' den (big enough for an orchestra), the eight men plugged in. The first hour was spent vamping: getting in tune, humming and wandering off for beer. Clemons then called a meal break. By mid afternoon, the tape was rolling. Both keyboards plunked; guitars slashed; drums (displaying a new taste for the octopuscular) pounded. All diligently studied their chord charts. Everything was flawless, top facilities, arrangements in exquisite taste – all that was missing was any creative snap. Despite a label-imposed deadline, there was no rush, nor tension; just release. For twenty years, Springsteen had been Hamlet-like in the studio. Now, he was all Falstaff, prowling the room, laughing, donning silly hats, and except for one or two tips, letting the band have their head. 'The most relaxed ever' was Landau's characterization of the week. By Friday, a revamped 'Secret Garden', Springsteen's mint-new 'Blood Brothers' and 'This Hard Land' (a holdover from *USA*) were done. Tentatively rated, all three were filler. Only the last was an unprecedented, late-term return to form, and it dated from 1983.

Also cut, though not making the edit, were 'Blind Spot', 'Back In Your Arms', 'Without You' (in the same frat-rock mould as 'Sherry Darling') and Tim Scott's 'High Hopes'. Around the third day in the Factory, they tried the title tune of what became *The Ghost of Tom Joad*. Springsteen quickly dropped the idea.* He was spinning a spare, acoustic yarn and, as on *Nebraska*, the band took it flat-out, modal and loud. So they mildly clashed. Along with such spats, though, were the long nights, hunched round the piano or sharing a smoke, that, Springsteen said, were 'like glory days'. As then, he and Landau spent hours shuffling songs. Both were driven home around dawn. Plotkin and the rest then went to work on the far side of the plate glass.

Fritz's rocumentary, *Blood Brothers*, was out in 1996. It was an unusual idea – following a reunion that could have ended in tears, not triumph. (Clemons, for one, was still silently 'crazy' at his role.) The film never quite lived up to its premise. At times it curled at the edges with knowing self-parody. For example, most of the band were paraded, something like the glazed-eyed POWs in Hanoi, in support of Springsteen's decision to fire them. With hindsight, wisdom was discovered that had somehow previously failed to show. It was obvious now that all of them, even the most hurt, deferred to the axe in a way which few had ever suspected. 'I was surprised,' said Federici, 'maybe naïve to what was going on . . . but I think it was a good thing.' Without exception, they paid Springsteen a respect that was as reasoned as, five years ago, it would have been rich. For its part, *Brothers* clung to the theory that the best way to treat the artistic process was to dog the artist going about his business – strumming a guitar, say, or romping with his son. Fritz shot a worthy vanity film.

Six weeks later, on 21 February, Springsteen and the band actually played live. For the record, it was their first gig together since 15 October 1988. Then, it had been an Amnesty gala in Buenos Aires. Now, it was a video shoot at Tramps, a club off Gramercy Park and hard by the Chelsea Hotel in Manhattan. The filming took five hours, for half of which Jonathan Demme did multiple

---

*John Steinbeck's estate, however, came on board with *Joad*, in a way that hadn't been true for other, doomed efforts to adapt classics, notably Bowie's half-baked '1984'.

takes of 'Murder Inc.' (remixed for *Hits* from the vault). That wrapped at eleven. Exactly at midnight, Springsteen cued in 'Backstreets', treating the fans to a ninety-minute party. It was as though 1992 had never been: a classic, seventies-era rave, not to mention the wildest crowd of all time. That New York knees-up was a thrilling hint of the lost age of 'rock and roll future'.

The *Greatest Hits* duly followed. Or, rather, they didn't. Strictly speaking, only nine of the eighteen tracks had ever charted, and there were few shocks among the rest. The whole concept dashed hopes of much new. Springsteen did it, obviously, because the market – sadly underserviced for years – would stand it. Never in pop history had so much been owed to so little: six studio albums in his first decade, and four in the next. Zealots and lost fans alike demanded more 'product'. Still, the stiff-backed title begged the question: why now? Springsteen himself told *Guitar World*, 'I love the classic idea of hits – it was sort of like 50,000,000 Elvis Fans Can't Be Wrong . . . The album was supposed to be fun, something you could vacuum the rug to.' A more cynical explanation was also forthcoming. According to Richard Williams, 'After the live LP comes the Best Of and, finally, the box set. As with everything since *Nebraska*, there was a sense of it being a smart move.' In another critic's view: 'the crap cash-in'.

As for track selection, there was little pre-1980 and even less of rarities or B-sides. Good as it was to hear 'This Hard Land', better résumés have been devised. Lost gems like 'Frankie' and 'Roulette' again failed to surface. Even with the bolted-on E Street coda, *Hits* seemed strangely flat, all action and no context. Springsteen, in retrospect, had been quite right to agonize over his song-cycles, giving them the all-important flow so lacking here. Liberated from their original albums, the tracks had all the fluency of drying resin. As *Rolling Stone* said, 'It comes over as a collection of familiar songs, each stellar in its own right, that adds up to something less than the sum of its parts . . . Spanning twenty years, isolated from the LPs that gave them meaning, they don't mix particularly well . . . [a] vivisection largely for dilettantes, come-latelies and radio pro-grammers.' Not to say *Top of the Pops*.

Still, raw song constructions and grainy riffs were there alongside Springsteen's true gift, the ability to hit the reality button at the
turn of a lyric. 'Thunder Road', in particular, was marvellous. The
emotional resonance of 'My Hometown' still worked. 'Badlands',
'The River' and 'Atlantic City' were often grim, yet always fluent
and fully 'there'. They couldn't have been improved by adding or
taking a note. 'Brilliant Disguise' was masterly, the sole cut from
Springsteen's optimal LP. Even without the smashes – most, bar
'Cover Me', present and correct – Springsteen's best was a blast.
There could be few moans under the Trades Description Act. Sure
enough, it was a great hit.

He went straight from there to the Grammys, virtually a
Springsteen sweep. As a song, 'Philadelphia' was as complex as its
author. On one level, it was a protest at the way Aids had been
seemingly stigmatized, or shunned, by the real – and even arts –
world (a point Tom Hanks made nonstop around Hollywood). It
was also, of course, a less clear-cut act of charity, never stooping to
a named cause. There was more than coincidence in the fact that as
Springsteen, career-wise, fell, his aim rose; all along, his wounds
had been his strengths. Writing 'Philadelphia' was therapy for him,
as film often is for rockers, and in that sense it was self-revealing.
He made long diary notes on his own case as he did it. Being
'unrecognizable', like the song's protagonist, was only one hint of
the way Springsteen himself felt in his forties, the soul split between
the pop Whitman and the maker of music 'you can vacuum the rug
to'. For all that, and as a sympathy vote for Aids victims,
'Philadelphia' deservedly won through. Springsteen spent much of
the next few months writing and recording something similar at
home. There was little in the way of public news. Ironically, his
most visible cameo was in a small-print ad for Audix. From
Chrysler down, he'd never previously endorsed anything, let alone
a tool of the trade. It was Springsteen's contradictions, above all,
that made him engaging.

Another *ad hoc* band reunion took place at Cleveland Stadium
that September. This one was to formally christen the Rock and
Roll Hall of Fame. Springsteen had little to say to the crowd, and

ended the short set on a dour, sustained 'Darkness'. He gave no interviews, showed for only a brief photo-op, and quickly left in a black car. One or two of the E Streeters, by contrast, made a weekend of it. Over the next four years, at least some of them put their 'own bag' in a blender with one overriding dream: to re-form with Springsteen. Most, as a rule, kept up. All – even Van Zandt – rang him, not vice versa. None, in creative terms, ever took their pasts to the bank.

There was Weinberg, for one, cooking up mood music for Conan O'Brien. It was a perfectly respectable gig. His seven-piece jump group duly furnished a vivid sense of swing and dynamic contrast during the show's breaks. But it was no E Street Band. Federici, unable, apparently, to take LA, made a solo LP called *Flemington*, his Jersey hometown. (They gave him the keys to it.) The album appeared on his own label. Tallent and Bittan had their successful, if modestly scaled, production and session jobs; Lofgren's own solo career was frustratingly stalled – at least until the one-off *Acoustic Live* – though he never quit. Van Zandt also plugged away on stage and screen, finally, in 1999, landing a part in HBO's *The Sopranos*. Clemons himself played with Ringo and various other constellations. Along the way he took his occasional raps, including one for domestic fray. He still, perhaps most openly, pined for Springsteen.

Aside from his own contributions, which he coyly slated, Springsteen always talked up the band where, as he said, 'up' and 'down' music rode together in the same saddle. It was the sheer scope of their act: from bazooka rock to ballads, a poised exercise in atmospherics. Above all, Springsteen owed them the true start of his career. For him, FM fame (in the form of 'Hungry Heart') had come only in 1980, fully eight years after the group. Their genius and sheer graft had kept the show on the road, as well as saving several of the songs from cliché. The E Streeters, then, were always more than a backing band, if something less than full equals. Real fans knew it. To them, it was impossible to ignore the snub by the very same Hall of Fame in 1999. For the hands, perhaps, it was more of a piece with their fate over twenty-five years. As one of them says, 'the riff was always that we were full of life. But the life was Bruce's, not ours . . . It wasn't his fault, but we weren't exactly blessed by association.'

Springsteen never shared the band's jag for nostalgic recycling. And he was right. In 1995, more than in '92, he gave himself up to a new audience for whom *Born* was quaint, and *Greetings* out of some lost Cenozoic era. That Grammy coup, following on the Oscars, was a grown-up version of what he'd had ten years before: a mass crossover. Not that it was, strictly speaking, policy. He'd never planned, before Landau prodded him, to write a 'Prince thing'. But he did. He didn't plan to charm tens of millions of middle-aged women either. But he did that, too. As the curtain rose that night on a backlit Springsteen, who sang 'Philadelphia' before walking off with four gongs, it also went up on a career in which sentiment – for some, too easily sentimentality – did for passion. Springsteen knew it. For public consumption, he tended to shrug off such gigs. 'I didn't win any awards for so long, so I devalued them,' he told the *New York Times*. But he was well aware of the ups, as well as downs, that came with a breakthrough. Tim Rice, backstage at the Grammys, calls Springsteen 'chuffed' there. A friend present three days later in Hancock Park, LA, for the 'Secret Garden' video, found him 'halfway between embarrassment and excitement'. Springsteen gave a third man, at Tramps, the sense that he was 'real comfortable trading on the new instead of the old'.

That was him. Springsteen believed in the past, hence *Hits*, but not at the price of a fresh creative stance. Nowadays, he leant to a music less rhythm and more blues, and to a social doctrine grounded, as he said, 'in the real world'. There was 'no going back to Peter Pan mode' in his late forties. But he turned a deaf ear to certain men who would have junked everything – the oldies – in a frenzied bid for MOR populism. For Springsteen, a controlled duality, Fitzgerald's notion of warring ideas, was one of the boons of not having been born yesterday. Real artistic realignment didn't come on the nod from some spin-doctor; it arose out of 'growin' up' with a sundering of tectonic plates, leaving a new line on old truths. 'I know how many times this song was misinterpreted,' he told an audience that winter. 'But I also know more people bought the record than any of my others.' He meant, of course, 'USA'. 'I was misinterpreted . . . I sold a lot of records.' Springsteen chuckled, holding up invisible scales. 'That's my gig.'

So it was. Springsteen was always weighing roles, while playing one or other of them to the hilt. Each was the 'real man'. None was the 'whole bag'. Springsteen wanted, among other things, to be a husband, father, poet, folkie, rocker, regular guy, hard nut, activist, recluse; to be very rich, to be very poor, to play in front of a sea of anonymous faces, to connect with fans one-on-one. Each of these had its moments in 1995. The pop plutocrat paraded in *Greatest Hits*. Blokeism was represented by the Joe Grushecky gigs. Art and commerce, the yin–yang of Springsteen's career: and, running as a throughline, the well-rounded voice of America.

It was a kind of schizophrenia, the razor-fine line between versatility and play-acting, if not shammery. The only thing to do with such cases is to aim for the heart. Springsteen loved his family. Relations with Doug and Adele had thawed by the mid nineties. The latter cheered him wildly from her seat, front and centre, at the Oscars. Springsteen continued his *entente cordiale* with his father. Both sisters were regular guests in Beverly Hills. As a spouse, he was ever the objective narcissist, someone who enjoyed analysing himself for bad as well as good. It was with the children Springsteen shone. Despite Scialfa and the nanny, a good part of their care was his. He gave them their baths, washed their hair and, in his stumbling, only slightly muddled way, tried to make sense of their education: parochial school, for one, was out. When Jessie got sick over Christmas, he stayed at her bedside for days, and later in the summer he cancelled a trip for the same reason. Springsteen woke every morning at eight – an hour at which he'd been known to be finishing takes – to drive the two oldest to class. They went everywhere with him on the road. All the Springsteens toured as a band. The E Street reunion was held up for an afternoon while the five of them watched *Beauty and the Beast*. While Springsteen shot 'Secret Garden', Evan played, just off camera, by the tar pit. What his father stood for, as a counterpoise to the fat receipts and thin emotional pickings of Bossmania, were the rich, deep, adult virtues of family. 'I think that before I had kids I was waiting for my life to begin,' he told *The Times*. Springsteen presented himself as, literally, a new man. And it was true. Scenes that, a few years before, would have left Scialfa slack-jawed with shock now left her beaming with pride. When Sam began kindergarten, his father sat in his room, sewing buttons on his sailor suit, while helping him sing the alphabet. They also played charades. High-pitched laughter rang down the tiled halls. It was all a long way, mood- and otherwise, from the gothic hell of South Street. Springsteen himself liked to say so; he often made the point, 'I believe when your children are born, then, in some fashion, you're reborn.'

As Springsteen gave more of himself, he still had a powerful lone streak. Particularly in the autumn, he liked to drive down the canyon trails, into the desert, though nowadays he was always home for supper. For too many years, solitude had come naturally. It was ever thus. As Grice says, 'that was just Bruce . . . the loneliness was as much a part of him as the Fender'; the one related to the other as 'a train does to rails'. Most or all of the 'shit' dated from those days in Jersey. But he'd been that way later, too, on the road. Ultra-coy one-on-one, incantatorily fluent with a crowd – Springsteen was still the same in middle age. Just as in the music, there was a spiritual push–pull to the man. Paradox cried out to be heard. In one glaring example, Springsteen duly had guilt pangs over his money. For every night at Spago, there was one at a diner. He'd follow a Rodeo Drive jag by another to the food bank. He gave cash to recovering addicts and alcoholics. Springsteen himself drank milk at home and tequila or vodka, with beer chasers, on the town. He still made the move from (Ryle's phrase) family man to soul man better than most. Both Springsteens were inexhaustibly 'up'. Whether trouncing guests at pinball or cutting deals with Columbia, there was a self-will – if never vanity – which in turn stemmed from the narrow groove in which he lived and worked. One ex-friend calls Springsteen a 'well-meant guy, not too bright, whose conscience owes everything to Jon'. Yet the ego, positive or negative, which so fuelled his smaller-hearted and shorter-fused peers, rarely got in his way. Springsteen rallied to causes, like the Rainforest Foundation, in a flash. It was in 'booting something back' that he rightly claimed to be centred and rooted. Art Rosato met Springsteen at a second Bridge gala, for autistic children, in San Francisco. '"Nice guy" is kind of a cliché, and most folks there were on their best behaviour. I've got to say, though, Bruce was sweet. He *was* real.'

As to his time. What did Springsteen actually do with it?

He loved the pram in the hall, but he wasn't the soul of domesticity. Though Springsteen rarely indulged in anything more than a shot of Cuervo, he liked a night out. Recording in the home studio went on most mornings. Nowadays, when friends called, they were apt to be west coast types like Jackson Browne, or actors trying to coach him in whales or the ozone layer. Such scenes, already seemingly dark, promptly turned black. He hung with Sting. The two men went cruising on a private yacht that summer. It's no wonder rock proves, time and again, such fertile turf for parody. But even it could have seen no odder sight than these figures with hoops, chains, and shirts splayed as if for surgery – at least in Sting's case, modelling a tandoori tan – the Jerseyan and the milkman's son traversing the Aegean. Later, in the fall, Springsteen and Scialfa drove to their neighbour Frank Sinatra's. After dinner, they hunched round the piano to sing 'My Way' and 'Send In The Clowns'. It was another stunning realization of a Freeholder's dream. The triumph of guts and glory that had, almost incredibly, brought this scene had begun forty years ago when Springsteen and his mother, out searching for Doug, heard Sinatra's voice over the jukebox of an Asbury bar. That he was then promiscuously chasing heroes, not just an Elvis or Dylan, was one of the better-kept secrets of Springsteen's twenties and thirties. 'I wanted to make songs *just* like Frank's.'

For all his double life as a crooner and boulevardier, Springsteen kept at his day job. As in 1982, some form of acoustic reinvention was due. Even those *Hits* sessions, not least 'Brothers' itself, had really been electric folk. If not quite at *Nebraska* pitch, the key instruments were Springsteen's voice, guitar and harp. For the most, the E Streeters were welcome but passive accompanists. 'The Ghost of Tom Joad' – based on that timeless read he'd never quite had time to read – was followed, in turn, by two songs broadly linked by a felon's tale. 'Straight Time' and 'Highway 29' dwelt, respectively, on the man's release and rapid disillusionment with home life; a thematic and musical bolt to the world of Woody Guthrie. Springsteen's friend Bill Bradley calls him, and specifically *Joad*, in a line with 'Whitman and the other patriarchal heroes'. Largely solo, sometimes with a house band, Springsteen cut the key narrative tracks in midsummer. By Labor Day, when he played Cleveland – where the downbeat set was of a piece with it – he had his album.

All Springsteen's writing had gone, broadly, in three phases. There were songs about himself. Then work, love and all *they* meant to him had been vented on albums like *Darkness* and *Tunnel*. Now social issues were routinely on call. Springsteen turned to them as his own life, married and set, proved less fecund. As for plot-lines: the muse came during those road-trips, when home brooding on Oklahoma City, or, as always, reading. Late one night in Beverly Hills, Springsteen took up Dale Maharidge's *Journey to Nowhere* (which he'd bought, in fact, as far back as 1985), a classic saga of rustbowl America. Soon enough, that yielded the songs 'Youngstown' and 'The New Timer'. Or, equally, he might toss off a lyric for Joe Grushecky based on a *Time* exposé of right-wing militias. Springsteen took an hour every day for the press.

On 13 March 1995, the *LA Times* published a front-page story on methamphetamine labs – 'the worst problem facing the state' – operating in the San Joaquin valley. The reporter's name was Mark Arax. Springsteen not only read the piece. He worked it, too, into a song. Using journalism for raw material went back, of course, as far as he did: the opening line of 'Atlantic City', for one, immortalised Philip Testa, a.k.a. the 'chicken man', a Mafia boss slain in 1981. Down the years, newsprint provided Springsteen with the locales and sub-texts of songs from 'For You' through to 'Souls Of

The Departed'. Drums seldom roll for living or recently dead writers, even of Arax's skill, as they did when Springsteen caught their copy.

'Not long later,' says Arax, 'I got a call. It was Terry Magovern saying, in effect, "Bruce liked it. He wants me to ask you some questions." I gave him a few colloquial phrases and local colour. Apparently Springsteen wanted some, quote, evocative images, such as what type of trees grow in the valley. Eucalyptus, I told him. Later, I got a second call. This one was for "cheat notes", mainly Spanish-language terms. Eventually, I worked up a memo called "Images From the Meth Fields" and sent it on . . . Bruce's own heroes would probably have gone to Fresno – our very own banana republic – and seen for themselves. He put it together his way. I liked the job he did on *Tom Joad*.'

Even while adapting Steinbeck for song, Springsteen still gave vent to his party side. With him, the sub-personalities seethed and mingled with the frenzy of eels in a net. In virtually the same musical breath, he could play with the blues-rock band The Blasters, root out Dylan and casually patronize Wayne Kramer, jobs taken on the fly, as ever, and without much self-questioning. Springsteen still covered the waterfront. At a midpoint between the *Hits* reunion and the artfully conceived, if morose *Joad*, he decided to redo his Beach Boys pastiche, 'Hungry Heart'. He even shot a live video for it. This compound of the up and down – the latter's fuse lit by 'Philadelphia' – was, coldly put, the schizo Springsteen, a quiet man who could still be loud, lewd and a 'fuckin' maniac', so often and so much that one of the crew thought him 'wacko'.

After his summer tour with Sting, Springsteen found himself doing Europe in July. On the night of the 9th he walked down Pappelallee in east Berlin. Number 73 was a down-at-the-heels dive in flaking red brick, squeezed by rising new construction. A heavy metal door gave on to mouldy green drapes and a bar lit by ugly, geometric-patterned neon. It was hard to imagine it being in any bloc other than the ex-Soviet. Here, upstairs in the Café Eckstein, Springsteen plugged in and worked.

After multiple takes, all fuelled by König-pilsener, of 'Heart',

Springsteen then jammed with one Wolf Niedecken and his Leopardefellband. 'Twist And Shout' duly gave way to an off-key Stones medley, and went on from there to get rootsy. The forty dazed customers shouted themselves hoarse. Dawn was already coming over Eberswalder when Springsteen finally set off in search of food at the Yogi Tilla. An Indian restaurant always represented fun for him. Once inside, he looked over the heaped bowls of curry, beans and rice; 'heaven', he called it. One of Niedecken's band told a long, broken joke, in fractured English, the rip being 'harass'. ''Ow you pronounce it?' he said. '*Harass? Her ass?*' Springsteen pounded the table and gave his wheezy laugh, whereupon the Tilla's manager, a half-clad Asian shaken from bed, balked at the whole brilliant, linguistically inventive party. He entirely missed the gag. 'You,' he barked. 'Down.' Springsteen nodded mildly and went back to his beans. After an hour of this, during which he struck the band as 'cool', 'warm-hearted', 'hot-headed' and, running as a theme, 'real', Springsteen paid the bill and walked out to his car. Hundreds of people were pouring off the trams for work. No one on Pappelallee recognized him. Springsteen then flew soft-class to London. Overnight, via Concorde, he was home in Rumson. The rereleased 'Hungry Heart' duly grazed the UK and US charts. Kevin Kline managed a bit of *shtick* with it in the film *Fierce Creatures*, as Tom Cruise had before him. Thus Springsteen conjured a multi-media hit, in his spare time, between writing, reading, recording, touring, fund-raising, parenting and 'goin' Cali'. For an 'off' year, the quick, bit parts and intense, creative spurts all bridged the gap between albums. Springsteen was as restless as a native Jerseyan, even in Hollywood.

In the same vein, he'd descended from Beverly Hills to co-write, produce and play on Grushecky's LP *American Babylon*. The two did clubland together. For anyone still after the soggy days of the Upstage and Pony, this was a fair shot: in one show, Springsteen sweated so much he actually shorted out the wiring on his Fender. Above all, the tour was a true collective. Both men travelled in the same bus. They were interviewed together, usually in the shacks' back rooms, with no airs, graces or other PR arabesques. (One

Time writer unkindly compared it to 'dating the girl of your dreams, only in a sewer and chaperoned by her ugly sister'.) As well as giving *Babylon* a send-off, Springsteen also inadvertently raised hopes of an E Street revival. If he was going back to the world of loud, electric rock, the theory went, it might as well be with them. At least one of his old band took badly to the Grushecky gigs. The in-house lobbying still went on. Among the hard core, the betting was on a box set or studio LP following up the Factory dates. Springsteen himself wasn't oblivious to his fans. 'I can understand how they found [1992–93] disorienting,' he said. 'With the E Street guys, we were like a family, like neighbours. In some ways, they were the physical realization of the community I imagined and sang about . . . There was a deep symbolic importance, and a lot of people missed that.' Asked about the status of the ex-band, Springsteen said, 'It's open.'

Some insiders, and especially Grushecky, saw *Babylon* as a last chance to raise Cain. 'Bruce is here,' he announced, 'before he has to go all arty with his own stuff.' He meant it as a gag, but it was a spot-on hint of Columbia's worst nightmare, what a man there calls the 'twitchy, poetic soul'. With Springsteen, not only was the art in permanent session; so was the antsy mind that brought Asbury into the plains and united Roland Barthes with Elvis. Even as he'd finished work that fall, the label had sued for an E Street, not to say 'Heart'-like sound. In the words of one high-level memo, 'Pray God it's Bruce in any state but Nebraska.'

The Ghost of Tom Joad followed in November. While both management and public cried out for more alchemical rock–dance smashes, it took guts for Springsteen to cut an album that barely worked as pop. Guts and vision: what he was doing was making music, not a record. *Joad* took its sound, broadly speaking, from 'Philadelphia'. Thematically, it followed from Steinbeck, Ford and Guthrie to, striking a lower chord, Ry Cooder's 'Across The Borderline'. As for locales, most tended to the American southwest and the zone around Fresno on Route 99, a road Springsteen knew from his trips to Doug and Adele. The lower-key, more gauzy style and plumbing of depths only hinted at on *Nebraska* was a revelation. (*Joad* made that LP sound like *Sticky Fingers*.) Doubly so, as there were also songs that were wry, witty and potent. It was Springsteen's boldest album, one of his best.

Nor was it exactly a U-turn. Springsteen's first LP had been a nine-gun salute; this, his thirteenth, swapped greetings for ghosts, volume for dry reportage, haste for things done in measured sequence, skilfully, with factual ease. It was an archivist's album. He seemed to have been heading there for years. From the very off, no other rock nova had dramatized in a body of work what it was actually like to live a life – to start out as Baby, become the Boss, and then end up, creatively speaking, an OAP. It was exactly two decades since *Born to Run* went gold. Springsteen's refusal to truck with decorative flourishes, but simply to wire back on the subclass, made for 'mellow drama': set at that age where everyone surveys the wastelands of their own, and other lives. He didn't preach. The songs carried real people on the lip of rhetorical waves, never too far from the ballad of folk-tale which accommodates life, death, despair within set confines. As Springsteen said, 'they're violent stories told quietly'.

In particular, the spoken-word hook of 'Tom Joad' (ideal colloquialism for the broken, relentlessly non-poetic verses) caught the album's mood. In Springsteen's yarn, hobos lurch down the line, then squat by a campfire, 'waitin' for when the last shall be first, the first/shall be last' and, specifically, on Steinbeck's hero. Like Godot, he never comes. Springsteen's goal on *Joad* was clearly to trip through the moral maze, not stooping to pat hopes of salvation. There may not be any. The ex-con of 'Straight Time' and 'Highway 29' certainly found none. 'Youngstown', too, pumped out an effortless, steel-guitar groove over lyrics notably short on laughs. In another internal link, the song's laid-off mill hand would migrate west, stoic, alone and quietly human in the face of insane savagery, as 'The New Timer'. In 'Sinaloa Cowboys' (Mark Arax's cut), Springsteen wove breathy rhymes and a basic I-IV-V chord change round his best vocal of the album. He nearly matched it on 'Dry Lightning'. Shifting his songs to a Latino or Okie perspective was one thing; but aside from the social comment, the shades of

Dylan and the stark beauty of his melodies, Springsteen scored time and again as a storyteller. In fact, *Joad* above all was a quiet synthesis – Twain's 'not too much zeal' – of folk lore. In 'Galveston Bay' alone, he fused Morris Dees's book *A Season for Justice*, Louis Malle's *Alamo Bay* and the amiably dim Forrest Gump. This shouldn't have added up to a song, but that came from the voice, the phrasing and the Biblical fable. Musically, 'Galveston' was shallow as a mirror. Lyrically, it revisited the scene of 'USA' and another returning vet's tale, thus making it more 'real' on war than anything happening in, say, *Private Ryan*. 'Galveston' worked. Like the other eleven tracks, it represented Springsteen's best shot at making America his own through a national reading. His snapshot album was a classic.

No doubt in part because there was no hope of a hit, Columbia, for whom a Top 40 smash always acted like musk on a bull in the rutting season, kept stum on *Joad*. There was minimal PR. Landau, too (uncredited as producer), may have been, a staffer says, 'mathematically sure it'd hit the bin ends' before Christmas. Even Springsteen had his doubts. 'I cashed in every chip I had in the bank over twenty years,' he told a friend. 'If it didn't work, I was fucked.' Needless to say, he wasn't. *Joad* clicked with most critics, while briefly exciting the vultures. In *Q*'s phrase, 'it's the ghost of Springsteen himself . . . the blue-collar god who went missing at the end of the eighties'. Richard Williams calls it 'well-crafted but contrived': mild compared to most *USA* lovers. Yet even crass nostalgia for the big beat couldn't deny *Joad*'s strengths, where humble scenes – that soup bowl, that hand slipped up a skirt, those mills, that valley – worked up no less a mood, were even better, than *Nebraska*. Like the earlier LP, it may have tipped the fine balance of rock economics – it barely met costs – yet still reminded fans of what the original fuss was about.

In particular, a row broke out as to whether *Joad* was an aberration, or Springsteen's true musical home. At least half the album was drawn from his 1972 filing cabinet. In some, if not most ways it returned him to folkie type. Lenny Kaye, for one, calls it 'blunt and brave, like the best of Bruce's early stuff'. According to this school, his creative rethink brought him, albeit on a higher budget, full circle. Among those who praised *Joad* were titles as far-flung as *The Times*, *Pork*, *NME*, *Rolling Stone* and *Village Voice*. Its more enduring fame, however, would flow from the extraordinary congregation of 'real dudes' who saw it as Springsteen's boldest work. Spare, harsh, brooding, compassionate, *Joad* was a pivotal record for its era and its author. If the true artist is the one who wrestles with, and flouts, his own best-known style, then the fans were right to cheer. It was precisely in those terms that Springsteen's dark vision earned its restless niche in both the Hall of Fame and the Smithsonian alike. Not too many documents are, in equal parts, touchy, wry, acid, cohesive and sweet. Above all, it simply encouraged people to think. *Joad* was a glorious antidote to *Top of the Pops*.

All Springsteen's career plans seemed to have followed broadly the same course: they worked, then he moved on. Following this pattern, he could back both Chuck Berry and Dylan at the Hall of Fame, début *Joad* at the Bridge gala, redo 'Hungry Heart' and randomly duet with everyone from Melissa Etheridge to Sinatra, all the time ducking the pigeonhole by constant, creative mobility. Endurance and abundance were his trademarks. He'd already been a musician for thirty years, an icon for twenty. There again, it'd be hard to find another star whose field of operation spread over so many sounds and styles. He channelled everyone from the Civil War minstrel Stephen Foster through to Social Distortion. If you wanted a pop god who could sing folk, reel from a random mixture of gospel to maudlin balladry and simultaneously win an Oscar before resuming his day-job as a polymath rocker, Springsteen was for you.

The initial premise for his fame had been radically different. Until his thirties, in fact, his chief stock-in-trade was single-mindedness. Springsteen himself was the mainstay of his enterprise. At least through *The River*, his natural sensitivity gave way to an imperviousness to anyone in the way, even seemingly, of the Mission. Van Zandt is just the star witness to the fact that 'Bruce was a very strong and mysterious person in those days. People were afraid of him.' Down the years, the blinkers fell from Springsteen's eyes. Divorce, remarriage and a family were merely the tokens of a man more on the move than his music. That he was only semi-credible as a pop grandee after 1987 in no way dished him. On the contrary, Springsteen soon fanned out into the mainstream. Thus, after 'Philadelphia', he wrote the theme for *Dead Man Walking*. He was heard on the soundtracks of *Jerry Maguire* and *The Crossing Guard*. Having shunned it for decades, Springsteen was suddenly on anything with a tube. As well as the Oscars and Grammys, he could be seen on *Saturday Night Live*, two Letterman shows, sundry VH-1 and MTV awards, and, ultimately, *60 Minutes*. Two Springsteen documentaries were out in 1996. It's tempting to say that, by pandering to TV, he tossed depth for breadth; though, at heart, there was still the sort of arch, wise cynic who wrote *Joad*.

A year that had begun with a frat party ended in a Jersey graduates' reunion. That December, forty million viewers saw Springsteen serenade Sinatra on his eightieth birthday. This local tribute from, as it were, one bank of the Raritan to another drifted dangerously close to a roast. It began with a rap. Springsteen gave full vent to the Chairman's ups and downs. Yet, in the end, the tale he had to tell was one of ceaseless triumph over adversity and rank 'shit', the Nelson Mandela of the Garden State. He repeated the saga of Doug, Adele and that song on the jukebox. 'It was a voice filled with bad attitude, life, beauty, excitement, a nasty sense of freedom, sex, and a sad knowledge of the way of the world,' Springsteen said. 'But it was the deep blueness of Frank's voice that affected me most, and, while his music became synonymous with black tie, good life, the best booze, women, sophistication, his blues voice was always the sound of hard luck and men late at night with the last ten dollars in their pockets, trying to figure a way out.' He'd never have said it, but the last part could have been autobiography. The Shrine Auditorium rose. Sinatra himself led the applause. Then Springsteen sang 'Angel Eyes'. What made it possible for him to operate in the proximate spheres of pop and rock with such cheerful, unstinted flair was the fact that, in terms of both his own and the fans' rationalization, he'd good cause to think he could carry it off. Even if it wasn't quantifiable, it was part of the night's sub-text that the two Jerseyans now traded on level terms. The old saloon standard ended in a choric scene of clapping and crying. Poignantly, Sinatra turned to his wife. It seemed to her that he, too, was dewy-eyed. 'I love him,' he said, nodding to the stage. 'Most of those guys don't sing. They gargle. The kid moved me.'

That kind of endorsement was proof that even older greats approached Springsteen with a kind of awe, one shared by his peers. In an indication of the way the pop *zeitgeist* was still going, the Right Stuff label now began culling their double tribute LP. Meanwhile, artists from Etheridge through to Counting Crows all re-created something of the *USA* blare. Springsteen himself, for his Olympian status, remained level-headed and amiably slouchy. He specialized in the self-snub. The very word 'genius' sent him into paroxysms. Even 'great' came out as a snort. The grass-roots network of clubs and fanzines, with their buffs and completists swapping news on bootlegs, related to Springsteen's own mood of almost defiant modesty. By selling the pass that way, he not only downplayed the cult but virtually denied his history.

Viewed with two decades' hindsight, Springsteen was arguably as famed for his personality as his aesthetic gifts: what he stood for as much as what he did. There was no lack of anomalies. He was warm and supportive of total strangers, yet pulled back from old mates like the band. He loved hearth and home, but still liked the road. He was a living icon, constantly in the spotlight, onstage and off, but shy around people and nearly petrified by women, with whom he managed to be simultaneously awkward and butch. Above all, he was the blue-collar plutocrat. Springsteen himself was well aware of the number of masks he lugged about. It showed in his take on the past. While he spoke of 'fucking up [the] myth' to get to the man, he made the journey from the other direction, too – using the fame as the ultimate ego prop. He may have told the best jokes against his glory days, but still hymned the Boss's praises, suggesting at least some lure to the beast. This love–hate dependency was at the heart of Springsteen's decision, in November 1995, to spend a full week listening to every track, released and unreleased, in his vault. Not only that: he gave Scialfa a sort of oral Ph.D. thesis on the oldies, delineating the roots of the very first tunes he wrote. Then he picked up his guitar and went on tour, playing songs so gaunt they could have been strummed in a coffee bar.

Springsteen's first Joadshow was on 26 November 1995 at the Wiltern, Los Angeles. He did his last exactly eighteen months later. In point of gigs played, if not customers paying, it nearly matched the *USA* extravaganza. There comparison ended. There was no mania. Onstage, Springsteen was obstinately bleak and austere, a sawdust Steinbeck whose hoarse, put-upon voice turned even the rootsy thangs into blues. Most of the repertoire drew on *Joad*. 'USA' and the odd hit were sung in a key, and arrangement, alien to the originals. There was no backing. The hoopla and stock rock star's entourage were equally pared down. Among spots Springsteen took in while in New York was a soup kitchen. This was doubly disconcerting to the tour Sherpas, who learned first that he'd driven off without notice or proper escort, and then that he was loose in the Bowery. Later, Springsteen turned up alone at the Beacon Theater, simply ringing the back bell and waiting patiently until a caretaker responded. He carried his own gear.

Musically, Springsteen's one-note shows were dour and downbeat or breathtakingly intimate, vivid and absorbing, to taste. They were certainly spare. Aside from the guitar, the only other accompaniment was from an offstage piano on three numbers. There were few lighting cues and no props. Springsteen lapsed into spoken verse at various points, with one or two key syllables punched up for effect. Even then, there wasn't much real tone in his voice. A conscientious effort was made to toss anything coming between the lyrics and the listener. The gruff, pinched melodies created a harsh contrast with the echoey riffs and Abba beat of 1992. If that set had been about choral pop, this one was anything but. At heart, they weren't so much even songs as recitals. Often, they seemed oddly alike, slivers of Springsteen's own brooding, blues–rock mood. But when they came alive across the pit, they did so with a furious vitality. Even though he was funny enough and could be windy, he'd never have made it, as some hoped, in politics. He was too human.

Springsteen worked hard to inject some between-times levity. The various raps, jokes and self-deflating intros contributed rapidly to warm up the house. 'Don't clap,' he told the New York crowd. 'If you feel like singing along, you'll be led away in cuffs. It happened to some supermodels in LA, and it wasn't a pretty sight.' Even setting up *Joad*, Springsteen cracked wise so often you wondered if he'd paid his dues, after all, in a beach bar or a comedy club. As a narrator, he coped brilliantly with the snags of the material, without stooping to flashy tricks that would have done for his well-chosen rendering. Above all, Springsteen's ability to flesh out the starkest set was still intact. The result was both mesmerizing and stylish, with the odd barb or tart aside, as if he were running the gamut of his own emotions. Much the same could have been said for Springsteen's fans.

Mark Arax caught the two shows in Berkeley and Fresno. He met Springsteen backstage. 'Bruce was pleasant, nice in a hazy kind of way. Very accessible. He didn't come on like a statue of himself.' A second man agrees that the real-life Springsteen was the same 'friendly, funny guy', droll enough for an improv night, he'd been portrayed. There were no airs. Having said that, nor was he 'over zoomed on anyone' but family. If strangers looked to Springsteen for an ego trip, they made a mistake. When cuing up his songs, for example, he might acknowledge his sources, or he might not. The fickleness extended offstage. An ex-lover who saw him again in Berkeley says she doesn't think Springsteen 'even realized we'd met'. Arax adds that he, too, wasn't sure 'if Bruce knew who the hell I was'. His public spiels could equally reflect the sentimental debris that was all that was left of a friendship, an affair or a film like *Grapes of Wrath*. At the Fresno concert, deep in *Joad* country, Springsteen made, says Arax, a 'semi-heavy-handed' pitch for the plight of migrant farm-hands. Despite several pleas from the stage, not a single cent was collected for their cause among the audience. A handful of fans even asked for – and were given – their ticket money back. Later, Springsteen wrote the local workers' union a personal cheque.

For their part, the E Street Band were well versed in Springsteen's ability to be an affable but essentially unreachable boss, who, says one, 'belonged in the 100-watt-bulb category – brilliant but no heat'. Their hopes of a recall were again dashed that winter. It was the old saw that journalists know, and fans could take into account: in rock, long-term careerism and low loyalty thresholds go hand in hand. Not only didn't Springsteen call, he allegedly hung up when, in turn, one musician rang him about work. Later in the tour, he shredded a friend's note similarly asking 'How about it?' When, by sheer fluke, another E Streeter arrived unannounced at a gig, Springsteen was civil. The two men jammed for an hour in the dressing room. Around the fifth or sixth song, there was a knock at the door. A thickset woman wearing headphones peered in and said, 'Ready, guys?' The old blood brothers looked at each other. 'Well,' Springsteen said, 'I guess so. You know me.'

He went on alone.

10

Legend

Springsteen let up but he didn't rest. For the past quarter of a century, he'd been brooding on the ancient war of needs and choice, limits and illimitability, on Olympian judgements between Bruce and Boss. 'I was always the kind of guy who liked to walk round and slip back into the shadows. What you dig is the respect for what you're doing, not the attention. Attention, without respect, is jive.' Springsteen had no idea what this meant when he first said it in 1976. He was relating fame to a few magazine clips and Landau's ill-starred hype. But to use the tag in its more global sense, meaning to rationalize the kind of frenzy he'd known in 1984–85, there's no doubt Springsteen levelled out in his mid forties, when he first put down the guitar. Between then and 2000 he attributed other symptoms besides ageing to the process: an identification with the underdog, a new moral code, a gradual toning-down of the music. In practical terms, Springsteen's duality meant playing small clubs and theatres, while leading a secret life as a Name. Not too many solo folk tours attract, like his, two thousand requests for press passes.

Thus, in the space of six weeks, Springsteen starred at the Hall of Fame; loomed out on *60 Minutes*; and swept a hatful of prizes for

Joad. On 25 March 1996 he sang 'Dead Man Walkin'' at the Oscars. It wasn't as though he squandered his unplugged shows by being a pop god from time to time. Springsteen's low-key dates fulfilled their one and only obligation: to move. Each and every one was episodically strung out on angst-ridden tales about people loosely connected by 'shit'. They made their point. Whether, had Springsteen not been an icon, he would have sold out 130 full-length acoustic gigs remains moot.

Those half-million fans (paying an average of £40 each in Europe) came not only for the two-hour set but out of mild awe, just as one might visit a listed pile, whatever its current state of ruin. A certain type of benign neglect – in the way he deconstructed his hits so they scarcely functioned as tunes – now went with the act. This wasn't a turn with which most rock idols would feel easy. Yet, for Springsteen, it was as though the Joadshows were the shining acme of thirty years' probation. 'I'm really happy doing them and I'm happy with the response,' he told *The Times*. 'I feel like I've kinda dug into a place where I finally feel comfortable . . . Like I've got something to do, something I can be good at. Really, that's my only concern.' If, in the past, Springsteen had been a 'dude' aiming to be a star, now he was Ganymede shooting for earth. This was reassuringly retrograde. As he saw it, playing 2,000–5,000-seat halls (the very ones he'd filled in the '70s) was his natural state. 'I've always felt that whole Boss thing is fundamentally silly . . . I never for a second had the slightest idea or interest in going out and trying to [copy] *USA*. I knew what it was the minute it happened – it was an anomaly. I knew my audience would go back to its regular level. I didn't see that it *might* happen. I knew it *would* happen.'

For their pains, the hard core got a twenty-two-song set, dense with *Joad* but rotating a few depressive takes on 'Darkness', 'Point Blank' or 'USA'. He might do 'Johnny 99' or 'Atlantic City'. It duly ended with 'The Promised Land'. Springsteen came on in jeans and workshirt, his hair swept back, jangling turquoise jewellery, resembling a truck driver with submerged New Age tendencies. He looked older. This particular model hauled a Takamine guitar – still playing it as though wrestling a gator – and a harness-fixed harp, which, endlessly and endearingly, banged him in the teeth. At the top of the show, Springsteen would read from *The Grapes of Wrath*. After encore time, fans queued up to shake his hand. Every night, he signed hundreds of autographs.

Aside from the foreign leg, there were three climaxes in 1996. On each occasion, Springsteen's staging an *ad hoc* bash coincided with lulls, or crises, in the calendar of his long and often lugubrious solo tour. Yet again, it was schizophrenia superbly done. First, on 9 August, in town for Toby Scott's wedding, he crashed amateur night in Whitefish, Montana. The Great Northern Bar & Grill reeled to a medley of party hits like 'Mustang Sally'. Six weeks later, Springsteen did a set in Cleveland to honour Woody Guthrie. And, that November, he played in the gym of his old school. It was, he rightly said, a 'sweet gig'. In 1956, Springsteen had trudged around the corner to St Rose, dour and wearing bib overalls, where he duly took eight years of 'ritual shit'. Exactly four decades on, he hit Lincoln Place in a black BMW. The staff stood in line to be introduced, shuffling up like a Cup Final team at Wembley. For them, the real surprise was what one Sister calls the 'gentleness and goodness' of their star alumnus. The central paradox in Springsteen's middle age was the way he combined a rage at human 'shit' with a yen for embracing those who dealt him it. It was, above all, this buried hatchet – a 'very Christian act' – noted by the nuns; also the way he 'broke down defences', 'got through', cracked people's codes. Whatever the limitations of Springsteen's act, local 'aqua velves' and greasers alike, both bending knee to the father-confessor of Jersey sinners, admired the light it let him shed into dark corners. With that show, yet another ghost was laid. The night raised thousands for the school and a county Hispanic Center, as well as Springsteen's own profile as a native hero. He left town waving and laughing.

Later in the month, Springsteen did three homecoming gigs at the Paramount, Asbury Park. Despite cameos by the likes of Federici and Van Zandt, the rumoured wholesale 'special guests' didn't show. Some of the crowd, mired with hopes of a reunion, slid out early. 'Last night, something was missing,' led the *Post*. On this point, Springsteen himself told a man backstage, 'Don't rule any-thing in, don't rule anything out.' Estimates were that a full E Street tour would gross him $150 million.

There was more to it than money. Whether or not he initiated the split, his actual sacking of the band was characterized by a curt, offhand rap that was full of half-truths, evasions and gripes, hurled at such pace that the listener couldn't keep up with them. Springsteen had promised the group a 'new chance', but what he gave them was the chop. And that puzzled many of those who'd known him for decades. To at least one of them, it was 'Mr Hyde time'. This particular man recalls how 'Bruce didn't have a mean bone in him in the early days.' In his view, the U-turn was all due to 'hitting forty . . . the usual crap'. Yet Springsteen, whatever one thinks of *Human Touch*, made a sane, smart move in 1989. Sooner or later, every star has his own epiphany, tossing cranked-up pop with big drums for the moody joys of *Unplugged*. (Even the Stones *Stripped*.) What's more, Springsteen still harboured deeply ambiva-lent ideas on a reunion. According to his ex, 'There's not a doubt in my mind Bruce wanted it. But he wanted it on his terms. You couldn't raise it, he did.' In more sentimental moments, Springsteen was known to literally cry over the fates of his blood brothers.

Once he got maudlin, he couldn't stop. Springsteen loved to tour the past. Distance, of course, helped make the relationships better, as they couldn't meddle in his life. So long as the musicians knew it, they got on well. In March 1996 Springsteen was in Dublin for the first of his European dates. Late at night, he rang Danny Gallagher, the ex-Dr Zoom draw (and early E Street roadie) now living locally. They talked for nearly an hour. Stars often briefly meet and greet their old staff, frequently with a camera handy, but Springsteen never showed off his endorsements by ex-flaks. Most were also good friends. Gallagher, a 300-pounder with a full beard, next found himself being whisked to dinner and the gig. 'I'm sitting there,' he told *Backstreets*, 'by Bono and the Edge. I asked [them], "Hey, you mind keeping it down? I'm trying to listen to my man, here." I was like, Jesus, this is just like the old

days. My man with a guitar and me . . . After the show, we went to
Little's Bordello. It used to be a whorehouse. Now it's a nightclub.'

Later still, a woman called Liz Else bumped up against
Springsteen at the bar. 'It was wild. Bruce was actually standing
drinks, and he was being mobbed. Photographers were trying to
get him to pose with Bono, but he seemed to want to hang out with
[Gallagher]. Finally, some wally grabbed him. "Hey, Boss, come on.
Who the fuck's this git from ZZ Top?" Bruce just gave him that
squinty look of his, staring him down. "This is my friend Danny.
He made it possible for me to be here," he said. You never saw
someone shrivel up faster. That guy slung his gear and *left*.'

Glumly horizontal in tone where the three Dr Zoom gigs had
been giddily vertical, the UK Joadshows won warm reviews, if few
new fans. Trades and tabloids alike were respectful. As for the
heavyweights: in David Sinclair's words, 'Bruce was epic. Over two
hours, there wasn't a second's slack. Personally speaking, I thought
Joad was too grey. But to anyone lucky enough to have been there,
the live set was riveting.'

It was the same in Pittsburgh, Providence and Kalamazoo; in
Akron, San Jose and Seattle. Springsteen played the last on 29
October 1996. 'Getting old is an uphill race against cynicism,' he
said: a challenge that, as America's documentarian, he radiantly
met. The dispossessed should have something more than welfare if
the Dream was to work, Springsteen believed, and that 'something', in his view, was the knowledge and certainty that
communities would join in like-minded protection of them. Hence
his line to Northwest Harvest that he 'tried to boost causes wherever he went, instead of just writing a cheque'. It was a pattern of
charity Springsteen repeated time and again. Recognition of the
'human factor', of personal loyalty, was at its core. He met organi-
zations, hand-picked individuals and shifted responsibility to them,
on the basis of what even three or four people could do for the
cause as a whole. The result was a small but highly motivated legacy
of aid workers who ran hostels or kitchens, and prided themselves
on doing Springsteen's work. It was a different kind of Bossmania.

It helped that he was naturally charming, and even when the

policy cloyed – as when Springsteen harangued a home crowd on Ulster – he got away with it. The format of lecturing, singing and deputizing a few volunteers was an odd one, but his obvious sincerity (and vestigial fame) made it work. At another British stop, Springsteen talked about his being 'a grunt in Uncle Sam's army'. The modesty was appealing, though the point of the tale was to twit his ex-Commander-in-Chief again. Springsteen himself didn't provide Reagan's own brand of evangelical fire. He was rather less of the armchair moralist. The wrecking crew of cretinous Republicans – 'rabid fascists', he called them – were still the obvious foe; but Springsteen, to his credit, adapted his war to 'making a difference', so becoming increasingly pragmatic. A radical act, to him, was funding a food bank. As usual, he was less stuck on conventional pieties than on the bottom line. Springsteen had that lethal mix, energy and sound instincts – the sort of character a real fascist would have had shot, lest the energy won power and the instincts made for change. It had: they did.

From Ireland, the spring tour wove a loop through Manchester, Birmingham, Newcastle and Edinburgh. At the last moment, the London shows were shunted back to let Springsteen play the Oscars. He didn't win anything. But it was another well-spent night. Just as Springsteen's celluloid complex had sparked dozens of songs, so his biennial turn now kindled his fame. Global recognition wouldn't come, nor the mainstream be won, nor every nook and cranny fall – in short, stardom couldn't convert into celebrity – unless, like him, you were ready to truck with Hollywood. While Springsteen went to the mat, as it were, with the likes of Elton, Landau stepped over the ropes from ringside to the second's stool. The feat of assimilation that had, against the odds, led to this coup had begun twenty-two years earlier, outside a bar. It was a mutual triumph.

Next to that, let alone the kind of gigs he'd done in the '80s, the Brixton Academy must have seemed like a rehearsal shed. ('Bruce's dogs have better kennels,' says Else. Not big, in other words.) Springsteen twice brought down the house there that April. Backstage, with the cricketer Mark Nicholas, Tim Rice found

'Bruce and Patti [with] all the familiar attributes: wit, charm and a total lack of airs and graces'. Another source confirms that the family provided a welcome contrast to the 'overcaffeinated thugs' who minded them. What Springsteen called the 'uptown shows' at the Albert Hall duly featured droll intros and raps, as well as some serious music. Overall, the latter won through. Seated and suited, the capacity crowd greeted *Joad* with the sort of polite *éclat* Nicholas might have got at a match. Notices were good. The album's title track briefly grazed the singles chart. With that, there followed his contrary sub-set, the one which still indulged a few harmless vanities. Before leaving the country, Springsteen drove out to Sting's house. They celebrated the latter's son's baptism. *Hello!*'s effervescent spread and glossy snaps of the two stars in tails (fresh from singing 'Jerusalem') were just the latest proof that the self-coined 'Jersey punk' and 'Geordie yobbo' had been deep-sixed for good.

And then there was the final jag – less well received – through France, Italy and Spain. Here the shows had little going for them beyond his name. Due to problems of context and translation, Springsteen had been expected with a band, if not *the* band. Speech-singing songs about meth labs, most of which they couldn't fathom, struck some as churlish; as though he'd set out to bite the hand that fed him. The music was of minimum interest. The story of the music, however – or, rather, of the way in which it was swamped by Springsteen's fame – had its own appeal for students of cultural meltdown. There were a few boos. On that note, the European tour ended in Madrid.

Speaking to Katharine Tulich of *The Australian*, Springsteen revealed that, nowadays, even the Joadshows were a family affair. Before agreeing to anything, he held a summit with Scialfa. Tours proceeded on her say-so. At least in the US, he only played during the week, flying home every Friday night. When in Rumson or California, Springsteen worked away at Thrill Hill, his own studio. But, at least in 1996–97, he wasn't there much; not, anyway, in the sense of the average commuting parent. When Springsteen rolled up, it might be for hours or days at a time. But, absent or not, his presence was felt, his voice heard. The Springsteen brood never doubted that they had a strong, demanding, protective father.

Life, in summer, now included two Jersey addresses – Rumson and a ranch at Colts Neck – as well as trips to the shore. Springsteen rose early, breakfasted at eight, wrote, happily 'bec[ame] a five-year-old kid', played, worked again, then rode out to Stope Brook. Scialfa, meanwhile, had a strictly arranged day cutting her second album. The whole tribe might set off in the evening for Asbury, or, if a show were on, New York. Nowadays, their strict rule was to be back by midnight. Springsteen would describe feeling 'centred' on home turf, particularly the farm, 'just wanderin' around with the cows'. This rural idyll was spoken of as if no one else was there. In fact, the Springsteens employed gardeners, cooks, nannies and maids. Terry Magovern bulked large as a joint PA–minder. Security arrangements were elaborate.*

A local woman, Brenda Cooper, once blundered into the tripwires for Springsteen's privacy. She and her daughter decided to 'case' Colts Neck. 'There was a long driveway leading to the house, at this time not even blocked off with a rope or anything else, and she went to drive into it, amongst my protesting, but after about fifty feet she realized that there was no way to discreetly get anywhere near the house, and there were cars at the end of the road, and suddenly two men appeared. She stopped the car, tried to turn around, but the driveway was so narrow, it was almost impossible, and at the same time, these guys came running to the car and asked us for identification. They were Bruce's guards for the joint. One of them took my ID and went back inside, which I later decided I probably shouldn't have given him anyway, since he didn't show me

---

*In October 1996, a 35-year-old man called Blane David Nordahl was arrested on suspicion – though not necessarily guilty – of having stolen millions of dollars of antiques in burglaries up and down the east coast, including one at Springsteen's Rumson house. Nordahl had been wanted for theft in at least six states, according to Lieutenant Richard Yunk of the local Sheriff's Department. 'He specialized in stolen silver goods and even took a test kit along on his heists to check whether the stuff was plate or the real thing,' says Yunk.

his, and I really didn't know for sure who he was, but he said he guarded Bruce, and the other guy watched the kids. He turned out to be okay, but warned us to STAY AWAY.' That gateway was soon blocked off with a chain. A screen of trees was duly planted off Route 54. Three separate signs read 'Beware of the Dog'. The field where Springsteen and Scialfa went riding was, however, fully visible from the road. Brenda Cooper saw them trotting out two weeks later.

The middle-aged Springsteen was richer, happier and more radicalized than the young one. Yet much of it wasn't politics, but ethics. The 1996 presidential election prompted a burst of good citizenship. 'If my work's about anything, it's the search for identity, for personal recognition, for acceptance, for communion, and for a big country,' Springsteen said. 'I've always felt that's why people come to my shows, because they *feel* that big country in their hearts.' Back on tour, he gave freely of his time to the Democratic plank. Those stump speeches and galas won over, even if, as usual, Springsteen listened more than he spoke. He put down two specific markers that autumn. Both were, in part, larks of a kind more popular with the summer-stock crowd. On 7 October, Bob Dole's bus rolled into Red Bank, between Springsteen's Jersey homes, blaring 'Born In The USA'. It was as though 1984 had never happened. Next morning a fax arrived at the *Asbury Park Press*. 'I'd like to make clear that it [the song] was used without my permission,' Springsteen wrote. 'For the record . . . I'm not a supporter of the Republican ticket.'

Three weeks later, he stood in downtown Los Angeles, speaking against Proposition 209 (reining in state affirmative-action laws). Even then, Springsteen leant more to 'good conservatism' than the virgin ideological left. His actual words could have just as well been a Dole's or Reagan's. 'I believe the Promised Land is still attainable . . . Let's stand together in defence of that great Land.' Springsteen did his song of the same title, along with 'No Surrender'. Then he hugged Jesse Jackson.

The vignette confirmed, yet again, that making enemies didn't come naturally to Springsteen. Even after his turn with Jackson, he was working the rope, assuring one woman, 'See, we gotta be inclusive. You, me, even those guys in DC – we're all the same.' Joel Bernstein re-met Springsteen in 1996. He was 'vintage Boss'. Another bottom-line verdict: 'Bruce hated to say no, didn't bear a grudge and, all in all, was dear.' Pete Seeger got much the same impression. The two men co-starred at the Guthrie hootenanny that autumn. Early in 1997, both were then backstage at the Grammys. 'I was in the green room, watching it on a monitor . . . Bruce came in, very quiet, polite. Like me, he enjoyed seeing it on TV more than actually performing. A sweet guy . . . charming.' By the base standards of the pop industry, of course, his reputation as 'sweet' and 'charming' was practically Powellite (Colin, not Enoch). Such extreme niceness, cynics said, could only be masking something ugly. Yet Springsteen carried on much the same way in private, with no hype. Later that year, a producer named Jim Musselman began soliciting songs for a – long overdue – Seeger tribute album. He approached Springsteen and Landau. 'I trusted them, and they followed through. They delivered on their promise.' Springsteen's seven-minute take of 'We Shall Overcome' duly led the bulging, two-CD *Where Have All the Flowers Gone* in March 1998.

To those outside the club, Springsteen in his mid forties was a relic whose easier, not to say effete work flowed from his drearily 'mellow' life. In the Seattle *Times*'s tart view, 'At the moment . . . Bruce himself isn't terribly hip. The music is as good as ever, but he's yesterday's news.' This sort of reaction typified the mainstream. He'd created a cult that was more loyal, more excitable, yet also more mature than anything yet come to the *Times*'s glazed eye. The tabloids, meantime, and those who like to read quickly or need to read slowly, had given up on him in 1988–89. Only rockers with 'attitude' made their cut. And it was precisely his care for the human race, not hatred of it, that fired the vision he put over. (Springsteen's most prized possession, outside of his family, was a signed copy of *Grapes of Wrath* from the author's widow; he had it mounted.) For critics who liked their gods along the lines of Kurt Cobain, the timeless leads – words like 'bold', 'brave' and 'ballsy' going round like drunks in a revolving door – all spoke to a grim truth. Springsteen *was* 'dear'. He used albums, gigs and civics alike to break down some of the arch rock follies, and nurture at least the illusion of community. True, he drove a hard deal, and didn't carp – he was no fool – when the lawyers sued over 'Unearthed', the latest bid to flog his 1972 tapes. During 1996, Springsteen spent almost as much time in attorneys' offices as in the studio. Those who thought of him as above sordidly commercial life were too credulous by half. No one gets so rich, for so long, by fluke. But he was also kind, tough, strong as oak, warm and 'real'. He cared. In any attempt to understand the man it's vital to keep one point clearly in mind. Springsteen was both boss and the Faithful Servant.

He was prodigal son, too, if only because, over the last year, he'd also mellowed towards his past. The St Rose gig was followed by Asbury. By late 1996, Springsteen was regularly doing the new 'In Freehold' alongside 'Adam' and 'My Hometown'. Between them, the three formed a sort of emotional Black Mass for youth. Springsteen's own lost Eden was one where, he said, 'folks talked to folks'. While at his old school, he struck one friend (who showed the requisite local ID in order to purchase a ticket) as 'just a pussy-cat, kind of road-stained but still Bruce'. A second man, who spoke to him backstage, found Springsteen 'nostalgic for the type of fifties vibe he took to a hell of a lot more now than then'. Sentimentally, he was a reactionary, even a 'good Republican'. Above all, Springsteen wanted to save the world that had made men like him.

The American tour signed off in Charlotte on 14 December 1996. Springsteen marked the gig – his 102nd in a year – by making a donation to two local labour unions. Then he flew by Learjet to California. His whole Hollywood life was still mulled over, particularly by Freudians, who made it a field day for theses on Springsteen's divided self; it was at worst a time-out, over which fans shouldn't have been so, he said, 'bent', nor Springsteen so cagey. (Or defensive: he'd moved west, after all, at exactly the same age as his own father.) 'Goin' Cali' was a breather, not a death warrant. As shown by his diaries, and an interview with *Rolling Stone*, Springsteen still rationalized his life in terms of 'booting something back'. The hard core found their most eloquent tribune in a man born, more than ever, to run. 'I certainly don't feel like stopping now,' Springsteen confirmed. By late January, he was back on the road in Tokyo.

When he hit Australia, five shows at the Capitol Theatre, Sydney, sold out in thirty minutes. Scalping was brisk. A local tribute band, They Call Me Bruce, duly took up the slack. (When Springsteen himself slid in to see this skit, at the Crow's Nest Hotel, no one recognized him.) As always, he enjoyed his overseas rides. Springsteen's days generally followed a fixed line. He rose early, a habit beaten into him by fatherhood, ate simply but well, and read slabs of his mail – there were 200 letters daily – before, as he said, 'hauling ass'. Those who watched him yomp up high streets or stop in for a beer saw a darkly clad figure, somewhat short, well proportioned, tailed by Magovern. Springsteen walked slowly, with a hawk eye for detail. (Sidling into a church, he still remembered an unusually tinted side window years later.) He made sightseeing utterly American by being both blandly bonhomous and naïve. Springsteen toted a camera. By what weird alchemy, then, did he also happen to be one of the most admired guests in Australia? For one, he had a natural dignity that seemed to add gravitas. He visited food banks as well as clubs and bars. Springsteen checked the normal rhythms of tourism by working nonstop. Late afternoon would be spent at the sound-check, signing again and ringing home. After the gig proper, Springsteen mingled with the network and mating group which dogged him everywhere. As well as the fans and charities, he always made time for CBS or Sony chiefs. Despite his quiet loathing of 'suits', when it came to practical politics, Springsteen went out of his way to charm. Corporate entertainment took up twelve of his fifteen nights Down Under.

Early in 1997, it was announced that Springsteen had scooped the annual Polar Music award in Sweden. He won $151,000 and a citation for 'his exceptional career as a composer and artist, whose authority is unshakeable . . . an uncompromising steward of the essential qualities of rock'. Six weeks later Springsteen was at the Grammys in Madison Square Garden. *Joad* took Best

Contemporary Folk Album; he did the title track live on TV. There were glittering prizes in London and Rome. Down the way, Springsteen mixed with everyone from Elaine Steinbeck to Gary Bonds. Festooned with medals and gongs, he was lionized both home and away. The ovation he got at St Rose approached that tendered Voltaire on his last trip to Paris, or a campaigning Kennedy. Strangers embraced, men sobbed and swore to love each other. Women became ecstatic. Not only that: Springsteen was the rocker other rockers turned to. He gave career tips to Brian Setzer, Sheryl Crow and Jakob Dylan, huddled with Bono and 'picked up on in a flash' (though didn't produce) Darlene Love. When Sting bought a new, 'must-have' villa in Malibu, he spent first $6 million and then a day in Benedict Canyon. For once, the two superstars discussed not Amnesty or Brazil, but property taxes and zoning. Advice of this sort was vital, but Springsteen, ideally, wasn't the man to give it.

His influence lay under much that was best in modern pop, and under much that was best in modern life. Taking just the first: *Born To Run* gave rise to Graham Parker and most of pub rock, which in turn was a primary source for punk. Even the most wizened folkie loved *Nebraska*. *USA* wooed the Bic-flicking vote, while the three T's – *Tunnel*, *Touch* and *Town* – surrendered themselves up to love. The spooked resonance of *Joad* was unfussily done and, in retrospect, fit well in the tight career plan. No quality of Springsteen's music was rarer than its tilt at these different markets, on so many different levels, in such different ways. Even Dylan, who stood apart from most peers, didn't lag behind them in his tribute to the man who – he told his son – 'can block out a novel in two lines'.

It was ironic, then, that, when Springsteen tried writing in March 1997, he couldn't. The few tracks doodled in Beverly Hills were among his self-styled 'stinkers', dross largely salvaged off *Joad*. The carefully contrived air of spontaneity hid weeks of despair. Writer's block led to the back catalogue. 'Long Time Coming' and a revamped 'Brothers Under The Bridge' were both duly exhumed from the crypt. Later in the year, Springsteen listened to a dozen demos, a medley for the most part of bloodless, nondescript pop.

Played back behind firmly closed doors at Thrill Hill, the tapes revealed a hard fact. All twelve cuts wove cat-and-mouse variations on the same out-take. He ditched the album.

If 1997 was a crisis period, and there were dry months and torn-up songs, what was remarkable wasn't the slump but the speed of recovery; and in the thick of it, Springsteen's refuge, as usual, in the music itself. He went back to the vault. By winter, he was again mining his past – everything from 'Mary Queen Of Arkansas' to 'Brothers'. Work picked up in 1998. Box-set rumours first swirled that spring; stewed over the summer; and swung to a frenzy in the autumn. *Tracks* followed on 10 November. It was a critical and popular hit, if lacking the hoped-for 'legs'. As the album bore down the same line as *Live* (out exactly a dozen years before), few of its fans could have known it was a cry of frustration, or that Springsteen had – in one take – 'literally wept' over his block. The solace wasn't long coming and, when it did, it rebooted him as a chart star. Few improvisations work as well.

Or pay such dividends. Springsteen was Croesus rich. By 1998, he qualified as one of California's top 500 wealthiest people. Financially, he traded on par with the likes of his friends Marlon Brando and Warren Beatty. For Springsteen, releasing *Tracks* amounted to a kind of therapeutic recuperation; he'd made something live again that wasn't even born in the first place. But it did much more. As a happy by-product, the LP also fed a full-scale revival in 1998–99. Even Springsteen's back pages turned gold. Donating 'Philadelphia' to the Princess Diana tribute album (where more people heard it than on film) and seeing *USA* voted one of the 'top hundred records of the millennium' were just the latest proof of Sony's PR blitz, BRUCE IS BACK. The very hint of Springsteen's appearance, that autumn, at a London club caused a riot. His beautifully sustained pose of artlessness paid off. Springsteen *was* back. Even now, he was still clocking up annual sales globally of five million units.

Meantime, the dealers – wild fauna with the added power of reason – circled for scraps. As well as the newsletters, hotlines, flyers, comics, zines and swap-meets, there was both a transatlantic mailing-list and website. A chain of trade-marts trafficked in dregs. In one souk, an old *Born* poster went for $500. In terms of vinyl kudos, *One Step Up/Two Steps Back* was out that winter. Kurt Neumann flung 'Atlantic City' at the chart. The band Glory Days, among others, plied a lucrative covers trade. In London, the singer Mark Wright sold out an 'Acoustic Feast of Boss Music'. These were all great 'daylight fans', who tended to skip the torments, horrors, fears, pain and angst in the black night of their hero's CV. Among depth writers, only Richard Williams, perhaps, pursued the man to his final meaning – and Williams had been first to 'rock and roll future'.

Between hard covers, Springsteen's view of himself in *Who's Who* aimed for altitude. He was an 'International Singer and songwriter; producer; winner of Grammy Awards'. It may be unfair to single out an entry in the reference books, but the worse he got, it seemed, the better his copy. Both Gene Santoro's *Stir It Up* and Chuck Werner's *A Change is Gonna Come* treated Springsteen as a cultural icon. More was to come: his rebirth as Lincoln's heir, and a key influence on American civics. This culminated in 1997 in an entire book on the subject by one Jim Cullen, which gave the impression that Springsteen's whole life jogged down a track from 'Thoreau, Whitman and Steinbeck . . . as a chronicler of his society and a catalyst for social change, [he's] every bit the equal of his illustrious antecedents'. That the epic view of Springsteen was something of a stretch the preceding pages have, perhaps, shown; and, at another end, a reaction set in which nailed him as an ephemeral chancer – a musicologist not a musician, who, in Charlie Gillett's phrase, 'stepped back inside' as early as 1975. This, too, was an inadequate snap of the man.

Springsteen certainly had his court. Without, men like Cullen offered a nice face on the cover and solid pulp inside. Within, Landau, Carr and Magovern, among others, acted as a DMZ between him and the world. Springsteen was now less the party animal, more the spouse; long since pension-funded against the market. His own commercial Dow Jones still rose on hints of a full tour. It wasn't likely. Springsteen only rarely saw the band. He didn't keep up with many of his old gang. Knowing him, they understood the reason was simply that he was too busy with other things and rapt with other people in other places. Most accepted it, and were still as vigilant of him as ever. But there was some sense, not least in E Street, of rejection, of being dumped.

Springsteen himself was unaware of this, since it was an experience he hadn't had for years; nobody ever refused him anything, one man says, simply because you didn't refuse a force of nature. That's how many of them saw him, as outside the norm, above and beyond the trivia of 'real dudes'. 'You call, and he may not call back,' one says. 'You have to leave that up to him.'

To his credit, Springsteen *was* aware of the mad, celebrity-crazed culture that had made him, whose ghosted, pat fiction fed the myth. He made a study of it. 'The size is tricky, it's dangerous,' he told *Rolling Stone*. 'You can become purely iconic, or you can become just a Rorschach test that people throw up their own impressions on . . . with size, and the co-option of your images and attitudes – you know, you wake up and you're a car commercial.' He was speaking of Bossmania, but Springsteen still hammered the point years later, in 1995, when he called himself a 'meat by-product in the US food chain'. As a star who could be both arch and real, sometimes at once, he knew all about the trivializing side of fame. That same year, *Joad*'s 'My Best Was Never Good Enough' fused Jim Thompson's *zeitgeist*-alert *Killer Inside Me* with the pop-struck *Forrest Gump*. Another friend tells the tale of Springsteen sitting in Beverly Hills 'regaling nine or ten of us about how American heroes – he jerked a thumb in the direction of Hollywood – become cartoons. He counted himself.' These weren't the acts of a 'half-bright *putz*', as Springsteen put it, 'from Jersey'.

He spent the summer there, 'hanging with the kids' and occasionally surfacing at some dive on the shore. Springsteen stage-hopped less than before. By retreating so fully – with no photo ops or interminable *Hello!* spreads – he turned the tables on the celebrity game. He became an absence, not a presence. Springsteen could have supercharged his oldies with an E Street tour or flamed his message on more films. Instead he chose a six-month blockbuster of domesticity. He plied his art not in domes and stadia but in the nursery. Springsteen sang his brood to sleep every night. Then he and Scialfa might sit on the porch, picking their guitars. A friend reports their duets to have been 'largely Bruce's odds and sods'. The off-duty equivalent of editing *Tracks*.

The couple did travel together, to Europe, that May. On the 5th, Springsteen was in Stockholm to receive the *de facto* Nobel prize for music, the Polar. He met the King of Sweden. Then he mini-toured *Joad*. Those dozen dates (none in Britain) were less to do with Steinbeck than with Springsteen himself, who, with the liber-ation that only a man with his wife's panties in his pocket can know, did his randiest gigs in years. In particular, 'Red Headed Woman' became a skit. For anyone missing it, Springsteen's cunnilingus rap – mimed on his knees – slaveringly made the point. The critics' own failure to give tongue was oddly reminiscent of the respect shown an Elton or Clapton, in that even their gaffes become such a part of the public vocabulary (those gushy, empathetic lows and manic highs) that everyone gets in on the act. The crowds lapped it up. Next, he floored them in Warsaw with a catchy riff about Prince Charles wanting to be a tampon. And finally, Springsteen told fans at the Palais des Congrès, Paris, that he used to feel 'kinda dorky around *les chicks*'. He loved himself too much for that now. The rest of the turn, *Joad*'s last ever, Springsteen had the dopey look of someone, as he said, 'blissed out', sex- and otherwise. He went on to tell the audience that he'd enjoyed playing his acoustic sets 'more than anything else I've done . . . And I don't just go down. I go *back*.'

Springsteen was generous to younger acts whenever possible because he knew their terror himself. As late as 1997 he wrote: 'I always feel like shit when I start a new job.' He was also completely free of petty jealousy. 'Any rock and roller who thinks of himself as a man would rather die so someone better can live,' he said. Springsteen's confidence and code moulded his own policy. Thus, he befriended Jakob Dylan. Not only that, he played host, for sev-eral days, to the Wallflowers. That fall, he graced the MTV awards (where 'Secret Garden' lost out) and led the group through 'One

Headlight', itself an up-tempo take on 'Independence Day'. Springsteen sat in with Grushecky and Bobby Bandiera. He specifically authorized (as he hadn't *Cover Me*, let alone *Songs from the Boss*) *One Step Up*. For long chunks of 1997–98, in the absence of anything new, he was kept alive largely through the patronage of Right Stuff and the Princess Diana LP. As the year wore on, Springsteen's block continued. He wasn't doing any serious work, not even pretending to write, though he still doodled with *Tracks*. Various producers, and production means – involving his own satellite uplink between LA and New York – were tried. Avon Books came calling. A lyrics anthology was mooted. Even that didn't help. Springsteen was also depressed by the flood of guests, some welcome, some not so, at Colts Neck and Rumson. Sting visited with his wife.

Not mingling with, or even much liking the glitterati – as opposed to starving artists – was very profoundly what Springsteen was about. He preferred family. When in Jersey, he spent weeks with them on the two estates. After Memorial Day, seclusion might not rule out a stint on the public beach at Sea Bright. Or Springsteen would spend an afternoon with his clan at the Chaple Club. He not only ferried his children round, but rapidly became a kind of car-pool for their six- and seven-year-old peers. First-graders at Markham Place school found themselves picked up by the VIP in his black Explorer and chauffeured to parties the length of Monmouth County. According to one parent who prefers anonymity, 'It was sort of weird, but cute to see him running around, kids all over, yelling things like "Giddyup" and " 'Board for the Chaple choo-choo." There was no stopping him. I mean, Bruce was always the designated driver.'

'The last time up, I had a very supportive audience,' Springsteen said. 'And what went on between then and now was getting together a whole part of me I never had in focus.' He was speaking in Sydney, where, in 1985, he'd been met by BOSSY headlines and brawls at the airport. It was the very town where he admitted 'not even know[ing] how to act' offstage. Now, a dozen years on, Springsteen was trying to learn about life beyond the boards. It was the late nineties, and he appeared more new boy than boss. Like so many Boomers around the world he was, as he said, 'starting over'. Again, he was right on the *zeitgeist*; after all, he was Springsteen. Motor-pooling was only one sign of the male paragon, not above housework, wearing jeans and a baseball cap. The look said: Ignore me.

In fact, no one took advantage of Springsteen's informality and public forays. Whether in Jersey or California, a cortège followed at a safe distance. More minders were detailed on tour, much to Springsteen's unease, since he hated violence. A secretary and valet rounded off the train. Meanwhile, two full-time offices operated in Los Angeles and New York. Springsteen was both well advised and seemingly cool about money; yet he couldn't seem quite to ever get off the topic, harping on about how he 'gave a shit' until, in the end, friends had no choice but not to believe him. He was run like an empire. Landau, not indifferent to his own interests, was rabidly defensive of his charges'. (By 1999 he also handled Scialfa, Natalie Merchant and Shania Twain.) The daily grind of paperwork and visitors was precisely his forte. At fifty-two, Landau was a squat, soft-looking man who favoured rumpled clothes and blade-sharp deals. He spoke straight to the gist. Lawyers and bankers took to him as one of their own. Landau's spiels never disintegrated into vacuous trendiness. Royalties and residuals were famously his bag, as much as charts and click tracks. If he was a businessman, he was also a Renaissance Man. Landau was happily married. It wasn't thus for all his colleagues. According to a female friend, one of Springsteen's inner court would enjoy a kind of anal-erotic romp with groupies 'trying to hump their way to Bruce'. The bottom line that vexed Landau, by contrast, was his client's annual $8–10 million turnover. The woman's slur about such sums 'puckering Jon's nipples' is obviously vile; but still speaks to a view people had of him. As a critic, Landau had arguably conformed to the type of limited souls recycling the values of their equally so-so models. As a rock tsar, he was peerless. If, despite sharing a name, he wasn't producer of *Titanic*, that must have been his sole ship not to come in. At the level of dealing with Sony (whom he only ever met at board level), in particular, Landau stalked the jungles of corporate HQ, impressing even a prey as 'brilliantly organized. Jon's skills are numerical and instinctive . . . there's nothing of the "teen tycoon" there. What you're dealing with is a suit.'

It was much to Springsteen's credit, therefore, that he voluntarily began making amends to his old E Street alumni. Now the caddie at a golf club, Lopez, for one, banked his first cheque in 1998. 'It makes me feel like all the work I put in was worth it,' he says. 'Bruce did it all on his own. His lawyers, working with Sony, came up with figures to pay us.' The band's *ex gratia* fees would rise in 1999. Springsteen also quietly lent or gave money around Freehold. Not surprisingly, he continued to do the right thing by Phillips. He and his ex, groping her way back in films like *Big Bully*, were fully friendly again. When he reviewed his conscience as regards family, especially Doug and Adele, Springsteen, now more than ever, made his point. He'd grown. He *had* developed a part of him he 'never had in focus'.

If, from time to time, Springsteen's music had depended on the kindness of strangers, fans or even hacks, he reciprocated in full. As for his extended family, he was a warm, considerate boss, sincere in his belief in what they were doing and, an insider says, 'the kind of man who, when he talked to you, you thought he was homed in like a radar'. Following down a line from Landau and Carr, a woman named Jan Stabile ran the office. Sandra Choron did Springsteen's art and, in time, helped broker his lyrics book. Like Batlan before him, Kevin Buell (also, with Magovern, a 'graduate of Clemons U') tuned the gear. Marilyn Laverty, the photographer Neal Preston and untold lawyers and agents all padded his well-heeled existence. Witness his comments in Sydney, the more Springsteen grew, the more he described what he was doing in self-analytical terms. He told one crowd, for instance, he'd had the same affair 'for twenty years with a few chicks' before a shrink 'charged me a fuckin' *lot*' to learn how to change; a variation on the theme he'd flogged, mainly in interviews, for a decade. As a rule, his breast-beating expanded in parallel with the bliss of his home life. For certain audiences, it could grate. But, to those who knew him best, it made Springsteen a model husband, a loyal colleague and, above all, a good friend. His office life was marked by an unheard-of niceness – equally to serfs and tsars. Springsteen was kind to juniors, open with partners, generous even toward rivals. He was, one says, 'supremely fair'.

The year rounded out with two anniversaries. Following on his St Rose gig in 1996, he showed his charm and unfaltering nostalgia for his hometown fans. If he was also curious, he wasn't alone. On 28 November 1997, Springsteen attended his class's thirtieth, and his first, high school reunion. Even the Holiday Inn at Tinton Falls, east of Freehold, could have seen no stranger sight, nor one less likely a few years earlier. His sixty peers, long since vanished into sales or drudge jobs in the system, stood in line as he and Scialfa orbited through the room, laughing – and there were no airs at all. One of the documents turned up by the roadies' lawsuit had been a 'waiver of rights' by which Springsteen's employees absolved him of 'any and all . . . monies, debts, damages, obligations' as well as 'any and all oral promises' he might make them; on top of which was a confidentiality contract signed by all staff. Something like the latter was tacitly understood at Tinton Falls, where, according to one woman breaking ranks, 'the gag order was sealed by phone calls binding us to silence'. In the end, all, initially, went well. 'Bruce slapped a lot of backs. He was funny, warm, looked you dead in the eye. You never met anyone less like a pop star.' After three hours of this a middle-aged man, refuelled by trips to the bar, made a speech. His list of demands of Springsteen was long – very long. The least of it was that he sing 'Glory Days'. As people shuffled from foot to foot, the woman turned to her companion. 'This stinks,' she said. 'Bruce doesn't want to be treated like Elvis. What will he think?' She'd never know. In true Presley style, Springsteen had already left the building.

A week later, another side of life entirely – Washington. Springsteen was there to play the twentieth annual Kennedy Center gala, specifically to honour Bob Dylan. On the night of 6 December, he shaved and climbed into the soup-and-fish for a formal banquet at the State Department. Later, as Clinton rose and a band in dress uniform struck up, Springsteen peered round the hall, all marble and candelabras – a 'morgue with protocol', as Lauren Bacall puts it. Even in that dark, bomb-proof suite, chopped-up moonlight came through the flecked glass. The art deco lifts had gilded gates. Springsteen, says his partner, was the 'bland good guy. Very shy; very – as he put it – shitstruck.' Another guest swears she heard him rasp, 'Well, we ain't in Kansas any more.' Clinton himself (as other matters, pertaining to impeachment, claimed his time) declined to comment for this book. But it's certain he asked Springsteen for his autograph. The show itself, next day, was a staged-spoken extravaganza. Springsteen vied with the ilk of Bacall, Jerome Robbins and Lynn Redgrave. Even in that company, his act shone. Aptly, he chose to dwell on Dylan's role in the '60s. 'The yearning in America for an open and just society just exploded. Bob had the courage to stand in that fire and capture the sound . . . It was a beautiful call to arms.' As a final salute, Springsteen sang 'The Times They Are A-Changin''.

For most of 1998, Springsteen was a boy at a table groaning with sweets. Uncharacteristically, he didn't eat them all. Nowadays, he turned down as many gigs, at least formally, as he took. As for bar-hopping, there's no doubt he still enjoyed the chance to belt a few oldies from the poky stages, bulging out with knots and lumps, of shacks like the Pony. He played these fire-traps for fun, not fame. Springsteen refused anything that might have been considered self-aggrandizing or hyped. In fact, some nights, singing from under the peak of his cap, swathed in scarves, he came on as the Invisible Man – an unconscious metaphor for his later life. Whether roasting the Dylans or mugging with fellow Jerseyans like Bon Jovi, Springsteen's sub-career of matey cameos continued, though less so than before. As his friend says, 'you call, and he may not call back'. Particularly in summer, rumours regularly did the rounds of the shore clubs. Many of these dives, already dodgy enough, had question marks routinely, if figuratively daubed over their signage.

Thus, in the space of a few months, Springsteen joined Steve Earle at Sea Bright's Tradewinds. He read verse from a stage in Red Bank. And he jammed with Joe Grushecky (launching the latter's second album, *Coming Home*). More to the point were the sort of gigs he missed. On 29 March, Springsteen was a no-show at the 'Dead Man Walking' gala in Los Angeles. Hosted by Tim Robbins and Helen Prejean (who wrote the book on which the film was based), it helped float a raft of social-uplift charities. The likes of Earle, Lyle Lovett and Eddie Vedder all sang. There was a rare set from Tom Waits. Yet most of these modestly gifted, if worthy turns were accorded the same ovation as death-row clemency appeals: muted. The hoped-for headliner never showed. Quizzed on Springsteen's absence, Robbins would say only: 'Ask his management.' A wry story, in this vein, is told by a staffer, who was once asked 'how Bruce picks his dates'. The woman answered that if Springsteen got a whiff of his name being used, or the show milked, the problem was solved if he pulled out. To outsiders, it might seem odd, even quirky, that an act, once booked, would cry off. Not everyone made the same distinction between being coy and capricious. But most stars of Springsteen's magnitude, knowing his guest policy, would recognize its sense. Even with no advance billing, such gigs as he did instantly became orgies. At least fifty times every performance, a cry of 'Rosalita!' or 'Hungry Heart!' would surge up from the pit.

It could have been this very factor at work over Easter 1998. That Good Friday, one Belfast daily carried the front-page splash that Tony Blair (a known fan) had asked Springsteen to 'come over to toast the Irish peace'. It didn't happen. Apparently the commonest mistake by even celebrity promoters was to assume that he wouldn't mind being co-opted. But Springsteen did mind. Hence his snub to both political camps in 1984. Those had been rebuttals; this, in PR lingo, a 'prebuttal'. He missed the Stormont gig for an NBA game in New York. Similarly, Springsteen failed to make a Beverly Hills smoker after officials there leaked his name. He did, however, play at *Rolling Stone*'s thirtieth birthday. That was for love.

Probably Springsteen's childhood and his fear of exploitation kept him dancing out of reach. But the occasional fit of truculence didn't, and couldn't, detract from the core truth: his obvious devotion, his almost paternal pride in America, his self-effacing charm and concern with the lost. It had been clear, for some time now, that Springsteen wasn't out of the Sid Vicious school. That he still cared – cared more than ever – rang out in the interview he gave Anthony DeCurtis. 'People deserve the right to work, and when you rob someone of that right, you're robbing them of an enormous part of their life . . . There's got to be some rebalancing of the fundamental forces that move American society and the American economy. I wouldn't presume to know what the answer is. There are many complicated issues, but, hey, there are many people of good will. There are some ports in the storm. But there aren't enough right now.' This local variation on 'something must be done' bore a personal edge. As Grice says, 'it's a cinch, buried there in the lyrics, Bruce never quite got over them closing that rug mill'. After more than thirty years, Doug's own 'shit' still cut deep.

That same spring, the 300-seat Bay Street Theatre in Sag Harbor, New York, honoured Elaine Steinbeck. Apart from her marriage, she'd been among the first female managers on Broadway, an author and activist. There was also the fact that she was a red-headed woman. It was hard to conceive of a life more full of resonance for Springsteen. He not only sat next to her in the front row. At the finale, he serenaded the house with 'Tom Joad'. To call it a quietly dramatic tribute, low-strung and lazy, would be to pay it the highest compliment. Even Springsteen's odd tantrums paled once a hero, or friend, hove into view. Of the latter, Mitch Ryder says simply, 'Bruce gave more than he took.' Another man adds: 'If you got past "management channels", Springsteen was always or usually cool. He came through. A very steady lad.'

To Springsteen, the basic reward of public life was working with such people, notably – after some mutual dirt in the early '90s – Jerseyans. Most of the spring and autumn, and all summer were spent in his home state. More and more, Springsteen gravitated to the Colts Neck farm. It emerged, after years of repair, as one of those idylls where a red barn rises from a dip in the hills with fields and pastures beyond, browned in the heat, and strains of music and laughter can be heard coming from the elegant, shingled house. Horses and chickens roamed about. Only a double row of

Range Rovers and BMWs, choking the narrow lane out front (now bathed in spotlights) testified to it being a pop star's lair. It was that kind of spread. Springsteen not only came back to roost; witness the local gigs, his class reunion and bonuses for the likes of Lopez, his Jersey life rested on a deep-seated love of its people.* Early that year, he reunited two-thirds of the E Street Band to join, among others, Bon Jovi at the Count Basie Theatre, Red Bank. The night was a benefit for the widow of Patrick King, a slain New Jersey lawman. Hit after hit soared out of the full-length set, the nearest to classic Springsteen in ten years, and further proof that, to him, 'where you come from is like your family and best friend'. Nowadays, he didn't distinguish between the two.

It was sad, then, and poignant, that Doug Springsteen died that April. He was seventy-three. In a statement, Bruce said: 'My father and I had a very loving relationship . . . I feel lucky to have been so close to my dad as I became a man and a father myself.' A funeral mass was held at St Rose. It was among the most sorry ironies of a life not untouched by shadow that Doug's death should have come at the very moment his son, after ten years of gradual thaw, had finally warmed to him. This blow, too, contributed to Springsteen's block. He still ground out tunes on his Takamine, but mostly for himself. Now, under management pressure, he had to kiss off his career or somehow rationalize his slump by turning back. He chose the archive.

Then came word, sifted through the mists slowly, like an old Soviet health report, that Springsteen was ill. He was in seclusion. Sessions with Gary Mallabar had been ditched. Springsteen was resting, he was working; he was on either coast, or in between. The hotlines fanned the rumours all summer. In fact, Springsteen wasn't physically sick. He was, though, depressed, forgetful and edgy, painfully aware, in clear-eyed moments, of betraying his own code of constant creativity. This increased his gloom. As well as his

---

*Springsteen's kindness and nostalgia didn't, however, in the end stretch to saving the Stone Pony. In late 1998, after a series of crises and near-closures, it converted into a dance hall.

family and odd forays to Hollywood, his few work projects had 'stopgap' written all over them. There were plans for Scialfa's second LP. He cut a tune, salvaged from *Touch*, called 'Gave It A Name'. Mostly, Springsteen flicked through his back pages, combing the material that became *Songs* and *Tracks*. (Predictably, mixing, or remixing, the latter took months, an epic involving the uplink, Landau, Plotkin, Clearmountain and two studios.) In the meantime, he had to cope. Just three weeks after Doug, Frank Sinatra also died. When America came to mourn at the funeral, there was Springsteen alongside Sophia Loren and Nancy Reagan.

It wasn't a great summer. But Springsteen himself, in his best moments, dissipated the whole Freudian syndrome of 'guilt-angst-sado-shame' which might have applied to lesser mortals. At the worst moment of his block – the day he threw a master tape out of the window – he could still seize on the liberation of art, or the part of it based on self-insight, affection and humour. *Tracks* cured him. (After the final edit of the final cut, he even began writing again.) Even now, there was enough to thrill any sentient friend. Jim Mahlmann met Springsteen one night at the T-Bird Club in Asbury. 'I got drunk and kind of mouthed off at him, but Bruce just smiled.' Similarly, a builder working on the Colts Neck farm speaks of him as a 'wink-and-nod guy – sort of gruff, but not one to lord it. He always brought out the coffee and Danish.' At least one of Springsteen's navvies guessed what only intimates fully knew; that he 'had a bark' but, in fact, 'not much of a bite'. He'd changed, of course. These days, Springsteen vented in his therapist's office more than backstage or at the studio. Musically, he'd long since shifted down. 'People don't stay the same,' he informed the *New York Times*. 'When I wrote *Greetings*, those lyrics felt like life to me. I wouldn't know how to do that now. I couldn't write another "Thunder Road", either. I wouldn't want to.' Physically, too, not much remained of the tow-haired Newarky. Springsteen had a fuller face and the start of a double chin. (The teeth, though, were exquisite, and much in evidence at his few public appearances.) Of late, his swagger had become a creaky, two-legged stutter. He loped.

In terms of his own job spec ('My gig is to write new songs'), there'd been little to cheer in three years. Even his soundtracks were of a piece. 'Missing' and the rest – like the ones he licensed to Demme or Ed Burns – were fine distillations of both the intensity of life and the abyss under it, but they basically retrod *Joad*. Springsteen returned to it time and again. Even now, he was in discussion with HBO over a series of films based on the album. By 1998, his cult, arguably, was built on the flimsy ground of a slow revolve. That and residual loyalty still kept the clubs and bazaars open all hours. As well as *Backstreets* and *The Ties That Bind*, there were 'Boss' titles in Spain, Holland and Hungary. Belgian fans could dial a Flemish-language chatline. From the mid-Atlantic states to Manila, thousands of scholar-squirrels went about their theme-spotting and hoarding. Springsteen's own personal Dow Jones, the collectibles and covers market, showed no signs of crashing. Of the tribute bands and clones, Melissa Etheridge and Bryan Adams were only the most brazen. In Berlin, a truck-driving singer called Gerhard Gundermann styled himself the 'Bruce of the east' – until he died unexpectedly in 1998, aged forty.

Early that fall, Springsteen mixed the sixty-sixth and final cut of *Tracks*. He declined, ultimately, to enter into the briar patch of the Pony's finances; the club took its last ride as a rock venue on 20 September. Springsteen did, though, celebrate his forty-ninth birthday by throwing a hoedown at Cheers in Long Branch. (A C&W band murdered 'Red Headed Woman'.) Aside from the editing suite and the beach, his main natural habitat was the ballpark. Anyone who knew Springsteen – the man who'd seriously offered himself as a strike buster – was well aware of the constant yearning for Arcadia, for anything redolent of a world governed by leather on ash. He loved baseball. At Rumson, Grammys and Oscars jostled for space with his Little League Hall of Excellence gong. (Springsteen coached his son Evan's team.) He was a fixture in the New York Yankees' clubhouse. There was the ritual exchange of guitar and bat with Mark McGwire. When Joe DiMaggio fell critically ill that Christmas, Springsteen did more than send flowers. He broke down when he heard the news. Not that he pined just for the Yankee Clipper *per se*. It cut deeper than that. Reflecting on the past and good old days, he told one co-worker, 'Even the bees don't buzz the same any more.' It was funny, and had the bonus of being sad. That bittersweet quip spoke volumes for Springsteen's sense of age and regret.

As for taking a shine to that other old gem, the band, Springsteen still faced down the pop equivalent of PM's Questions. There were few answers. Even when he did broach the subject, orchestrated 'corrections' promptly followed. Thus, on 17 July 1998, Springsteen announced *Tracks* at a Sony sales meet. Asked about tour plans, he smiled and said, 'Everyone . . . I mean . . . you guys'll be happy.' The suits rushed to the obvious conclusion. Not so fast, Springsteen then warned. 'Everybody's got their own lives and families, which they didn't have before,' he told the press, helpfully. Still, 'if the opportunity [to play] presented itself, I think we'd enjoy it. It's always a sub-text.' For the rest of the autumn, the spin-doctors and flaks teased the story, with various unlikely types taking turns to play good and bad cop. No sooner did agent say 'no' than manager said 'maybe'. Sources close to Springsteen, meanwhile, yielded to pressure to brief pet hacks, who in turn fed the frenzy. So it went. It was a strange, sometimes low year, but even he must have sat up at how it ended: with grown men debating the exact nuances of 'you guys'll be happy'.

For Springsteen, then, the *fin de siècle* meant business as usual. Comeback rumours buzzed. The circulars and zines made use of the concept of positive thinking. 'People' columns copied. In fact, for a host of reasons, an E Street tour was more likely now than ever. For one thing, the band themselves no longer cared quite as much. Ten years on, most or all of them had finally reconciled to being dumped. Some of the stress – the kind that led one member to call them 'blood donors, not brothers' – had given way to a wary consensus. 'We didn't hold our breath,' the same man says. Meantime, Springsteen pulled back from his own policy ('I'll fix their hash'), largely in response to 130 straight Joadshows. He duly missed what he called the 'chemistry and shit'. The regular reports on public opinion, of which he was well aware, also showed a majority in favour of reviving the group from behind their marble slab. For that matter, this rock equivalent of the unquiet dead, it now emerged, had never been buried in the first place. Springsteen told one writer he'd always planned to alternate E Street gigs with solo ones. 'I simply want to do both things, like Neil Young does with Crazy Horse,' he explained. 'He'll go off with different musicians, and then he'll come back and play with Crazy Horse when he has something that feels right for them.' Fair enough: it was the line about 'the guys still [being] my bridge to the fans' that took the breath away. In fact, they were part of a continuum: he wrote for them, they played for him. This particular fantasy could only have come from the same source that drafted 'My father and I had a very loving relationship.' It wasn't that Shore Fire lied, of course. They just chose among different versions of the truth.

Reunion gossip was well timed. Not only was Springsteen banking his past in 1998. He also took it to law. An old hand at the piracy and bootlegging wars, he fought on two related fronts that winter. First, Springsteen defended a writ by Pony Express Records, denying their claim to own rights to his 'early recordings', a point he also made to JEC Music. The second suit was a sequel of the long-running *Prodigal Son* saga. Springsteen had reached a deal with Dare International as far back as December 1994. He acted when much the same material re-emerged, in 1996, as 'Unearthed'. Now, yet again, Springsteen's copyright row got its regular biennial airing. The events of late 1998 won him his most 'straight' press since 1985. Then, of course, he'd been the man of whom a High Court justice had been heard to ask, 'Who is he . . . a pop star?' This time round, the judge not only knew all about Springsteen. He, too, asked for his autograph.

Springsteen first appeared in court on the morning of 6 October. Dressed in a dark grey suit, grey shirt and tie, he could have been taken for one of his own counsel. He was accompanied by a Sony manager, his barrister Nigel Davis and a bodyguard. They took seats in the front row, immediately opposite Masquerade Music and their lawyers. For most of the first two days, Springsteen sat bolt upright, frequently scribbling notes and poring over the documents as they were read. 'I must say I'm finding it fascinating,' he allowed at the adjournment, just before the minder cut off any more heady remarks. Later, he entertained the press pack, posed and hummed snatches of 'Sandy'. He went for a pint. On the 8th, Springsteen made his sole appearance in the witness box. Although imagining himself in a death feud over 'control of my art', he wasn't gag-free. At one stage Davis asked him if he wanted a glass of water. 'I'm fine,' said Springsteen. 'I always sound like this.' The actual grilling had more to do with the Appel era than arcane patent law. Spectators saw a man clearly edgy, often evasive, gamely insisting, for instance, that he was 'flat broke' until 1977. He kept his anger in check, though, and most of the media seemed to sympathize with the target of what appeared to be a rip-off. Springsteen flew home on Concorde that weekend; came back to London early Monday; listened to Masquerade's case on Tuesday; then left.

He was in court again for the actual verdict two months later. Mr Justice Ferris allowed him his injunction. He also awarded Springsteen £500,000 costs against Masquerade, whose lawyers said they would appeal. According to the terms of the judgement, he was free to seek damages of £2 million. 'I wasn't here for the money,' Springsteen said. 'I came to defend my right to my music . . . What you release is the way you shape your career. It's a big part of what you say and the way you say it. What you come up with when you're sitting alone with your guitar late at night is one of the most personal things in your life.' With that, Springsteen left for Paris, where he performed at a charity gig for Amnesty.

One-sided or not, the tabloids set a tone for coverage of the hearing and raised awareness, among non-fans, that Springsteen was alive and well. BRUCE SHOWS WHO'S BOSS was only the set headline. Into the arid pages of law reports flocked words like 'gig' and 'track', while the broadsheets wandered to the new territory of 'rock-biz' like gaunt Tennessee farmers and their families in mule-drawn carts. The wisdom was that his case had been well put. Not for the first time since 1976–77, he'd enshrined pop in principle. The judge was quite right to award him the cash. Most of the home media, up- and down-market, splashed the story on their front pages. Two classes benefited from this ritual: the press them-selves, who sold more papers, and Sony chiefs, who saw Springsteen stock soar in the weeks ahead. For the latter, one says, it was a 'very boss Christmas'.

By happy timing, the official back catalogue, *Tracks*, was out that fall. As well as the four CDs of sixty-six songs (fifty-eight previously unreleased), there was a fifty-six-page booklet and a mini photo album. Logistically, if nothing else, it was a coup. *Tracks* became both a substantive and substantial hit. Springsteen's ploy worked. If the best records, like ships, are measured by their displacement, then there, too, he scored highly. *Tracks* displaced everything. This holy grail of LPs was like *Live* once again. Even the pre-hype, in the months leading up to 10 November, reminded those with ele-phantine memories of his last box set. By mid September the trade and press were in overdrive. In October, WNEW in New York began playing 'three leaked songs' in heavy rotation. As the clock ticked off to B-Day, there was no doubt the Maniacs (so named again) would impose their ecstatic vision on cynics. It was a second coming. Anyone with $70 and four hours to kill would, and did, love it. Springsteen's first LPs had set an early standard that led fol-lowers to await each new project with fanatical glee. Though *Tracks* mildly dashed such hopes with questionable choices – where was 'The Fever'? – the album duly rose as though stoked by Viagra. It was a critical and popular smash.

In particular, some of the chrome-plated *River* cast-offs chimed in with those that actually made the cut. The acoustic 'USA', done before it was bludgeoned to death, was exquisite. Even the later material rustled up a fair quota of Springsteen's finest hours, such as 'Lucky Man'. The fluid yet bruising E Streeters had never sounded better. Yet again, it was the band's versatility, the way they could swing out or keep it short and sharp as a ransom note. Clemons' bag, for one, was delightfully of no fixed abode. With an alchemist's touch, he turned sweet soul into pop flash. Both keyboardists offered their own virtuoso twists. Even Weinberg gave due expres-sive weight to the grave beauty of a 'Roulette'. Yet, ultimately, it was Springsteen's triumph. *Tracks* showed how one man could lyrically speak for millions and then throw in twenty or thirty classic tunes. It worked a cryogenic miracle. The box set was a well-deserved showcase for genius.*

Further daylight came in on the myth in *Songs*, Springsteen's coffee-table tome of photos, lyrics and linking text. Often the essays were rich stuff; the story of his writing 'Born To Run' was masterly. But the quality that most shone out of the book was innocence. The best bits, and the best songs, were fables by a man who still believed in truth, justice, happiness and the pursuit of good, while being well aware of their opposites. The class of the individual entries could even make Springsteen's doggerel seem better than it was. No one would guess from *Songs* how over-the-top *Greetings* had been, and the way he humanized *Nebraska*, an album about as warm and cuddly as a razor, bore the imprint of a true author. Springsteen's prose was vivid, uninhibited and crisply phrased, with enough jolts of insight for any fan. 'You can follow a song from its inception through to the finished product and see all the bad verses I threw out,' he told *USA Today*. Any such glimpse of the creative process would have been unthinkable a few years before. 'I've always enjoyed working in private,' he said. 'But over time, you tend to have more flexibility. Everything seems like less of a big deal now.' Except, of course, it wasn't: that winter there was one fit after another, starting with *Tracks* and all fuelled by E Street gossip. Once again, as the *Post* put it, 'Bruce [was] back' – official.

When the copy came to be written, there was no doubt it would be hard. The coverage that began to well up in October had a special quality, a kind of mania. There were raves in the *Wall Street Journal* and *Washington Post*. Even *Time* revisited the scene of 1975. A few friends worried about how Springsteen would take to being duly exhumed. As it happened, he was utterly at home with the hype. For once, he even collaborated in it. Breaking his no-TV rule, Springsteen sat for an hour on the *Charlie Rose Show* and performed a decidedly 1982 'USA'. That same night, he turned up on

---

*Also out that winter, the altogether chunkier affair *Deep Down in the Vaults* went the bootleg equivalent of gold.

MTV. Next he was the star of *Legends* and *A Secret History* on, respectively, VH-1 and BBC2. All that was missing, by then, was his own Christmas special. Springsteen was an acutely self-conscious interviewee – at once studied and casual – and an active stage-manager of his own myth, with a bent to wordy screeds on humanity. But he could also debunk the PR. Nor was he averse to laughing at himself. The overall impression was of a well-meant man, self-educated, who, for all his particular gifts, his love–hate for America, and its concomitant hate–love for fame, wasn't untypical of most adults who've 'worked' on themselves. His therapy shone through.

Some remarked on the ingenious way Springsteen pointed up his enthusiasms – the way he'd mention, for example, reading Erskine Caldwell late into the night. 'I think there's a little insecurity,' says an old friend. 'But he's street-wise, catches on fast and works like a dog. He may not be Einstein, but he's sharp.' For many, it was Springsteen's good sense and graft they most admired, his negotiation of give and take, not any abstract smarts. By now, three years on from *Joad* and two into creative block, he rarely stopped. Whether fronting for Amnesty, honouring Johnny Cash or winding a loop through Scandinavia, Europe and back home to flog *Tracks*, he took almost every gig offered. Between times, early in 1999, Springsteen again began recording. *18 Tracks*, making a greatest-hits of an anthology, duly followed. He planned to 'ship something', he said, this side of the millennium.

The deadline wasn't generous. Even the acoustic songs he cut in March and April went through scores of edits. Most listeners might not notice what he was doing, adding carefully detailed guitar parts over deceptively spare riffs – not to mention buffing the words. They might even think it sounded spontaneous. But Springsteen worked hard on these effects: deconstruction of even his worst lyrics shows a feel for motivation, mood, context, tension and release. Precious few others of pop's top table were still writing as carefully, and well, as in their pomp. Springsteen's style – now more than ever – seemed to break into two parts. There were more sheer, monochrome folk-tales. Here, the plots were about real people. Springsteen was obviously much taken by the format, and the stories were often moving, with a downright churchy quality about them. But he still liked to rev up the Fender. Looking at his career as a whole, it's possible to see a kind of spiritual–carnal tug, a throughline, from the off. He never gave up on the latter. When Springsteen went electric, he tended to use symptoms of his own 'growin' up' saga in the narrative. Thus most of his best rockers charted his slow evolution from Loner to Loser, to Lover. The protagonist's point of view was a natural product of his personal history. Over time, Springsteen developed and refined his writing. But that was the basis he worked from.

The creative allsorts, from acoustic strum to *USA* bombast, and most stops between, also underlay events in March 1999. Debate over whether, in fact, Springsteen was or wasn't a solo act went back to 1972. Both Appel and John Hammond, in a rare show of unity, had been stunned when he first cut with a group. They were expecting a bard-singer like Dylan (or, in Appel's case, Cat Stevens). Twenty-seven years on, not much had changed. Just the scale: now the Rock and Roll Hall of Fame inducted him without the E Streeters. Worse, the citation didn't even mention them. (In yet another twist, the Hall's executive panel, sifting candidates for a year beforehand, had been co-chaired by Landau.) At least seven albums and seventeen years on the road were thus dubbed down to the bones. 'Springsteen fused influences from Woody Guthrie, Bob Dylan, Roy Orbison and Hank Williams, while onstage he demonstrated the awesome emotional and physical power of rock with legendary four-hour marathon shows.' All that was true. But he was no one-man band, and the Hall's hype, elliptic logic and auto-delusion came off as abject and, at best, absurd obduracy. Both sides deserved more.

Springsteen's sometimes slightly antique view of employee relations – seen in a no-fraternizing policy after 1985 – was duly jolted that same winter. Yet again, he rang each of the brothers. It was the call they, and millions more, had been hanging on. Springsteen finally announced reunion tour plans. Certain fans flayed him for waiting so long. They weren't afraid to submit Springsteen to raking criticism, knowing that he could take it like a dervish crossing hot coals. Many more were ecstatic. Among them were most of the actual musicians, exactly a decade on from the sackings. Nineteen ninety-nine became their, and Springsteen's, biggest year since the bygone era of Reagan and Hueys swooping down over Tualatin. Opening night was 9 April in Barcelona. Of the twenty-five-song set, an operatic 'Youngstown' and evangelical 'Light Of Day' duly vied with the hits, along with formation posing by the front line. By July they were back in the USA.

It'd been a long haul for the band, the fans, and for Springsteen himself. Even as the tour fired up, he still had doubts. 'I'm no Mick Jagger,' he said. An odd sort of rock god; trying to stop them cashing in is usually the problem. There was nothing of the Peter Pan in Springsteen. The quinquagenarian shared many of his age group's disdain for sweating out the stuff of their youth – there was no 'Rosalita' in 1999 – though neither dotage nor gammy knees stopped him hammering it one last time. It was almost surreal, seeing Springsteen and the group suit up again; probably one reason why he was stalked by so many devotees, anxious to touch the hem of his cloak.

In fact, he'd helped re-boot the whole essence of fandom into something like a religion. With his old-time revival, he also regrouped the cult. In purely worldly aspects, Springsteen's career swept anything before it, and probably most after it. His royalties were vast; his tour was a mass rally – and he had the maniacs. As well as his core customer base, addicts and archivists all preserved something of the myth. Clubs, websites and auctions still spoke to a Springsteen sect. Aside from the CD buff, there were those for whom he was the conscience of America, an inner voice in crazed times. Some in turn became the completists who rode a tidal wave of Springsteen relics. On top of the books and zines, there were calendars, caps, T-shirts, promos, programmes, posters, mobiles, mousepads, backstage passes and 'boots'. Notably the last. There were Springsteen experts, *Mastermind* types and a man called Billy Smith who authenticated lyrics and autographs. A collector who came on a first draft of titles for *Darkness* (bearing, as it turned out, little connection to the final LP) was akin to a dealer finding a lost

Monet. These were the sort of fans who bought *Bruce Springsteen Complete* – thick as a Sears catalogue – or the pirated, twenty-one-CD *Lost Masters*. They spread from the grass roots through to the late Princess, with everyone, including Clinton, between. Some were obsessed cases. An Olympic skater named Jozef Sabovcik choreographed his whole act to *USA* cuts. There was a restraining order out on another fan. Many more were sane adults who spoke of Springsteen's ability, like Diana's own, to reach out and move them. Thirty years on, the moral fervour of the movement was intact.

Spring came, and the sound of hammers and the flash of coloured bunting across the ballroom of New York's Waldorf-Astoria set up the ritual of another pop coronation. The fans didn't forget that it was both the twenty-fifth anniversary of 'rock and roll future' and also the year Springsteen himself hit fifty. Added to the twin drama of *Tracks* and his tour, it wasn't surprising he was at a historic premium. When the day itself dawned, the din of conflicting cults rolled through the Hall as the two camps – pro and anti his induction as a solo act – staked their turf. As well as being fêted, Springsteen also knew the major prestige of controversy.

He deserved the fame. For too many years before *Born*, fans had been starved; true romance, grit and pop-smithery had been tossed; old icons had been shown to have hoofs of clay, and latter-day gods revealed as ultimately gaudy and flat as a dud cracker. Something that people needed, if rock was to be more than wallpaper, was missing. And all at once Springsteen provided it. It was as if he'd been bred for the job. The hard case of Doug and Adele's stoic cheer, the strong fruits of a lone, unsettled childhood and of Springsteen's brooding years – all merged into the epitome of 'rock and roll future'. By 1999, of course, he was also the hero of campaigns past. Pushing fifty and festooned with more medals and gongs than Marshal Zhukov, he'd long earned his niche among McCartney and the rest. But, when the Hall of Fame came to decide on its favourite sons for the last time that century, only one name struck sparks. As Springsteen was announced, the house came down. His speech, singling out Adele, and set (with, as it turned out, the band) shamelessly worked the decks, even down to the Tom Jones impersonation on 'Tenth Avenue'. All in all, it was a night of rowdy whoops, sweat and tears. The all-star jam on 'People Get Ready' was glorious, if ragged. But the band's snubbing would shed bad blood. As one of the more classically minded, not to say scholarly of them adds, 'Don't forget it was the Ides of March, a good day for a backstabbing.' This terrible tyranny of the mute and enfeebled wasn't, though, Brutus's work; Springsteen, to be fair, had done his best to get them in. 'They exploded the definition of a back-up band and my work would have been different without them,' he put it. '[But] I conceive my career individually and independently' (the very hint of ambivalence first heard in 'Blood Brothers'). 'They should be there,' he told Charlie Rose. The fault lay with the Hall's rules, which say that an act can only be inducted twenty-five years after a first LP, and then in the exact form shown on the sleeve. *Greetings*, famously, was a solo album.

Springsteen was right. The E Streeters did 'explode the definition' of a group. They were all good-time musicians, with an imposingly Apolloesque stock of groans, yells, grunts, stifled moans and loud suits to pad out the set. Despite that potentially hammy act, they were also down and dignified when the mood called. They could hack it all. Always much more than a 'dinosaur in flight', as one writer puts it, the exes had been, for the most, publicly civil ever since 1989. In private, at least some of them burned with the rage of a scorned disciple. Judas and, especially, Clemons kissed with the same hurt fury. 'Whenever we do play together,' he said, 'you look at each other thinking: This is the way it's supposed to be . . . so why isn't it?' Behind this lay a broad streak of nostalgia, but also Clemons' self-reproach that, 'No, I don't anticipate it happening again. Everything's gone.'

It certainly had, especially in Asbury. All that was left of the lost world of 'Sandy' was Madame Marie's and a dive called Club Seduction, once the Student Prince. The old Palace Amusements complex, toasted in 'Born To Run', had been officially condemned. Nowadays, it was a sombre grotto of stress cracks and peeling paint. Walls on all sides had caved in, though, over the lintel, leering down on the boardwalk, Tillie the clown kept smiling. It was a suitably macabre relic. Of the Stone Pony's own new look, it's kindest to be silent; the place closed again in 1999. In a bizarre if well-meant tribute, the Council renamed the alley beside it Boss Boulevard. Overall, the town's feel was of pre-oil Benghazi, flowering weeds and heaped rubble set off by a last strand of puce neon: BEER. Beyond, on the far side of the flimsy pier, nothing remained of the drag strip but a furrow between slums, though, upshore, a few shacks still beat out a diet of R&B and pop covers. This was where a Bobby Bandiera plied his trade.

Springsteen himself, of course, was inland, mainly on his rambling 200-acre seat in horse country. Past the split-rail fences, up the long gravel drive, the Colts Neck house now became home. A friend saw how Springsteen straightened up as he entered the place; how the 'shitty look' went; how he could get down on his knees and 'goof off with the kids and pets'. The common denominator both there and in California was children. Re-creating an eden of cosmic merriment – a constant round of eight-year-olds' parties – dotted the wastes when Springsteen felt blocked, stale or spent. That was too often. More and more, the accent, so central to Springsteen, was on the world of innocence and youth, of the primitive emotions, even of regressing to the first flush of life. Every year, on Halloween, he threw open his gates to the Boy and Girl Scouts. But he didn't just load them with junk. Springsteen would haul out his guitar and play to them for hours, a kind of superstar jamboree that, says his friend, showed an unruffled and altogether pure childlike glee he found 'sweet but a tad odd'. That may have been him.

Clean-shaven and photogenic, usually smiling or with an air of mild humour, Springsteen physically most resembled a hip vicar. Politically, he *was* the Jesse Jackson of the mid left. Like many clerics and self-taught achievers who end up as judges or mayors, he liked long words. Thus a lyric would have a 'cumulative dynamic', a 'hemi-cognition' he'd harp on for hours. But Springsteen was still the Jerseyan who salted his speech with the odd 'fuck'. When he laughed, it was in a dry cackle. Garb-wise, nothing was certain but the cowboy boots. As for cars, he owned anything with wheels: from a '48 pickup to the '63 De Ville seen on the cover of *Tunnel*, as well as a fleet of Camaros, Chevys and bikes. He could have opened a dealership. While out west, he wasn't above dining at Le Dome or Chasen's. He enjoyed a drink. Even so, Springsteen wasn't, by the esoteric standards of most locals, a foodie. Grilled cheese sandwiches were okay by him. He watched nonstop TV. That didn't, however, normally include Weinberg's own after-hours gig. Most nights when not actually touring, Springsteen turned in at eleven. He read a lot.

This relative normality was a source of strength. Through musical technique, Springsteen converted it into art people wanted. Like many or most of his fans, he was no radical but a sentimental cynic – someone who cared. A friend asked Nick Dawidoff, a seasoned reporter who once 'did' Springsteen, whether his 'nice-guy bit' wasn't an act. The reply was blunt. 'I watched Bruce up close, day and night, on and offstage. He's for real.' And he seemed to get more so, less mired in his own neurosis, as he went. The beneficiaries of Springsteen's growth were both public and private. 'I used to get nada – zip – from life,' he said. He got very little. As late as 1989, Springsteen had been married to fear; to have gone with joy, Kern says, would have 'been like fooling around'. Patently, that wasn't the case now. On the basis that happiness was equilibrium, says his friend, 'Bruce shifted his weight'. In fact, his whole career demonstrated that if one's goal is to move on, flexibility offers a distinct bonus.

Still, the humbling surprise wasn't that Springsteen had changed, but that in certain ways he'd remained true to Doug and Adele. His work ethic, for instance, was classically '50s. What the hagiographers always attribute to Springsteen's brotherly love is always better understood by his affinity to the market. No one so grasped, or serviced, the needs of his core audience, at least from 1975 to 1985. He'd met the musical black hole of his times with better tunes, persuasively realistic lyrics, and sheer graft. It paid off. After *USA*, even critics gradually lost their lofty slant and began to have an emotional stake in Springsteen goods. Much as it was a feat in itself to tie fans in, it wasn't done on the back of a few well-meant yearnings of the ilk of 'Nobody wins unless everyone wins.' Accounts of non-careerism generally tend to collapse on close inspection: 'Born' went through thirty or forty takes, and 'Dancing In The Dark' was no fluke. Springsteen, like every long-running star, had a shrewd native feel for when to release what wares (one fully shared by Landau). 'Product' was specifically designed to milk – CBS's words – the 'healthy trading vibe' set up by more work. And so it did: faulting us for buying it is like moaning that our chests are poorly shaped for slipping off straitjackets.

Thus Springsteen released his first single from *Tracks*; shuffled his oldies yet again with an obsessive eye for the mix; and spent weeks rehearsing. Scattered throughout it all was the same graft, grind and need to win that a DJ recalls from 1970. 'Bruce phoned me every day. Then every week, every two or three days. I told him no. But he was very sweet. Finally I told him to send a tape. It was here, on my desk, exactly ten minutes later. He'd run across town with it.' Springsteen was then twenty. As a demi-centurion, he still worked long hours to connect with his public. In most views, he never quit.

Springsteen may have done little new, instead falling back on the old frontier values of hard work and play (a surefire export), though his vision was as expertly turned as the planes of his cars. First, like all true artists, he could find the general in the specific. His cruisings around Asbury and the New York street-jive of a *Wild* translated verbatim, whether in London or Lapland. For sheer relevance, his lyrics couldn't be matched. Or beaten: no one else quite sensed the poetry in the flow of pop. Then there was the fact that, well into his forties, Springsteen still wore his heart on his ragged sleeve. For several years past, he'd liked to drive out on I-10 to the spa called Truth or Consequences. It was the perfect tag for his whole career: feverish with change, crisis, upheaval, both Springsteen and his work were much more than stock cut-outs. Like him, his characters always questioned their own motivation. Such musings were intensely personal. How else with Springsteen? It was these two- and three-dimensional types that, above all, made his songs work the world over. The precision beat was only the echo of a master's voice he rightly described as 'inquisitive, concerned and curious' and which made other *auteurs*, including his highly touted '70s peers, sound like the Wombles. Springsteen was that good. Last, he brought to the job not just real insight, but range. He could write as though very young or very old, as if up or at the end of his rope; not too many sets would get away with, as his had, both 'Johnny 99' and 'Santa Claus Is Comin' To Town'. Such sweep was the very core of Springsteen's appeal. Part lay in the fact that almost anyone could 'relate' to him, spinning their own yarns off his. What fans most lit on was the application of a verse, chorus or title to themselves. Part came from his deft swings of sound and vision. And, overlaying it all, was Springsteen's key virtue: consistency. In studio LP terms, he was ten or eleven for twelve, a near ninety per cent hit rate that others could only feebly approximate. No one else, certainly not Dylan, combined such depth and breadth. Springsteen's best work, like *Tunnel*, was autobiography, civics and self-help all in one, with a message that rang true for America – and in the far universe.

So, what was he like? Sane, limited, conscientious, a Jerseyan to his marrow, Springsteen, a non-star star, famously – irresistibly – had a code. He was about growing up. Around forty, he radiantly achieved his theme. By means of disarmingly real songs, he'd created a window through which fans could make out a soul of rare fire, skill and sensitivity. In the years after that, he survived. By fifty, he'd gone from a moody mother's boy into a fully adult, fêted icon: a long haul for a half-ton. Springsteen's ups and downs, from dire youth to *Touch*-era breakthrough, read, in part, like a Nathanael West saga. Thus the moral sense in the man and his music. He'd lived, and it showed in the way he dealt with fears, shared them and moved on. Springsteen's vital sense of empathy was hard won. When he told people 'I've been there', he meant it.

Such drop-dead sincerity didn't merely affect Springsteen but extended to the art as well. To be passionate and real aren't the easiest of things over thirty years. He'd brought it off. Striking such a course had led him past even an Elvis or Dylan, let alone his dump-bin neighbours the Spice Girls. Above all, Springsteen kept faith with both his conscience and his constituency. 'Rock can offer a transcendent moment of freedom,' he'd told fans. 'A promised land.' He let them glimpse it fleetingly through the fog.

Appendix 1

Chronology

23 September 1949	Bruce Frederick Springsteen born at Monmouth Memorial Hospital, Freehold, New Jersey.
1955	He enters St Rose of Lima School, staffed by the Sisters of St Francis and a lay faculty of Catholics. It's the start of what he still calls the 'big hate'.
1958	Springsteen discovers Elvis Presley. In a not incidental move, he now plays a toy guitar.
1963	Transfers from parochial school to Freehold Regional High. It, too, is a flop.
1964	Springsteen joins his first band, the Rogues. He soon trades up to the Castiles, churning out a diet of Motown, Stones and Who hits on the local roller-rink circuit.
22 May 1966	The group cut two numbers, Springsteen's first ever on vinyl, in a booth at the Brick Mall shopping centre.

19 June 1967	He graduates.
	As well as dodging the Vietnam draft, Springsteen enrols in a Liberal Arts course at Ocean County College, thirty miles down Highway 9 from Freehold. He lasts a year there.
1969	After his family moves west, Springsteen hones his trade in *ad hoc* groups like Earth, Child and Steel Mill. Home now is an attic over a surfboard factory in Asbury Park.
1971	He becomes the 'Doc' in Dr Zoom & the Sonic Boom, a situationist prank that lasts three nights. A number of other nicknames are tried until buried under the weight of the final pseudonym. From then on, he answers to Boss.
	That November, Springsteen meets Mike Appel, a hyperactive showbiz hustler, whom he tells: 'I'm tired of being a big fish in a little pond.' The next spring, they sign three separate contracts, later slated as a 'slavery deal'.
2 May 1972	Springsteen auditions for Columbia Records. Ownership of the demos he cuts at 49 East 52nd Street, New York, is still being haggled over nearly thirty years later.
9 June 1972	The CBS contract inked.
12 November 1972	His group takes the stage for the first time as the E Street Band.
January 1973	*Greetings from Asbury Park, NJ* released in the US. Most reviews are good, but don't

	pull up any trees. The LP shifts an initial 11,000 copies.
14–15 June 1973	Springsteen opens for Chicago at Madison Square Garden. He won't be back there for five years.
November 1973	*The Wild, The Innocent and the E Street Shuffle* released. Like *Greetings*, it dies commercially; but the critics sit up.
9 May 1974	The reviewer and sometime producer Jon Landau sees Springsteen second-bill for Bonnie Raitt at Harvard Square Theatre. He goes home and types up a storm for Boston's *The Real Paper*. The strap-line will be quoted, and misquoted, the world over. 'Last Thursday . . . I saw my rock 'n' roll past flash before my eyes. And I saw something else: I saw rock and roll future and its name is Bruce Springsteen.'
	Unsurprisingly, the two men become close.
1974–75	While he cuts his third, make-or-break album, Springsteen also glosses his live act. He hires the best sound and lighting men in the business. His titanic shows, an alluring mix of originals and oldies, soon become lore.
13–17 August 1975	Five nights, two sets per night, at New York's Bottom Line.
	Born to Run released.
	A star is born.
27 October 1975	In Appel's last-gasp coup, Springsteen makes the cover of both *Time* and *Newsweek*.

18 & 24 November 1975	The Hammersmith Odeon, London.
1975–76	Despite the fame, Springsteen still exists on pocket money. He takes home $350 a week and has $3,000 in the bank. Tension with Appel now becomes a blood feud.
27 July 1976	Springsteen formally sues his manager. The suit, and counter-suit, will drag on for ten months. Under the terms of the settlement of 28 May 1977, Appel gives up most of his publishing and all his management rights for $800,000.
1 June 1977	Work begins on the long-stalled *Darkness on the Edge of Town*. Springsteen and Jon Landau co-produce.
23 May 1978	Seven-month, 118-date tour – his biggest yet – opens in Buffalo. Landau is manager.
	Darkness released.
	Everything now goes overboard: even other rock gods watch with mingled awe and envy as the press get behind Springsteen as for no other solo act since Dylan.
1 January 1979	The *Darkness* blitz ends in Cleveland, Ohio.
1979	'Born To Run' officially adopted as New Jersey's 'Rock Anthem'. Springsteen himself narrowly avoids being voted the state's youth ambassador. Even Jimmy Carter quotes him in the White House.
23 September 1979	Springsteen closes the last night of the 'No Nukes' smoker at Madison Square Garden by manhandling his ex-lover off stage. She threatens to sue for $3 million.

23 September 1979   He turns thirty.

3 October 1980   Hits the road again.

                       The River released. 'Hungry Heart' estab-
                       lishes Springsteen firmly and finally as a
                       major, mass-market star.

May–June 1981   For the first time in five and a half years, he
                       plays the UK. The house comes down.

2–9 July 1981   Springsteen opens the new Byrne, a.k.a.
                       Meadowlands Arena in Jersey. Home-state
                       fans go wild. As he later has it, 'I felt like I
                       was the Beatles.'

3 January 1982   Springsteen settles on to his bedroom chair,
                       turns on a four-track cassette deck and picks
                       up his guitar. Over three hours, he records
                       the album *Nebraska* and half the songs that
                       become *Born in the USA*.

September 1982   *Nebraska*.

1983   In a pivotal year, Springsteen buffs his *USA*
                       material, huddles with Landau and CBS and,
                       on a personal note, starts weightlifting. The
                       result will be a global bonanza, with himself
                       seen, by some, as a kind of guitar-toting
                       Rambo.

June 1984   *Born in the USA* released. It shifts twenty
                       million copies, with seven hit singles. The
                       title track, largely misread at the time,
                       becomes a fact of life. Springsteen himself is
                       the biggest white rock star on the planet.

29 June 1984   The fifteen-month world trek opens in St
                       Paul. In 460 days of 'Bossmania', five million

fans pay $110 million for seats alone. Merchandise rakes in another $60 million, with Springsteen netting $2 a copy for *USA*. When all the numbers are totted up, the tour grosses a quarter of a billion dollars.

19 September 1984	Ronald Reagan, in a campaign stop at Hammonton, New Jersey, mobilizes Springsteen as an unwilling character witness. Others also co-opt him.
October 1984	He meets Julianne Phillips, a 24-year-old model and aspirant actress. Springsteen later tells a friend, 'I knew.'
13 May 1985	They marry.
1 June 1985	European leg opens at Slane Castle, Dublin. Officially, the crowd is put at 65,000; thanks to gate-crashing and forgery, there are twice that on site.
3–6 July 1985	Wembley Stadium.
30 September 1985	The tour winds down at the Los Angeles Coliseum.
November 1986	*Bruce Springsteen & the E Street Band Live/1975–85*. It sells three million copies off the bat.
August 1987	*Tunnel of Love*, Springsteen's masterwork, suggests that all isn't well in his marriage.
25 February 1988	Tours again. Springsteen has changed: previously, because the gigs had been as much about graft as native talent, they'd tended to bring out the latent cheerleader, much like the audiences in *Rocky*; now, fans are rooting

for the lofty moral of a *Field of Dreams*. In another twist, he engages in several steamy duets with his backing singer, Patti Scialfa.

May 1988 — Phillips quits the tour party.

June 1988 — The tabloids make it official. Springsteen and Scialfa aren't just acting – they become rock's most famous onstage–offstage item.

30 August 1988 — Phillips files for divorce.

September–October 1988 — Springsteen headlines Amnesty's 'Human Rights Now!' tour, over Sting, Peter Gabriel, Tracy Chapman and Youssou N'Dour.

15 October 1988 — After sixteen years and thirteen tours, the E Street Band play their final full gig together for more than a decade.

23 September 1989 — Springsteen hits forty, lathered like a horse, sweaty and drunk on stage at McLoone's in Sea Bright, New Jersey. Several of the E Streeters join him; the band is broken up that fall. Scialfa, meanwhile, is pregnant with the couple's first child.

25 July 1990 — Evan James Springsteen born in Cedars Sinai Hospital, Los Angeles. He'll later be joined by a brother and sister. The family now spend most of their time on the west coast.

16–17 November 1990 — Springsteen re-emerges for two benefit shows, among his best ever, for the Christic Institute.

8 June 1991 — He and Scialfa marry.

21 January 1992 — The *LA Times* breaks the news that, after

years of silence, Springsteen will release two albums simultaneously. He also tours.

April 1992	*Human Touch* and *Lucky Town* hit the chart at, respectively, numbers two and three. Both ignite sales expectations, but ultimately fizzle.
15 June 1992	Springsteen's comeback tour, without the E Streeters, opens in Sweden. Most sets are solid, if uninspired. While there are a few empty seats for the first time in seventeen years, he grosses $30 million in ticket sales and millions more in spin-offs.
1993	Springsteen plays more European dates; raises cash for hunger programmes and the Kristen Ann Carr Fund; and writes the theme for Jonathan Demme's *Philadelphia*.
21 March 1994	The 'Best Song' Academy Award duly goes to a rock star for the first time. Springsteen's acceptance speech is, almost uniquely for the Oscars, genuinely moving.
1994	For one of the first times ever, he suffers writer's block.
9 January 1995	The E Street Band regroup in the studio. They cut three new songs (and do a lone gig) for Springsteen's *Greatest Hits*. Hopes of a full-bore reunion are, however, dashed.
March 1995	*Hits* released.
November 1995	*The Ghost of Tom Joad*. The gauzy style, dust-bowl theme and plumbing of depths only hinted at on *Nebraska* is a revelation. Rage Against the Machine later flay the title tune.

26 November 1995	First of 130 Joadshows, spread over eighteen months.
5 May 1997	Springsteen accepts the *de facto* Nobel Prize for music, the Polar, in Stockholm.
7 December 1997	Toasts Dylan in front of a blue-chip audience, including the Clintons, at the annual Kennedy Center gala.
November 1998	*Tracks* and *Songs* both out.
10 December 1998	Springsteen awarded £500,000 against Masquerade Music in their bid to market his 1972 demo tapes.
Winter 1998–99	Home to the studio.
March 1999	Cuts 'My Love Will Not Let You Down', as well as a new song, 'Lift Me Up', for the John Sayles film *Limbo*.
15 March 1999	Springsteen inducted into the Hall of Fame.
9 April 1999	Opening night of the E Street revival tour, Barcelona.
9 June 1999	Also enters the Songwriters Hall of Fame. Springsteen's music becomes a sub-plot of the play *High Life*. Students at Oxford University, meanwhile, read his lyrics as part of a Philosophy, Nature and Politics of Geography degree.
15 July 1999	Back in the USA: Springsteen opens American dates.
23 September 1999	He turns fifty.

December 1999	Springsteen and the band take a well-earned break from the road for three months.
23 February 2000	'The Promise', a track he wrote in 1976, garners Springsteen two Grammy nominations, which, in the event, he doesn't win.
28 February 2000	Second and climactic leg of the US tour kicks off at the State College, Pennsylvania.
4 April 2000	The infamous Tacoma Dome, Tacoma, Washington.
June 2000	Springsteen and the band's reunion ends, at least temporarily, at Madison Square Garden, New York.

Appendix 2

Bibliography

The place of publication is London unless specified.

Cullen, Jim, *Born in the USA*, New York: HarperCollins, 1997.

Duffy, John, *Bruce Springsteen in His Own Words*, Omnibus, 1993.

Eliot, Marc, with Mike Appel, *Down Thunder Road*, New York: Simon & Schuster, 1992.

Frankl, Ron, *Bruce Springsteen*, Broomall, PA: Chelsea House Publishers, 1994.

Gambaccini, Paul, with Tim Rice and Jonathan Rice, *British Hit Albums*, Guinness, 1990.

Goodman, Fred, *The Mansion on the Hill*, New York: Random House/Times Books, 1997.

Humphries, Patrick, and Chris Hunt, *Blinded by the Light*, Plexus, 1985.

Humphries, Patrick, *The Complete Guide to the Music of Bruce Springsteen*, Omnibus, 1996.

Lynch, Kate, *No Surrender*, Proteus, 1984.

Marsh, Dave, *Born to Run*, New York: Doubleday/Dolphin, 1979.

——, *Glory Days*, New York: Dell Publishing, 1991.

Monroe, Marty, *Back in the USA*, Robus, 1984.

Rolling Stone, Editors of, *Bruce Springsteen: The Rolling Stone Files*, New York: Hyperion, 1996.

Sandford, Christopher, *Demolition Man*, Little, Brown, 1998.

Springsteen, Bruce, *Songs*, New York: Avon Books, 1998.

Sources and Chapter Notes

As ever, the author has his debts. There are over a hundred dues. The following notes show at least the chief sources used in writing each chapter. Copyright holders of lyrics quoted for review are also given. As well as the formal interviews and taped conversations, I also spoke to a number of people who prefer not to be named. Where sources asked for anonymity – usually citing the 'paranoia' of Springsteen's office – every effort was made to persuade them to go on the record. Where this wasn't possible, I've used the words 'a friend' or 'a musician', as usual. I apologize for the frequency with which I've had to resort to this formula. No acknowledgement thus appears of the help, encouragement and kindness I got from a number of quarters, some of them, as code has it, well placed. The sources for Springsteen's first-person quotes are his published interviews, *In His Own Words* or the memory of those who know him.

For better flow, please note that a few proper names and titles have been re-punctuated in the text – for example, *Born in the USA*.

'Point Blank' (Springsteen) © Bruce Springsteen (ASCAP)

Chapter 1

The 'No Nukes' gala (a.k.a. Woodstock 2) of September 1979 has been well mined. As well as the album and film, I sifted the *New York Times*, *Q* and *Rolling Stone*. Lynn Goldsmith, Joel Bernstein and a source who prefers anonymity also gave compelling accounts. Jean Allenbach kindly filled in details of Springsteen's support of Northwest Harvest and others in 1996. Printed reviews, and my own memory, are responsible for the rest of the chapter.

Chapter 2

Institutional help in recalling the 'Growin' Up' years came from Freehold Regional High, the *New York Times*, Ocean County College and St Rose of Lima Church; I should particularly thank Ed Shakespeare and Carey Trevisan. Springsteen's birth certificate was supplied, at a pinch, by the New Jersey Department of Health. Jacob van de Rhoer helped with etymology. The late Andy Warhol, whom I met in 1983, gave me his views on '*Feinschmecker*' Catholicism. Further comment on the world of Freehold and Jersey came from Todd Grice, Toni Hentz and Judy Kern; on Springsteen's early career by John Entwistle, Lenny Kaye and Jim Mahlmann; and, on his love life, by Phil Woodruff. It's a pleasure to acknowledge, as any Springsteen author should, Dave Marsh's *Born to Run* – a major source on the Castiles era – and Marc Eliot's *Down Thunder Road*, the latter with its new twist on Mike Appel.

Springsteen's first arrival at the Upstage, Asbury Park, is from *Rolling Stone* of 10 October 1985.

'No Surrender' (Springsteen) © Bruce Springsteen (ASCAP)
'Growin' Up' (Springsteen) © Bruce Springsteen (ASCAP)
'Human Touch' (Springsteen) © Bruce Springsteen (ASCAP)
'Independence Day' (Springsteen) © Bruce Springsteen (ASCAP)
'4th Of July, Asbury Park (Sandy)' (Springsteen) © Bruce Springsteen (ASCAP)

Chapter 3

Springsteen's breakthrough years were well recalled by, among others, Joel Bernstein, Randy Brecker, 'Doc', Todd Grice, Robert Lamm, Jim Mahlmann, Dave Motz and Mitch Ryder. Vital help on his first UK blitz came from Allan Clarke, Charlie Gillett, Jeff Griffin, Bob Harris, the late Dick James, Paul Jones, Andy Peebles, David Sinclair, Richard Williams and a source at Sony. I'm grateful to Noel Chelberg, Hugh O'Neill and Keith Richards.

I should especially mention Fred Goodman's *The Mansion on the Hill*, as well as profiles of Springsteen in *Crawdaddy*, *Melody Maker*, *New Musical Express* and *Sounds*. My own travels took me to New Jersey, New York and Tin Pan Alley.

'Blinded By The Light' (Springsteen) © Bruce Springsteen (ASCAP)
'Born To Run' (Springsteen) © Bruce Springsteen (ASCAP)
'Rosalita (Come Out Tonight)' (Springsteen) © Bruce Springsteen (ASCAP)
'Thunder Road' (Springsteen) © Bruce Springsteen (ASCAP)

Chapter 4

Comment on Springsteen's post- *Born to Run* fame was provided by the late William Burroughs, Charlie Gillett, Bob Harris, Richard Williams and a number of others who prefer anonymity. Noel Chelberg, as ever, deftly decoded the music. It was among the greatest joys of the book to interview my old hero, Graham Parker. Lenny Kaye, widely and rightly called the 'nicest man in rock', set out the whole saga of 'Because The Night'. Litigation being what it is, most sources who spoke on Springsteen's suit against Mike Appel did so off-record. Any biographer, though, should cite the full account in *Down Thunder Road*. Valuable comment also came from Lynn Goldsmith and her *Photo Diary*.

Secondary source material included *Cashbox*, the *Chicago Tribune*, *Crawdaddy*, *Creem*, *Newsweek*, the *New York Times*, *Rolling Stone*,

Time and *The Times*. Specific quotes first appeared in *The Mansion on the Hill*, the best field guide ever to the twinned worlds of art and commerce.

'The Promise' (Springsteen) © Bruce Springsteen (ASCAP)

'Jungleland' (Springsteen) © Bruce Springsteen (ASCAP)

'Rosalita (Come Out Tonight)' (Springsteen) © Bruce Springsteen (ASCAP)

'The Promised Land' (Springsteen) © Bruce Springsteen (ASCAP)

'Darkness On The Edge Of Town' (Springsteen) © Bruce Springsteen (ASCAP)

Chapter 5

Springsteen's reaction to the second wave of fame was vividly recalled by Joel Bernstein, Bill Bradley, Pat Fosh, Todd Grice, Graham Parker and others. Richard Williams also put his memories of the 1981 tour at my disposal.

I read Joe Klein's biography of Woody Guthrie and watched *Video Anthology/1978–88*. Of the published material, I should single out *The Mansion on the Hill*, Dave Marsh's *Glory Days*, *Rolling Stone* and the fanzines *Backstreets* and *The Ties That Bind*, not least for quotes from Max Weinberg.

The lines by Ken Erickson are from the *San Francisco Chronicle*, 4 March 1979.

My thanks to the source at the Stone Pony.

'Racing In The Street' (Springsteen) © Bruce Springsteen (ASCAP)

'Ramrod' (Springsteen) © Bruce Springsteen (ASCAP)

'The Price You Pay' (Springsteen) © Bruce Springsteen (ASCAP)

'Crush On You' (Springsteen) © Bruce Springsteen (ASCAP)

'Wild Billy's Circus Story' (Springsteen) © Bruce Springsteen (ASCAP)

'Nebraska' (Springsteen) © Bruce Springsteen (ASCAP)
'Reason To Believe' (Springsteen) © Bruce Springsteen (ASCAP)

Chapter 6

Bossmania was crisply brought home by Joel Bernstein, Jim Eddy, Todd Grice, Arthur Rosato, Mitch Ryder, Celia Ryle and George Will. Vince Lorimer plugged the gaps from Australia. Richard Williams, meanwhile, enlightened me on his views of *Born in the USA*, which I partly share.

Further colour on Springsteen's softball and sex lives came from Brian Pringle and an ex-friend who prefers not to be named. I leant on interviews with, or data from, Tom Modi, Oregon Vital Records and Our Lady of the Lake Church for the saga of May 1985. Other published sources included the previously named books, most notably Dave Marsh's *Glory Days*, and articles in *Billboard*, *Melody Maker*, *People*, the *Seattle Times* and the *Weekly*. *Q* was also invaluable. I should acknowledge ASCAP, Bookcase and Helter Skelter.

'I'm On Fire' (Springsteen) © Bruce Springsteen (ASCAP)
'Downbound Train' (Springsteen) © Bruce Springsteen (ASCAP)
'My Hometown' (Springsteen) © Bruce Springsteen (ASCAP)

Chapter 7

Springsteen's road life is charted, with trainspotter's detail, in Dave Marsh's fine *Glory Days*. *Blinded by the Light* also boasts a chronology. For first-hand comment on his time in the UK, I'm grateful to Julia Collins, Paul Jones, Piers Merchant and Andy Peebles; and, in Europe, to Vasily Yatskin. Randy Brecker provided colour.

As for Springsteen's home life, 'Doc', Todd Grice and Kathleen Stanley all put their views on record. I again trawled the various fanzines, the *Guardian*, *Newsweek*, the *New York Times*, *Q*, *Rolling Stone*, the *Sun*, *Time* and *The Times*. For a take on the 'Human Rights Now!' tour, I'm indebted to Cat Sinclair. Sting returned my fax.

I watched *Sweet Lies*; and, for that matter, *Fletch Lives*.

'Ain't Got You' (Springsteen) © Bruce Springsteen (ASCAP)
'Tunnel of Love' (Springsteen) © Bruce Springsteen (ASCAP)
'Brilliant Disguise' (Springsteen) © Bruce Springsteen (ASCAP)
'One Step Up' (Springsteen) © Bruce Springsteen (ASCAP)

Chapter 8

Sources for the period 1988–92 included Allan Clarke, Amy Frechett, Rose Macnab, Graham Parker, Tim Rice and Richard Williams. I again used, among others, *Billboard*, *Entertainment Weekly*, the *Los Angeles Times*, *Mojo*, the *New York Times*, *Rolling Stone*, *Today* and *USA Today*. Much of the comment from Mike Batlan appeared in his letter to *Q*; Max Weinberg's quote was published in *Backstreets*; Robert Sandall's review is from the *Sunday Times*.

For descriptions of Springsteen's west coast life, the LA County Assessor's Office, the memory of two friends and my own trek to California are all responsible. Birth and marriage certificates came through the state's Vital Records.

Springsteen's *mea culpa* that he 'avoided closeness' is from his interview with *Rolling Stone*, 6 August 1992.

Bruce Springsteen in Concert: MTV Plugged is on video.

'57 Channels (And Nothin' On)' (Springsteen) © Bruce Springsteen (ASCAP)
'Real World' (Springsteen & Roy Bittan) © Bruce Springsteen/Roy Bittan (ASCAP)
'Better Days'(Springsteen) © Bruce Springsteen (ASCAP)
'Ain't Got You' (Springsteen) © Bruce Springsteen (ASCAP)

Chapter 9

Major sources for this chapter included Bill Bradley, Toni Hentz, Lenny Kaye, Jim Mahlmann, Tom Modi, Tim Rice, Arthur Rosato,

Kate Rous and Tony Yeo. I must warmly thank Mark Arax, who related his experience of dealing with Springsteen and Terry Magovern. The Café Eckstein, in Berlin, was charm itself.

Newspapers and periodicals again included *Mojo*, *New Musical Express*, *Q*, *Rolling Stone* and *Village Voice*. I watched the various awards shows and documentaries. Ernie Fritz's film *Blood Brothers* is on video.

'The Ghost Of Tom Joad' (Springsteen) © Bruce Springsteen (ASCAP)

Chapter 10

Parting comment came from Brenda Cooper, Luis Gleick, Jim Mahlmann, Tom Modi, Mitch Ryder and David Sinclair. Of all the sources tapped for *Point Blank*, none was more genial than Pete Seeger; it was a thrill interviewing him. I should also acknowledge, again, Vince Lorimer, Northwest Harvest and the source at Freehold High. Tony Yeo once more put his views on record. I consulted the excellent *Backstreets* and *The Ties That Bind*.

The above-named secondary sources, as well as *Who's Who*, were all used. I read more than a dozen news reports of Springsteen's war with Masquerade Music; thanks to Terry Lambert. The 'Bruce . . . isn't terribly hip' quote first appeared in the frankly dire *Seattle Times*; Nick Dawidoff's full profile was published in the *New York Times* magazine, 26 January 1997. I read Jim Cullen's *Born in the USA*.

Finally, I should mention the *Backstreets* hotline, an inexhaustible mine of data over the last year; and my wife Karen, who stood it all.

Index